✢   THE CULTURAL TURN

✢   IN LATE ANCIENT STUDIES

✝ THE CULTURAL TURN

✝ IN LATE ANCIENT STUDIES

✝ Gender, Asceticism, and Historiography

✝ Edited by Dale B. Martin and Patricia Cox Miller

✝ Duke University Press   Durham and London   2005

© 2005 Duke University Press

All rights reserved

Printed in the United States

of America on acid-free paper ∞

Designed by Amy Ruth Buchanan

Typeset in Quadraat by Keystone

Typesetting, Inc. Library of Congress

Cataloging-in-Publication Data appear

on the last printed page of this book.

✢   ✢   ✢

Essays by David Brakke, Virginia Burrus,

Patricia Cox Miller, James Goehring,

David G. Hunter, Averil Cameron, Susanne

Elm, and Dennis E. Trout originally appeared

in "Rereading Late Ancient Christianity," a special

issue of the *Journal of Medieval and Early Modern*

Studies 33.3, published August 2003 by Duke

University Press.

FOR ELIZABETH A. CLARK

✛   CONTENTS

✝   HISTORIOGRAPHY

✝ ACKNOWLEDGMENTS

Putting together a collection of invited essays necessarily incurs debts. The editors thus have many persons to whom we owe sincere thanks. First, we gladly thank the different contributors, who have worked diligently and at several different stages of revision to produce outstanding examples of the best in current scholarship in late ancient studies. The essays were read by generous but critical scholars who offered insightful suggestions for improvement. We are especially grateful to Elizabeth Castelli, Derek Krueger, Georgia Frank, Michele Renee Salzman, Ann Matter, Rebecca Krawiec, and Karen King. Eight of the essays were previously published as a special issue of the *Journal of Medieval and Early Modern Studies*. We are grateful to the journal's editors, Annabel Wharton and Sarah Beckwith, for their support of the project and especially to Annabel for suggesting the idea in the first place. We thank the journal for permission to republish the essays here. We would like to thank Emily Bennett for assistance with the bibliography, Timothy Marquis for the index, and Deborah Pratt, Theresa Boustead, and Christopher McDaniel for help with multiple mailings.

These essays were commissioned and written in honor of Elizabeth A. Clark, whose career has been an inspiration to us all. But more than that, her mentorship for many of us, her hospitality and friendship to all of us, and her visionary leadership for the entire academic community are and will long be deeply valued.

DALE B. MARTIN

Late ancient studies as a relatively discrete discipline is a recent invention. Only since the 1970s have scholars, who in a previous generation might have identified themselves as classicists, church historians, Roman historians, or patristics scholars, come to identify themselves as scholars of "late antiquity." But more has changed than just the name. The methods of analysis—both historiographical and literary—of the period (itself newly delineated within academic discourse), its characters and texts, have also changed significantly. The essays in this volume, concentrating for the sake of coherence mainly on Christianity in late antiquity, exemplify those changes.[1]

A New Discipline

"Late ancient studies" designates the study of the civilizations clustered mainly around the Mediterranean from the period between roughly 100 and 700 C.E. The earlier terminus is intended to indicate that New Testament history and literature lie outside the purview of late ancient studies. Although some New Testament scholars publish on noncanonical early Christian texts and even non-Christian materials of later periods, the field of New Testament studies has its own scholarly organs and identity markers: journals, associations, job descriptions. Late ancient studies generally leaves the New Testament and earliest Christian history (for example, the historical Jesus or the social organization of Pauline communities) to others and begins where the study of New Testament history and literature leaves off.

The latter terminus (700 C.E.), on the other hand, is less firm. When Peter Brown published *The World of Late Antiquity*, one of the first books that helped define the new field, he added "AD 150–750" to the title. Averil Cameron, on the other hand, entitled one of her books, with an admittedly narrower focus, *The Mediterranean World in Late Antiquity*, AD 395–600. But we may be excused for settling on the round number 700 by pointing out that when the *Journal of Early Christian Studies* was founded in 1993 as the first journal explicitly devoted to covering the period and embodying the discipline's methodological innovations, the editors designated the period "C.E. 100–700."[2]

In previous generations, scholars who dealt with the texts and history of this period and region were trained in other disciplines. Those who dealt primarily with Christian texts approached the field from either New Testament studies or the broader history of Christianity. As David Brakke explains, "Before the 1980s scholars of ancient Christianity, if they were not trained in patristics programs mostly at Catholic universities, received one of two kinds of education. Some trained in doctoral programs in New Testament that extended beyond the canon to include the first few centuries, usually to Constantine, sometimes to Chalcedon. Others came out of programs in the history of Christianity, in which they took doctoral exams in all the major periods, but specialized in the ancient."[3] As Brakke notes, although the first option is still possible, many New Testament scholars limit their scholarship to the New Testament or at most to Christian literature (with often some attention to Jewish, Greek, and Roman sources) of the first two centuries of the Common Era. The latter option, training in a broader doctoral program that covers all of Christian history, "has become very rare."[4]

Other scholars, though, approached late ancient studies from training in classics or history departments, in which they had concentrated on the political, social, or economic history of the late empire. The work of M. I. Rostovtzeff, Moses Finley, A. H. M. Jones, and Ramsay MacMullen, to name only some of the scholars most often cited, shows its influence in the early writings of late ancient studies.[5] Increasingly in the 1970s, scholars educated in ancient history began to treat religious issues with more care, while scholars trained in patristics brought social, economic, and ideological issues to bear on their own studies.[6] For example, Peter Brown came to the study of traditionally "patristics" material (Augustine, in the beginning) from a background in ancient and medieval history.[7] Elizabeth Clark, on the other hand, was trained in Columbia University's doctoral program in the history of Christianity, and her first book, a version of her dissertation, may be deemed a fairly traditional philological and theological study.[8] In the work of these pioneers of (what has come to be) late ancient studies, interests of previously discrete disciplinary divisions were combined: a greater role for society and culture was brought to patristics; a greater role for religion and religious studies was brought to ancient and medieval history.

Religious Studies

Certain institutional shifts, related to the *location* of the study of late antiquity, have proved important for redirecting scholarly attention and method. Scholars in previous generations who read Christian literature of this period— "patristics"—often did so in theological seminaries as part of philosophical and theological training. Robert Markus, for instance, remembers immersing himself for a year in the scriptural commentaries and homilies of Augustine during his Dominican novitiate on the instructions of his novice master, who had forbidden him from reading philosophy, in which he had just received a doctoral degree.[9] Non-Catholic scholars would also have been introduced to "the fathers" as a topic in historical theology during their ministerial education.

In the United States the situation changed significantly beginning in the 1960s with the establishment of departments of religious studies in what either had become or always had been secular colleges and universities. Thanks to the 1963 Supreme Court decision (Abington School Dist. v. Schempp, 374 U.S. 203) that permitted teaching "about" religion even in state-supported institutions, religious studies departments began springing up in public universities.[10] Moreover, even private universities with ecclesiastical ties or histories (Yale and Duke stand as two examples) retained their divinity schools but moved the undergraduate and sometimes doctoral education of students to separate departments of religious studies. This institutional change had two notable effects on late ancient studies in the United States. First, the study of late ancient Christianity entered the general curriculum of "arts and sciences." Theology was understandably deemphasized and other aspects of historical and literary study were strengthened. Second, the centrality of "religion," understood as a historical, social, and cultural phenomenon, became more visible, to be studied in its own right. Moreover, the *way* religion was studied was also affected by its new embeddedness in the culture of "arts and sciences." The nature of late ancient studies in its current form is hardly imaginable apart from the institutional shift from the seminary to the secular faculty, particularly to departments of religious studies. To gauge the extent of the innovation, one has only to note that of the sixteen scholars contributing to this collection, only one teaches in a theological school, whereas all have appointments in arts and sciences faculties.

Social History, Sociology, and Anthropology

The institutional realignment of the discipline is thus one important reason that late ancient studies has become more historically and less theologically oriented, but it doesn't explain other methodological changes in the discipline from 1970 onward. For those changes we must look to broader developments that were taking place in wider academia. One was the growing centrality during the last half of the twentieth century of *social* history. As social history increasingly replaced institutional or intellectual history as the prima donna of historiography, so scholars of late antiquity also turned their attention to the methods and concerns of social history, addressing issues such as class and status, family and household, slavery, patron-client structures, travel and communications, and the influence of economics and urban life on developments in early Christianity and late antiquity.[11]

To some extent, scholars of late antiquity were following the lead of New Testament scholarship, which began appropriating social-scientific approaches in the 1960s and 1970s.[12] Studies by New Testament scholars such as Gerd Theissen, Wayne Meeks, John Gager, and Bruce Malina are sometimes cited as precursors to the adoption of social-scientific methods in late ancient studies.[13] Elizabeth Clark, one of the first to move from "patristics" to "social history" in late ancient studies, has often noted the influence on her own work of a 1977 National Endowment for the Humanities seminar on sociological and anthropological approaches to ancient Christianity led by Wayne Meeks.[14]

More important than sociology, however, has been the influence of cultural anthropology.[15] One of the earliest and most influential pieces that self-consciously appropriated anthropological work was Peter Brown's classic article, "The Rise and Function of the Holy Man in Late Antiquity," published in 1971.[16] Reflecting on the writing of that article and some of his other works from the same period, Brown has emphasized the huge impact exerted on him by his acquaintance with Mary Douglas and her scholarship.[17] As Susanna Elm explains, for late ancient studies Brown's article "effected a paradigm shift. It posited that the most significant shift in the Roman East of the fourth to fifth century occurred in the *locus* of civic and religious power from temples and institutions to the 'holy man' himself as a 'blessed object' mediating between the divine and the human."[18] Averil Cameron identifies the study as offering a "functionalist" anthropological treatment: Brown studies the "social function" of the holy man as a "rural patron, defusing the tensions and difficulties felt by the villagers."[19] In general, one cannot over-estimate the impact cultural anthropology, mostly though not exclusively in its "functionalist" mode, has had on late ancient studies, especially via the scholarship of Mary Douglas and Clifford Geertz, to cite perhaps the two anthropologists most influential for late ancient scholars in the 1970s and 1980s. Rather than simply commenting on texts and ideas, scholars of the period began to see themselves as attempting to "enter a world"—a different and somewhat odd world—much the way an ethnographer would enter a foreign culture.

Cultural History

The new tenor of the discipline can be seen in the first paragraph of Brown's (also now classic) book *The World of Late Antiquity, AD 150–750*: "This book is a study of social and cultural change. I hope that the reader will put it down with some idea of how, and even of why, the Late Antique world (in the period from about AD 200 to about 700) came to differ from 'classical' civilization, and of how the headlong changes of this period, in turn, deter-mined the varying evolution of western Europe, of eastern Europe, and of the Near East."[20]

Several details in this short paragraph may be recognized as signs of what would come to characterize the new field of study. The very designation of the subject as the "Late Antique world" (capitalized) is one, along with the realization that the period will be treated as a transition between the "classi-cal," on the one side, and "Europe" and the "Near East," on the other. Four other words, though, are also more significant than they may initially ap-pear. First, by using the word "world," Brown signals that he will be dealing not merely with the church or the fathers; his subject is an entire social and symbolic "world." "Social," as by now should be evident, invokes social history and all the various structures that make late ancient society what it was. But "social" is supplemented by "cultural," which nods in the direction of "high culture," "popular culture," and cultural anthropology all at once. Finally, the word "change" shows that Brown's study has not abandoned the traditional historiographical concern with development and evolution. Late ancient studies is self-consciously a subfield of historical studies, *and* it represents a period narrated as transitional, liminal, between the "ancient" or "classical" and the "medieval." The subject has become a time in need of a narrative, but it is also a period with its own personality or character—or at least a period in search of one.

Several years later, in *The Mediterranean World in Late Antiquity*, Averil Cameron cites Brown's book as one of the first along the lines of the new "cultural history."[21] Benefiting from the perspective possible after the intervening twenty years, Cameron is understandably clearer about the central role of "culture" in her own study: she designates her book a "cultural and social history" and identifies the importance for her study of the relatively new field of "cultural studies" (she is writing in the early 1990s): "But while questions of culture and 'mentality' are familiar enough when applied to other periods of history, they have only recently begun to impinge in their current form on the study of the later Roman empire."[22] Here we see evidence that the earlier "social history" has been giving way, at least in part, to the history and study of "culture," a term and a development we must examine more closely.

Culture

As several studies have noted, "culture" is simultaneously a near ubiquitous term in contemporary discussion (both academic and popular) *and* one that is extremely difficult to define. As Raymond Williams has remarked, "Culture is one of the two or three most complicated words in the English language. This is so partly because of its intricate historical development, in several European languages, but mainly because it has now come to be used for important concepts in several distinct intellectual disciplines and in several distinct and incompatible systems of thought."[23] This is not to say that the term cannot be defined. In a recent introduction to cultural studies, Mark Smith begins by noting, "Culture is an important but can be a slippery, even a chaotic, concept," yet he proceeds to explain that the study of culture involves "the exploration of the representations and lived experiences of everyday life," which may include "rituals, family structures, courtship patterns, gift relationships, the transition from childhood to adulthood and old age."[24] Lest one think that Smith is referring only to what others might call "social structures," his treatment also invokes less tangible objects of study, such as feelings, perceptions, and values. The meaning of "culture" for his study is thus broader: it refers to an entire "way of life" of a group of people.[25]

Intellectual historians have noted that this understanding of "culture" is only several decades old. Recent theorists of "culture" and "cultural studies" have sketched the history and development of the term itself. In a survey of that history, Kathryn Tanner has limned the variety of meanings of the term from the beginning of modernity until today. From the use of "culture" in the language of agriculture ("culture" as the care of plants and animals), "culture" came to refer, in some quarters, to what we would today call "high culture," the correctly developed sense of aesthetics or taste usually available only to those of high status and proper socialization. For other nineteenth-century authors (Tanner notes Matthew Arnold in particular), "culture" becomes something universal or universalizable. It is "the best that has been said and thought," "the same for all mankind."[26]

In other nineteenth-century contexts, though, "culture" was used to designate the more particular aspects of, say, German tastes and values that should be retained and nurtured in opposition to hegemonic French trends. As Tanner explains, "The German pluralistic use of the word culture also approximated an anthropological use in making culture a marker of a society's influence over individuals. The cultured individual is bound by the culture of his or her group, and therefore should be no cosmopolitan figure, haplessly aping the external manners of a French-dominated, European-wide elite."[27] This more "particularistic" notion of culture, in which one imagines many different and noncommensurable cultures of different peoples, anticipates meanings of "culture" that become dominant only in the twentieth century.

It was in anthropology, itself an invention of the twentieth century, that the use of "culture" gradually came to mean what it does to most contemporary academics. Although the word can still, of course, be used in many different ways ("He's cultured" is readily understandable apart from the anthropological meaning of the term), "culture" in its modern anthropological sense includes "everything about the group that distinguishes it from others, including social habits and institutions, rituals, artifacts, categorical schemes, beliefs and values."[28] As should be obvious from this description, the term "culture" may indeed be in danger of becoming so all-inclusive as to be rendered in the end too universal to be analytically meaningful. But the very popularity of the notion may be due in large part to its universality, capaciousness, and malleability.

The Cultural Turn

When scholars speak of "the cultural turn" in various recent intellectual pursuits, they invoke this universalizing though particularizing notion of culture (it is universal since every human society has culture; it is particular since no two cultures are exactly the same), appropriated mainly from cultural anthropology and used as an organizing rubric for the study of history, literature, and society. In many cases, however, and certainly in this book, "the cultural turn" refers to more than just the influence of cultural anthropology. It includes the observation that late ancient studies, like many other disciplines, has also been influenced by recent theories of language and literature.[29] David Chaney, explaining the rise of contemporary "cultural history" and "cultural studies," suggests that "the cultural turn" could be said to have grown out of "the linguistic turn," a phrase used to describe shifts in philosophy and the human sciences from the first half of the twentieth century.[30]

The philosophy of language of Wittgenstein and the structuralist linguistics of Saussure have both had enormous impact on disciplines far removed from philosophy or linguistics per se.[31] For one thing, merely becoming convinced that language provides the "given" by which human reality is constructed in any meaningful way has forced all sorts of scholars to concentrate much more self-consciously on language and its structures, rather than assuming that they could sail past the "epiphenomenon" of language to arrive at the "real stuff" or "phenomena" behind or below language. Many historians have begun to realize that they are, after all, always dealing with language, not directly with "the thing itself." As scholars have become increasingly convinced about the centrality of language for human meaning and society, they have become more willing to consider themselves readers of "texts," even if the term "text" here refers also metaphorically to reconstructed social practices, symbolic codes embedded in "realia," or even to "history" itself. The "cultural turn" in its embodiment in the 1980s and 1990s is not understandable apart from its predecessor of the mid-twentieth century: the "linguistic turn."

In this regard, the various methods and theories sometimes lumped under the umbrella term "poststructuralism" are key, the work of Michel Foucault being the most, though certainly not the only, important influence on late ancient studies. Peter Brown's *The Body and Society*, for instance, resulted in part from his friendship and collaboration with Foucault.[32] The book's concentration on the way the human self is shaped by means of rhetoric and discourse invokes a prominent Foucauldian theme.

The combination of approaches borrowed from cultural anthropology and literary theory can be seen in Averil Cameron's introduction to her *Christianity and the Rhetoric of Empire: The Development of Christian Discourse*, delivered as the Sather lectures in 1986 and published in 1991.[33] More than once, Cameron identifies herself, at least in this project, as a "cultural historian" (see, e.g., 13, 19), and she points out, as we might expect by this time in late ancient studies, that her study is not a "theological book" but a historical one, though one that makes use of insights from the sociology of knowledge (6, see also 12). Yet she goes beyond these familiar points to emphasize that her study also takes its lead from literary theories, "discourse analysis" of the sort made famous in the works of Foucault, and rhetoric broadly understood—that is, not the "technical" rhetoric of Greek or Latin education, but rhetoric understood as the function of language to persuade in a variety of social situations. Cameron also invokes poststructuralist theories and the study of ideology. The combination here of "culture" with a diverse set of literary and social theories marks Cameron's book as a representative of "the cultural turn" in late ancient studies in its assumption also of "the linguistic turn."[34]

"The cultural turn" in late ancient studies thus refers not to one particular theoretical or methodological innovation, but to a broad shift in textual and historical analyses of a newly defined field of study, analyses influenced, to be sure, by cultural anthropology and the social sciences, but more recently by a wide diversity of theories and methods borrowed from poststructuralism: various literary theories, discourse analysis, ideology critique, theories of the construction of the body and the self, feminist and gender studies, ritual studies. Indeed, the very diversity of new theoretical approaches is one of the remarkable characteristics of "the cultural turn" in recent late ancient studies.

A Representative Journal

To illustrate these rather abstract observations with more concrete examples, let us survey, if only briefly, articles published in the first volumes of the *Journal of Early Christian Studies*, founded, as noted above, in 1993 as the first journal specifically dedicated to the new discipline and its methods. In the first issue, the founding editors, Elizabeth Clark and Everett Ferguson, write, "The editors hope that the *Journal of Early Christian Studies* will publish traditional articles of the highest caliber, but will also become a showcase for work in newer fields, such as women's studies and literary theory, that were not incorporated into the older 'patristics.' We also hope to include articles using some of the newer methodologies, as well as those that employ traditional historical and philological scholarship." Noting also that traditional patristics scholarship has increasingly expanded to include attention to materials outside the Greek and Latin orbits, such as Syrian, Egyptian, Armenian, and Jewish, they conclude, "We would like to include articles that explore how the various religions of late antiquity intersected with and influenced each other, and how disciplines such as archaeology and art history illuminate our textual studies."[35] The foundation of the journal reflects the broader scope of recent work geographically and linguistically, the move toward more historical study of theological documents, and the appropriation of new theoretical methods of analysis.

As the editors of the journal point out, there was no attempt to exclude more traditional methods or articles that carried on the historical and patristics scholarship of earlier generations. And the volumes of the journal bear this out. The first article in the first issue, for instance, is a study by Robert Wilken on "historical" versus "typological" or "allegorical" interpretation in the fathers, a topic that has exercised patristics scholars for many years.[36] Other articles in the same volume, though, reveal the influence of cultural anthropology and the social sciences we have seen above. Harry O. Maier's essay, "Purity and Danger in Polycarp's Epistle to the Philippians: The Sin of Valens in Social Perspective," explicitly invokes Mary Douglas and investigates the social stratification in early Christian churches,[37] while J. Patout Burns commandeers Douglas's work on "purity and danger" as well as her "grid-group" model to analyze the different ways Christian leaders in Rome and North Africa responded to the aftermath of the Decian persecution.[38]

With Dennis Trout's article in the next volume we see both the appropriation of social-scientific methods as well as developments in still other directions. "Re-Textualizing Lucretia: Cultural Subversion in the City of God," to be sure, cites anthropologist Clifford Geertz on "reading public symbols as the bearers of culture,"[39] and Trout refers to social science studies of honor and shame (64 n. 48). But the article also shows just how central feminist theory and gender analysis have become for the discipline as a whole. Scholars have increasingly realized that gender is everywhere in the ancient world, even when women are not. Feminist theory, therefore, is indispensable for analyzing ancient texts, even those not explicitly about women. Trout's article also shows, even in its title ("Re-Textualizing Lucretia," emphasis mine) that gender is socially constructed, textually inscribed, and literarily interpreted.

Other articles in early volumes of the journal likewise illustrate the "linguistic turn" and the new attention to rhetoric, discourse, and textuality. Theodore S. DeBruyn draws on rhetorical studies and Foucauldian discourse analysis in his "Ambivalence within a 'Totalizing Discourse': Augustine's

Sermons on the Sack of Rome." In his article, "The Encroaching Desert: Literary Production and Ascetic Space in Early Christian Egypt," James E. Goehring emphasizes that the "withdrawal to the desert" (anachôrêsis) is a textual portrayal. Although anachôrêsis doubtless existed in the fourth century, Goehring urges his readers to keep in mind the rhetorical, literary nature of all our sources for whatever the "actual history" may have been.[40]

Gender

Several articles in the first issues of the *Journal of Early Christian Studies* illustrate the role of feminist and gender studies and the variety of approaches employed. Inspired by the women's movement in the 1970s, scholars began to search history for the experiences and voices of women in the past, who had been ignored for the most part in previous historiography. "Women's studies" grew in importance throughout the 1970s and 1980s, and those developments expressed themselves also in late ancient studies. Biblical scholars, most notably Elisabeth Schüssler Fiorenza, attempted to tell the history of the beginnings of Christianity from "the woman's point of view," both the women of antiquity and the female scholars of modernity.[41] Several groundbreaking studies by Elizabeth Clark on largely neglected women in late ancient Christianity and their relationships with different church "fathers" opened up entirely new fields of exploration.[42] This sort of "women's studies"—the "recovery" of history about women, their experiences, social roles, and voices—is represented in the first volumes of the *Journal of Early Christian Studies* by such articles as Judith Evans Grubbs, " 'Pagan' and 'Christian' Marriage," and Susan Ashbrook Harvey, "Sacred Bonding: Mothers and Daughters in Early Syriac Hagiography," both excellent social-historical studies of ancient familial structures and their impact on women's roles and experience.

In the 1980s and 1990s, however, feminist theory and gender studies began to move beyond both social history and the "recovery of woman" project.[43] As Elizabeth Clark has argued, "It seems clear that we must move beyond the stage of feminist historiography in which we 'find' another forgotten woman and throw her into the historical mix. I do not mean to belittle the enterprise of 'recovery'—after all, I have done a good bit of it myself, and I believe these labors have served some useful functions." But Clark urges also a different kind of gender analysis: "The current moment, more attentive to linguistic and social theory, is considerably less celebratory in its conclusions: we cannot with certainty claim to hear the voices of 'real' women in early Christian texts, so appropriated have they been by male authors. Yet interesting work may continue to examine how 'woman,' how gender, is constructed in early Christian texts, but will also move beyond purely linguistic concerns to explore the social forces at work in these constructions."[44] Clark had earlier, in the second volume of the *Journal of Early Christian Studies*, made some of the same points, especially about the need for "ideological criticism," the realization of the "textuality" of the construction of the ancient woman, and the need for attention to poststructuralist literary and gender theories.[45]

Indeed, in the very first issue of the journal an article by Patricia Cox Miller provides an outstanding example of the kind of feminist analysis urged by Clark. "The Blazing Body: Ascetic Desire in Jerome's Letter to Eustochium" begins with a literary moment: the quotation of a poem on love and the body. Building on the "women's studies" works of Elizabeth Clark and others on various church fathers' relations to women and their writings pertaining to gender and asceticism, the essay quickly summons Foucault and literary theorist Roland Barthes to divert attention away from authorial intention, and indeed from "the author" at all (23 n. 14); rather, it "will follow the metaphorical figurations of the text rather than Jerome's explicit intention" (23). And, alluding both to poststructuralist concerns with the implicit erotic and to its themes of textuality and body, the essay focuses the reader's attention on the "metaphorical female body which is a creation of language, a 'textual' body that is the object of Jerome's desire" (24). Appropriating French feminist theory, especially Julia Kristeva's, Miller interprets Jerome's use of the erotic and the female body to encourage asceticism (see 29–30). The body is spoken of as a text constructed and written by someone, a text to be read. This collusion of body with language and textuality, and the collusion of reading with other forms of cultural interpretation, are all elements familiar to us from various practices of social and literary interpretation that have been labeled "cultural studies."[46]

Another innovation arising from "gender studies" that should be mentioned at least in passing is the new concentration on the cultural and textual construction of "masculinity." This scholarly development is also represented in essays from the journal in the early 1990s. Steve Young's article, "Being a Man: The Pursuit of Manliness in *The Shepherd of Hermas*," provides an example of the use of contemporary feminist and gender theory to analyze the cultural construction of masculinity and "man." Though the articles on gender published in *The Cultural Turn in Late Ancient Studies* concentrate on women in antiquity, it should be noted that many scholars in the discipline—including some represented by our collection—have elsewhere followed the study of gender into the construction—and deconstruction—of "the male."[47]

"Gender," it is clear—even with all the debates and diversities of its meanings and uses—has indelibly shaped the nature of late ancient studies. And the rise of gender analysis more broadly conceived—that takes, for example, the construction of masculinity to be no less important ideologically than the construction of femininity—has led to exciting new studies of early Christian morality, power, rhetoric, and the body. Gender therefore has been one of the organizing themes of the essays in this collection.

Asceticism

All this emphasis on the body, discourses of the body, the body and power, and the cultural construction of the self has stimulated a new interest in *asceticism*. To be sure, the history of Christianity has long considered monasticism an important social and cultural force, meaning that asceticism was bound to be of importance in late ancient studies. But the recent centrality of asceticism in the discipline also owes much to the fact that it is here that the body, gender, the cultural construction of the self, and textuality intersect.

Scholars in the discipline for the past twenty years have spent much energy attempting to define and theorize asceticism. For many years, individual scholars studied monasticism and its attendant practices of self-control, but the self-reflective study of asceticism received a huge boost from the Project on Ascetic Behavior in Greco-Roman Antiquity, a collaboration among many scholars that took place over several years within the Institute for Antiquity and Christianity in Claremont, the Society of Biblical Literature, and the American Academy of Religion. The project culminated, first, in the publication of a sourcebook illustrating *Ascetic Behavior in Greco-Roman Antiquity*, edited by Vincent L. Wimbush, which contained introductions to and translations of many important, and in many cases hitherto neglected, ancient sources. In the preface, Elizabeth Clark listed the ways in which older ideas about asceticism had been displaced. No longer, for instance, was asceticism seen as evidence of pathology or considered an invention of Christianity in reaction to the "profligacy" of ancient "pagan" society. Scholars were no longer convinced that Judaism in the ancient world was essentially antiascetic in contrast to Christianity, and no longer were scholars content to think about asceticism as necessarily the denial of "world" and body. Although scholars had not agreed upon a definition of asceticism, they were united in signaling its importance and the need for further, more theoretically sophisticated analysis.

The study of asceticism advanced further with the organization of an international conference held at Union Theological Seminary in New York in 1993. Led by Vincent Wimbush and Richard Valantasis, the conference brought together scholars working on issues of asceticism in different periods and cultures. The collected papers, published in 1998 under the deceptively simple title *Asceticism*, constitute a remarkable testament to the growth of interest in asceticism and to the value of comparative approaches, but also to the conundrums associated with producing an adequate definition and theory of asceticism.[48]

There is still no real consensus on the meaning of asceticism. Attempts have been made, of course, to break through the impasse. One of the most recent proposals of a "new theory" of asceticism that will be truly universal and comprehensive has been offered by Richard Valantasis. Rejecting many notions of asceticism as too limited to particular cultural locations or as focusing too exclusively on notions of "deprivation" or "denial," Valantasis insists that scholars should accept a "positive understanding of asceticism" that "revolves about the intentional reformation of the self through specific practices. . . . That ascetical refashioning of the self consists of two simultaneous movements: a rejection of the existent self and the conditions for its maintenance, and a positive movement toward the construction of a new self and the conditions for its survival."[49] Valantasis attempts to turn the attention of scholars away from using culturally specific practices of self-denial as a way of identifying asceticism. "The asceticism relies not so much on the specific renunciatory practices, but rather on the articulation of a newly fashioned self, one inconsistent with the past, one confidently knowing the all, one new and sufficiently different from the old to be spoiled by contact with it. . . . Only the positive agenda for creating a newly refashioned self in conflict with the old self matters in describing the gospel [the *Gospel of Thomas* being Valantasis's focus here] as ascetical."[50]

Though Valantasis is to be applauded for attempting to broaden the analysis of asceticism and introduce comparative methods, it is not clear that his new definition and theory of asceticism will move that project along. Valantasis's definition of asceticism, boiling down to "the positive refashioning of a self in contrast to the previous self," is far too broad to be analytically useful for talking about what people normally mean by "asceticism." The term loses so much specificity as to be analytically useless. Valantasis's definition, for example, describes perfectly what happens, say, to a homosexual young man who decides to "come out" and refashion himself as an "out"—perhaps even wildly sexual—gay man in contrast to his closeted, controlled, previous self.

Many similar examples could be readily proposed: a previously staid housewife who intentionally remakes herself into a prostitute; a teenage girl who struggles to be the "popular cheerleader"; a frightened, urban youth who refashions himself to become a hardened, violent gang member. It may be interesting to analyze such behaviors by invoking the category of asceticism—by portraying the "coming out" process *as* "ascetic" or gang violence *as* "monastic." But it should be recognized that doing so constitutes an *extension* of the term "asceticism" to apply it in counterintuitive and innovative ways that depart from the "normal" meaning of the term.

In his attempt to come up with a definition and theory of asceticism that could include every form of human behavior that anyone might want to identify as ascetic, Valantasis has neglected a fundamental notion of definition: that in order to define words we must look, at least to a significant degree, to the "ordinary," "everyday" *uses* of the word. Precisely because the sorts of behaviors scholars regularly identify as "ascetic" are more limited than all "refashionings of a new self," Valantasis's definition fails.

Leaving aside any attempt at a new definition or theory of asceticism, I will merely point out that for the purposes of our title the word refers to those human impulses and practices of self-control, training, and discipline that reject or avoid, for the purpose of attaining a "higher good," the enjoyment of "goods" normally thought appropriate for human use in the society in question. In other words, some notion of "renunciation" as part of "discipline" must be included for asceticism to be recognizable as such. Moreover, other practices may be adopted or intensified in an attempt to train the self. In the ancient world, for example, asceticism often included fasting, renouncing sexual or erotic contact, avoiding bathing, giving up wine, and depriving oneself of familial and customary social connections or other comforts. Giving up these "goods" can be identified as ascetic precisely because they are considered more broadly in the society as properly enjoyed in normal circumstances (unlike, say, bestiality or eating dung). And they are ascetic because they are done for the purposes of acquiring some higher good (rather than avoiding sex, say, simply because one finds it personally unpleasant). Moreover, certain behaviors that may be considered "normal" when practiced to a limited degree (prayer, fasting, standing, kneeling) become "ascetic" when practiced to an extent considered by most people of the society to be beyond the "normal." What counts as "ascetic" in this view is dependent on what is considered a "good" or "normal" behavior by the broader society. Asceticism in any of its particulars is culturally specific *and* parasitic on the "normal."

At this point it is less important to provide a universal definition of asceticism than to note that studies of asceticism—and debates about its meaning—have come to characterize much of the work of the past thirty years in late ancient studies. Asceticism has been and continues to be a central focus for the study of late antiquity precisely because it was a central factor of late ancient society. Moreover, asceticism has become an important organizing rubric for thinking about both ancient culture and the shape of modern scholarship on ancient culture. Experimenting with the meaning and interpretation of asceticism provides much of the structure for the work of many scholars in the field, as several of the essays in this collection attest.

Historiography

The third organizing theme of our collection is *historiography*, and it should already be clear how the reading and writing of history has changed in the past thirty years within late ancient studies. As sketched above, the move from institutional and intellectual history to social history, which scholars of late antiquity borrowed from broader movements in twentieth-century historiography, constituted an important development. Moreover, some innovations in the field were due simply to the fact that scholars cast their nets in wider areas under the influence of interdisciplinary approaches. Syria and Egypt were added to Greece and Rome as areas of interest; Judaism and Manichaeism were allowed to rub shoulders with Christianity and "paganism." Though the essays here included center mainly on Christianity, they also indicate their authors' cognizance of recent research in non-Christian phenomena. Scholars of late ancient Christianity increasingly keep their eyes on developments in scholarship on non-Christian late antiquity also.

The study of "culture" introduced above, moreover, allows us to delve deeper into how and why the writing of history has changed in the ways it has. When one begins with the category of "culture" and all it has come to mean, one begins to "see" the questions of history differently.

Tanner has noted, in her study of culture mentioned above, that according to modern usage of the term, "Culture in an anthropological sense is an originary formative influence on individual persons and as such must be exercised primarily through unconscious means."[51] Note what this may mean for historiography. When the "culture" of the early church in its "cultural" environment becomes the focus of attention, the object of study shifts to concentrate less on the intentions and conscious thinking of the ancient author. Those are still a matter of interest and conjecture, but they can scarcely claim even the most central, much less the only, role. Rather, the unspoken, unreflected assumptions of the author are sought, which, since they are precisely not "named" by the author, must be garnered from the broader culture. The goal of the historian becomes not the conscious or even unconscious intentions of the author, but the larger matrix of symbol systems provided by the author's society from which he must have drawn whatever resources he used to "speak his mind."

Moreover, the emphasis on culture shifts attention from the universal to the particular. The modern anthropological notion of culture refers to *different* cultures; a "universal culture" is not conceivable in this sense of "culture."[52] This observation may also be used to illustrate one of the innovations in late ancient studies. Previous patristics scholarship tended to take as its goal the explication of Christian theology that, for many, was seen as enduring through the ages, unchanged in at least its "essential" aspects. If Christianity is true, according to the traditional notion, then its fundamental doctrines were understood as universally and always true. Thus, the patristics scholar may have been less inclined to locate the "meaning" of theology in the particularity of its late ancient, upper-class *culture*. But that is precisely the goal of much scholarship today: illustrating how ancient Christian doctrine, debates, language, and social institutions were part and parcel of late ancient *culture*.

There are other ways the category of "culture" itself may have influenced the practice of writing late ancient history. For example, Tanner points out that analyses of culture, certainly those of most twentieth-century anthropology, have usually been synchronic rather than diachronic, a feature of the structuralism that marked anthropology in the mid-twentieth century. In some schools of thought, ethnographical analysis *was* structuralist analysis. The kinds of societies traditionally analyzed by anthropologists were often presented as if outside the changes of history. If anything, they were taken as representing some prehistorical state of primitivism from which we all emerged.[53] It may be no accident, therefore, that many studies of late antiquity in the past thirty years—though by no means all—tend to emphasize *synchronic description* of late ancient culture over *diachronic explanation* of the various changes from the classical to the medieval world. Understanding the changes in historiography in late ancient studies in the past thirty years requires some attention to the ways in which modern notions of "culture" have influenced how historians think about their task.

Last, though, I should reiterate the importance for historiography of the "turn to language" and the realization of the centrality of textuality for the writing of history. Scholars working in late ancient studies no longer think of history as involving the objective discovery of the way things "really were." They realize that they deal almost exclusively with *texts*—with highly literary, rhetorically sophisticated texts at that. The importance of attention to literary theory, therefore, has been thrust upon them. History is seen as a *hermeneutical* enterprise in a way more traditional historians would have abhorred (as many still do). Scholars have also come to realize, for another thing, that "history" is itself available only *as text*. History itself, insofar as it is discernible by any human being, is just like a text in that it is constructed by a particular person in a particular time and place. And it must be interpreted like a text. There is, in the end, no escape from language and textuality. And many scholars working in late ancient studies, I would venture, are quite content to live with those limitations. After all, texts may be imagined as prisons, but they may also be imagined as infinite universes. In any case, this combination of recent notions of "culture" and "textuality" has profoundly shaped the historiography practiced by scholars of late antiquity.

✛ ✛ ✛

The various essays here collected are organized around these three central topics that have engaged scholars of late antiquity for the past thirty years: gender, asceticism, and historiography. Taken together, the essays illustrate the recent history of the discipline and its current state with regard to late ancient Christianity. We believe they also contain elements that may point the discipline in still new and exciting directions. The essays witness to the scholarly ferment of the past thirty years that constitutes "the cultural turn in late ancient studies."

Notes

1. The one article in this volume that focuses on non-Christian materials, that by Daniel Boyarin, is nonetheless closely related to the study of late ancient Christianity. In the first place, Boyarin is taking his lead from the methods and questions that have driven the "quest for the historical Jesus." Second, interpreting the significance of Yavneh (Jamnia) has been an ongoing concern of scholars of early Christianity.
2. Clark and Ferguson, "Editors' Note."

3. Brakke, "Early Church in North America," 476.
4. Ibid., 477.
5. Note, for instance, the centrality given to Jones by Cameron, *Mediterranean World*, 5–6; the use of MacMullen's social history of the late empire is quite evident in Brown, *Making of Late Antiquity*.
6. Note Elizabeth Clark's praise of Robert Grant for bringing "ancient political, economic, and social history to patristic scholarship": "The State and Future of Historical Theology: Patristic Studies," in *Ascetic Piety*, 7.
7. Brown, *Augustine*.
8. Clark, *Clement's Use of Aristotle*.
9. Markus, "Evolving Disciplinary Contexts."
10. Note the discussion of this shift in Meeks, "Irony of Grace," 47–48 and n. 7.
11. Hans Hillerbrand notes these developments for all of church history: see his introduction to the special issue on *Present Trends in the Study of Christian History*. Hillerbrand mentions "new methodologies," but the only one he explicitly names is social history, which testifies to its importance in the recent development of historiography. See also, for such changes in the broader field of history, Hunt, introduction to *New Cultural History*.
12. Different scholars have wanted to distinguish their own work with different terms, including "social history," "sociological," "social-scientific," or even "ethnohistoriography." I have narrated the debates about these terms and their different usages elsewhere. See Martin, "Social Scientific Criticism." For the purposes of this essay the general term "social-scientific" is used to include all those approaches that take significant inspiration or methodological guidance from any of a number of disciplines often included in "social science," especially sociology, cultural anthropology, and sociology of knowledge.
13. Theissen, *Sociology of Early Palestinian Christianity*, and *Social Setting of Pauline Christianity*, both of which publish English translations of articles published earlier in German; Meeks, "The Man from Heaven" and *First Urban Christians*; Gager, *Kingdom and Community*; Malina, *New Testament World*. Note the influences mentioned by Maier, *Social Setting of the Ministry*, and "Purity and Danger in Polycarp's Epistle."
14. Personal communication. See also Klutz, "Rhetoric of Science in *The Rise of Christianity*," 163 n. 3. For a brief introduction to the use of social-scientific methods in New Testament studies, see Martin, "Social Scientific Criticism."
15. Cf. Hunt, Introduction, 10.
16. The "classical" status of the article is witnessed by the intense attention given it in retrospectives and celebrations of the twenty-fifth anniversary of its publication: see the special issue of the *Journal of Early Christian Studies* devoted to it, vol. 6, no. 3 (fall 1998); see also Cameron, "On Defining the Holy Man."
17. Brown, "Rise and Function of the Holy Man"; see 359–62 in particular on Douglas.
18. Elm, Introduction, 343.
19. Cameron, *Mediterranean World in Late Antiquity*, 73. Cameron also refers to Brown's *World of Late Antiquity* as "cultural history" (ix). See also Cameron, "On Defining

the Holy Man": "With the article on the holy man [Brown] could be seen stepping more confidently into the territory of social anthropology, using a wide range of 'data' to construct a social definition, not of a saint, but of the 'holy man' in late antiquity as a typically interstitial figure exercising a patronage role based in the symbolic capital of his perceived authority" (27).

20. Brown's *The World of Late Antiquity* has also been the subject of retrospectives. See, e.g., the special issue of *Symbolae Osloenses: Norwegian Journal of Greek and Latin Studies* 72 (1997).

21. Cameron, *Mediterranean World*, ix–x.

22. Ibid., 128.

23. Williams, *Keywords*, 87. Williams says that he first noted a significant shift of the meaning of "culture," from referring to a well-trained or educated person to referring to the "way of life" of a group of people, in the immediate postwar years after 1945 (see 12–13).

24. Smith, *Culture*, 4, 21.

25. "*Culture as social, as a way of life* whereby it expresses the structure of feelings of a social group and therefore should be analysed, clarified and valued in terms of the (sometimes tacit) meanings and values of ordinary behaviour and social institutions as well as in terms of their place in art and learning," Smith, *Culture*, 22–23 (emphasis his). See also Chaney, *Cultural Turn*, 2: "[M]embers of a group have characteristic and persistent forms or patterns of thought and value through which they understand and represent their life-world (culture, in a well-established phrase, is a form of life). Within this set of shared understandings culture (or some equivalent) will be one of the terms they use to describe their own and other groups' symbolically important occasions, practices and objects."

26. Arnold, *Culture and Anarchy*, 204; Tanner, *Theories of Culture*, 4, 14.

27. Tanner, *Theories of Culture*, 11.

28. Ibid., 27.

29. For the same development in the broader discipline of history, see Hunt, Introduction, 17.

30. Chaney, *Cultural Turn*, 2.

31. The most important works being Wittgenstein, *Philosophical Investigations*; and Saussure, *Course in General Linguistics*.

32. On the influence of Foucault and other French scholars on Brown, see Cameron, "On Defining the Holy Man," 28–29.

33. The shift from the "socioanthropological approach" to "more structural and literary analysis" and the "study of discourse" is discussed further by Cameron in ibid., 36–43.

34. Bonnell and Hunt discuss the importance of poststructuralist and literary theories for recent historiography in their introduction to *Beyond the Cultural Turn*.

35. Clark and Ferguson, "Editors' Note."

36. Wilken, " 'In novissimus diebus.' "

37. See 242–43 of Maier's "Purity and Danger" for his citation of Douglas, and 233–34 for references to New Testament scholarship he is following.

38. Burns, "On Rebaptism."

39. Trout, "Re-Textualizing Lucretia," 55 n. 9.

40. See esp. 282 of Goehring, "Encroaching Desert."

41. See esp. Fiorenza, *In Memory of Her* and *Bread Not Stone*.

42. Several of Clark's important essays are collected in *Jerome, Chrysostom, and Friends* and *Ascetic Piety and Women's Faith*. See also Clark, *The Life of Melania the Younger*.

43. For a good idea of the varieties and changes in women and gender studies, see the anthology *Women, Gender, Religion*, ed. Castelli with Rodman.

44. Clark, "Holy Women, Holy Words," 430.

45. Clark, "Ideology, History, and the Construction of 'Woman.' "

46. See also, in the first volume of *Journal of Early Christian Studies*, the article by Blake Leyerle that appropriates feminist film theory to analyze John Chrysostom's rhetoric of feminization: "John Chrysostom on the Gaze."

47. An influential example is Gleason, *Making Men*. See also Brakke, "Problematization of Nocturnal Emissions"; Burrus, *Begotten, Not Made*; Keufler, *Manly Eunuch*. For a similar study of earlier and non-Christian sources, see Martin, "Contradictions of Masculinity."

48. Wimbush and Valantasis, *Asceticism*.

49. Valantasis, "Is the Gospel of Thomas Ascetical?" 61.

50. Ibid., 63.

51. Tanner, *Theories of Culture*, 13.

52. See ibid., 14.

53. See the discussion in ibid., 35–36.

✢ GENDER

✢ ASCETICISM

✢ HISTORIOGRAPHY

✢   The Lady Appears:

Materializations of "Woman"

in Early Monastic Literature

DAVID BRAKKE

According to a famous monastic saying, the Egyptian desert in late antiquity was the place where, as in some recent theory about gender in history, "there are no women."[1] To be sure, the desert was filled with thoughts of women, memories of abandoned wives and mothers, and demonic specters of women, but monks claimed that there were few, if any, flesh-and-blood women in their desert. Likewise, Elizabeth Clark has invited historians of Christianity to consider the prospect that our sources present us not with real women from the past, but with male authors' fantasies about or rhetorical uses of women, no more than the gendered literary "traces" of elusive "real women."[2] Imagine, then, the surprise of a group of lay tourists—and perhaps our surprise as well—when their representative monk turned out to be really a woman:

> Some worldly people visited a certain anchorite, and when he saw them he received them with joy, saying, "The Lord sent you so that you would bury me. For my call is at hand, but for the benefit of you and of those who hear (your report), I shall tell you about my life. As for me, brothers, I am a virgin in my body, but in my soul up to now I have been inhumanly under attack by fornication. Look, I am speaking to you, and I behold the angels waiting to take my soul, and Satan meanwhile standing by and suggesting thoughts of fornication to me." Having said these things, he stretched himself out and died. While dressing him the worldly people found that he truly was a virgin.[3]

The radical confirmation of the monk's claim about himself—"a virgin in my body"—made possible by the appearance of a female body only underscores what the monk presumably left unsaid about him/herself. Whatever truths the monk may have told his admiring visitors "about my life," perhaps only summarized here, his body, once he stopped talking, told a different truth: he was a woman. At the end of the male monk's discourse, the lady appears. So the story, presumably told by the visitors, says. This surprise was too good to tell only once: a longer and more complicated *apophthegma* about Abba Bessarion likewise climaxes with a monk revealed to be a woman at his death (*Apoph. patr.*, Bessarion 4). The heroine of the later *Life of St. Pelagia the Harlot* lives for three or four years disguised as a male monk in Jerusalem, until her death reveals her ruse.[4] From here the motif of the transvestite ascetic multiplied in early and medieval Christian literature; the abundant detail of these later narratives provides fertile ground for complex scholarly readings on several levels.[5]

In contrast to later medieval tales, the two *apophthegmata* in which dead monks are revealed to be women are spare. For example, the *Life of Pelagia* explains why its heroine chose to disguise herself as a man: a reformed actress and "prostitute," she sought to escape her wealth and notoriety in Antioch for a life of ascetic anonymity. "She held her fortune to be worse than blood and fouler than the smelly mud of the streets"; wearing clothes given her by Bishop Nonnus, she fled to Jerusalem to live as a monk.[6] In contrast, the *apophthegmata* narrate only the postmortem discovery of the monks' cross-dressing, leaving it to scholars to offer plausible reasons for an ascetically inclined woman in fourth- or fifth-century Egypt to have impersonated a male monk. First, solitary women in the desert faced the risks of robbery and sexual assault: passing as a man provided some (but not complete) protection from such dangers.[7] Second, sayings about and attributed to Amma Sarah, one of the very few named female anchorites in the *apophthegmata*, indicate that some male monks did not accept female colleagues and were even openly hostile to them.[8] There were, then, good practical reasons for women who wished to pursue the eremitical life in the desert to disguise their sex. If so, then why are such stories so few? And why are they only of these women being discovered at their deaths? The compilers of the sayings appear to have been interested only in successful cross-dressers—or rather, *almost* successful—they made it through their lives without being discovered, but at their deaths the masquerade ended.

This essay, then, analyzes these two *apophthegmata*, along with certain kindred monastic sayings and anecdotes about "real women." I ask about these women, "What were or are they doing there?"—not in a positivist quest for the actual motivations of real cross-dressing monks but to explore the relationships between the literary and the social, the rhetorical and the real. On the one hand, I explore the rhetorical effects, in literature produced by and for men, of stories about such unexpected women. What purposes do these women serve? How do these stories construct "woman"?[9] On the other hand, I draw on the metaphor of "performance," recently influential in studies both of asceticism and of gender, to argue that monastic discourse about real women was not "merely" literary but materialized "woman" as embodying "the world" of sexuality, embodiment, and discourse, that which for the male ascetic was the "strictly foreclosed, . . . the nonnarrativizable."[10] Such materializations had concrete effects for real women.[11]

On one level our short anonymous *apophthegma* plays on the gender ambiguity of the Greek word *parthenos* ("virgin") and on the definition of true virginity. Unlike the male body, the female body could provide evidence of whether a person "truly was a virgin," and in the fourth and fifth centuries Christian authors increasingly identified female virginity with physical intactness, as the debate over Mary's virginity illustrates. The case of men was more difficult: John Cassian quotes Basil of Caesarea as saying, "I do not know woman, but I am not a virgin," and comments, "Well indeed did he understand that the incorruption of the flesh consists not so much in abstaining from woman as it does in integrity of heart, which ever and truly preserves the incorrupt holiness of the body by both the fear of God and the love of chastity."[12] Our anonymous monk echoes Basil by claiming that his body is virginal, but his soul has been vulnerable to temptation; yet the anecdote seems to take the dead monk's integrity of body as evidence of the virginity of his soul, caught between the angels and Satan even at death. Only a female body could provide proof of the monk's virginity "truly."

Or, drawing on antiquity's equation of virtue with manliness, we could say that only a female body could provide proof of the monk's manliness. Through her ascetic discipline, especially through her battle against the "inhuman" temptation of fornication, our anonymous virgin proved herself to be manly; she achieved the masculine virtue of self-control. A variety of early Christian writings portrayed virtuous women as being "made male" or becoming "men."[13] In monastic works, the metaphor of the ascetic life as warfare with demonic forces of temptation portrayed the monk as a combatant, an *agônistês*, a masculine figure (e.g., *Apoph. patr.* 7.58). The monks inherited this metaphor from the literature of martyrdom, which understood the captive Christian's struggle with beasts or gladiators in the arena to be combat with Satan. A female martyr such as Perpetua displayed masculine courage in her triumphant defiance of the demonic forces: "I became a man," she says. The anchoritic life in the desert succeeded martyrdom as the arena in which a woman could prove herself to be a female man of God.[14]

Like our anonymous monk, Amma Sarah epitomized this masculine ideal, waging warfare against the demon of fornication for thirteen years without asking God for relief. At last, "the spirit of fornication appeared corporally [sômatikôs] to her and said, 'Sarah, you have conquered me.' But she said, 'It is not I who have conquered you, but my master, Christ' " (Apoph. patr., Sarah 1–2). Rightly then Sarah was able to say to two male anchorites who sought to "humiliate" her, "According to nature [physis] I am a woman, but not according to my thoughts" (4). To another set of brothers she stated, "It is I who am a man, you who are women" (9). Sarah's assertion that she is a woman "according to nature" parallels our anonymous apophthegma's identification of the anonymous monk as a (female) virgin "truly" based on her body. Bessarion and his disciple Doulas, as we shall see, discover that their anonymous monk "was a woman by nature [physis]" (Apoph. patr., Bessarion 4). Thus the sayings present an ancient version of the modern assignment of sex (man or woman) to the body or to nature, and of gender (masculine or feminine) to practices or to culture. Naturally or truly Sarah and the anonymous monk are women, but in their thoughts, by their practices, due to their virtue, they are masculine, that is, men. Successful cross-dressing shows that they exemplify the power of the monastic regime to lift the human being above human nature and the sinful body, both associated with femininity.

In recent years modern scholars have developed their own vocabulary of the "performative" for the transformations, gendered and otherwise, that ascetic and other practices produce. Drawing on theories of performance, Patricia Cox Miller has called ascetics "performance artists, enacting the spiritual body in the here-and-now," and Richard Valantasis has developed a nuanced and highly persuasive theory of asceticism as "performances within a dominant social environment intended to inaugurate a new subjectivity, different social relations, and an alternative symbolic universe."[15] Here scholarship on ancient asceticism dovetails with recent theory on gender. Contesting the assignment of sex to the body and gender to culture, Judith Butler famously argued that gender is performative, "a stylized repetition of acts . . . in which bodily gestures, movements, and styles of various kinds constitute the illusion of an abiding gendered self."[16] Amma Sarah and our anonymous monks appear to embody these theoretical positions: they became "male" by performing ascetic acts. Yet the concept of performativity questions the apophthegmata's insistence upon the persistence of a "natural" and "true" gendered identity, female, grounded in a body impervious to the transforming power of performance.[17] It pushes us to ask how this seemingly "natural" and "true" female body may actually have been rendered "real" or "materialized" through monastic performance. A fuller analysis of the rhetorical context of the appearing women will lead us to perhaps the most powerfully transformative of monastic ideologies, Origenism.

The version of the monk-as-woman anecdote preserved under the name of Bessarion amplifies the figural dimension of its presentation and thus its rhetorical utility:

> On another day, when I (Doulas) came to his cell I found him (Bessarion) standing at prayer with his hands raised toward heaven. For fourteen days he remained thus. Then he called me and said to me, "Follow me." We went into the desert. Being thirsty, I said to him, "Father, I am thirsty." Then, taking my sheepskin, the old man went about a stone's throw away and when he had prayed, he brought it back, full of water. Then we walked on and came to a cave where, on entering we found a brother seated, engaged in plaiting a rope. He did not raise his eyes to us, nor greet us, since he did not want to enter into conversation with us. So the old man said to me, "Let us go; no doubt the old man is not sure if he ought to speak with us." We continued our journey toward Lycopolis, till we reached Abba John's cell. After greeting him, we prayed, then he (John) sat down to speak of the vision that he had had. Abba Bessarion said that a decree had gone forth that the temples would be overthrown. That is what happened: they were overthrown. On our return, we came again to the cave where we had seen the brother. The old man said to me, "Let us go in and see him; perhaps God has told him to speak to us." When we had entered, we found him dead. The old man said to me, "Come, brother, let us take the body; it is for this reason that God has sent us here." When we took the body to bury it, we discovered that it was a woman by nature. The old man marveled and said, "See how women triumph over Satan, and we behave shamefully in the cities." Having given thanks to God, who protects those who love him, we went away.[18]

This version makes explicit that the story is told by and for men. The speaker is Abba Doulas, the disciple of Abba Bessarion. Bessarion gives the discovery of the woman its moral: "See how women triumph over Satan, and we behave shamefully in the cities." As soon as she is stripped of her male monastic garb and revealed to be a woman, this "brother" is expelled from the (male) monastic community, as Bessarion speaks of "we" monks in contrast to "women." The function of this woman is to shame male monks.

Shaming men, Clark has taught us, is one of the most ubiquitous functions of the "woman" that ancient Christian authors constructed.[19] They inherited the tactic from the gospel writers (e.g., Luke 24:22–25),[20] as well as from pagan moral philosophers, whose talk of virtuous ("manly") women scholars are now inclined to see less as indicative of a belief in the equality of the sexes in achieving virtue and more as a "rhetorical strategy designed to provoke the male moral subject."[21] Bessarion only makes explicit the implicit function of our sparer anonymous *apophthegma*, in which the monk's identity as a woman provides physical confirmation of his claim to be "a virgin in my body." The possibly less pure male monastic reader should feel shamed by this woman, as he should by Sarah's statement, "It is I who am a man, you who are women." The *Life of Pelagia* carries this motif to a higher level. As a group of bishops sits outside a church in Antioch waiting for a meeting, the actress Pelagia, adorned with expensive jewels, passes by in a late ancient version of a promotional photography spread, seated on a donkey, accompanied by a throng of boys and girls. Exclaiming on the great attention that Pelagia has lavished on her body in order to please her potential lovers, Bishop Nonnus chides his dumbstruck colleagues, "We have paid no attention to our souls in the attempt to adorn them with good habits so that Christ may desire to dwell in us. . . . And maybe we should even go and become the pupils of this lascivious woman" (*Vita Pel.* 4–11). When the dead monk Pelagius is discovered to be a woman, the monks "wanted to hide this astonishing fact from the people but were unable to do so. This was to fulfill what is written in the holy Gospel: 'There is nothing hidden which shall not be revealed, and nothing concealed which shall not be made known' (cf. Matt. 10:26)" (*Vita Pel.* 50). As actress and as monk, Pelagia serves to broadcast a moral to men: if a woman exhibits such care and devotion, how much more should a man?

In monastic literature the real women that instruct male monks by shaming them with their virtue inhabit the same world as the real women who tempt male monks by seducing them with their sexuality, often as the instruments of demons (e.g., *Apoph. patr.* N175–77, N189–90). As Arsenius famously put it, "It is through women that the enemy wars against the saints" (*Apoph. patr.*, Arsenius 28). In some stories these two identities combine: a tempting woman prevents the wavering monk from succumbing to his sexual urges.[22] For example, a washerwoman dissuades a monk who wishes to sleep with her by warning him of the guilt he will suffer afterward: the rescued monk and his abbot marvel at this blessing (*Apoph. patr.* N49). A young widow finds it not so easy to cool down her ardent monastic suitor: finally, she says, "I am in my menses, and no one can come near me or smell me because of the foul odor" (N52). In both of these stories the monks are on errands, temporarily in the secular world, and they thank God for the "wisdom" that appears in these women, a theme seen as well in more developed literature about holy women who instruct men, such as Macrina.[23] In a story about a monk named Simeon, the wise woman of the world who instructs the monk becomes nearly abba-like. When Simeon, still a layman, wishes to marry the widow of his deceased wealthy friend and business partner, the unnamed woman puts Simeon through an elaborate parabolic spiritual exercise worthy of any esteemed elder training his disciple. The story uncharacteristically refers to the woman's attraction to Simeon's "youth and beauty," thus further conforming her to a (male) monastic identity by portraying her as tempted by a beautiful body.[24] Displaying her "intelligence and temperance," the widow persuades Simeon to become a monk and declares herself "to have renounced my husband" (Apoph. patr. N84). A variety of monastic literature's female roles coalesce in this real woman—temptress, woman of the world, shamingly virtuous monk—and amplify into the role of a female abba, a miniature version of a Macrina. These wise, instructing "real women" retain the monastic association of women with "the world" by their location: the monk meets the woman in the world while on an errand or in his premonastic life, and she sends him (back) to the desert.

Our monks who are really women are located in the desert, but the problem of the world sticks to them as women and follows them into their stories. In the anonymous anecdote "worldly people" (kosmikoi) form the audience who witness the revelation of the monk as a woman: monastic life itself seems to suffer an embarrassing exposure of its truth to the secular admirers upon whom monastic prestige depends. It does not describe the reaction of the "worldly people" to the revelation of a woman's virginal body, but its concluding announcement that "he was truly a virgin" both confirms and draws a question mark over the story of his life that the monk had told his visitors. The monks who discover that Pelagius is actually Pelagia try to hide this fact, but the gathered crowds do not permit it. These moments open out the shaming function of the revealed women: they suggest not only that male monks are failing to live up to their monastic calling, but also that the reality of monastic life fails to live up to its narrated form. The female body's appearance makes evident a gap between reality and representation, not only in how monks see themselves but also in how their lay admirers see them. In the Life of Pelagia, this awkward, even dangerous moment of potential monastic inauthenticity is quickly resolved with the quotation of Matthew ("There is nothing hidden which shall not be revealed") and with the glorious funeral procession for Pelagia "as for a righteous woman" (Vita Pel. 50). The gap between reality and representation opened up by the appearance of the woman holds in it not only shame and embarrassment, but also pleasure and productivity—a new good story about the desert for the worldly audience. It is a lesson perhaps both for the ancient monks who feared exposure and for the (post)modern historian who may lament the loss of positivist certainty.

The Bessarion story presents a more indirect and complicated engagement of the revealed women with the world and thus with the problem of representation. At the center of the anecdote lies Bessarion's meeting with John of Lycopolis, in which he interprets the famous monk's vision to mean that "the temples would be overthrown." The narrator Doulas informs us that this is indeed what happened. Framing the encounter with John are the two meetings with the unnamed brother. In the first, the brother refuses to speak with or otherwise acknowledge Bessarion and Doulas; in the second, the brother is dead. At its extremities, the story begins with Bessarion standing in prayer for fourteen days and miraculously producing water, and it ends with the revelation of the woman's body and Bessarion's moral, "See how women triumph over Satan, while we behave shamefully in the cities." What are "we" monks doing "in the cities" that they should feel shamed by the cross-dressing monk? Unlike the anonymous anecdote and the sayings of Sarah, there is no reference here to a struggle by the monk with fornication. The clue seems to be John's vision of the temples being overthrown and its fulfillment: Bishop Theophilus of Alexandria led the violent attack on the Serapeum in 391 and, it seems, enlisted monks in his campaign of destroying pagan images and worship sites. It is this monastic involvement in antipagan violence that Bessarion condemns.[25] The female monk's resolute withdrawal, exemplified by her refusal even to acknowledge the presence of other monastic visitors, contrasts favorably with the male monks' abandonment of desert withdrawal for violent action in the cities.

The presence of John of Lycopolis and the allusion to Theophilus and his campaign against images provide the context for the opening scene of prayer in our apophthegma—the Origenist controversy. Elizabeth Clark has dubbed the 390s "the decade of the image" in Egypt: the antipagan iconoclasm of its early years developed into the anti-images Origenism at the end of the decade.[26] Theophilus, of course, played a notorious role in this drama. At first he followed the decade's iconoclastic path by opposing first pagan images and then the mental images for prayer entertained by the so-called anthropomorphite monks. In 399, however, he did an about-face, supporting the anthropomorphites and attacking the anti-images "Origenist" monks, who followed the teachings on "pure prayer" of Evagrius Ponticus. His actions belie the continuity that Clark persuasively describes: "Evagrius is, then, the quintessential iconoclast, radicalizing and internalizing the historical anti-idolatry campaign waged by Theophilus in the last decade of the fourth century. Before 399, Theophilus's iconoclastic moves against Egyptian paganism found a seamless whole with a theology that set itself against 'imaging' God."[27] Our saying mimics the slipperiness of Theophilus: on the one hand, it condemns the monks' violent participation in the campaign against pagan images; on the other hand, it endorses imageless prayer in its praise of John of Lycopolis and its opening vignette of Bessarion at prayer. In both these moves, however, it condemns the unnamed Theophilus, who led monks into their shameless behavior in the cities and later persecuted the Origenists exemplified by John.[28]

Although the "Origenism" that Evagrius taught addressed a variety of issues in the ascetic life, at its heart was the practice of pure, imageless prayer, an aspect of Evagrius's teaching with which John of Lycopolis is particularly associated (elimination of the passions is another).[29] Evagrius himself reports that he and Ammonius consulted John on the origin of the "light" that one sees during pure prayer.[30] In the Historia monachorum, John exhorts his visitors to preserve "the purity of your understanding" in prayer and warns them against "distractions," including "recollection of indecent images" and "opposing thoughts."[31] Monks "should cultivate stillness and ceaselessly train yourselves for contemplation, that when you pray to God you may do so with a pure mind" (Hist. mon. 1.62). When he translated the Historia into Latin and revised it, Rufinus made the pro-Origenist John more prominent and gave him a new sermon that even more explicitly calls for "pure prayer" and considers the problem of the monk giving God "some kind of appearance or image in his heart in some corporeal likeness" (Hist. mon. 1.22–28). The miraculous production of water for the thirsty Doulas suggests that Bessarion's fourteen days of prayer achieved the purity that John was known to have commended. This saying, then, engages in an acute conflict over representation, the problem of images in thinking about and praying to the divine, while leaving the particulars of that conflict implicit, unsaid.

The complicated allusions that run through this brief narrative render the unexpected revelation of a woman even more puzzling: what is she doing here? In her exhaustive study of cross-dressing in (mostly recent) Western culture, Marjorie Garber argues that "the apparently spontaneous or unexpected or supplementary presence of a transvestite figure in a text (whether fiction or history, verbal or visual, imagistic or 'real') that does not seem, thematically, to be primarily concerned with gender difference or blurred gender indicates a *category crisis elsewhere*, an irresolvable conflict or epistemological crux that destabilizes comfortable binarity, and displaces the resulting discomfort onto a figure that already inhabits, indeed incarnates, the margin."[32] In our anecdotes, as I have suggested earlier, the discomfort occasioned by the female brother is partly rooted in the deception of the monk's cross-dressing: he has misled those who meet him and the readers of the story. In general, the unmasking of this deception calls into question the truth of monastic discourse, especially as it is narrated to outsiders. More specifically in the Bessarion *apophthegma*, the deceptive brother makes explicit and thereby draws to himself the duplicities to which the story alludes, most immediately that of the unmentioned Theophilus, who drew monks into his campaign against images and supported those monks who argued against anthropomorphite images of God, but then who (in the view of our pro-Origenist anecdote) traitorously turned against the Origenist monks. In turn, the female brother incarnates the duplicity of the story itself, which covertly scores political points against Theophilus in a story that ostensibly simply commends complete withdrawal and monastic avoidance of "the cities."

The Origenist subtext speaks further in the female brother's silence: it is his reluctance to enter into conversation without a signal from God that Bessarion commends. The brother's refusal to enter discourse, followed by the undermining of discourse that his female body occasions, indicates the danger of talk, which may produce the representations (*noêmata*) that can obscure pure prayer. "Prayer," Evagrius wrote, "is a state of mind destructive of every earthly representation."[33] The monk who would reach such a state must "deprive himself of all representations" (*Skemm.* 2). Hearing speech— "through the ears"—is one way "by which the mind grasps representations" (17). In Evagrius's view, hearing was an ambiguous and therefore particularly dangerous mode of sense perception. On the one hand, unlike the representations that are grasped through vision, those that come through hearing do not always "imprint a form" and obstruct pure prayer "because a word (can) signify both sensory objects [bad] and contemplative objects [good]" (17). On the other hand, the "most dangerous" thoughts "come by hearing, since it is true, as the proverb says: 'a sad word disturbs the heart of man' [Prov. 12:25]" (19). The silent brother's renunciation of discourse embodies a condition necessary for the pure prayer that Bessarion achieves. It is appropriate that the silent brother be a woman, for like other ascetic authors, Evagrius considered women especially prone to "empty talk" and stressed in his directives to female virgins the virtue of silence, even while praying in church.[34] This woman provides, then, a particularly pointed example of silence triumphing over speech.

Ironically, however, the female brother makes this point through a dramatic visual image, the discovery of his female body, and thus generates a particularly striking representation. As a woman, the brother accomplishes his embodiment of silence literally as a body, female "by nature," and so introduces that which troubles Evagrian Origenism, its "category crisis," the body and its nature. Like Origen, Evagrius criticizes those who would "speak in an evil way of our soul's body"; God's assignment of human intellects to bodies, in which they could learn virtue, is an instance of God's "grace."[35] To have a body is nothing more than to be in "the world" (Keph. Gnost. 6.81). Some monastic ideologies inspired by Origen confidently envision transforming the body itself.[36] On the other hand, Evagrius calls monastic withdrawal (anachôrêsis) a "flight from the body"; the goal is liberation from the body, which obstructs true knowledge (gnôsis) of God.[37] For those intellects that have achieved contemplation, "the entire nature of bodies shall be removed" (Keph. Gnost. 2.62). Unlike the monks who behave shamelessly in the world, the anonymous brother has transformed himself and has left behind a corpse, the body, "a woman by nature."

The real "woman" that these stories construct is the detritus of monastic performance, the material body of sexuality, discourse, and the world that the monastic regime rejects and thereby creates as its opposite. The gendered body is not simply there for the monk to transcend; rather, it is an instance of "matter, not as site or surface, but as *a process of materialization that stabilizes over time to produce the effect of boundary, fixity, and surface we call matter.*"[38] The monastic "man" and "woman," "soul" and "body," are real, but as instances of "the power of discourse to materialize its effects."[39] The appearance of the real woman disturbs because it unmasks the chain of performances that produces the monk as male, beyond sexuality, discourse, the world, as performances.

> To think of "sex" as an imperative in this way means that a subject is addressed and produced by such a norm, and that this norm—and the regulatory power of which it is a token—materializes bodies as an effect of that injunction. And yet, this "materialization," while far from artificial, is not fully stable. For the imperative to be or get "sexed" requires

a differentiated production and regulation of masculine and feminine identification that does not fully hold and cannot be fully exhaustive. And further, this imperative, this injunction, requires and institutes a "constitutive outside"—the unspeakable, the unviable, the nonnarrativizable that secures and, hence, fails to secure the very borders of materiality.[40]

As the "nonnarrativizable," the appearing woman interrupts both the late ancient monastic myth of the desert as male space, without women and apart from "the world," and any late modern scholarly myth of gender as merely rhetorical, unrelated to women and apart from social and material concerns. Even the most radically transformative of monastic ideologies, Origenism, in order to gain traction on the materiality it sought to transcend, made use of gender stability and gender-based practices of renunciation and separation that situated women as that left behind, even when women were themselves performing that ideology.[41]

One strategic value of performativity as an interpretive concept is its recognition of "the power of discourse to materialize its effects."[42] Real women were indeed left behind by husbands and fathers and sons, renounced as temptations and representatives of the world, segregated into their own ascetic communities, legislated to by men. The story of one such eerily real woman displays the power of monastic performance as its most extreme.

> We visited another priest in the district of Achoris called Apelles, a just man who in his former life had been a blacksmith and had abandoned his trade to turn to discipline (*askêsis*). One day when he happened to be forging utensils for the monks, the devil came to him in the form of a woman. In his zeal he snatched up a red-hot piece of iron from the fire with his hand, and badly seared her face and whole body. The brothers heard her screaming in the cell. From that time the man was always able to hold red-hot iron in his hand without being burned. He received us courteously, and told us about the men worthy of God who had been with him and were still living there. (*Hist. mon.* 13.1–2)[43]

Here, too, a real woman unexpectedly appears (as the empirically minded historian might insist). In a striking transfer of corporeality, the body of the male monk loses its reality as a human body, becoming impervious to searing heat, while the thin, attenuated body of the demon acquires feminine corporeal solidity, enough to be seared and to produce audible screaming.

This anecdote incorporates and transcends the story of the dead monk revealed to be a woman. If the "natural" woman who dresses as a male monk seems to vanish into the rhetorical, here the supernatural demon/woman incarnates into the real. Apelles renounces woman/body and, even before his death, achieves a state of passionlessness that defies corporeality. He then begins to talk, to spin the monastic narrative for his admiring visitors. We see here in chilling fashion the power of monastic discourse to materialize the "woman" it constructed.

Notes

For their suggestions and corrections, I am grateful to Virginia Burrus, Dyan Elliott, Bert Harrill, and an anonymous reviewer of the *Journal of Medieval and Early Modern Studies*.

1. *Apophthegmata patrum*, Sisoes 3, in Ward, *Sayings of the Desert Fathers*, 213. For the evidence that Sisoes's saying "represents more an ideal than an accurate description of reality," see Elm, *"Virgins of God,"* 253–82. The Greek *Apophthegmata patrum* (hereafter *Apoph. patr.*) that I cite are found in three collections: (1) the alphabetical collection, denoted by the name of the monk and a saying number (text in Migne, *Patrologia Graeca* 65:71–440; translation in Ward, *Sayings*); (2) a series of anonymous sayings that follows the alphabetical collection in some manuscripts, denoted by N (text of the first four hundred edited by François Nau in *Revue de l'orient chrétien* 12–18 [1907–13]; partial translations in Stewart, *World of the Desert Fathers*, and Ward, *Wisdom of the Desert Fathers*; and (3) the systematic collection, denoted by chapter and saying numbers (text edited by Jean-Claude Guy in *Les Apophthegmes des Pères*, no translation). Hereafter I will cite the *Apoph. patr.* parenthetically in the text, giving the Greek original only for the sayings that I discuss in detail.

2. Clark, "Lady Vanishes" and "Women, Gender, and the Study of Christian History."

3. *Apoph. patr.* N63, in Nau, *Revue de l'orient chrétien* 12 (1907): 393. The translation by Stewart, *World of the Desert Fathers*, 30–31, is inaccurate.

4. The Pelagia literature is vast and complicated. See Séminaire d'histoire des textes de l'École normale supérieure, *Pélagie la Pénitente: Métamorphoses d'une légende*, vol. 1, *Les textes et leur histoire* (Paris: Études Augustiniennes, 1981). See also the treatment of the account by Patricia Cox Miller in this volume.

5. See Anson, "Female Transvestite in Early Monasticism," and many other studies, most recently Davis, "Crossed Texts, Crossed Sex."

6. *Vita Pelagiae* (Syriac), 40–41, in Brock and Harvey, *Holy Women of the Syrian Orient*, hereafter cited parenthetically in the text (using the abbreviation *Vita Pel.*).

7. Cloke, *"This Female Man of God,"* 196.

8. Ibid., 196–97. It is not certain that Sarah was in fact a desert anchorite. See the discussion of her in Harmless, *Desert Christians*.

9. Cf. Clark, "Women, Gender, and the Study," 424.

10. Butler, *Bodies That Matter*, 188.

11. Thus, the essay works in the spirit of Elizabeth Clark's desire to pursue both "women's studies" and "gender studies" in the history of Christianity, yet recognizes with her that the evidence for the ancient period may be more congenial to the latter ("Women, Gender, and the Study," esp. 419).

12. Cassian, *Institutes* 6.19, trans. Ramsey, *John Cassian: The Institutes*, 161. Of course, Cassian did find a means of measuring integrity of heart through the male body—nocturnal emissions. See Brakke, "Problematization of Nocturnal Emissions."

13. Castelli, " 'I Will Make Mary Male.' " See, e.g., *Gospel of Thomas* 114 and *Acts of Paul and Thecla* 25, 40 (where Thecla cuts her hair short and dresses as a man).

14. *Martyrdom of Saints Perpetua and Felicitas* 10.7, in Kraemer, *Maenads, Martyrs, Matrons, Monastics*. See the summary of Elm, "Virgins of God," 267–69; also Cloke, "*This Female Man of God.*"

15. Miller, "Desert Asceticism"; Valantasis, "Constructions of Power," 797.

16. Butler, *Gender Trouble*, 140.

17. Cf. Burrus, *Begotten, Not Made*, 69.

18. *Apoph. patr.*, Bessarion 4, in Migne, *Patrologia Graeca* 65:140–41. I have used but altered the translation of Ward, *Sayings*, 41.

19. Clark, "Lady Vanishes," 29.

20. Coon, *Sacred Fictions*, 82.

21. Goldhill, *Foucault's Virginity*, 136–43, discussing esp. Musonius Rufus.

22. The three examples that follow are found in Stewart, *World of the Desert Fathers*, 13–16.

23. Clark, "Lady Vanishes," 22–26.

24. Although Sarah and our anonymous cross-dressing monk refer to their long struggles against fornication, "no text presents Satan disguised as a handsome boy in order to provoke a girl who has devoted herself to God" (Giannarelli, "Women and Satan," 201).

25. On the attack on the Serapeum and monastic involvement in it, see Clark, *Origenist Controversy*, 53–57, citing our saying as well as *Apoph. patr.*, Theophilus 3. Cf. Ward, *Sayings*, 40.

26. Clark, *Origenist Controversy*, 55, and passim 43–84.

27. Ibid., 84.

28. As Ward puts it, "the ambiguity of his (Theophilus') relationship with the monks is mirrored" in the sayings transmitted under his name (*Sayings*, 80), esp. *Apoph. patr.*, Theophilus 2–3.

29. On pure prayer, see Stewart, "Imageless Prayer," 173–204; Clark, *Origenist Controversy*, 67–71.

30. Evagrius Ponticus, *Antirrheticus* 6.16, in Frankenburg, *Euagrios Ponticus*, 524; Clark, *Origenist Controversy*, 70; Stewart, "Imageless Prayer," 194.

31. *Historia monachorum* 1.23, 25, in Russell, *Lives of the Desert Fathers*, hereafter cited parenthetically in the text, using the abbrev. *Hist. mon.*

32. Marjorie Garber, *Vested Interests*, 17, emphasis original.

33. Evagrius Ponticus, *Skemmata* 26, hereafter cited parenthetically in the text, using

the abbreviation Skemm.; cf. Evagrius, On Prayer 71, in Evagrius, Greek Ascetic Corpus, 200. For a clear discussion, see Stewart, "Imageless Prayer," 186–91, esp. the references gathered at 190 n. 81.

34. Evagrius, Sententiae ad virginem 13, 15, 25, 33, in Nonnenspiegel und Monachsspiegel, ed. Gressmann, 152–65. Cf. Athanasius's directions to virgins, described in Brakke, Athanasius and Asceticism, 72.

35. Evagrius, Kephalaia Gnostica 4.60, in Les six centuries des "Kephalaia Gnostica," ed. Guillaumont, hereafter cited parenthetically in the text, using the abbreviation Keph. Gnost.; Evagrius, Praktikos 53, in Évagre le Pontique, ed. Guillaumont and Guillaumont.

36. For example, see the Letters of Antony, discussed briefly in Brakke, "Problematization of Nocturnal Emissions," 436–38.

37. Evagrius, Praktikos 52 (flight); Keph. Gnost. 1.58; 2.6; 4.70, 74 (liberation); and Gnostikos 23 (obstruction).

38. Butler, Bodies That Matter, 9, emphasis original.

39. Ibid., 187.

40. Ibid., 187–88.

41. Compare Rebecca Krawiec's analysis of Shenoute's "universal monasticism" as one that "existed for all monks 'whether male or female,' thus retaining gender, and was not a monasticism that recognized 'neither male nor female,' suggesting repression of sexual difference" (Shenoute and the Women of the White Monastery, 132).

42. Butler, Bodies That Matter, 187.

43. I have used but altered the translation of Russell, Lives of the Desert Fathers, 93.

✛   No Friendly Letters: Augustine's
Correspondence with Women

MAUREEN A. TILLEY

Augustine's opinions about women are usually mined from his treatises and
sermons, where he treated women as types of approved or disapproved conduct.[1] The women whom Augustine described there were notional women,
not women who actually existed.[2] But notional women do not always bear
strong resemblance to living women.

The women in the *Confessions* likewise are problematic. Much has been
made of Monica, but the only Monica there was shaped by the exigencies of
his texts.[3] She appears at convenient moments, a *mulier ex machina*, to provide
the womb from which the constantly evolving Augustine was repeatedly
reborn. But like women in theories of reproduction in antiquity, she does not
serve any active purpose, only a passive one. Even Augustine's long-time
companion and mother of his son fares no better. Her story is less the tale of
a particular woman than an account of one woman's emotional impact on
Augustine. She is a wall on which the shadow of Augustine's emotions
mimed his inner journey from self-absorption to attention to God.

On the other hand, Augustine's correspondence with women provides
some relatively underutilized evidence for enriching his biography.[4] These
women are not mere foils for Augustine's theology or his self-portrait. They
often have independently verifiable biographies and interests other than
those of Augustine. His representations of the women to themselves had to
bear some resemblance to their own self-image in order for his letters to find
fruitful reception. So there is in the letters, more than in his other writings,
some control on the picture he painted of them.

Yet in antiquity the letters functioned not only as private correspondence.
They were copied and circulated among friends—and enemies. Some, as
Augustine often attests, might circulate in spite of the author's wishes. The
contents of letters functioned as extended discussions in a time before elec-
tronic mail. In that respect, ideals about women did appear. But, in order to

be convincing to readers beyond the primary addressees, comments on real women had to bear some resemblance to the way in which those women were more broadly perceived. Thus information about historical women may be garnered from them, as well as hints of the authors' attitudes toward real and ideal women. Considering Augustine's correspondence with women helps round out knowledge of the women as well as of Augustine. It also shows how he avoided women who approached him as friends and provides verification of his deliberate distancing of himself from women during his episcopate, even women potentially useful to him.

Augustine, Friendship, and Women

Augustine was imbued with classical concepts of friendship: a relationship of equals in which neither was debtor but both wished the best for each other, the union of two souls. Augustine added that Christian friendship had to be ordered in the sight of God. No friend could be valued more than God.[5] Thus his friendships, at least as recorded in the first half of the *Confessions*, that is, before his conversion, were troublesome and unsatisfactory precisely because his earthly friendships in that period were more important than his relationship with God.

Because of classical concepts of male and female inequality, Augustine excluded the possibility of a woman as an equal, even before the Fall.[6] If God had wanted Adam to have an Edenic equal, that is, a stimulating conversation partner, God would have created another man. Any friendship between a man and a woman, even in Eden, was ordered to an exclusive relationship for the sake of progeny, a relationship not appropriate for celibate men. Not only did Augustine's theory of friendship thus exclude women, he practiced what he preached. An analysis of his letters shows that he made the exclusion of friendship with women an art. It was effected in two ways: first by turning them into debtors, thus excluding them as equals, and second by turning their appeals for pastoral help into occasions for using personal correspondence as an outlet for the publication of theology.

Augustine and Women in Correspondence

Augustine's correspondence includes several letters to women. None appears to date from before 395.[7] Thus all were correspondence between the bishop of a diocese and the women under his pastoral care—women from wealthy and influential families, some from around Hippo, others from farther away. Who were these women and how were they related to one another and to Augustine?[8] What does his correspondence reveal of Augustine's attitudes toward women and the impressions they made on him? In answering these questions, I will consider the women in Augustine's letters roughly in chronological order, varying the series to discuss members of the same family or related letters. I begin with a short biography of each woman, then discuss the letters, commenting on the gendered relationships in them. I conclude with a summary of what may be learned from his letters to reveal his general attitude toward the women.

THERASIA

Little is known of Therasia, the wife of Paulinus of Nola, other than the fact that she married Paulinus (355–431) in Spain, where the couple lived when Paulinus was baptized in 389. By 393 they had begun to live an ascetic life, divesting themselves of her property and his. In 395, a year after Paulinus became a priest, they moved to Nola where they established monasteries for men and women. Therasia died between 405 and 415. The couple's friends included her husband's teacher Ausonius, Ambrose of Milan, Augustine's friend Alypius, his patron Romanianus, and Licentius, Romanianus's son.[9] Although the couple never met Augustine in person, they enjoyed a lively correspondence, despite their connections to Augustine's Pelagian opponents.[10]

There is no extant correspondence between Augustine and Therasia apart from that written to both members of the couple jointly. *Epistles* 25, 30, and 94 from Paulinus and Therasia to Augustine begin in a plural authorial voice but quickly give way to the singular. An imaginative reading of the plural sections as reflecting Therasia's voice runs up against various anomalies that can only be solved by attributing the plural language to Paulinus or his (male) religious community. Similarly, Augustine's *Epistles* 31, 42, and 45 to husband and wife indicate that he was writing to Paulinus and his clergy rather than to the couple.[11] So the content of the letters tells us nothing about Therasia. They do, however, illuminate their author. Augustine's letters to couples do not differ in tone and content from letters written to husbands alone. In the case of Therasia and Paulinus, when they jointly addressed him, he addressed them jointly. It appears that Augustine deferred to his correspondents' sensibilities, addressing his letters to couples as they signed theirs to him even when he actually wrote only to the husband. Thus this set of letters to and from Augustine reveals his single-mindedness in correspondence. He addresses the responsible party directly and gets to the heart of the issue immediately, even if politely addressing a wife too. This is paralleled in his correspondence with men. When compared to many other letter writers of antiquity, Augustine spends very little time on preliminary or closing niceties.

ALBINA AND MELANIA

Albina and Melania were at the heart of a family network that included the most distinguished homes in Rome. Augustine and Jerome cultivated their support against the Pelagians.[12] Albina's father was probably Rome's prefect in 360; her mother was the ascetic Melania the Elder. Albina married her daughter, Melania the Younger (ca. 385–439), to Pinianus, a cousin and the heir of a wealthy family, when she was thirteen. After the birth of their second child, Pinianus accepted the ascetic life his wife desired. After 410 they traveled with the widowed Albina to family estates in Africa, temporarily living near Thagaste, Augustine's hometown. This was when Augustine sent Albina *Epistles* 124 and 126.[13]

Elizabeth Clark is correct in saying that there is no evidence that Augustine had face-to-face contact with aristocratic women such as these before the second decade of the fifth century.[14] But Augustine was already acquainted with the family through correspondence with Albina's husband, Publicola (396–99).[15] When Albina, Melania, and Pinianus came to Africa, Augustine already knew them sufficiently well that his *Epistle* 124 shows familiarity both with their plight as exiles from the sack of Rome and with their characters. He expresses regret that health and pastoral cares at Hippo kept him from visiting. Unless one accuses the bishop of dissembling to comfort them, he seems to have had genuine affection for them and personal distress at their plight.

In 411 Melania and Pinianus came to Hippo without Albina. Some of the Christians at Hippo attempted to force ordination on Pinianus. They doubtless recognized piety and administrative talents but were probably also interested in the wealth that would come to the local church at his death. The prospect of the endowments, however, would make Augustine the envy of other bishops.[16]

The pressure to ordain Pinianus was immense. Augustine blamed it on lowlife agitators and explained to Albina how he had tried to stem the frenzy by threatening that he would resign if the ordination took place. Pinianus's refusal to be ordained placed Augustine as host in an awkward situation. If he honored his guest's wishes, he faced a hostile church. If he persuaded Pinianus to be ordained, he would be in the position of helping to alienate large tracts of land from the family and from the control of Albina. For her benefit and in his own defense Augustine wrote *Epistle* 126. He described weighing all the alternatives. He reported that Pinianus himself cut the Gordian knot, avoiding both violence and ordination: Pinianus said that if they forced him, he would immediately leave Hippo, but to placate the crowd he swore a carefully worded oath that if he ever were ordained it would be in Hippo.

What was Melania's role? How did Augustine react? She wanted to prevent the ordination, protesting that the weather at Hippo was deleterious to her husband's health, but, according to Augustine, Pinianus himself brushed this aside (Ep. 126.4). Later, when the congregation forced some bishops to countersign his oath, she persuaded Augustine not to join them. He seems to have understood neither her actions nor her motives and did not justify them to her mother. He says only that the daughter might have been looking for some loophole to invalidate her husband's promise (Ep. 126.5). He was not particularly close to Melania and did not consider her wishes significant, at least not as significant as that of his congregation. He deferred to her only when it suited his purposes in defending himself. Again, Augustine's single-mindedness pushed a wife from the stage on which her husband was the significant actor.

His relationship with Albina was more important to him. Augustine was concerned to defend himself and his congregation in her eyes. No, he had not suggested that Pinianus take an oath. No, he did not force him, though he did admit helping him find the right words. In his letter he even tries to show how his congregation is not avaricious and that Pinianus's ordination would be a good thing. He tries most of all to convince her that no one is trying to bilk her of her property (Ep. 126.6–8). He supports his version of the events with strong words: those who proffer a different version either have their facts wrong or are lying (Ep. 126.6).

All this he relates under oath to Albina, to preserve his reputation (Ep. 126.8). Finally, he defends his role in Pinianus's taking of the oath by supporting the goodness of oaths to do good and of the priesthood—even if exercised in Hippo.

This was a difficult situation for Augustine. He had to justify his own conduct and to confront a woman of remarkable financial means who had already donated large sums to Christians in North Africa (Ep. 126.7). Of all his correspondence with women, this is the only letter in which Augustine was at a distinct disadvantage. No matter what he says about the situation, he is not in control; he is doing "damage-control."

Augustine's damage-control must have been effective, since his relationship with the family continued, and in 418 he wrote *De gratia Christi* and *De peccato originali* to the mother, the daughter, and her husband. He wrote ostensibly because they had requested from him clarification of Pelagian doctrine. It is significant that such an extended reply was the answer. Yes, they had requested it, but it is difficult to believe that their inquiry was as detailed as the reply. The fact that he took this time to reply—amidst his professedly busy schedule—indicates the respect he had not only for Pinianus but primarily for Albina. This respect was not simply personal but reflected her position as the heart of a network of Roman correspondents whom Augustine wanted to reach. Finally, this is the first of several examples of Augustine's prolixity in his correspondence with women. But it should be noted that Augustine wrote extended explanations only when he composed a doctrinal treatise as a letter.

PROBA, ITALICA, AND JULIANA

Anicia Faltonia Proba was a member of the Roman aristocracy, the child of the very influential Anicii. Juliana and Italica, Proba's daughters-in-law, were correspondents of Augustine and of John Chrysostom too. Juliana's daughter Demetrias figures in Jerome's correspondence (Ep. 130) and Augustine's (Epp. 150, 188, and *De bono viduitatis* 18).

Augustine wrote Epistles 92 and 99 to Italica about 408. Epistles 130 and 131 went to Proba alone around 412–13, and Epistle 150 to Proba and her daughter Juliana in late 413 or early 414. In 414, after the death of Juliana's husband, Augustine wrote to Juliana *De bono viduitatis*. Later, between October 417 and April 418, he and Alypius wrote Epistle 188 to her. In all these missives Augustine is concerned to support the women's resolves to begin or continue continent lives and to dedicate their wealth to charity.

The first letters were to Italica. There were at least five letters, three from her and two from him (Ep. 99.1). Only his survive (Ep. 92 and 99). Epistle 92 is a letter of consolation on the death of her husband. He indicates that it might not be exactly what she wants to hear but that she will have to make what she can of it (Ep. 92.1). His consoling remarks open by exhorting her not to grieve as non-Christians do, who had no hope of eternity (1 Thess. 4:13). Instead, she should anticipate reunion with her husband in heaven, where she would have a closer friendship with him than on earth. Any friendship Augustine might have had with her is deflected toward her husband.

From this description of seeing a loved one in heaven, Augustine quickly turns to his real theme: the eyes of the body cannot see God; the beatific vision can be achieved only with the spiritual eyes of the afterlife. It is difficult to see how this letter would have been any consolation to a recently bereaved widow. It is as if Augustine was not really comfortable with the intimacy an act of consolation required. However, as he admits, he has to send something, so he is sending an essay the subject of which is comfortable for him, one that will counter the erroneous speculation on the vision of God circulating at Rome.[17]

In *Epistle* 99 Augustine expresses his disappointment that Italica had not sent more news of Rome. But he tries to show how God's promised suffering is a prelude to eternal life. Next, he reports that he is unable to exchange two properties as she requested on behalf of an otherwise unknown Julian. One belonged to his church at Hippo and the other to another church. The letter ends abruptly with Augustine's refusal to alienate property held by his church. His hands are tied, he claims—a nice excuse when denying an influential woman.

About four years later, Augustine wrote *Epistle* 130 to Proba. He tailored this formal treatise on prayer to Proba's state in life as a wealthy widow. He begins with the idea that he is discharging a debt in fulfilling his promise to write to her. Augustine was never comfortable being in debt to a woman, and he makes it clear that he considered each letter to her the discharge of his debts.

Elsewhere, in *Epistle* 155.1, Augustine says that this theme of owing and discharging debt is one contrary to true friendship.[18] In his letters to male friends Augustine never uses this language, but it shows up quite frequently to women, a subtle but clear indication that their relationship was not one of friendship, but of duty.

His theme is a paraphrase of 1 Timothy 5:5: "she is truly a widow who is desolate; she places her hope in the Lord and offers persistent prayer day and night" (Ep. 130.1). The suppliant's prayer in the second clause is a result of being a true widow as defined by Scripture. Given that Proba was bereft of neither family nor fortune, how could Augustine link the two clauses in their application to this wealthy woman? Augustine's approach was one he used consistently with the Anicii women. He made her—and them—participants in the fulfillment of prophecy. He tells her that she should feel desolate so that God's word would be fulfilled and that she should continue to pray until she was consoled as a person bereaved (Ep. 130.6–7). Like a widow too, she is to despise the things of earth, including her wealth, which she is to give to the poor, since it could not console her.

What is she to pray for in her insistent and incessant prayers? Augustine tells her to pray for happiness, that is, desiring what was proper, and counseling that the desire for money is the root of evil. Prayer, he tells her, is appropriate for all widows, and all—widows included—are desolate before the Lord (Ep. 130.8–11).

His final plea would have appealed to a Roman widow of more than modest means. In a city and society where competition on all fronts was the *modus vivendi* of high society, he entreats her to compete with the others in her household in praying for him (Ep. 130.14–15). Augustine followed this letter with the short but not sweet *Epistle* 131. In this letter, he reminds her that she cannot truly pray for heaven if fortune is smiling on her. She needs to enter fully into the desolation of a true widow by divesting herself of her fortune.

Epistle 150, from Augustine to Proba and Juliana, and *Epistle* 188, from Augustine and Alypius to Juliana, concern Demetrias, Juliana's daughter. In the first letter Augustine encourages her family to support her. The family, he writes, will be more glorious by her virginity than by her family's consuls. Again Augustine appeals to the family's sense of competition, but he adds a motif of reversal already used in *Epistle* 130 to Proba. He plays off the reputation of a young woman against senior men, angelic purity versus mortal fame, and virginity versus marriage. He appeals to the grandmother and mother to enjoy in Demetrias what they lack; through her they might be vicarious virgins. He ends by acknowledging receipt of, though not expressing explicit thanks for, a souvenir of Demetrias's profession ceremony. Outright thanks might have made him indebted to them.

Between *Epistles* 150 and 188, Pelagian teaching seems to have been making headway in the family Augustine had cultivated, so the response of Augustine and Alypius is strong and to the point. Where Pelagius appealed to Demetrias's position, family wealth, and physical beauty as her ornaments, they focus on these not as personal accomplishments but as the gifts of a heavenly spouse from whom she has received them.

De bono viduitatis, written between the two letters in 414, addresses the same issues. In this letter-treatise, Augustine expresses his view that just as the ability to vow virginity is God's gift, so also is the widow's continence. While Demetrias had vowed virginity, her mother Juliana had already vowed the continence of widowhood when Augustine wrote to her in 414. Though the treatise is addressed primarily to Juliana, Proba is also explicitly included in the intended readers.

As in many of his letters to women, Augustine begins *De bono* with language of the debt he is discharging in answering her previous letters. Not wishing to be in debt to a woman, he turns the tables and suggests that her distribution of her wealth as a widow will make others indebted to her, although, of course, he is not suggesting that her largesse be distributed to him and thus make him her debtor.[19]

The prime reason for this treatise was to encourage women who have vowed continence as widows to remain firm in their vows. By assimilating widows to virgins, Augustine and Alypius could use 1 Corinthians 7 to encourage the women to persevere in the same gift as virgins (De bono vid. 3). The authors of the letter thus are doing what Augustine had done in Epistle 130: they place themselves in the sweep of biblical history and make themselves the fulfillment of prophecy (De bono vid. 10).

Epistle 188 and De bono viduitatis were, with the exception of Epistle 126 to Albina, the longest of Augustine's missives to women. Where doctrine was concerned Augustine and Alypius were alert. They took the time and energy to make sure that the nuances of Pelagius's appeals might be thoroughly deconstructed. They did so perhaps not so much because of intimacy with the family as because of the influence these women wielded over the other women in their households and over the larger society of Roman ascetics. Similarly with Epistle 126 to Albina, the issue was not only one of setting straight what had actually happened but also of not alienating a woman of influence and wealth. With both women, their actual or potential status as donors and women of power was significant.

FELICITAS (411–30) AND THE CONSECRATED
VIRGINS AT HIPPO

About 423 Augustine wrote Epistle 210 to "Mother Felicitas, Brother Rusticus, and the sisters who are with you." She was the successor of Augustine's sister as praeposita (superior) of a monastery in Hippo. Her brother may have been Sixtus Rusticus Julianus, proconsul in Africa in 371–73.

Augustine addresses Felicitas and Rusticus first about taking warranted criticism. One ought to be grateful for the complainant who has brought the critique. Unity and peace might spring from bearing one another's faults in community. With no rhetorical transition at all he moves from a positive consideration of criticism to the negative issue of dissent. He pleads with his addressees to come to agreement lest the dissent corrode the community.

In Epistle 211, written about the same time, Augustine addresses the whole community.[20] The congregation had appealed to him as their bishop and expected a visit from him to unify them. He almost sounds glad not to have gone, not to have become more involved in their wrangling and the issues that brought their dissension to birth. If Epistle 210 stressed the good that can come from living together and from mutual correction, and the benefits of unity, *Epistle* 211 is just the opposite. Dissent and schism are plainly excoriated. Augustine compares the congregation to Paul's quarreling Corinthians. The letter reveals what was hidden in *Epistle* 210: that some of the women had revolted against Felicitas. They relied on Rusticus as leader. Felicitas had been at the monastery longer than anyone else and perhaps was already the *praeposita* when the most senior nuns entered. Soon after the arrival of Rusticus as *praepositus*, the women broke into groups that accepted or rejected Felicitas's authority based on their relationship to Rusticus. Augustine exhorts the women to repent and to accept Felicitas's authority.

The strong language of this letter, compared with the guarded language of *Epistle* 210, may indicate a lapse of time or a worsening of conflict, but it reveals, first, that Augustine expected more of those in higher rank, and, second, that he strongly favored the authority of the woman who had been leader over the man who had more recently arrived. Her authority was prized over whatever status Rusticus enjoyed.[21] Augustine's position was both authoritarian and hierarchical. Felicitas was in charge—however that headship was gained—and nothing ought to have been done to weaken the preexisting order. Like others in the Roman Empire, such as Paul lecturing the Corinthians and Ignatius the Ephesians, Augustine valued order.[22] He would not disturb order within the monastery because Felicitas was the properly constituted authority there. Disturbing her authority would set a precedent for continued disorder. Under those circumstances, the small society of monastic women would never achieve harmony.

Augustine's other letters, which deal with issues of authority or dissension in the community, show what similarities and differences there are between his treatment of men and women on issues of authority. In a similar situation with monks, Augustine did intervene. *Epistles* 214 and 215 and the treatise *De gratia et libero arbitrio* relate how in 426/427 he received news that a controversy over grace and free will had split the community of monks at Hadrumetum. Augustine uses the situation of division at Corinth as a biblical model for both the women's and the men's communities, but the similarities in his replies end there. The women are exhorted to unity and charity, while the men were cautioned against pride and a lack of logic. One may initially be tempted to find these differences to be exhortations crafted for sexist reasons: the women were catty and behaving like children, and men were striving as intellectuals. The letters, however, may address the situations as much as Augustine's patriarchal attitudes. While the women's situation split the community over the question of leadership and obedience and made life uncomfortable in the short run, it did not entail doctrine directly or have clearly eschatological consequences. Augustine considered the men's split more severe because it concerned doctrine, which might have led the monks into heresy and entailed the loss of their eternal souls.[23] Anytime doctrine was concerned, Augustine wrote at length and carefully.

The situations of *Epistles* 78 and 213 are even more instructive. In *Epistle* 78, written around 403/404, Augustine says that he hesitates to remove from the list of clergy a priest accused of a crime. He was predisposed to favor the priest in his office over his lay accuser. For the sake of the order that would be breached if he barred an innocent person and was later forced to retract his ban, he refuses to strike the priest's name from the list. The future order of the church made the temporary disorder worth risking. In *Epistle* 213 Augustine shows that he was willing to violate the canons of Nicaea in appointing his own successor in order to promote order in his fractious diocese. It appears from these letters that Augustine was concerned with upholding authority and order within the local church whether dealing with women or men.

PAULINA

Epistle 127 is addressed both to Paulina and Armentarius, her husband, and *Epistle* 147 to Paulina alone. For our purposes, I will presume that the Paulinas addressed are the same woman. In *Epistle* 147 Paulina is greeted in the salutation as *famula dei*. The term was often used of monastic women, but Augustine also used it for married women living lives of continence.[24]

This second letter, written about 413, is a lengthy treatise of fifty-four chapters on the vision of God. There are only a few things to note. First, Augustine casts himself as a debtor to Paulina in his promise to write in answer to her request. He seems to be anxious not to leave himself indebted. While this debtor relationship was a commonplace in epistolary writing, it gains even more force in connection with Augustine's desire never to be indebted to a woman, as we have seen in earlier letters. Second, he mentions Galatians 3:28, "There are not Jew and Greek, slave and free, male and female," in his comments on the eyes of the body seeing God.[25] While this verse has often been cited as an appeal for female equality in the church, here the citation simply reinforced Augustine's contention that any body of either gender would be unnecessary for the vision of God. Finally, one might think, here we have Augustine discoursing long and broadly on a truly abstruse subject—and to a woman. But perhaps we ought not to take his remarks too seriously. While the letter is indeed in answer to a woman's request, it need not indicate her readership alone, and it is of a piece with *Epistle* 92 to Italica.

He is discharging a personal debt and simultaneously using the letter to reach a wider circle. Thus the letter actually reveals very little concerning Augustine's thought about or relations with women other than the theme of debt, which keeps them from true friendship.

The first of these letters, *Epistle 127*, was written in late 410. It is more personal and does reveal a little more about Augustine and women. It is addressed to Paulina and Armentarius, who had agreed to a celibate life. Augustine is concerned that the strain of their vow might tempt them, more specifically the husband, to break it.

While the heading of the letter and its conclusion seem to indicate that the letter was meant for both husband and wife, the grammar of the body of the letter contains direct speech only to the husband. Like the correspondence with Therasia and Paulinus, this is a letter to a woman in name only. Only when he issues the direct command, "Pay what you have vowed," does Augustine slip into the plural.[26]

In the body of the letter Augustine appeals to the nature of love and exhorts Armentarius not to make his wife dependent on him and needy and not to treat her the way Romans treated their city in the days when the Goths were attacking: "Let us not despoil our beloved in order to hold her as they do."[27] Toward the end of the letter, Augustine admits that there is one reason why Armentarius should not fulfill his vow, that is, if Paulina, for any reason, refuses to implement the vow, "for such vows are not to be made by married people without a mutual will and agreement. . . . God does not exact of us what is vowed at another's expense; rather, He forbids us to trespass on another's rights."[28] Augustine reinforces his opinion with Paul's admonition that husbands and wives do not control their own bodies (1 Cor. 7:4). Yet this statement should not be read as an indirect appeal to Paulina—as if she were reading over her husband's shoulder. Rather, it is a direct command to Armentarius to consider the unity of the couple and not to request what she is unwilling to give. If she is willing to make and fulfill the vow of continence, he should play the man and be continent, motivated by a pun on *vir* (man) and virtue.

In this case Augustine encourages a husband to defer to his wife's wishes. His appeal for unity is scriptural. We might wonder how Augustine would treat a couple if it were the wife who made the demand. We are fortunate to have such an example in our next letter.

ECDICIA

Epistle 262 is the only evidence we have for Ecdicia, a wealthy married woman, in charge of her own property. Both she and her husband were

Christian, but she was much more interested in asceticism than he. Her letter to Augustine does not survive, but his answer, written circa 418, reveals that after the birth of their son, she had vowed continence. On biblical grounds (Num. 30:10–15), her husband could have annulled her vow, but he too seemed to have been interested in asceticism, at least at first. Apparently, she went farther and faster in the project than her husband was ready to do.

The husband had several objections to her conduct. First, he was so pained by his abrupt loss of consortium that he took a mistress. Second, her conduct had an impact on his social status. She gave large donations to wandering ascetics, wore drab clothing, and went without makeup. She acted like a widow, which she was not. Their marriage appeared to be no marriage. Augustine once and only once tells her that she should have obeyed her husband as her head (Ep. 262.8). The bulk of his response focuses on the unity that should be theirs and is not. She should have brought her husband along, even if slowly, in the practice of asceticism by moderating her behavior. Augustine gives her many examples of how she might have done that.

Two particular items stand out in Augustine's exhortations. He excoriates Ecdicia's failure to support their son, perhaps a reflection of his own childhood penury.[29] Then he comments on her dress. To a modern ear, this is the least important issue, and the space he affords dress seems disproportionate. But the underlying issue for both property and dress is familial order. Things should be in good order and be perceived as such: Ecdicia should be an obedient wife, and her husband should see her obedience—in bed and at the bank. Also things ought not to be perceived as what they are not: she is not a widow and should not have dressed like one. On all counts, governance and order are as paramount here for Augustine as they were in his dealings with the women of Felicitas's monastery.

Epistle 262 shares another theme with Epistle 127: that a spouse who wants to be continent might bring an unwilling partner to the practice of continence. In both cases Augustine uses unity and Scripture as his appeals. But there are significant gender-based differences between the letters. When addressing a man, Armentarius, Augustine makes his prime theme love and unity. When addressing Ecdicia, a woman, his appeal is to the duty of obedience. These differences may be construed as misogyny, but there is more at stake here. Augustine did not know Armentarius and Paulina well, they were at the outset of their project, and they had not asked his advice. In Ecdicia's case, he knew her well, her project had advanced in time, and she had appealed to him for help. Even considering such differences, Augustine's basic advice—the contrast in virtues recommended, love and unity for a man and obedience for a woman—parallels Augustine's instruction to men and women in monasteries: virtues of the intellect are for men and those of submission are for women.

FABIOLA

This Fabiola is not the same woman who was a close friend of Jerome,[30] but she was at least an acquaintance of Jerome, who mentioned her to Augustine without introduction in one of his letters from 410, saying Augustine could borrow some of the works Jerome had sent her.[31] She apparently was a well-read woman whom Augustine knew shortly after 410. Mandouze places her in Africa by 411.[32] Many Romans fled there after the sack of Rome. Augustine's *Epistle* 267 answered her now lost letter. In it, he likens the communion of friends separated by physical distance to the contemplation of the One. This is classical friendship theory[33] and the closest Augustine ever comes to any expression of friendship for a woman, yet he is quite satisfied to retain the distance and makes no comments encouraging any diminution of it.

There is little reason to doubt that the addressee of Augustine's *Epistle* 267 is the same Fabiola addressed in *Epistle* 20*, written in 422. The salutations in the two letters are nearly identical. In this later letter, Augustine discusses Antoninus of Fussala, whom Fabiola had supported financially. Antoninus had been a disastrous episcopal appointee of Augustine to an area recently converted from Donatism.[34] To discipline him for his manifold crimes against his flock, the bishops of his province circumscribed his diocese to a small village. This effectively limited his influence without violating the norms of Nicaea against the deposition of bishops.[35]

In *Epistle* 20* Augustine attempts to distance himself from the miscreant and simultaneously tries to narrow the gap between Fabiola and Antoninus so that the woman who funded him would have more good influence over him than Augustine, his nominal superior. Augustine exhorts her to grant him not the funds for which he was sure to petition but the alms of spiritual advice (Ep. 20*.27–28). Augustine positions himself in the place of the Lord in calling her to do her duty (Ep. 20*.28).

When faced with a woman of wealth and influence, Augustine is able to ask favors, but he writes in such a way that the favor would seem to her to be the only just and honorable thing to do for the church and her own soul (Ep.

20*.33). Once again Augustine casts himself not as a friend but as someone avoiding indebtedness.

FELICIA

In 422 or 423, Augustine wrote *Epistle* 208 to Felicia, a consecrated virgin and former Donatist, in response to her concerns about pastoral leadership among the Donatists. But there is nothing particularly distinctive here. Augustine repeats the same arguments found in his earlier anti-Donatist treatises in a very simple manner. Here, as in his letters to Proba and Juliana, *Epistle* 130, and *De bono viduitatis*, Augustine places his correspondent in the text of the Bible. She is not to be upset by the conduct of Donatist clergy, "for the Lord himself predicted it in the gospel" (Ep. 108.2). He exhorts her to conduct herself correctly by making that conduct the fulfillment of prophecy. He encourages her also to concentrate not on the conduct of clergy but on the fulfillment of her vow of virginity (Ep. 108.7). In other words, she should tend her own garden.

FLORENTINA

Epistle 266 (408/409) reveals Florentina as a respected, upper-class ascetic living with and supported by her parents. Her mother already had written Augustine more than once about her daughter. Apparently Florentina was a self-willed young woman who had threatened her mother that she would write directly to Augustine. For whatever reason, the mother preferred to buffer her daughter's requests to Augustine. Augustine answered the daughter directly with a mixed message. He writes that she should feel free to ask him anything and that her questioning him would serve to perfect him. Simultaneously, he insists that the truly wise are not in need of instruction as they are taught by God. In essence, he appears to be saying, yes, I am humbly at your service, but also, if you were wise, you would not ask. Such a response must have put an end to the mother's letters; she no longer needed to write because her daughter had Augustine's direct permission to ask any advice she needed. But at the same time, it would have served simultaneously to both compliment and put off the young woman.

MAXIMA

Maxima was the author of a now lost letter to Augustine about the Incarnation. From *Epistle* 264 (418) one can deduce that she lived outside North Africa and that she was wealthy and independent enough, perhaps as a widow, for Augustine to address her as head of a household. She possessed theological tracts on the Incarnation to which Augustine did not have access. While the texts may not have been orthodox or at least raised doctrinal questions, in his reply to her, Augustine does not discourage her reading or thinking about the issue. The fact that she is distressed by what she has read encourages Augustine to approve her orthodoxy. He simply asks her for a copy of the book. As if her granting the request might somehow place him in debt to her, he immediately counters with the offer that in return he will oblige her with a copy of his writing on the subject if she sends scribes to Hippo to copy them. She should find it easy to do so, Augustine added, "because God has given you the means." Again Augustine wishes not to be in her debt. He offers to be a woman's benefactor but not at close range. In her response not only to him but to God, she is made the petitioner.

SAPIDA

Augustine wrote *Epistle* 263 to a woman formally vowed to virginity. She was the sister of Timothy, a Carthaginian deacon (fl. 395–430) who had been a messenger for Augustine.[36] So Augustine was related to Sapida because her brother worked on his behalf. According to Augustine's letter, she had made a tunic for her brother. After he died, she sent the tunic to Augustine. Augustine says he will wear it, not because she sent it—making him a debtor—but because she needs consolation at the death of her brother and his wearing it will console her—making her a debtor. By wearing the shirt Augustine becomes a donor (of consolation) to her. What we learn from this letter is that Augustine did not allow gift giving and receiving to bind him to a woman as debtor.

SELEUCIANA

About 408–9, in *Epistle* 265, Augustine replied to a now lost letter from Seleuciana. Like Maxima, she was literate enough to have written a letter on her own and wealthy enough to have a secretary who took dictation. Her letter concerns the opinion of a Novatianist friend who held that Peter had never been baptized. Augustine's reply indicates that this statement indirectly contradicts what she had previously written about her friend's teaching. He offers to have her letter to him copied and sent back to her, in case she had no copy of her own to which she could refer.

Why did Augustine delay the resolution by not simply sending the copy at once? The rest of the letter might provide a clue. Rather than embarrass her by contradicting her latest report, Augustine gives her the opportunity to rethink what she has written. Later in the letter he does not say that she is wrong about penance among the Novatianists, but merely that she does not express herself clearly. This tactic extricates him from having to solve what may be a nonexistent problem. It was less important to Augustine to make sure that Novatianists were or were not consistent: the presumption would be that error and evil are not necessarily even internally consistent. His more important task was to make sure that Seleuciana was not seduced by any error. By reviewing the letter she had written perhaps in haste, she could read what Augustine said to clarify her question.

One can interpret this response as the tactic of a bishop weary of his many episcopal duties, but Augustine never implies that her theological concerns were above her abilities. On the contrary, he seems to have engaged theological questions on her behalf while avoiding a more personal interchange.

Conclusions

After considering each of Augustine's writings to women individually and in small groups, what patterns emerge? What implications do these patterns have for a consideration of Augustine's relationships with women?

First, all of Augustine's extant letters to women date from the years of his episcopate. These years were filled with competing attractions for Augustine. He wished to do his duties as pastor and to do them well. At the same time, he understood his particular vocation as a Christian as being called to the life of a contemplative author with a monastic bent. He often commented on how the demands of both the active bishop and the contemplative writer pulled him apart. He found little attraction in correspondence with members of his congregation or people outside his diocese. Therefore many letters appear to be formal and to encourage no reply. These are largely letters associated with questions of praxis initiated by others. The first letter to Armentarius and Paulina (Ep. 127), the ending of the letter to Italica on the trade of property (Ep. 99), and the letters to Felicia, Ecdicia, Maxima, Seleuciana, Florentina (Epp. 208, 262, 264, 265, and 266 respectively) fall into this category. But this is not simply a tactic used solely with women. The same might be said even of a few of his longer letters to men during this period, for example, Epistle 47 to Publicola on the religious practices of his peasants. Augustine was a busy person who wanted more time for his intellectual pursuits, which he saw as his avenue toward God. Many modern academics and clerics might have sympathy for his desire to do what he saw as "his own work."

Second, Augustine defused any potential situations that might use up more of his precious time or create a debtor situation for him, for example, the letter in which he merely acknowledges the souvenir of Demetrias's veiling, Epistle 150. Even his acceptance of gifts such as Sapida's tunic (Ep. 263) placed women in his debt rather than vice versa. Epistles 130, 147, 208, 264, 266, and 20*, as well as De bono viduitatis, all present him as avoiding being indebted to a woman. The language of debt and debtor was peculiar to his correspondence with women. While avoiding debt might be taken as paving the way for true friendship, instead it functioned to sever incipient bonds and preclude any subordination of Augustine to women.

His formation as a young man and increasingly as a Christian encouraged his bent away from socialization with women as friends or anything like equals. To become a Christian was for him to vow celibacy. His initial attempts to live out that vocation in the idyllic company of men at Cassiciacum reinforced the tendency. He institutionalized it in the living arrangements of men at the Basilica Pacis in Hippo. The social context in which he lived out that particular vocation rarely placed him in the company of women, much less as his social equals. Thus he developed the habit, as his biographer Possidius wrote, of never being together in the same room with a woman alone.[37] Hence, many of his letters to women stand as monuments to a lifestyle he chose, a postconversion lifestyle in which women played no significant role and, when present, were treated as inconsequential or dangerous.

Third, taking a cue from the ambient culture, Augustine regarded women as the weaker sex physically and intellectually. Beyond his treatises on notional women, his letters to real women bear this out. His encouragement of virtue was highly gendered in a pattern that reflected his social formation. In Epistle 147 he counsels Armentarius not to lord it over his wife, but in Epistle 262 he advises Ecdicia to be obedient to her husband. In Epistles 214 and 215 Augustine warns the monks at Hadrumetum not to be intellectually conceited in their study of theology, but in Epistle 266 he implies that Florentina was conceited for even asking intellectual questions.

Fourth, some letters to particular women were extensive and specifically requested replies. They show him as less uncomfortable with some specific women and their concerns than with the rest of his female correspondents. But this category is very specific. It contains letters not about praxis but about doctrine, for example, his letter to Maxima on the Incarnation (Ep. 264). Likewise, in Epistle 130 to Proba on prayer, he takes Proba's mundane concerns about prayer, which were practical issues, and answers her request through an exegesis of Scripture, removing the issue from the realm of praxis to that of biblical theology. De bono viduitatis certainly was written for the situation of Juliana, but Augustine specifically says that he means it also as a general tract, again an exposition of theology, this time, on grace. *Epistle* 92, a letter of consolation, becomes an essay about the vision of God. Similarly, *Epistle* 147 moves to the same subject and shows him more comfortable as the topic grew more theological. In *Epistles* 150 and 188 the theological stakes are the highest as Augustine battled Pelagius. Here the specific situation of Demetrias may be the ostensible subject of the letter. But for Augustine the body of the young woman is simply the battleground in the war against Pelagius. He never addresses her personally. Concern for purity of doctrine in these letters, whether it comes from the woman or is manufactured by Augustine, stands like an altar rail between him and the women, protecting him from too close contact. Given this protection, he can write more expansively.

Finally, there are the letters to women of higher social or financial rank. Here Augustine is at his most vulnerable and is downright awkward. He finds it difficult to ask Maxima (Ep. 264) for a copy of a treatise he needed, and, like the social climber he had once been, he asks for it with reference to her personal wealth. His long letter to Albina (Ep. 126) is the best example. He takes time with his missive precisely because he was in a socially inferior position. In the face of wealthy women, especially those he exhorted to divest themselves of their wealth, his tactic is to appeal to them in terms of both classical Roman and Christian honor. They are to compete in doing good and to become the fulfillment of prophecy.

One might not have expected Augustine to be uneasy among the wealthy. After all, he had participated in the circles of well-placed Manichees in Rome and Milan. Had they not provided him with an apprenticeship in gentlemanly arts? Yes, but during that time he had learned to be an inferior seeking advancement, not a man of social and financial largesse. Later in life, as a Christian bishop, his social life was most relaxed with his closest male friends, who happened to be his ecclesiastical equals socially and in the episcopate. It is their letters that most closely approach exchanges of true friendship. Bonds forged before Christianity with men of equal rank survived and prospered but only as they were subordinated to the good of the Church. There were no really wealthy male companions in Augustine's later life—and no powerful women friends. Unlike Jerome or Chrysostom, Augustine had not come from a wealthy family, nor had he socialized with upper-class men or women as an equal before he became bishop.

To such a social context, one must add the religiophilosophical construct of containment in Augustine's commitment to celibacy and his vocational lifestyle. Peter Brown reads the *Confessions* as Augustine's account of his own struggle with sexuality and his hope that others would find the peace he did in continence.[38] Spiritual delight displaced his fascination and attraction to sexual joy.[39]

In her rereading of the *Confessions*, Margaret Miles highlights the important role continence played in Augustine's life. Continence and containment are etymologically related in Latin. To be continent is to contain one's self sexually, physically, and, in Augustine's case, even sensually: "Augustine's understanding of his past and present experience coalesced in images of concupiscence and continence. At present, he is collected, gathered, no longer spilled and scattered. He no longer loses energy and vitality—like seminal fluid—on the pursuit of sex, power, and possessions. He now contains himself.[40]

Augustine's containment and continence were not so much a rejection of the senses as evil as a perception that attraction to sensual objects as creatures was a distraction from God, the One and the Good.[41] Augustine's sensual, sexual, and rational containment applied especially to his relationships with women. Before his conversion he had been incontinent sexually with women. His pleasure depended on their presence. The closer he came to Christianity and to continence, the farther he distanced himself from women. As a young man he had frequented the fleshpots of Carthage. During his long search for truth, he had confined himself to a single woman, the mother of his son. Once he had found the truth of Christianity, he withdrew as much as he could from associations with women: his engagement was broken, and eventually he entered the monastic lifestyle that he continued even as a bishop.

Not only was this withdrawal one from sensuality and sexuality and some forms of rational intercourse; it was also one of financial continence. Before his conversion and ordination to the episcopate, he had been content to receive the largesse of patrons, for example, the Manichees and Romanianus. As he matured, he withdrew from such arrangements. Even when he needed books from literate women or when, for the sake of the local church, he received donations from wealthy women, he endeavored to avoid relationships of dependence on women by making them his dependents or at least by keeping himself from becoming indebted to them.

So in the end, what do Augustine's letters to women reveal about him? That he avoided being their dependents and often made them his, certainly. Under those circumstances, true friendship was not possible. He preferred men to women and God to all creatures. For all his pastoral duties as a bishop, Augustine saw women as a greater distraction from the life of the mind intent on God than men were. Augustine had told Juliana not that virginity was good and marriage was not, but that the good of virginity was better than the good of marriage. So too Augustine saw his relationships with women as inferior to those with men. Only when the life of the mind was engaged in godly conversation or in the deconstruction of heresy, its opposite side, did he prolong conversation beyond the necessary.

The reasons Augustine did not form friendships with women are closely related to his own formation. Whether this formation was imposed on him by the social class of his birth or self-imposed as in his use of classical theories of friendship, it was a different formation from that of his patristic companions. Augustine was friend to a few, but none of them was a woman.

Notes

1. I would like to acknowledge the research assistance of Judith Amey, M.A. student at the University of Dayton and the editorial assistance of the anonymous reviewer of this article and of the editors of this volume, Patricia Cox Miller and Dale B. Martin. References to the letters of Augustine (hereafter Ep.) are to S. Aureli Augustini Hipponensis Episcopi Epistulae, ed. Al. Goldbacher, Corpus Scriptorum Ecclesiasticorum Latinorum 34, 44, 57, and 58 (Vienna: Tempsky, 1895–98); and Oeuvres de Saint Augustin: Lettres 1*–29*, Bibliothèque Augustinienne 46B, ed. Johannes Divjak (Paris: Études Augustiniennes, 1987).

2. It is difficult to evoke women's experience from men's writing and even from the writings of women themselves. Patriarchal expectations and the expectations of male editors and transmitters influenced even women's letters and diaries. See Simpson, "Women and Asceticism in the Fourth Century," esp. 39; Clark's address "Women in the Early Christian World" and her article "Women, Gender and the Study of Christian History," esp. 423–26.

3. Clark, "Rewriting Early Christian History," esp. 96–106.

4. The best use made is Clark's short biographies of the women in "Theory and Practice in Late Ancient Asceticism," Journal of Feminist Studies in Religion 5, no. 2 (fall 1989): 25–46.

5. Both classical notions of friendship and Augustine's own are discussed in detail in White, Christian Friendship in the Fourth Century, esp. 189–217.

6. De Genesi ad litteram 9.5.9, in De Genesi ad litteram, ed. J. Zycha (Vienna: Tempsky, 1894). For Augustine's progressively more positive view of Eve as Adam's companion, see inter alia Clark, "Theory and Practice," 34, where she shows that even this approbation of Eve as a sort of friend did not have an impact on Augustine's relationships with women in his life.

7. For the dates of Augustine's letters I usually rely on Robert B. Eno, "Epistulae," in Augustine through the Ages, ed. Allan D. Fitzgerald (Grand Rapids, Mich., and Cambridge: Eerdmans, 1999): 298–310 (volume hereafter cited as Fitzgerald).

For the dating of Paulinus and Therasia's letters I rely on Teske, *Works of Saint Augustine*.

8. For the prosopographical details, I am indebted to Jones, Martindale, and Morris, *Prosopography of the Later Roman Empire*; and Mandouze and La Bonnardière, *Prosopographie chrétienne du Bas-Empire*. Other information comes directly from the letters.

9. For more on the couple, see Trout, *Paulinus of Nola*, and Joseph T. Lienhard, "Paulinus of Nola," in Fitzgerald, 628–29.

10. Lienhard, "Paulinus of Nola," 628.

11. See, e.g., Augustine, *Ep.* 31.4.

12. See Jerome's letter to Augustine and Alypius, *Ep.* 202 in Augustine's letters.

13. On both Melanias, see "Melania the Elder" and "Melania the Younger" by Elizabeth Clark in Fitzgerald, 552–53.

14. Clark, "Theory and Practice," 38–39.

15. Publicola to Augustine *Ep.* 46, and vice versa *Ep.* 47.

16. Clark, "Theory and Practice," 40.

17. Augustine wrote here and in *Epp.* 147 and 148 against the anthropomorphite idea that one could perceive God with corporeal eyes. See Frederick van Fleteren, "Vivendo Deo, De," in Fitzgerald, 869.

18. See White, *Christian Friendship*, 191–92.

19. Augustine, *De bono viduitatis* 1, in *De fide et symbolo*.

20. Since sections 5–16 cannot reliably be attributed to Augustine, I discuss only sections 1–4.

21. There is no convincing evidence that Rusticus was or was not ordained. *Propositus* does not indicate clerical status, but is a general term, even in Augustine, for a person in charge of others. In *Ep.* 64, *praepositi* are expressly opposed in canon law to *clerici*. It is entirely possible that Rusticus was the *praepositus* of another monastery and/or became the *praepositus* of Felicitas's monastery. Given Augustine's use of the word here, Rusticus was not an abbot with authority over the entire monastery. Perhaps Sister Wilfrid Parsons, O.P., is not far from a good translation in "spiritual director." See her translation in Augustine, *Saint Augustine: Letters*, Fathers of the Church 32:41.

22. 1 Cor. 1:10–17; Ignatius, *Ephesians* 4.1–2. On Augustine's desire for order and its impact on sexual hierarchy, see Power, *Veiled Desire*, chap. 4. Augustine was not unique in his relationship to a dispute over authority in a women's monastery. In the same era, across the Libyan desert in Egypt, Shenoute in the White Monastery of Atripe (383–466) faced a similar situation. He tried to interfere in the leadership of Amma Tachon's monastery by appointing a priest from his monastery to be the chaplain. Augustine would not have known of the ills that would befall Shenoute for his attempts, but they do indicate that Augustine was not alone in facing this challenge to monastic authority. Unlike Shenoute, Augustine prized the authority internal to a monastery or any community, and he refused to support anyone usurping authority. He simply forced the women to solve their own problem.

23. *Ep.* 214.2–3, *De gratia et libero arbitrio* 5 in Migne, *Patrologia Latina* 44.

24. E.g., *Ep.* 44 of Albina and Proba.
25. Augustine's Latin ("ubi non est iudaeus et graecus, seruus liber, masculus femina") matches the wording of neither the Vulgate nor Paul's Greek text, but it is similar to wording used by Ambrose in *De fide* 5.14.
26. Bible verses in the plural are the exception.
27. *Ep.* 127.5, in *Saint Augustine*, trans. Parsons, Fathers of the Church 18:360.
28. *Ep.* 127.9, in *Saint Augustine*, trans. Parsons, Fathers of the Church 18:363–64.
29. *Ep.* 262.8 and *Confessions* 2.3, ed. James J. O'Donnell, 3 vols. (Oxford: Clarendon, 1992).
30. See Jerome, *Ep.* 77 (400), in which he consoled her brother Oceanus on her death. Oceanus's sister is the more likely subject of *Corpus Inscriptionarum Latinarum*, vol. 6: *Inscriptiones Urbis Romae Latinae*, ed. Wilhelm Henzen and Giovanni Battista de Rossi (Berlin: G. Reimerus, 1876–1933), 6.31974, than Jerome's close friend of the same name.
31. Jerome to Augustine, *Ep.* 126.2 = *Ep.* 165.2 of Augustine.
32. Mandouze and La Bonnardière, *Prosopographie chrétienne du Bas-Empire*, 380, with references to DeBruyne, "Les anciennes collections et la chronologie," 290 and 294; cf. Delmaire, "Contributions des nouvelles lettres de saint Augustin," 85.
33. See White, *Christian Friendship*.
34. Cf. Augustine, *Ep.* 209.
35. See Jane E. Merdinger, "Antoninus," in Fitzgerald, 47–48.
36. He may be the person mentioned in *Ep.* 110.1; cf. *Epp.* 62–63.
37. Possidius, *Vita Augustini*, 26.
38. On Augustine's struggle, see Brown, *The Body and Society*, ch. 19.
39. Brown, *Body and Society*, 394.
40. Miles, *Desire and Delight*, 101.
41. Cf. Power, *Veiled Desire*, 36–41. While I disagree with Power's judgment that Augustine saw women as positive evils, my views are less influenced by an application of Platonic theories to Augustine's writing than by a reading of his Christianization of them in *De Trinitate*. By the logic he manifests there, women are a lesser good than God. So too would men be if considered instrumentally or as ends in themselves.

✛ On Mary's Voice:

Gendered Words in

Syriac Marian Tradition

SUSAN ASHBROOK HARVEY

Syriac Christianity is noteworthy for the early prominence it grants to the
Virgin Mary, both in devotional activity and in doctrinal instruction.[1] In a
particularly interesting development, beginning with Ephrem Syrus (d. 373
c.e.), Syriac hymnographers and homilists often chose to present Mary
through the rhetorical technique of imagined speech, endowing her character with ample and eloquent words, sometimes in the form of soliloquies
and sometimes in dialogue with other biblical characters. Through these
speeches, Syriac writers explored Mary as a character in the drama of biblical
events, considered her own salvific role, and utilized her as a mode of instruction in the teaching of right Christian faith, above all for matters of
Christological import. Hymns and homilies about Mary throughout the ancient church often used architectural and spatial metaphors to exalt Mary's
body as a location of unique power in which God's work was enacted.[2] My
focus will be the Syriac emphasis on Mary's speech as a vehicle of divine
truth.

In this essay, my principal interest is the late antique Syriac construction
of Mary as speaker, a presentation of complex rhetorical strategies in dynamic tension with prevailing social values and expectations of the time.[3] I
will consider three groups of texts from the fourth through sixth centuries
c.e.: Ephrem Syrus's *Hymns on the Nativity*, the anonymous dialogue poems
(*soghyatha*), and the Marian verse homilies of Jacob of Serug. These texts
treat a number of the major themes in Syriac Marian tradition. They also
present different literary forms, and contrasting methods of performance in
liturgical settings.[4] Ephrem's hymns were often sung by women's choirs,
while the dialogue hymns were sung antiphonally apparently by both male
and female choirs. Jacob's verse homilies, by contrast, would have been
chanted by the male preacher.[5] I will argue that the construction of Mary's
voice in each instance is strongly shaped by both the literary and the perfor-

mative requirements of the composer's chosen form, in addition to the particular emphases of content. Further, I argue that the Syriac liturgical presentation of Mary develops over the course of late antiquity in ways that strongly constrain the social and political implications of how her character is configured.[6]

To the hymnographer or homilist, Mary's voice—the words Mary might have said—was a matter of rhetorical strategy. What was said in an imagined dialogue, in a retelling of a biblical story, was qualitatively changed by who said it, and from which narrative perspective.[7] In this essay, I will use the Syriac representation of Mary's voice to ask how and why gendered speech could contribute to doctrinal teaching in the late antique Syrian Orient. As we will see, at no point could the imagined memory of Mary's voice stand wholly apart from the present world of those men and women who voiced and heard these compositions.[8]

Ephrem's Mary: The Prophetess Sings

Ephrem the Syrian (d. 373) wrote on Mary's doctrinal importance in various works.[9] But in his cycle *Hymns on the Nativity*, Ephrem granted Mary a strikingly prominent place in Christian worship, a place both figurative and participatory.[10] Written to celebrate Christ's incarnation into human reality, these hymns often incline to dwell on the marvel of Mary's role in the salvation drama and on the significance of her place in human history as the one through whom God's plan was brought to fruition. However, Ephrem here presents Mary not only as the subject of liturgical and devotional attention, but further as a subject who participates in the larger task to which these hymns contribute: that of collective worship. In these hymns, Ephrem represents Mary as one who offers her own voice as a vehicle for teaching the faithful, proclaiming God's wondrous actions and revealing the fullness of divine dispensation. Interestingly, Ephrem does not set Mary's voice in the context of a musically dramatized narrative, as will be done by other Syriac writers, to retell the nativity stories of the Gospels. Instead, he locates Mary at once within and outside of time, speaking both from within the biblical world of the past and yet as present among the gathered faithful of the church community. Since these hymns would most likely have been sung by women's choirs, their performance would have heightened their rhetorical content: women's voices would have raised Ephrem's words, fashioned as Mary's song.[11]

In Ephrem's *Hymns on the Nativity*, Mary does not participate in an active dialogue with other characters. Rather, she is presented as a singer whose voice joins that of the congregation in raising songs of praise to God. Most often, Ephrem addresses her song to Christ, her newborn son, on the day of his birth.

> My mouth knows not how to address You,
> O Son of the Living One. I tremble
> To dare to address You as son of Joseph,
> For You are not his seed. Yet I shrink
> From denying the name of him to whom I have been betrothed.
> . . . . .
> Although You are the Son of the One, I shall call You henceforth
> Son of many, for myriads of names
> Do not suffice for You, for You are Son of God
> And Son of Man and Son of Joseph
> And Son of David and Lord of Mary.
>   (H. Nat. 6.1–2)

Directed to her child, Mary's voice sings out from within the community, leading the task of praise. Even so, her voice is distinct from all other voices because of her unique identity.

> Most of all those healed, I rejoice, for I conceived Him;
> Most of all those magnified by Him, He has magnified me,
> For I gave birth to Him.
> I am about to enter into His living Paradise,
> And in the place in which Eve succumbed, I shall glorify Him.
> For of all created women, He was most pleased with me,
> [And] He willed that I should be mother to Him,
> And it pleased Him that He should be a child to me.
>   (H. Nat. 2.7)

Awed and empowered at one and the same moment, Mary sings to her son in terms that cast her voice across the vast swath of biblical history. From Eve's tragic silencing at the Fall to Mary's song, Ephrem reminds the congregation that women's words have woven the very fabric of God's salvific plan. With songs and lullabies, he recalls, with tears, vows, voiced and silent prayers, women called upon their Lord in shadowed types of the exalted role that awaited Mary's consent. Sarah sang lullabies to Isaac; Rachel cried to her husband; Hannah with bitter sobs prayed for a child; Rebekah and Elizabeth made their vows through long years of barrenness (H. Nat. 8.13–

15). Leah, Rachel, Zilpah, and Bilhah sang their lullabies with "soft words" (H. Nat. 10.1); the Hebrew daughters sang the laments of Jeremiah as they intoned biblical lullabies (H. Nat. 13.1). Beyond the faith of these, Ephrem admonishes, Mary began with silence: "Blessed is Mary, who without vows / and without prayer, in her virginity / conceived and brought forth the Lord of all" (H. Nat. 8.16). From the silence of her perfection then sounded a song unlike any sung before:

> Who will sing a lullabye to the child of her womb
> As Mary [did]? Who will dare
> To call her son, Son of the Maker,
> Son of the Creator?[12]
>   (H. Nat. 8.17)

Mary's song is sung to her child, himself at birth a silent infant. But the wonder is this: the silencing of God through incarnation as a newborn brings speech to his mother, the one who had been silent and now brings forth not only a son, but a birth of new words. In Ephrem's hymns, Mary sings a new song:

> With You I shall begin, and I trust
> That with You I shall end. I shall open my mouth,
> And You fill my mouth. I am for You the earth
> And You are the farmer. Sow in me Your voice,
> You who are the sower of Himself in His mother's womb.
> . . . . .
> . . . Blessed be the Babe
> Who made His mother the lyre of His melodies.
> And since the lyre looks toward its master,
> My mouth looks toward You. Let Your will arouse
> Your mother's tongue. Since I have learned by You
> A new way of conceiving, let my mouth learn by You
> A new [way of] giving birth to new glory.
>   (H. Nat. 15.1, 4–5)

In her new lullabies, in her new song, Mary sings to her Lord in a voice that crosses from the biblical past into the historical present of the worshipping church. In a voice that addresses her son with imagined speech, Mary's imagined figure offers Ephrem's congregation instruction in right faith on the occasion of the feast commemorating the Nativity event of biblical—and present—time. Never spoken in reality, the words of Ephrem's Mary proclaim a reality unspeakable.

> . . . A new utterance
> Of prophecy seethes in me.
> What shall I call You, a stranger to us,
> Who was from us? Shall I call You Son?
> Shall I call You Brother? Shall I call You Bridegroom?
> Shall I call You Lord, O [You] who brought forth His mother
> [In] another birth out of the water?
> For I am Your sister from the House of David,
> Who is a second father. Again, I am Your mother
> Because of Your conception, and bride am I
> Because of Your chastity. Handmaiden and daughter
> Of blood and water [am I] whom You redeemed and baptized.
>
> (H. Nat. 16.9–10)

Ephrem could grant Mary a voice by following the model from Luke's Gospel. There, Mary not only speaks when she questions the archangel Gabriel (Luke 1:43), but sings to her cousin Elizabeth a song of prophecy and wonder (Luke 1:46–55), echoing the one sung many generations before by Hannah, mother of the first prophet Samuel (1 Sam. 2:1–10).[13] Ephrem grants Mary a prophetic voice, one that declares God's intention in the presence of God's people. In his hymns, hers is not a hidden voice, spoken in the sheltered space of a household—the expected space for women's speech. Rather, her words of prophetic truth ring out amidst the gathered congregation of the believing community. Ephrem is both imagining the words Mary would have said, had anyone been there to hear her, and proclaiming those words as a public presentation, sung in the presence of all. Into the silent absence of Mary's voice from most of the Gospel accounts, Ephrem pours the voiced presence of her figure. What voice could better state the paradox of God become human, uncontainable greatness confined to the contained smallness of a mother's womb?

> I shall not be jealous, my Son, that you are both with me
> And with everyone. Be God
> To the one who confesses You, and be Lord
> To the one who serves You, and be brother
> To the one who loves You so that You might save all.

While You dwelt in me, [both] in me and outside of me
Your majesty dwelt. While I gave birth to You
Openly, Your hidden power
Was not removed from me. You are within me,
And You are outside of me, O Mystifier of His mother.

(H. Nat. 16.1–2)

Ephrem's Mary reiterates themes that Ephrem delights to highlight elsewhere, or by other rhetorical means.[14] Voiced from her perspective, these
themes become embodied rather than observed, enacted rather than considered. The paradoxical wonder of the human mother who bears, suckles, and
nurtures the divine Creator was a favorite theme across patristic authors of
the time.[15] In Hymns on the Nativity 4, Ephrem offers a veritable cascade of
images to present the conundrum as one of irreconcilable extremes. His
imagery includes startling play with gender, for he follows a Syriac tradition
that can grant feminine characteristics to a creator God more often portrayed
in masculine terms.[16] Thus in this hymn the very Word of God is born as a
mute infant to the young girl Mary; the One older than the universe is carried,
helpless and tiny, on the elderly Joseph's shoulder. The newborn drinks the
mother's milk he himself created; he who suckles all creation to give it life,
nurses at the breast of Mary. He whose womb contains the universe, who
himself burst the womb of Sheol, yet confined himself to Mary's womb,
allowed his greatness to be carried and cradled by her smallness.[17] The
polarities of divine/human, great/small, exalted/humble recur throughout
the hymn cycle.[18] Voiced by Ephrem the hymnographer, these paradoxes are
proclaimed as observations whose contemplation elicits our astonishment.

O Lord, no one knows
How to address Your mother. [If] one calls her "virgin,"
Her child stands up, and "married"—
No one knew her [sexually]. But if Your mother is
Incomprehensible, who is capable of [comprehending] You?

(H. Nat. 11.1)

Voiced by Ephrem's Mary, these same paradoxes become encountered
experiences. Beholding her child, murmuring and wide-eyed, in her lap
preparing to nurse, Mary sings with awe, "How shall I open the fount of
milk / for You, the Fount [of Life]? . . . How shall I approach / with swaddling
clothes the One arrayed in streams [of Light]?" (H. Nat. 5.24) As speaker
herself, Mary provides an enactment of Ephrem's favorite images of the

paradox of God become human. In Ephrem's construction, Mary is young, female, poor, and from a place of no account (Bethlehem): a "needy girl" from "a small town" (H. Nat. 25.12). Who is she to speak? Yet her very insignificance is what Christ found "worthy" when he sought a person to indwell, a place to inhabit (H. Nat. 25.12).

Wealth and poverty, honor and shame, could provide further imagery for the wonder of divine glory rendered in the humbleness of human life. Ephrem underscores the imagery by grafting its literal example into the Mary he represents in song. Portraying her as materially poor, vulnerably young, and scandalously female, Ephrem can raise sharp critiques of class, gender, and other social markers. In so doing, he displays the dazzling breadth of power evoked by the notion of universal salvation. This he demonstrates in hymns without Mary's voice.

> Women heard that behold a virgin indeed
> Would conceive and bring forth. Well-born women hoped
> That He would shine forth from them, and elegant women
> That He would appear from them. Blessed is Your height
> That bent down and shone forth from the poor.
> Even little girls taken by Him [as brides]
> Spoke prophetically. "Yours, Lord, let me be,
> For I am ugly, to You I am fair,
> And if I am lowly, to You I am noble."
>
> (H. Nat. 8.23.20–21)

When Ephrem gives Mary voice from that precise social location, she is presented through her words as the sudden instance of paradox and inversion. The marginalized stands at the center, the voiceless becomes heard, eloquent and clear.

> All the chaste daughters of the Hebrews
> And virgin daughters of rulers
> Are amazed at me. Because of You, a daughter of the poor
> Is envied. Because of You, a daughter of the weak
> Is an object of jealousy. Who gave You to me?
> Son of the Rich One, Who despised the womb
> Of rich women, what drew You
> Towards the poor? For Joseph is needy,
> And I am impoverished.
>
> (H. Nat. 15.2–3)

In his construction of Mary, then, Ephrem takes theological themes of grave philosophical weight, and reifies them into the specific, and literal, person of the young virgin mother. For the social and political markers of poverty and wealth in a civic order stand in place of their metaphysical counterparts: the unbounded enormity of divinity compared to the small specificity of human life; the limitless wealth of divine meaning counterposed to the frail limits of human language; the divine being and the human person. Casting Mary thus as the Poor One, Ephrem sets theological discourse as a social reality all too familiar to his congregation. Nonetheless, he engages a social reality within which these familiar doctrinal teachings are shown to have concrete social ramifications.

Hence, Ephrem's Mary laments that despite her exaltation by divine choice, in the human realm she is but a cause of scandal and scorn. Repeatedly, she sings of the slander to which she is subjected by virtue of the sheer unlikelihood of her position: "Behold, I am slandered and oppressed, / but I rejoice. My ears are full / of scorn and disdain, but it is a small matter to me" (H. Nat. 15.7). The voices Mary reports through her sung verses articulate moral and religious outrage at the glorification of her poverty, at the apparent violability of her betrothal, at the decency of her abrasive declarations.[19] Mary's identity as human mother of the divine Son shatters the illusory stability of a moral universe known through familiar social order. Ephrem the hymnographer addresses the Christ child triumphantly, "The womb of Your mother overthrew the orders."[20] In turn, Ephrem's Mary embraces her social suffering as an act of power, the effective means of redemption:

> For Your sake, behold, I am hated,
> Lover of all. Behold, I am persecuted
> Because I conceived and bore the One Place of Refuge
> For human beings. Let Adam rejoice
> For You are his key to Paradise.
> (H. Nat. 6.4)

Ephrem's hymns draw Mary's voice across biblical history and into the present gathering of the church community. At the same time, the voice he grants her embodies theological comprehension amidst the social vulnerability of the civic world. What time and location frame Mary's character into a morally ordered narrative within these hymns?[21] When and where does she speak? For there is a certain permeability to time and place in Ephrem's *Hymns on the Nativity*. The figures of the biblical past are suddenly rendered present and active in the persons of the singer's congregation. Thus the widows and young virgins who had slandered Mary in her biblical time, become the widows and consecrated virgins who now—as Ephrem's choir—sing her glory.[22] And the figure of Mary as the maligned virgin takes shape within this singing chorus as those consecrated virgins within the Christian community, now slandered and scorned by a civic society offended by their asocial choice of celibacy.[23] When Mary's voice sings out for Christ to vindicate her blackened reputation, the women's choirs who sing these hymns become themselves the objects of his divine advocacy and protection. This elision of time and location, between biblical past and contemporary congregation, allows Ephrem to trumpet the valuation of consecrated virginity in the midst of a social order which, in the mid-fourth century, was genuinely struggling to accommodate its consequences.[24] Ephrem's Mary was a figure who embodied dramatic challenge to civic order.[25] The sociopolitical critique her representation opened passed further, in these hymns, into the life of the hymnographer's contemporary Christian community.

> Blessed is the woman in whose heart
> And mind You are. She is the King's castle
> For You, the King's Son, and the Holy of Holies
> For You, the High Priest. She has neither the anxiety
> Nor the toil of a household and husband.
>
> . . . . .
>
> O chaste woman, eagerly await my Beloved
> So that He might dwell in you, and unclean women, too,
> So that He may purify you; churches, too,
> So that He may adorn you. He is the Son of the Creator
> Who came to restore the whole creation.
>
> (H. Nat. 17.4, 7)

Ephrem's *Hymns on the Nativity* articulate sharp tensions within the Christian community, represented and embodied through the voice of Mary. The hymns are presented without a stated historical narrative frame, presuming the familiar narratives of the Gospel nativity accounts. Yet they do not follow those accounts, rather locating Mary's speech in unidentified moments of the larger story. Their content does not contribute to the narrative lacunae of the Gospels. Instead, these verses engage the work of interweaving Old and New Testaments, providing an exegesis that sets the nativity and its characters typologically within scripture as a whole. Performed as the worshipping song of the gathered church, their content is also contextualized in the present life of the civic Christian community. Mary's voice is thus a teaching voice, instructing the faithful in right doctrine.[26] Her words can be such because by his incarnation Christ transformed utterly Mary's body and mind (H. Nat. 28.4, 7). She herself could then become the means of his revelation because to her and in her and through her Christ had made his hidden truth wholly, openly known (H. Nat. 16.3–7; 17.1).

Yet even in these hymns where Mary's voice is proclaimed and celebrated, Ephrem curtails its effect, blunting its consequences. For if Ephrem's Mary challenges the confines of biblical narrative by speaking outside its limits, the voice he grants her remains safely within the ritual structure of the church—a structure that supported and sustained the Christian community as a viably constituted social body. Within the sphere of sacred ritual, the constraints of civic order could be challenged, negotiated, and upheld through redefinition as the instruments of divine dispensation.[27] Hence Ephrem reminds his congregation that Mary's voice could be active and outspoken, yet obediently deferential. She might challenge a fallen world order, but she would not question divine initiative. For that would be speech of a truly dangerous kind: the heretic's hubristic inquiry into matters beyond human ken. Ephrem's celebration lays the boundaries for Mary's words:

> Blessed are you also, Mary, whose name
> Is great and exalted because of Your child.
> Indeed you were able to say how much and how
> And where the Great One, Who became small, dwelt in you.
> Blessed is your mouth that gave thanks but did not inquire,
> And your tongue that praised but did not investigate.
> Since His mother was awed by Him, although she bore Him,
> Who is sufficient [to know] Him?
>
> (H. Nat. 25.14)

Dialogue and Narrative: The Constraints of Story

Ephrem's towering genius invariably dominates the landscape of Syriac hymnography. But late antiquity was a fertile period for Syriac composers, and a vibrant diversity of hymnographic forms and poets flourished especially between the fourth and seventh centuries. The exploration of biblical characters through the medium of imagined speech, voiced in song, was a favorite activity for Syriac writers. Mary's voice remained a popular subject in this context. At the same time, Marian hymnography after Ephrem shows distinct lines of development that redirect the liturgical expression of her character as well as the congregational experience of her voice. A brief consideration of two representative blocks of material will make the relevant points: the anonymous dialogue hymns (soghyatha) of late antiquity, and the Marian verse homilies of Jacob of Serug (d. 521).

A large body of anonymous hymnography survives in Syriac in the form of dialogue poems (soghitha in the singular; soghyatha, plural), many of them composed in the late antique period. As a literary genre of verbal contest, the soghitha has its roots deep in the Ancient Near East. In Syriac and in Christianized form, it was a favored mode of liturgical poetry.[28] The soghitha presented a dialogue between two characters, set between a brief narrative frame at the beginning and a closing doxology at the end. Sung antiphonally by two choirs in alternating verses, it set up a conflict or contest of competing positions. The argument moved back and forth until finally one side prevailed through persuasion (sometimes aided by divine inspiration on the losing side). Often these dialogue poems presented biblical stories, retold not through an elaborated narration but rather through the conflicted exchange of two biblical characters. The Virgin Mary was one of several biblical women whose stories were treated in this manner.[29] In her case, the dialogue poems provided generous opportunity for imagining Mary's voice as an active agent in God's salvific plan. At the same time, the conventions of the literary form, as well as what emerged as the conventions of the liturgical presentation of Mary, combined to shape a highly stylized construction for her voice.[30]

The Syriac dialogue poems about Mary are set in specific Gospel scenes:[31] the exchange between Mary and the archangel Gabriel at the Annunciation, the (imagined) argument between Joseph and Mary when he learns of her pregnancy, the discourse between Mary and the Magi at the Nativity, and the exchange between Mary and the Gardener in the resurrection narrative of John 20 (in Syriac tradition, it was the Virgin Mary and not Mary Magdalene who was the recipient of this first resurrection appearance).[32] In related anonymous hymns, Mary sings lullabies to the newborn Christ child, marvels at her conception and birthgiving, and engages a shorter dialogue with the prophet Simeon the Righteous at the presentation of Christ, couched in a longer narrative frame.[33] For each of these dialogues, there is a biblical basis in the Gospel texts, whether explicitly (as with the Annunciation in Luke 1) or implicitly (as with Joseph's doubts in Matt. 2). The scene and its place in the Gospel narrative are familiar, clear, carefully delimited.

The *soghyatha* are straightforward in content, unadorned by elaborate artistry. Lacking the exquisite imagistic play of Ephrem's hymns, they are nonetheless effective in presenting the major themes of Marian doctrine. In general, the Marian *soghyatha* revolve around an exchange of the basic argument between faith and reason. Gabriel speaks the wonder of God's choice of incarnation, while Mary argues that her conception would be impossible; insisting on the power of divine prerogative, Gabriel convinces Mary to acquiesce and affirm faith in an action she experiences but cannot explain (*Bride*, 41). In turn, Mary insists on the marvel of God's activity in opposition to the protests of a doubting, bitterly self-righteous Joseph, until he is persuaded by her witness (*Bride*, 42). Again, a canny and clever Mary tests the Magi who arrive with their gifts, refusing to acknowledge the identity of her son until they have persuaded her of their own true faith (*Bride*, 43). In the resurrection exchange, Mary stubbornly and uncomprehendingly spars with the enigmatic Gardener until at last he reveals that he is the one she seeks (*Bride*, 44). In each case, the opposing sides are standardized in argument, offering conventional objections and rebuttals. The antiphonal format expresses the conflict and its resolution in stately simplicity: a lucid, cogent method of congregational instruction.

But if the verses of these hymns present standard formulae, Mary's voice is nonetheless problematic. Although the *soghyatha* lack the sharp-edged challenges of Ephrem's *Hymns on the Nativity*, where Ephrem's Mary is represented with stark critiques of the sociopolitical order, Mary's character cannot be voiced in the given exchanges without gender—and occasionally class—as complicating factors. Hence these hymns repeatedly express puzzlement, frustration, and even dismay that Mary speaks in opposition to the male partner in the dialogue. The complication adds dramatic friction to the familiar narrative context.

In the *soghitha* on the Annunciation, Mary refuses to accept Gabriel's greeting, asking, "Who are you, sir? And what is this that you utter?" (*Bride*, 41.12) The angel's replies do not convince the wary virgin, whose suspicious hesitation elicits the angel's astonishment: "It would be amazing in you if you were to answer back, / annulling the message which I have brought to you" (*Bride*, 41.17). But Mary holds her ground. Citing the disastrous model of Eve, who received the words of the serpent without question, Mary refuses to accept from Gabriel a pronouncement she cannot understand. As the verses alternate, the angel's exasperation mounts. He sings:

The angelic hosts quake at His word:
The moment He has commanded, they do not answer back;
How is it then that you are not afraid
To query the thing which the Father has willed?

(Bride, 41.23)

"I too quake, sir, and am terrified," Mary sings in reply, but still she questions (Bride, 41.24). The constraints of metered verse do not diminish Gabriel's annoyance: "It is appropriate you should keep silence, and have faith too" (Bride 41.25). A further eleven verses of argument ensue before Mary's mind turns, and the dialogue changes to one of shared praise for the wonder of divine activity.

In the soghitha with Joseph, Mary insists on her virgin conception in the face of her husband's anguished disbelief. The exchange carries a harshness ill-concealed by the dignity of antiphonal singing.

> JOSEPH These words are inappropriate,
>   Mary, for a virgin; keep silent,
>   For falsehood will not stand up.
>   Speak the truth, if you are willing.
> MARY I repeat the very same words—
>   I have no others to say.
>   I remain sealed, as the seals of my virginity,
>   Which have not been loosed, will testify.
> JOSEPH You should not contradict,
>   But confess that you have been seduced.
>   Now you have fallen into two wrongs:
>   After getting pregnant, now you tell lies.
> MARY You should believe my words,
>   For you have never seen any falsehood in me:
>   My chaste and truthful life bear me witness
>   That I am a virgin and have not lied.
> JOSEPH I am astonished at what you say:
>   How can I listen to your words?

(Bride, 42.9–13)

Demure and unassuming as this representation of Mary may be, her voice grates against social convention. Expectations of socially correct speech are violated not only by the content of her words, but by the act of her speaking in opposition to her husband. Instead of the humorous frustration of the archangel Gabriel, we are here given Joseph's anger. But their message is the same: "Woman, be silent; do not contradict." Still the exchange continues. Mary is not silent. She does contradict.

In the soghitha of Mary and the Magi, the problem of Mary's voice is further complicated by issues of status. Trying to protect her son from his enemies, Mary flaunts her poverty to conceal his identity, asking defiantly, "When has it ever happened / that a poor girl has given birth to a king? / I am destitute and needy" (Bride, 43.12). The Magi, mistaking her ruse for lack of comprehension, patiently and condescendingly attempt to instruct her on the nature of her child; repeatedly, they call her "young girl," speaking as if she were naïve. But it is she who is wise, knowing, and rightly concerned about persecution: words are her only weapons, and she uses them well. As if to sum up the cultural discordance of granting such importance to a woman's speech, the soghitha of Mary and the Gardener has Christ in the guise of the Gardener attempting vainly to fend off Mary's persistent inquiries about her son. He exclaims, "How you weary me with your talk, / how you vex me with what you say!" (Bride, 44.13). Yet Mary prevails, and the truth is revealed because she will not silence her words.

Because of their rhetorical form, the dialogue poems set the significance of Mary's speech in high relief. In each soghitha, an equal number of stanzas must be sung in her voice as in that of her male opponent—stanzas intoned by women's choirs, in a performative voice that enhanced their sung content. Moreover, the opening and closing frames to the hymns do little more than identify the narrative context; they do not describe or fashion a character for her. Instead, whatever sense of character she is given derives from the dialogic exchange: the words she speaks, those spoken in return, the engagement of verbal contest, and its resolution by spoken reconciliation. In these hymns, speech is the action that defines Mary. Indeed, as action, her speech is extraordinary in its power: it can stem or bring to effect God's salvific plan.

Nonetheless, at the same time that these hymns highlight the import of Mary's words, they constrain them to a far greater degree than is evident in Ephrem's hymns. Though presented and performed as dialogue—as liturgical drama—these words are rigidly embedded in a narrative of defined temporal and spatial location.[34] They are located in the time and place of the biblical account; they are precisely set within its narrative bounds. Antiphonally sung, the verses remain those of the biblical characters in their sacred past. There is no slippage across time, no elision into the present worshipping congregation. Although performed as sung conversation, the dramatic dialogue is performatively constructed to preclude any intersection between Mary's imagined voice and the voices of those who sing her words. This is not only a matter of hymnographic form. In content, Ephrem's hymns crossed the whole spectrum of biblical time, across Old and New Testaments, and they crossed the spectrum of historical time, past, present and future. The presentation of Mary's voice as prophetic contributed to this dynamic of open temporality. In the dialogue hymns, Mary speaks not as prophetess, but as a character in a given moment. The salvific consequences were surely understood to be eternal (if not timeless), but the moment is precisely demarcated.

The verse homilies of Jacob of Serug provide one more instance of Mary's voice within Syriac tradition.[35] Unlike Ephrem's hymns or the *soghyatha*, these were not sung by choirs, female or male, but rather chanted by the homilist in a simple metrical pattern (Jacob used couplets with twelve syllables in each line of the couplet). Hence the performative quality of these homilies is immediately and strikingly different from that of the hymns we have considered thus far.[36] On the other hand, Jacob's homilies on Mary are presented as long, even leisurely, retellings of the Gospel stories with excurses on major doctrinal issues; they focus on the same scenes already emphasized (with the addition of Mary's visit with Elizabeth). Into his narrative accounts, Jacob adds substantial blocks of dialogue at the expected interludes: between Mary and Gabriel at the Annunciation, the two women at the Visitation, Mary and Joseph upon her return from her cousin's home, the lullabies of Mary to her newborn son, and the exchange between Mary and Simeon at the Presentation.[37]

In different homilies for different liturgical occasions, and particularly for the feast days associated with these episodes, Jacob recalls and recasts the same scenes and interactions, each time with different points of emphasis, imagery, or doctrinal instruction. As is characteristic of Jacob's writings in general, these homilies follow familiar, standardized presentations of theological and doctrinal positions. If Ephrem's artistry dazzles as much by his peerless originality in imagery as by poetic technique, Jacob's prominence in the Syriac literary memory rests on the genius of presenting traditional materials in familiar yet well-crafted form, occasionally polished with strokes of poignant beauty.

In comparison with the hymns we have considered thus far, Jacob's literary form allows him the fullest construction of Mary's character and voice. The long narrative passages tell the story explicitly, following and embellishing the Gospel accounts. The portions devoted to imagined speech, whether monologue or dialogue, are concretely embedded in a narrative that not only frames the passages of speech but also laces through the encounters. The homilist not only tells his congregation *what* to hear (the imagined words of Mary), but further, *how* to hear—for her words are surrounded by accompanying comment. In some respects, Jacob's homilies control Mary's presentation as speaker far more tightly than any other text this essay has treated. On the other hand, Mary's voice remains a volatile entity, even in Jacob's homilies. Jacob makes this point by devoting much ink to discussion *about* Mary's speech, in addition to crafting its expression; he refers to it and describes it more often than he presents it. Ephrem had represented Mary as subject: figurative subject of devotion, and participatory subject as speaker. Jacob, by contrast, firmly locates Mary as object: she is the object of his text, as she is the object of the congregation's devotional piety.

In his treatment of the Annunciation, Jacob presents the paradox of Mary's position by stressing the enormous frailty of her stance in contrast to Gabriel's celestial splendor. The whole weight of human-divine relation rested on the words they exchanged. Mary's voice held the entire hope of humanity, its only recourse. In Jacob's reckoning, the cosmic order itself hinged on this exchange.

> That moment was full of wonder when Mary was standing conversing
>   in argument with Gabriel.
> One humble daughter of poor folk and one angel met each other and
>   spoke of a wonderful tale.
> A pure virgin and a fiery Watcher spoke with wonder: a discourse
>   which reconciled dwellers of earth and heaven.
> One woman and the prince of all the hosts had made an argument for
>   the reconciliation of the whole world.
>   (Jacob, *Hom.* 1; p. 29)

The moment was itself the replay of an earlier conversation, which had first set things awry. In that instance, too, a woman's voice had carried the weight of all humankind. But in that first exchange, when the serpent had spoken in Eden, Eve had listened without questioning: she had kept silent.[38] Now, Jacob stressed, Mary chose differently. Faced with a messenger of non-human form, she was not swayed as her foremother had been. Instead she questioned and queried; she badgered, she tested. Not until she had received answers sufficient to her understanding would she grant her consent—and her consent, the human action necessary for God's redemptive plan, would come only as an act of her own deliberate choice. For Jacob, Mary's voice was proof that humanity had not lost its free will. Alone, with no assistance, encouragement, or guidance from others, Mary had made her decision, and made it well. If Ephrem had focused attention on Mary's character as the paradoxical extreme of human insignificance—female, poor, young, of no account—Jacob took these attributes and emphasized two further elements discordant with the ancient social order: Mary as a sharp-minded intellectual, and Mary as the exemplar of human autonomy: "She rose up to this measure on her own" (Jacob, *Hom.* 1, p. 38).

Jacob's Mary thus spoke a voice that raised dangerous tension with the late antique social order. But laying open that tension, Jacob would also immediately curb its impact. For no sooner had Mary spoken her great feat of consent, he claimed, than she turned to a more seemly stance: "she inquired, sought, investigated, learned and then kept silence" (Jacob, *Hom.* 1, p. 33). It was in fact the measure of her contrast to Eve that Mary knew when to speak and when to be silent. In that difference lay the fate of the human condition.

> As reprehensible as Eve was by her deed, so Mary was glorious,
> And as the folly of this one, so that one's wisdom is shown up.
>
> . . . . .
>
> By Eve's silence, guilt and the fouling of a name;
> By Mary's discourse, life and light with victory.
>
> (Jacob, *Hom.* 1, p. 33)

Jacob enjoys the play on Eve and Mary as one of foolish silence righted by wise speech, and vain words repaired by discerning silence. Elsewhere, he sets up Mary and her cousin Elizabeth as the conduits of divine inspiration and revelation—women who spoke a new teaching. They, too, must act on their own: the men are speechless, silent, uncomprehending, just as Luke's Gospel had explained in its first chapter. Joseph was absent, while Elizabeth greeted Mary in the presence of her mute husband, Zechariah, and the voiceless infant John in her womb. The women themselves carried the language of truth in their pregnancies, Jacob declares, for Elizabeth carried the Voice—the Forerunner who would cry in the wilderness—while Mary carried the Word, the divine Son. Elizabeth spoke first, mirroring the role of her menfolk had they power to speak:

> And she [Elizabeth] became a mouth for her husband who was not
>   speaking
> And a harp for the sounds of her baby who was making merry.

. . . . .

She was explaining what Zechariah was seeking to do;
She was expressing what the lad was eager to say.

(Jacob, Hom. 2, pp. 53–54)

Emboldened by their circumstances and filled with divine inspiration, Mary and Elizabeth spend the time of their visitation engaged in speech: "For three months," Jacob intones, "the sublime and divine story / was being told in the house of the priest on account of Mary" (Jacob, Hom. 2, p. 55). Together, Jacob proclaims, the women read the scriptures and interpreted their readings; together they encouraged, narrated, meditated on the prophets, explained, showed, and discussed. Together they spoke. What contrast, Jacob marvels, when Mary returns to her husband to be greeted by his scandalized disbelief. "Secretly" Joseph attempted to speak with Mary about her pregnancy. But Mary had gained words of power:

The Virgin also, with loud voice and uncovered face,
Spoke with him, without a bride's veil.
And with the revelations and interpretations of the prophecy,
She was urging him not to doubt on account of her conception.
. . . . .
She was telling him the words which she heard from the angel,
And she was narrating to him how the priests in Judea had received it.
She was also reminding him what the prophets spoke.

(Jacob, Hom. 2, p. 57)

By her speech with Gabriel, Mary had acted to effect the divine incarnation; by her speech with Elizabeth, she acted to place that event rightly in the sacred history of scripture, to understand its biblical foretelling and its historical consequences. By her speech with Joseph, Mary acted to bring biblical witness into living history. Elsewhere Jacob would marvel that "by the mouth of Mary" Christ reached out into human encounter, and "with Mary's voice" the Holy Spirit stretched forth into human experience (Jacob, Hom. 3, p. 78). Indeed, Jacob's Mary rejoices that her words will become the source of new speech by others, even calling forth the women's choirs who would continue the exaltation and praise begun at the Visitation when the two women spoke.

In the world I will be a great parable full of wonder;
All mouths will speak of me, profusely.
. . . . .

Let all the multitude of virgins praise Him with wonder,
Because the great Savior shines forth from them to the whole world.
Let the voice of the young women be lifted up in praise,
Because by one of them, behold, hope is brought to the world.

(Jacob, *Hom.* 3, pp. 82–83)

In this passage, Jacob allows his Mary to summon the women's choirs who would come to sing the hymns and dialogue poems we considered earlier. It is in fact from Jacob that we know something about these choirs. In his panegyric homily in commemoration of Ephrem, Jacob claims that Ephrem himself had founded the choirs of consecrated virgins[39]—choirs declared mandatory for the civic churches of every city, town, and village of the Syrian Orient in the late antique canons and church orders.[40] These choirs were a distinctive feature of the Syriac-speaking churches, differentiating them from their Greek-speaking counterparts, who disallowed the practice. In his homily on Ephrem, Jacob defends the tradition, claiming that Christ offers one salvation for all people, male and female; therefore all are freed to sing God's praise. He further argues from Eve-Mary typology, that where Eve had closed the mouths of women in shame, Mary had opened them in glory. The passage forges an explicit link between the voice of Mary, chanted by the women's choirs and intoned in his own verse homilies, a link earlier enacted in Ephrem's hymns. Ironically, although Jacob controls Mary's speech far more carefully than Ephrem had done, he, too, will use Mary's voice to justify the liturgical practices of his church in terms that recognize their tension with normative social reality beyond the church doors. There are spaces and times appropriate for women's words in Jacob's view; within the church (building and community), and within its historical memory of the biblical past, Mary's character as Jacob represented her could provide the proper voice for those words.

✛ ✛ ✛

The Syriac texts I have considered in this study differ in literary form and in liturgical presentation: Ephrem's hymns would have been sung, perhaps by choirs together with the congregation, and by women's choirs; the dialogue hymns would have been sung antiphonally with women's choirs; Jacob's verse homilies intoned by the preacher. In performance, then, they differed in the degree to which they were inclusive of women's voices in the ritual context of their presentation. In content, they also differed in where and when they located Mary's voice. Ephrem's fashioning of Mary's voice as that of prophetess leading the congregation in songs of praise caused an elision between biblical past and historical present, locating her speech in the midst of the gathered congregation in its present worship. The dialogue hymns performed Mary's voice as liturgical drama, yet placed the exchange within specific narrative moments of the church's salvation story. Jacob of Serug enclosed Mary's voice within the clear boundaries of narrated story; within that narration, he constructed the social spaces of her speech as domestic rather than public. Jacob's Mary speaks in the household of female relative or husband, not in the gathered community of faithful. Instead, her words are intoned in the spaces of public ritual through the mediation of the male priest, perhaps to be echoed by the ritually contained voices of the women's choirs.

A growing gravity toward greater social control of women's religious roles characterizes the era of late antiquity in the Syrian Orient as elsewhere in the Roman Empire of the time.[41] Apparently, that gravity was felt also in the liturgical exploration of biblical imagination. Narrative play with biblical stories and biblical characters was a much loved activity of Syriac hymnographers and homilists. It was also an effective, efficient form of instruction. In the beauty of poetic verse, the biblical past was retold and interpreted through the clear lenses of accepted church doctrine. In this context, the prominence of attention to Mary's voice reveals much about the richness of Syriac Mariology as a developing theological tradition. But I would suggest it tells us something more: that the imagined, consciously fashioned voice of this biblical woman did not sit easily in the ears of the men who wrote these pieces or the congregations whose worship they adorned. In the voiced expression of normative Christian teaching, an expression in Syriac often carried by women's choirs, Mary's words yet echoed with challenge to normative social and political order.

Notes

1. *Odes of Solomon* 19, depending on how it is dated, is not only one of our earliest references to the virgin birth, but specifically one of the earliest to highlight the significance of painlessness in Mary's birthing of Jesus (the undoing of Eve's punishment from Gen. 3:16). The *Odes* have been dated to the late first, mid-second, or third centuries; see Charlesworth, *Old Testament Pseudepigrapha*, 2:725–71 (Ode 19 at 752–53). The strong possibility of Syria as the provenance for the second-century apocryphal text the *Protevangelium of James*, and certainly the immediate popularity of that text in the Syrian Orient, indicates an early attachment to Marian devotion in the region. See Schneemelcher, *New Testament Apocrypha*,

1:421–39; and for the argument for Syrian origin, see Smid, *Protevangelium Jacobi*. Although these are small glimmers amidst the general dearth of knowledge for Christianity's growth in the Syrian Orient, they give some hint that the sophisticated Mariology and Marian devotion found in Ephrem Syrus's hymns do not appear out of thin air but rather are built upon a strong existing tradition.

2. The greatest example is surely the Greek *Akathistos Hymn*, traditionally ascribed to Romanos the Melodist. See Limberis, *Divine Heiress*, esp. 62–120. Important for the ethos out of which the *Akathist* emerged is Constas, "Weaving the Body of God." Although there are problems in the presentation, Gambero, *Mary and the Fathers of the Church*, makes important points, and the selection of texts for Proclus, Theodotus of Ancyra, Romanos, and the *Akathist* itself are illustrative of this point: 249–71, 325–51.

3. McClure, *Spoken Like a Woman*, offers a variety of helpful models for consideration of gendered speech. See further the collection edited by Lardinois and McClure, *Making Silence Speak*, again for suggestive comparisons.

4. For an introduction to Syriac liturgical poetry, see Brock, *St. Ephrem the Syrian*, 36–39. See also Husmann, "Syrian Church Music."

5. According to Jacob of Serug and also an anonymous sixth-century *vita* of Ephrem, Ephrem established the women's choirs explicitly for the presentation and teaching of right doctrine to the Christian community and to counteract the harmful effects of heretics who taught through hymns of their own composing. Jacob of Serug, "A Metrical Homily on Holy Mar Ephrem by Mar Jacob of Serug," ed. and trans. Joseph P. Amar, *Patrologia Orientalis* 47 (1995): 5–76, esp. 35, vv. 40–45; Joseph P. Amar, *The Syriac "Vita" Tradition of Ephrem the Syrian*, 158–59 (Syriac), 298–99 (trans.). The fifth-century Rabbula Canons indicate that the antiphonal singing was divided between male and female choirs, comprised of members of the Sons and Daughters of the Covenant (*Bnay* and *Bnat Qyama*). The hymns were performed in different ways. For *madrashe*, such as Ephrem's *Hymns on the Nativity*, sometimes the verses were sung by a soloist, punctuated with choral refrains; sometimes the stanzas were alternated antiphonally with verses of the Psalms. With the *soghyatha*, a subset of the *madrashe*, the verses alternated between two choirs. The Rabbula *Rules for the Qeiama*, canon 20, state that the male choir should chant the verses of the Psalms, and the female choir the verses of the *madrashe*, again stressing the important role of women's choirs specifically for the singing of doctrinal hymns. The Rabbula Canons are edited and translated in Vööbus, *Syriac and Arabic Documents*, esp. 41.

6. Beyond the scope of this essay, but of great importance to its issues, are the questions of how the texts fit into the development of the Marian feasts in the Syriac liturgical calendar. Crucial studies are van Esbroeck, *Aux origines de la Dormition de la Vierge*; Raes, "Aux origines de la fête de l'Assomption en Orient"; and Mimouni, *Dormition et Assomption de Marie*. For the broader Byzantine developments of Mary's liturgical presentation, see Ledit, *Marie dans la liturgie de byzance*.

7. Scholes and Kellogg, *Nature of Narrative*, remains an excellent study for issues of narrative and narrativity.

8. No one has done a better job alerting us to the difficulties of assessing late

antique literary and rhetorical representations of women than Elizabeth Clark. See especially her articles "Holy Women, Holy Words" and "Ideology, History, and the Construction of 'Woman.' "

9. For the larger Syriac tradition to which Ephrem contributed, see, e.g., Murray, *Symbols of Church and Kingdom*, 144–50, 329–35; Brock, "Mary in Syriac Tradition" and "Mary and the Eucharist."

10. Ephrem, *On the Nativity*, hereafter cited as *H. Nat.* All quotations are from the excellent English translation of McVey in *Ephrem the Syrian*. The Syriac text is edited with German translation by Beck in *Des heiligen Ephraem des Syrers Hymnen*. For an overview of the cycle, see McVey, *Ephrem the Syrian*, 29–34. It is worth noting that the cycle originated as a collection of sixteen hymns (*H. Nat.* 5–20), which Ephrem seems to have collected himself and titled "lullabies." These are the hymns in which Mary's is often the dominant voice. In the course of the manuscript transmission, other Nativity hymns by Ephrem were added, to make up the present cycle of twenty-eight hymns. See McVey, *Ephrem the Syrian*, 29. Beck's edition contains a further thirteen hymns on Epiphany, mostly of dubious ascription.

11. See Harvey, "Spoken Words, Voiced Silence" and "Women's Service."

12. Cf. also *H. Nat.* 9.1, 3.

13. No doubt Ephrem also has in mind Miriam, the sister of Moses, who led the people in song after they had crossed the Red Sea (Exod. 15:20–21).

14. Brock, *Luminous Eye*, is especially helpful on Ephrem's primary themes. See further Murray, *Symbols*.

15. E.g., Limberis, *Divine Heiress*, 121–43; Brown, "Notion of Virginity." For the larger ramifications of the theme in cultural terms, see Cameron, *Christianity and the Rhetoric of Empire*, esp. 155–88 on the rhetoric of paradox.

16. The tradition was most prevalent for the Holy Spirit, since in Syriac the term *ruha*, "spirit," is a feminine noun. But the imagery of Christ's breasts, or God's womb, was also found, for example both in the *Odes of Solomon* and in Ephrem's hymns. See, e.g., the discussions in Harvey, "Feminine Imagery for the Divine"; Drijvers, "19th Ode of Solomon"; McVey, *Ephrem the Syrian*, 10 n. 28.

17. *H. Nat.* 4.143–214. Cf. *H. Nat.* 11.6–8.

18. E.g., *H. Nat.* 5.19–21; 11.1, 2, 6, 7; 13.7; 16 (passim); 23.11; 25.12, 14. See Brock, *Luminous Eye*, 53–84.

19. *H. Nat.* 6.3–6; 8.9; 12.4–11; 13.13; 14 (passim); 15.7–8; 16.12–3; 17.7.

20. *H. Nat.* 11.7. Cf. Luke 1:46–55. Ephrem has Mary present salvation history in like manner, recalling the scandalous women of Jesus' geneaology (Matt. 1:1–16: Tamar, Rahab, Ruth, and Bathsheeba) as women who reversed the social order: *H. Nat.* 9.7–14. See also *H. Nat.* 16.16.

21. On narrative as an inherently moralizing form of discourse, see Hayden White, "Value of Narrativity in the Representation of Reality," in Mitchell, ed., *On Narrative*, 1–24.

22. *H. Nat.* 7.9–13; 8.22; 22.N23.

23. *H. Nat.* 12.4–11; 14.11–19; 16.12–13; 17.4–11.

24. Brown, "Virginity," makes this point especially well.

25. It is clear that the challenge raised by Mary's character was meant to encompass

the entire social order. In *H. Nat.* 17, Mary is borne on divine pinions in a heavenly ascent. From the heights, she sees a new order in which slave and free, male and female will be able to attain perfect freedom for devotion to Christ; in like manner, the sick will find their health, the lepers their cleanliness.

26. Exactly the point emphasized for the role of women's choirs in both Jacob of Serug's "Homily on Ephrem" and the anonymous sixth-century *vita Ephraemi*. See above, note 5.

27. See the discussion in Harvey, "Spoken Words, Voiced Silence." I am much influenced by Bell, *Ritual Theory, Ritual Practice,* 109–24.

28. The *soghitha* was a subset of the *madrashe,* the stanzaic hymns such as Ephrem's *Hymns on the Nativity* that dealt particularly with doctrinal matters. See esp. Brock, "Dramatic Dialogue Poems," 135–47; and "Syriac Dispute Poems: the Various Types," 109–20. Reinink and Vanstiphout's *Dispute Poems and Dialogues* is helpful for the larger literary context.

29. Sarah at the incident of Genesis 22 (the sacrifice of Isaac), and the Sinful Woman of Luke 7:36–50 are other favorites. See Harvey, "Spoken Words, Voiced Silence." For a sense of the contrast to other modes of exegesis, see Brière's translation of Severus of Antioch's *Homily* 118 (on the Sinful Woman) and Hill, "St. John Chrysostom's Homilies on Hannah."

30. For the intersection of dramatic dialogue and liturgy in Greek tradition of the same period, see esp. Dubrov, "Dialogue with Death." Also important for the broader traditions of literary and rhetorical disputes, see Reinink and Vanstiphout, *Dispute Poems and Dialogues,* esp. Averil Cameron, "Disputations, Polemical Literature, and the Formation of Opinion," 91–108.

31. I use here the examples collected and translated in Brock, *Bride of Light,* nos. 41–44, pp. 111–34; cited hereafter as *Bride,* with hymn number and stanza.

32. On the Virgin Mary rather than Mary Magdalene for this Gospel episode, see Murray, *Symbols,* 146–48; and now Shoemaker, "Rethinking the 'Gnostic Mary.' "

33. *Bride,* 24 (Soghitha 3), pp. 78–86.

34. In comparing the narrative aspects of Ephrem's hymns, the *soghyatha,* and the verse homilies of Jacob of Serug (below), I have been much helped by the essays in Mitchell, ed., *On Narrative,* especially Hayden White, "The Value of Narrativity," 1–24; Frank Kermode, "Secrets and Narrative Sequence," 79–98; Paul Ricoeur, "Narrative Time," 165–86; and Robert Scholes, "Language, Narrative, and Anti-Narrative," 200–8. See also Dubrov, "Dialogue with Death."

35. Narsai (died ca. 502) would be the other obvious Syriac writer to consider. However, Narsai makes little use of dialogue in his verse homilies, in contrast to Jacob. The difference in presentation is strikingly clear in Narsai's "Homily on Our Lord's Birth from the Holy Virgin," which covers the Gospel episodes from Luke, from the Annunciation all the way through to the Presentation to Simeon. In this long homily (508 lines), Narsai has Mary speak only three lines—an immediate acceptance of Gabriel's announcement of her conception! The text is edited with translation by McLeod, *Narsai's Metrical Homilies,* 36–69.

36. Consider the discussions in Harvey, "Spoken Words, Voiced Silence," and Dubrov, "Dialogue with Death."

37. Jacob's homilies on Mary are in S. *Martyrii, qui et Sahdona*, edited by Paul Bedjan, 614–17. I cite the homilies (abbreviated *Hom.*) as numbered and translated by Mary Hansbury in *Jacob of Serug*; since Hansbury does not give line numbers, I indicate the page in her translation. Several others from the Bedjan collection, as well as from other editions of Jacob's homilies, are translated by Thomas Kollamparampil in *Jacob of Serugh: Select Festal Homilies*; for Mary, these are thematically very similar to the ones in Hansbury's collection.

38. For the larger theme in Syriac tradition, see Murray, "Mary, the Second Eve."

39. Jacob of Serug, "Metrical Homily," 5–76, esp. 35, vv. 40–45.

40. I have tried to collect the major canonical evidence in Harvey, "Women's Service," and "Spoken Words, Voiced Silence." The fifth-century canons from the East Syrian Synod of 410 convened by Maruta of Maipherqat demand that every village set aside children to be trained as Sons and Daughters of the Covenant, explicitly to maintain the spiritual life in less populated regions (canon 26); and moreover, require every civic church to have a women's choir, trained in psalmody (canon 41). These are edited and translated in Vööbus, *Canons Ascribed to Maruta*.

41. Harvey, "Women's Service," traces the changes in the Syriac canon collections and church orders into the medieval period.

+ Is There a Harlot in This Text?

   Hagiography and the Grotesque

   PATRICIA COX MILLER

In her book *Christianity and the Rhetoric of Empire*, Averil Cameron argues that hagiography can be characterized as a "continual reworking and reenactment of idealized Christian biography, the pattern of Christian truth in action."[1] Found first and foremost in the Gospels, "the Christian story is itself a biography"; thus later Christians, through the writing of saints' lives, "could present an image of the life in imitation of Christ, the life that becomes an icon."[2] Following this line of thought, but taking it to a different part of the New Testament, Philip Rousseau and Tomas Hägg have remarked that "no Christian biographer or panegyrist could entirely escape the apostle Paul's evocation of the 'new man'—especially since the idea was linked with 'putting off mortality and putting on immortality.' "[3]

Surely it is this "new man" who provides the model for Peter Brown's holy man, most recently defined by Brown in terms of the " 'transformation' of his person, through a Spirit-filled ascetic discipline and through the imaginative alchemy associated with the return of Adam, in the desert, to his Paradise Regained."[4] With this new emphasis on transformation rather than translocation, Brown now finds "the issue of his male gender . . . that much more interesting," "for maybe holy men were not 'men.' " Figures such as the angelic Symeon the Stylite, he suggests, "had transcended the categories of gender as normally defined."[5]

While the rhetoric of the angelic life may well indicate a desire to construe the character of men like Symeon apart from sexual behavior (Brown specifically mentions procreation as what defined "normal" male-gendered identity), it does not indicate that maleness had ceased to function normatively as a measure of religious status. Although, as Elizabeth Clark has pointed out, "gender-bending" was a feature of Christian portrayals of ascetic heroes from early on, Thecla being a notable example, still the gender that was "bent" was typically female rather than male.[6] There was no male equivalent to the female transvestite, who by the fifth century had become a stock character in hagiography, and even in earlier biographies holy women were often portrayed as honorary men: the "female man of God" is Palladius's memorable phrase.[7] Just as there was no female equivalent to Brown's "holy man," as Clark, again, has shown, there was also a marked tendency to position the identity of holy women in terms of male-gendered norms.[8]

Although manliness and holiness seem to be virtually inextricable from each other, especially in early Christian literature that portrays historical women, there is a literature that takes a step in the direction of imagining holy women who are valued for more than their "manly" character. This is the hagiographical literature of the so-called holy harlots that, as I will argue, gestures toward a "pattern of Christian truth" that destabilizes the dominant maleness of the "life as icon," to recall Cameron's phrases. Yet my focus will be on the paradoxical quality of these portrayals, for these "seductively feminized figures" are nonetheless "spectacles of conflicting images that refuse to resolve into a visual whole."[9]

The two texts that I am going to discuss are the *Life of Mary of Egypt* and the *Life of St. Pelagia of Antioch*.[10] As Virginia Burrus has remarked, these *vitae* of loose women are themselves "promiscuous," so to speak, because they are difficult to locate historically, geographically, textually, and in terms of authorship.[11] Although the earliest written versions of both texts may be from the seventh century, each has a complicated literary and oral past, due at least in part to elaborations of anecdotes about reformed sinners. Both were translated into several languages and appear to have circulated rapidly.[12]

Briefly, the storylines of these two popular hagiographies run as follows. The *Life of Mary of Egypt* is framed by the tale of Zosimas, a Palestinian monk in middle age, who begins to be tormented by the thought that he has achieved perfection and so despairs of being able to advance in the spiritual life. At the behest of a vision, he retreats to a secluded monastery near the Jordan River, whose normally cloistered monks follow a Lenten practice of leaving the monastery to sojourn in the desert in solitary ascetic observance. For his retreat, Zosimas crosses the Jordan, "hoping that he might find some father there who would fulfill his longing" (VM 7). As Burrus remarks, "[T]he knowing reader appreciates the irony: what Zosimas will in fact find is a 'mother' who will not so much fulfill as intensify his longing and thereby finally shatter his self-satisfaction."[13]

One day while singing the Psalms, he glimpses "the shadow of a human body" (VM 7), a sunburned apparition that he fears is demonic.[14] Recognizing finally that this is no demon but a woman, he gives chase, she flees across a dried-up stream, and he collapses in exhaustion. A conversation ensues, as the woman eerily addresses Zosimas by name. Refusing to face him because she is naked, she requests and receives his tattered old cloak. They pray together, and Zosimas, sneaking a peek, is further astounded when he sees her levitating. He begs to know her story, which she tells in a lengthy first-person narrative. She describes her life of insatiable desire for sex, culminating with her seduction of pilgrims about to sail for Jerusalem for the festival of the Exaltation of the Holy Cross. Having offered the favors of her body as payment for the passage, Mary arrives in Jerusalem, but when she attempts to enter the church with the others, she is repulsed by a mysterious force emanating from an icon of the Virgin Mary. This is the moment of her conversion, and a voice instructs her to cross over the Jordan. When Zosimas meets her, Mary has been in the desert, alone, for forty-seven years. They agree to meet a year later, at which time Zosimas promises to bring her Communion; he does so, and experiences another eerie moment, as she approaches walking on water. Again they agree to meet in a year, and when Zosimas finds Mary this time, she is dead. A helpful lion assists in the burial.

The *Life of Pelagia* is similarly framed by events in the life of an ascetic male, one James the Deacon, who opens his account with a kind of ecclesiastical tableau: bishops, including his own bishop Nonnos, have gathered on the steps of a church in Antioch. While waiting for the assembly to begin, they are being instructed by Nonnos. Breaking the spell of this scene of holy teaching, an actress and her retinue pass by in debauched splendor. Dressed in little more than gold, pearls, and jewels, Pelagia parades by "with her head uncovered, with a scarf thrown around her shoulders in a shameless fashion, as though she were a man" (VP 6 [Syriac]). Understandably amazed, the bishops hide their faces to shield themselves from this sinful sight—all except Nonnos, who exclaims over her astonishing beauty and laments that he has not adorned his soul as she has her body.

In the next scene, the hand of God guides the harlot Pelagia into the very church where Nonnos is preaching; overcome and weeping, she demands to be baptized: "You must baptize me at once and so make me a stranger to my evil deeds; you will become a stranger to your holy altar and deny your God if you don't make me a bride of Christ this very day" (VP 26 [Syriac]). Nonnos complies, and helps Pelagia make a nocturnal escape from Antioch by giving her his clothing. Cross-dressed, she is now Pelagius, and takes up a solitary life of extreme asceticism in a cell on the Mount of Olives.

In the final scene, James—who is ignorant of Pelagia's fate—goes on pilgrimage to Jerusalem. Nonnos advises him to visit "a certain brother

Pelagius, a monk and eunuch" now renowned for working wonders (VP 13). Knocking on the monk's window, James doesn't recognize the cross-dressed Pelagia: "How could I have known her again, with a face so emaciated by fasting? It seemed to me that her eyes had sunk inward like a great pit" (VP 14). Pelagia recognizes him, however, and asks him to ask Nonnos to pray for her. James leaves, but is impelled to visit again some time later, and finds Pelagia dead, whereupon a crowd of fathers and monks preside over a lavish burial.

The literature of the harlot-saints of late ancient and early Byzantine Christianity has often been characterized as "dramatic tale[s] of a lust turned into love."[15] According to Benedicta Ward, "[T]he stories of the harlots belong to the literature of conversion" and "conform to the pattern of the great penitent of the New Testament, Mary Magdalene," understood in early Christian legend as a repentant prostitute. Further, "the sinful woman is also Eve, the mother of all the living, and therefore the image is of Everyman, of the human race alienated from the love of God." More particularly, continues Ward, these are stories told by monks for monks; using "the image of the courtesan to rebuke the life of a [male] monk," such stories—both here and in the *Apophthegmata Patrum*—serve to remind the monk about his sinful state.[16] Similarly, Lynda Coon argues that "only the conversion of sexually depraved women, such as Mary of Egypt and Pelagia of Antioch, could teach Christian audiences that redemption is possible even for the most loathsome sinners."[17] Indeed, she says, "such females serve as mediators of human salvation; they atone for the sorrowful life of the postlapsarian Eve."[18]

The heroines of this literature are thus constructed as depraved, licentiously sexual women who atone for humanity's primordial fall.[19] According to this perspective, holy harlots are images of repentance whose basic function is symbolic: either they are construed as images of human salvation,[20] or they are seen as a product of the male monastic imaginary that uses the figure of a courtesan to bring home to the monk his state as a sinner.[21] Both of these views vitiate the specifically female aspects of these hagiographic images, the one by universalizing them, the other by seeing them as objects of exchange between ascetic men.

While I do not deny that these are compelling readings, I want to explore a different understanding of these texts. Thus rather than rescuing the discordant figure of the harlot-saint from absurdity by reading her story as a morality tale, I propose to read this image as a realization of a contradiction central to the late ancient Christian (male) imagination, a contradiction expressed by the seemingly simple phrase, "holy *woman*." I will argue that the

figure of the harlot-saint is a grotesquerie—a not-quite-coherent construct—
and as such brings to its most acute expression the problematic quality of
early Christian attempts to construct a representation of female holiness.[22]

I was alerted to this alternative reading by a curious detail at the end of the
Life of Pelagia. As indicated above, following her conversion to Christianity
Pelagia secretly leaves Antioch dressed in the clothing of the bishop Nonnos,
takes up residence in a monastic cell on the Mount of Olives, renames herself
"Pelagius," and becomes famous for ascetic rigor and wonder working.
When the narrator of this story, James the Deacon, discovers that the monk
has died, monks from several monasteries arrive and break open the door of
the cell. Now comes the curious detail:

> They carried out his sacred little body as if it had been gold and silver
> they were carrying. When the fathers began to anoint the body with
> myrrh, they realized that it was a woman. *They wanted to keep such a
> wonder hidden* but they could not, because of the crowds of people
> thronging around, who cried out with a loud voice, "Glory to you, Lord
> Jesus Christ, for you have hidden away on earth such great treasures,
> women as well as men." (VP 15, my emphasis)[23]

Why the attempted cover-up? Of course this botched attempt to conceal
feminine holiness by the male monastic establishment introduces a comic
note, since the reader knows all along that "he" is really "she." But it is also a
notable revision of a standard topos in stories about transvestite saints who
are discovered to be female after they have died; unlike other stories, whose
disclosure of female identity is accompanied by wonder, astonishment, and
praise, here there is an attempt to undermine the revelation, reversing in a
striking way the motif of unearthing buried treasure that both opens and
closes this text.[24]

This failed ruse functioned for me as a "luminous detail," a phrase that
New Historicists Stephen Greenblatt and Catherine Gallagher borrowed
from Ezra Pound to describe moments when a text confounds itself in *ap-
oriae*, those "tears where energies, desires, and repressions flow out into the
world."[25] Unlike the hagiographic paradigm of ascetic women that stripped
such women of their femaleness by declaring them to be manly women or
"female men of God," vitae like those of Pelagia and Mary are not successful
in suppressing the femaleness of their subjects. No one in these texts says of
them what John Chrysostom is reported to have said about his friend and
patron Olympias: "Don't say 'woman' but 'what a man!' because this is a
man, despite her physical appearance."[26]

Yet these stories are not entirely successful in promoting a truly female model of holiness, either. Judith Butler has remarked about another anomalous figure, Antigone, that "what she draws into crisis is the representative function itself, the very horizon of intelligibility in which she operates and according to which she remains somewhat unthinkable."[27] Similarly, Mary and Pelagia draw into crisis the representative function of hagiography. It is this crisis, this perch at the limits of intelligibility, that I will explore under the figure of the grotesque, defined by Geoffrey Galt Harpham in his *On The Grotesque: Strategies of Contradiction in Art and Literature* as "phenomena that both require and defeat definition: they are neither so regular that they settle easily into our categories, nor so unprecedented that we do not recognize them at all; they stand at the margin of consciousness between the known and the unknown, calling into question the adequacy of our ways of organizing the world."[28]

Recent scholarly work on gender and asceticism has clarified the ideological difficulties, both physical and theological, that were involved in attempts of early Christian men to conceptualize how women might occupy the status of holy person. Physically speaking, women's bodies and sexuality were so closely allied as to be virtually synonymous, as in medical texts where "all symptoms in a woman must be considered in relation to the genital area."[29] This medical pathologizing of female sexuality was allied with one of the fourth century's major paradigms for female sanctity—virginity—by Basil of Ancyra. This physician and theologian argued that the virgin must "destroy the pleasure of the female in herself," making "her look masculine and her voice hard."[30] As Teresa Shaw has explained, "[T]he 'form' of the female body, made alluring at creation, is rendered 'pure' through virginity and asceticism." Yet, as Shaw also argues, "the virgin continue[d] to be crippled by her physical body."[31]

Theologically speaking, women bore the "weight of the abhorrence of sexuality that the church focused on women."[32] In Gillian Cloke's pithy summary, "Women were essentially sinful because essentially sexual."[33] Here is where the other major models that allowed for women to be constructed as holy persons are relevant: the manly woman and the transvestite saint displace the legacy of the sinfully sexual Eve by setting the virtuous woman apart from her sexuality altogether. As Judith Herrin has argued, this was a simulated holiness: "to the church fathers the very idea of a holy woman was a contradiction in terms, which women could only get round by pretending to be men."[34]

As I have already indicated, however, in hagiographic portraits like those of Mary and Pelagia, such male disguises begin to wear thin. Mary is not troped as a female man of God, nor is she ever in total disguise. Pelagia's grace, valor and virtue as a woman seem affirmed in her portrait, despite her transvestism. Others have noted the positive qualities of these portraits, particularly regarding transvestism. Teresa Shaw has cautioned that the "notion of becoming male can only be taken so far—in transvestite narratives, there is almost always a revelation of the true female identity of the disguised monk"; and Susan Ashbrook Harvey has written that "despite real and literary attempts to the contrary, in the end it was her true identity as a woman which was, by necessity, honored."[35]

While I applaud their avoidance of the explanatory strategy that some have adopted about transvestism, namely that it depends upon an ideal of androgyny, I am not so sanguine about the affirmative nature of these texts, since I think that affirmation is precisely what such texts are grappling with. These two lives of saints are riddled with interpretive oddities, especially regarding gender; their oscillations between male and female suggest that they are narratives of an emergent, not an accomplished, comprehension.[36]

The femaleness of both Mary and Pelagia is affirmed, but oddly, through multiple transgressions of gender identities and boundaries. Significantly, both are initially troped as phantasmal: Pelagia, clothed in jewels and gold, is said to be "dressed in the height of fantasy" ("cum summa phantasia") (VP 2); and Mary, "clothed" only in her naked femaleness, is seen as an apparition (VM 1, naming her as both *simulacrum* and *spectrum*). Such symbolic uses of clothing to position these figures as simulacra suggests that, like the grotesque, they are "concepts without form," just beyond the reach of coherence. As anomalous beings, they will continually pass in and out of focus.[37]

One of the ways in which these hagiographic portraits mark the "corrupted or shuffled familiarity" of their heroines is in the "typological incoherence" of their use of scriptural referents.[38] Fittingly allusive, these referents demonstrate the ways in which such texts both flirt with the erasure of female identity and inscribe it at the same time. Mary, for example, would seem to be the most consistently "feminine" of the holy harlots. Her divine intercessor is the Virgin Mary, who is often invoked, and only once does she don male clothing, when the monk Zosimas throws her his cloak to cover her nudity, but even this only partially covers her body, as the text says explicitly: "She took [his tattered cloak] and partially hid the nakedness of her body with it and then turned to Zosimas" (VM 9).[39]

However, she is repeatedly portrayed with scriptural images that are male.

As Lynda Coon has pointed out, "like Saul, Mary receives loaves of bread before beginning her spiritual journey," and "her independent life in the desert resembles the spiritual solitude of Elijah and Christ."[40] Furthermore, like Christ Mary walks on water and has a "Christ-like power of clair-voyance."[41] The most stunning allusion to Christ is this text's presentation of Mary as the eschatological Messiah: "the hair on her head was white as wool" like that of "the one like a son of man" in Revelation 1:14.[42]

Such allusions might seem to indicate that this nakedly female "she" is really a "he," were it not for the fact that in her monologue Mary insists that she is a "sinful woman," drawing on the concatenation of whorish images that came to cluster around Mary Magdalene in the late ancient imagina-tion.[43] And, in the very sentence in which Mary is cast as the apocalyptic Christ, she is also cast as the "black but comely" bride of the Song of Songs 1:5–6, with her "body black as if scorched by the fierce heat of the sun." Male or female?[44]

While this text attempts to move from the female margin to the male center, it never quite achieves its goal.[45] Mary's story, spoken in her own (female) voice and called by the monk Zosimas a "life-giving narrative" (VM 14), is paralleled by the Christological and thus male phrases "life-giving wood of the cross" and "life-giving body and blood" (VM 17, 20). Yet these parallels are undermined by her story, which is one of extreme female pro-fligacy and subsequent abasement. As Harpham has observed, "[I]n the case of both metaphor and the grotesque, the form itself resists the interpretation that it necessitates"; thus "we remain aware of the referential absurdity of the metaphor despite [the text's] attempts to transcend it."[46]

I have already indicated that the concept of the grotesque indicates not a mediation or fusion of opposites but the presentation or realization of a contradiction. This phenomenon of the "impossible split reference" also marks the hagiographic portrait of Pelagia.[47] Here also gender-crossings transgress boundaries without dissolving them. Like Mary, Pelagia is often biblically scripted as both female and male. Prior to her baptism, she pre-sents herself as both the sinful woman of Luke 7:37–38, who wets the feet of Jesus with her tears, and as the Samaritan harlot at the well, whom Jesus converts in John 4:7–39. After her baptism, however, she is like Jesus tempted by Satan, and no sooner is she declared by the bishop Nonnos to be a bride of Christ than she dresses in the bishop's clothing and goes off to Jerusalem to begin her career as Pelagius, performing miracles like her male model, Christ.

Furthermore, when the text moves Pelagia across the boundary between secular and sacred, it places her in an enclosed space, her monastic cell. As Lynda Coon argues, "Pelagia, who personifies the bride from the Song of Songs (4.12), has now become 'a garden locked, a fountain sealed.' The architecture of seclusion transforms a body that had been open to sin into an impenetrable fortress, and Pelagia transmutes into the New Eve and the immaculate Virgin."[48] I would only add that this "virgin" is no virgin; and, while she may conform to the image of the female virgin as enclosed garden, she does so in male disguise. In fact, as Pelagius she has had her femaleness "castrated," so to speak, by the bishop Nonnos, who says the monk is a eunuch (VP 13), a marker that actually intensifies her maleness rather than transporting her to some state of being beyond sexuality, as some have argued.[49]

Aside from these oscillations, however, the most stunning instance of "impossible split reference" is the entrance of the great mime of Antioch into this hagiography. Here is James the Deacon's account:

> Now while we were marvelling at [Nonnos's] holy teaching, lo, sud-denly there came among us the chief actress of Antioch, the first in the chorus in the theater, sitting on a donkey. She was dressed in the height of fantasy, wearing nothing but gold, pearls and precious stones, even her bare feet were covered with gold and pearls. With her went a great throng of boys and girls all dressed in cloth of gold with collars of gold on their necks, going before and following her. (VP 2)

This is an intensely feminized and degraded image: Pelagia appears as the whore of Babylon of Revelation 17:4, golden and bejeweled, an incarnation of lust, idolatry, and shamelessness.[50] At the same time, however, this pas-sage is a replay of another, more famous entry, that of Jesus into Jerusalem, riding—according to Matthew 21:1–9—on a donkey and a colt, with crowds going before and following him.[51] Split reference, indeed: as Harpham re-marks, "[T]he grotesque is always a civil war of attraction and repulsion, marked by the co-presence of the normative and the ideal and also the abnormal and the degenerate."[52]

Of course, this is not the only procession in Pelagia's story; the final one is her funeral, when the "sacred little body," carried as though it were gold and silver, discovered to be female, and declared to be a great treasure, is put to rest by a huge crowd of monks and nuns who, with much splendor, fill the air with singing and the scent of myrrh, just as the crowds in the first procession "fill the air with traces of music and the most sweet smell of perfume" (VP 2). Is her end in her beginning? What are we to make of the transformation of the gold-bedecked harlot, whose body becomes the ornament she once wore? Taking seriously the view that the body is a "surface of signification"[53] and that, in late antiquity, human subjectivity was rooted in the body and particularly in the body's sexuality, I turn now to the issue of the construction of a specifically female selfhood, a "holy woman," that I think is emergent in the tales of the harlot-saints.

As Harpham writes, "[T]he grotesque threatens the notion of a center by implying coherencies just out of reach," but "in its purposeful rearrangement of familiar elements, it teases us with intimations of deep or profound meanings"; "grotesqueries confront us as a corrupt or fragmented text in search of a master principle."[54] While intimating that a truly female, because fully sexual, woman can carry the designation "holy," the texts under discussion here founder on the difficulties involved in conceptualizing female *erôs* in religious terms without tainting it with excess. Does not a title like *Vita sanctae Pelagiae, Meretricis* state both sides of a contradiction at once? Yet this designation, *meretrix*, contains a hint of the "master principle" that the harlot-saint literature is trying to articulate.

Most scholarship on holy harlots has accepted the socioeconomic meaning of the term *meretrix*, "a woman who earns," without question.[55] And indeed, some of them are prostitutes in this sense: they operate out of brothels or, more independently, out of their own houses and take money for their services.[56] Mary and Pelagia, however, are not presented as prostitutes in Roman legal, social, and economic terms, despite the presence of the term *meretrix* in the titles of their stories. Neither is attached to a *leno*, a pimp, or indeed to any man, unlike most prostitutes who had very little control over their bodies and were subject to legal regulation and disabilities.[57]

In fact, neither Mary nor Pelagia takes money in exchange for sex. Unlike most Roman writing on prostitution, in which "male rather than female lusts were central," these hagiographies emphasize female eros.[58] In her monologue, Mary describes herself as a woman of ardent desire: "For more than seventeen years, I passed my life openly tarrying in the fires of lust. I had not lost my virginity for any gift of money, for I frequently refused what they wanted to give me. . . . Do not think that I was at all rich, for I lived by begging or sometimes by spinning threads of flax. It was just that what I did, I did out of insatiable desire" (VM 13).

Pelagia, an actress and so a member of a profession notorious for its questionable sexual mores, is presented as a woman who adorns her body to please her lovers.[59] Directed both at herself and at others, her eros is connected with "such great beauty that all the ages of humankind could never come to the end of it" (VP 2).

These women love sex, and in loving their sexuality they also value themselves, according to the late ancient code that identified women's being with their sexuality. For a moment, beauty, desire, and femaleness are positively valued. Furthermore, as autonomous lovers they are free agents and as such they disrupt male norms of subjectivity. And, as harlots typically did in the Roman imagination, Mary and Pelagia cross forbidden boundaries between domestic, private, female-gendered space and public, male-gendered space.[60] Even after their conversions, they continue to occupy positions of agency, not only by switching teaching and priestly roles with their male interlocutors but also by practicing their spirituality in solitude, apart from male ecclesiastical structures.[61] The grotesque violates categories and threatens to decenter cultural norms.

But, can a woman with a truly female, because female-sexed, identity be a saint? This, I think, is the "master principle" that these texts are struggling to articulate. They attempt to speak the unspeakable, "holy woman." But they don't quite succeed, for the identities of Pelagia and Mary are simultaneously affirmed and negated.[62] Because their beauty, agency, and love are connected with their sexuality, they are exposed as perverted, as indeed the term meretrix suggests, for it can designate not only literal prostitutes but also women "whose sexual morals the speaker wants to impugn."[63]

Yet however ephemeral, their beauty and eros have been valued. Through changes in angles of vision, the deformed is revealed as the sublime, but also the reverse.[64] "Sometimes," Harpham remarks, "only the context enables us to decide between devil and deity," depravity and holiness.[65] As embodiments of truly female holiness, Mary and Pelagia remain somewhat unthinkable.

So: Is there a harlot in this text? Yes, and no. Mary and Pelagia are grotesqueries and, as Harpham observes, "if the grotesque can be compared to anything, it is to paradox," which is "a way of turning language against itself by asserting both terms of a contradiction at once. Pursued for its own sake, paradox can seem vulgar or meaningless; it is extremely fatiguing to the mind. But pursued for the sake of wordless truth, it can rend veils and even, like the grotesque, approach the holy."[66] In their hagiographies, Mary and Pelagia both approach the holy, but their full embodiment of it is undermined by the gendered contradictions that cluster around them. Elevated and debased at once, they are paradoxes whose allure is the truth of female holiness.

Notes

1. Cameron, *Christianity and the Rhetoric of Empire*, 123.
2. Ibid., 91, 143.
3. Hägg and Rousseau, *Greek Biography and Panegyric*, 22.
4. Brown, "Rise and Function of the Holy Man," 371.
5. Ibid.
6. Clark, "Holy Women, Holy Words," 416. For a discussion of the destabilization of gender, see Castelli, " 'I Will Make Mary Male.' "
7. Palladius, *Lausiac History* 9 (ed. C. Butler, *The Lausiac History of Palladius*, 2 vols. [Cambridge, 1898]): "hê anthrôpos tou theou." On female transvestites, see the discussion and survey of literature by Davis, "Crossed Texts, Crossed Sex." For a catalogue of statements about the "maleness" of saintly women, a selection of which follows, see Cloke, *This Female Man of God*, 214. Palladius, *Lausiac History*, intro. 1: "God-inspired matrons, who with masculine and perfect mind have successfully accomplished the struggles of virtuous asceticism"; Paulinus of Nola, *Epistle* 29.6, on Melania the Elder: "What a woman she is, if one can call so manly a Christian a woman"; also, *Epistle* 45.3: "Melania, a perfect woman in Christ, yet retaining unaffected the courage of her manly spirit"; Palladius, *Dialogue on the Life of St. John Chrysostom* 56, on Olympias: "not a woman but an *anthrôpos*, a manly creature: a man in everything but body"; Gregory of Nyssa, *Vita Macrinae* 1, 14–17: "it was a woman who provided us with our subject; if indeed she should be termed woman, for I do not know if it is appropriate to describe her by her sex who so surpassed her sex"; Gregory of Nazianzus, *Concerning Himself* 116, on his mother Nonna: "displaying in female form the spirit of a man"; Gerontius, *Life of Melania the Younger* 39: she was received by the monks of Nitria "like a man" since "she has surpassed the limits of her sex and taken on a mentality that was manly, or rather angelic."
8. Clark, "Holy Women, Holy Words," 413–17.
9. Virginia Burrus, "Secrets of Seduction: The Lives of Holy Harlots," unpublished manuscript. I thank Prof. Burrus for sharing her manuscript and allowing me to quote from it.
10. *Vita Mariae Aegyptae* (hereafter VM), attributed to Sophronius, in Migne, *Patrologia Graeca* (PG) 87:3697–726; translation of the Latin text by Ward, *Harlots of the Desert*, 35–56; *Vita Sanctae Pelagiae, Meretricis* (hereafter VP) by James the Deacon, in Migne, *Patrologia Latina* (PL) 73:663–72; translation by Ward, *Harlots of the Desert*, 66–75. I have also consulted and occasionally quoted from the translation of this text from the Syriac in Brock and Harvey, trans., *Holy Women of the Syrian Orient*, 41–62.
11. Burrus, "Secrets of Seduction."
12. For a detailed analysis of the *Life of Mary of Egypt*, I have consulted Paul B. Harvey, Jr., "Mary the Egyptian: Sources and Purpose and New Notes." I thank Professor Harvey for allowing me to use his unpublished manuscript. See also Coon, *Sacred Fictions*, 84. For discussion of textual traditions pertaining to the *Life of Pelagia*, see

Brock and Harvey, *Holy Women of the Syrian Orient*, 40–41, 186; and Petitmengin et al., *Pélagie la Pénitente*.

13. Burrus, "Secrets of Seduction."

14. Both the Latin and the Greek texts emphasize the illusory quality of what Zosimas sees ("*aposkiasma . . . anthrôpinou sômatos*"; "*corporis humani simulacrum*"). In *Sacred Fictions*, 86, Coon suggests that "the hagiographer intends his audience to view this initial contact between male confessor and female penitent as an allusion to Jesus' first encounter with the devil in the desert." This may be so, but it is an allusion that the text itself complicates, since it is Mary, not Zosimas, who will be shown to be Christomimetic, while Zosimas has already been implicated in perhaps the worst sin of ascetic life in the desert, the claim to perfection. On the latter, see Harpham, *Ascetic Imperative*, 43: "Indeed, the illusion that one had reached an ideal or perfect identification with Christ the Word was the most notorious and insidious of temptations, slamming the door closed at the very moment when one had proven oneself worthy of entering."

15. Ward, *Harlots of the Desert*, 33.

16. Ibid., 7, 60–61.

17. Coon, *Sacred Fictions*, 94.

18. Ibid., 72.

19. Coon, *Sacred Fictions*, 72; see also 27: "female *vitae* duplicate the double-edged biblical *topos* of impenitent women as sinful humanity and repentant women as harbinger of universal salvation." Sargent, "Penitent Prostitute," 32–35, details the connection between the "new Eve" and Mary.

20. Coon, *Sacred Fictions*, 72; Ward, *Harlots of the Desert*, 7–8, 34; see also Ward, vii: "the *Lives of the Harlots* are texts about repentance, the return of everyman to the lost Kingdom"; Harvey, "Women in Early Byzantine Hagiography," 46.

21. Ward, *Harlots of the Desert*, 33, 60–61; Anson, "Female Transvestite," 5; Patlagean, "L'histoire de la femme déguisée," 622–23.

22. The concept of the grotesque will be developed further below.

23. In VP 49–50 (Syriac), the motifs of surprise ("They gasped with astonishment in their hearts") and hiding/revealing are intensified.

24. For the motif of buried treasure, see VP prologue and 15, alluding to Matt. 10:26. See Anson, "Female Transvestite," 13–28, for an analysis of stories of transvestite saints discovered to be female after death. He argues that the shedding of the "transvestite masquerade" (14) and the revelation of female identity are standard features of such stories. A brief but typical version is also in Moschos, *Spiritual Meadow* 170, p. 139. Two monks report that, after praying on Mt. Sinai, they got lost and, seeing a cave and human footprints around it, they go to investigate: "We carefully searched the place and we found something rather like a manger with somebody lying in it. We came near to that servant of God and begged him to speak to us. When there was no answer, we touched him. The body was still warm, but his soul had gone to the Lord. Then we realized that he had departed this life as we entered the cave. So we took his body from where it lay and dug a grave for him there in the cave. One of us took off the pallium he was wearing and wrapped the elder's body in it; and we buried him in it. But we discovered that it

was a woman—and we glorified God. We performed the office over her and buried her."

25. Gallagher and Greenblatt, *Practicing New Historicism*, 15, 109.

26. Palladius, *Dialogue on the Life of St. John Chrysostom*, PG 47:56; trans. Castelli, " 'I Will Make Mary Male,' " 45.

27. Butler, *Antigone's Claim*, 22.

28. Harpham, *On the Grotesque*, 3.

29. Rousselle, *Porneia*, 24 and passim.

30. Basil of Ancyra, *De virginitate* 19.16–18; trans. Shaw, *Burden of the Flesh*, 236.

31. Shaw, *Burden of the Flesh*, 237.

32. Harvey, "Women in Byzantine Hagiography," 46; Cloke, *This Female Man of God*, 33: "Women were essentially sinful because essentially sexual."

33. Cloke, *This Female Man of God*, 33.

34. Judith Herrin, "In Search of Byzantine Women," in Cameron and Kuhrt, eds., *Images of Women in Antiquity*, 179; see also Cloke, *This Female Man of God*, 213, 220; Karras, "Holy Harlots," 31; Susan Ashbrook Harvey, "Women in Early Syrian Christianity," in Cameron and Kuhrt, eds., *Images of Women in Antiquity*, 297; Harvey, "Women in Early Byzantine Hagiography," 40; Patlagean, "L'histoire de la femme déguisée," 597, 605, 615; Clark, "Holy Women, Holy Words," 429.

35. Shaw, *Burden of the Flesh*, 247–48; Harvey, "Women in Early Byzantine Hagiography," 48.

36. Harpham, *On the Grotesque*, 15.

37. Ibid., 3. On the rhetorical use of clothing, see Coon, *Sacred Fictions*, 52–70.

38. For these phrases, see Harpham, *On the Grotesque*, 5.

39. Harvey notes, in "Mary the Egyptian," that "the giving of the garment is nothing more than an attempt by an embarrassed male to clothe (and therefore conceal/deny) Mary's sexuality."

40. Coon, *Sacred Fictions*, 84–85.

41. Ibid., 86.

42. The fact that Mary's hair is also described as short, "coming down only to the neck," may be related to cutting the hair as a sign of female ascetic practice. See Castelli, " 'I Will Make Mary Male,' " 44: "It is striking that in all of these narratives, the women who perform these outward gestures of stretching dominant cultural expectations related to gender are also embracing a form of piety (sexual renunciation and virginity) which resists dominant cultural expectations vis-à-vis social roles."

43. Karras, "Holy Harlots," 17–18; Ward, *Harlots of the Desert*, 10–25.

44. See Coon, *Sacred Fictions*, 93: "The most iconoclastic features of the *Life of Mary of Egypt* are her physical description, her independent conversion, and her symbolic self-baptism in the Jordan. . . . The wizened desert hermit is both the eschatological Messiah and Christ's bride; she is a vessel of sin and a vessel of redemption; she is the devil's votary and a virginal male's spiritual guide. The Egyptian begins her life as a whore and ends it as a desert hero. Few women's vitae demonstrate better the paradoxical nature of sacred gender."

45. On the "margin swapping places with the center" as characteristic of the gro-

tesque as a discourse of transition, see Harpham, *On the Grotesque*, 47. Harvey also comments, in "Mary the Egyptian," 1–2: "the figure of the solitary ascetic marginal woman also appeals as an exotic creature marginal, and therefore cause for revulsion and attraction, to our western urban communal existence. Hence, the tradition of Mary the Egyptian also exemplifies a motif common in early Christian ascetic accounts: the sexually-attractive wild woman who tempts the ascetic in the wilderness."

46. Harpham, *On the Grotesque*, 178.
47. Ibid., 13.
48. Coon, *Sacred Fictions*, 82.
49. See Basil of Ancyra, *De virginitate* 57–60, on the danger of eunuchs, and the discussion in Shaw, *Burden of the Flesh*, 236–37. For a contrary view, see Patlagean, "Histoire de la femme déguisée en moine," 606, on eunuchs transcending the distinction between the sexes; and Davis, "Crossed Texts, Crossed Sex," 21–24, on eunuchs, "the third sex," as liminal and so as ambiguous as transvestites were in terms of gender.
50. See Coon, *Sacred Fictions*, 28–29, 83; perhaps also the apostate harlot of Ezekiel, Isaiah, and Jeremiah (29).
51. Note Coon, ibid., 83, who reads this scene as a satirical recreation of Jesus' entry into Jerusalem.
52. Harpham, *On the Grotesque*, 9.
53. This phrase is from Braidotti, *Nomadic Subjects*, 198. On the relation between self-understanding, the body, and sexuality, see Miller, "Jerome's Centaur" and "Blazing Body"; Burrus, *Begotten, Not Made*; Brown, *Body and Society*, esp. 428–37.
54. Harpham, *On the Grotesque*, 43; see also 16: "the interval of the grotesque is the one in which, although we have recognized a number of different forms in the object, we have not yet developed a clear sense of the dominant principle that defines it and organizes its various elements."
55. For the definition of "prostitute" in this sense, see Flemming, *Quae Corpore Quaestum Facit*. Karras, "Holy Harlots," 8, 13, is the only author I have found who questions this sense of *meretrix* in the cases of Mary of Egypt and Pelagia.
56. See Ward, *Harlots of the Desert*, 76–101, on Maria, the niece of Abraham and Thaïs.
57. Flemming, *Quae Corpore Quaestum Facit*, 42, 47, 50.
58. Ibid., 50.
59. See Barnes, "Christians and the Theater"; Karras, "Holy Harlots," 13.
60. See Ford, "Bookshelf on Prostitution," 129. On the grotesque and the violation of categories, see Harpham, *On the Grotesque*, 27.
61. Like Thecla, Mary baptizes herself and conforms to the biblical model of the woman of faith who is superior to men. Pelagia's beauty is used symbolically (and literally) to shame male ecclesiastics, and she effects her own conversion by writing to the bishop Nonnos. For discussion, see Coon, *Sacred Fictions*, 87, 93, 81–83.
62. The following observation by Davis, "Crossed Texts, Crossed Sex," 31–32, although directed at the phenomenon of transvestite saints only, applies equally well to the two texts under consideration here: referring to "[t]he creative tension

in the transvestite saint legends between 'manly' piety and female sexual identity," Davis sees an "interplay of competing cultural discourses about gender-discourses that operate simultaneously, but function at cross purposes."

63. Karras, "Holy Prostitutes," 5.
64. See Harpham, *On the Grotesque*, 20.
65. Ibid., 18.
66. Ibid., 20–21.

✛ Macrina's Tattoo

VIRGINIA BURRUS

When the time came to cover the body with the robe, the injunction of the great lady made it necessary for me to perform this function. The woman who was present and sharing the great assignment with us said: "Do not pass over the greatest of the miracles of the saint." "What is that?" I asked. She laid bare a part [meros] of the breast [stēthos] and said: "Do you see this thin, almost imperceptible, scar [sēmeion] below the neck?" It was like a mark [stigma] made by a small needle. At the same time, she brought the lamp nearer to the place she was showing me. "What is miraculous about that," I said, "if the body has a small mark [sēmeion] on this part [meros]?" She said: "This is left on the body as a reminder of the great help of God."
—Gregory of Nyssa, *Vita Macrinae*[1]

I find myself frankly fascinated by that little part of Macrina's body—indeed, no more than a part of a part, "a part of the breast"—that is marked as if by a "small needle." The "thin, almost imperceptible sign" on her breast, "below the neck," modestly veiled by the woman herself during her life, is nakedly exposed to her brother after her death. The miracle that the brother, Gregory, is instructed to read in this revealed sign lies as much in the presence of the mark itself as in the divine healing that it commemorates: Macrina's body, we subsequently learn, was in fact untouched by the steel of either needle or knife. As Vetiana, the woman who attends her body, explains to Gregory, "At one time, there was a painful sore [pathos] on this part and there was the risk that if it was not cut out it would develop into an irremediable illness if it should spread to places near the heart." Despite her mother's anxious pleas, Macrina refused the physician's services, for she "considered worse than the disease laying bare anything of the body to another's eyes." In the event, she was healed by her own prayerful tears (from which she prepared a mud poultice) and also by her mother's chastened faith: when the mother, following her daughter's stern instructions, "put her hand inside her bosom [kolpos] to place the seal of the cross on the part," the sore simply disappeared. All that remained in its stead was the "little sign," as "a reminder of the divine consideration, a cause and reason for unceasing thanksgiving to God," Vetiana concludes (Vita Mac. 31).

As Georgia Frank notes, "By inserting a scar where the story requires none, Gregory can insert Macrina into a long tradition of the saintly wounded"—threading from Christ through the martyrs, who, according to Augustine, would retain the visible marks of their wounds for eternity (City of God 22.19).[2] More than that, Macrina's "scar," which recalls the celebrated scar (ouē) of Odysseus (Odyssey 19), provides a fixed point for Gregory's recognition of his sister's complex and fractured identity and thereby "becomes the site of a locational memory, a place from which to remember the departed Macrina."[3] At this point, however, a question arises: If Gregory punningly equates Odysseus's scarred "thigh" (mēros) with Macrina's marked "part" (meros), as Frank suggests, why does he describe Macrina's "part" not as scarred by a wound but rather as inscribed by a "sign" (sēmeion) or "mark" (stigma)? The insinuated distinction—which only becomes perceptible in the light of the Homeric allusions identified by Frank—seems to me as important as the implied slippage between "scar" and "sign"/"mark." Gregory might, after all, have simply called the mark a "scar," if such it was meant to be, thereby tightening the link not only with the scar of Odysseus but also with the wounds of Christ and the martyrs. Instead he writes, "[I]t was like a stigma made by a small needle." It was, in other words, like a tattoo—a tattoo admittedly inscribed miraculously, but nonetheless also manifested visibly on the fleshly body.[4] God has written on Macrina's body; he has marked her with a sign, a stigma. But what might this imply?

Christianity and the History of the Tattoo

The history of tattooing is by now not altogether uncharted territory. The ancient Greeks and Romans used tattooing to mark the bodies of criminals and slaves, that is, to inscribe the violence of punishment or possession.[5] Cultures (for example, the Thracian) in which tattooing was a positive marker of social status were known but dismissed as "barbaric"; thus, in both Greek and Roman discourse, the voluntary tattooing of "foreigners" constituted yet another form of effective social stigmatization.[6] The tattoo is, then, a sign of shame and subjugation, whereby the body is marked by another and also marked *as* "other." Yet here as elsewhere—most notably in the discourse of martyrdom and the figure of the crucified Christ—ancient Christians subverted symbols of domination and submission, activity and passivity, honor and shame, appropriating the identity of slave or criminal in such a way as to translate the humiliating mark of political subjugation into an inscription of divine election. Mark Gustafson argues for "a kind of paradigm shift" taking place in the Christian appropriation of stigmata, constituting "a deliberate undercutting and reversal of the punisher's intent, and of the ambivalent nature of a tattoo."[7] As self-proclaimed "slaves" or "witnesses" of Christ, Christians not only mimed the voluntary submission of God's very Son, but also actively owned the marks of their holy otherness: "Henceforth let no one give me trouble, for I carry the stigmata of Lord Jesus on my body," the apostle Paul proclaims proudly (Gal. 6:17).[8]

The point is not only that such rhetoric symbolically inverts relations of power, but also that the stigma itself becomes, scarlike, a dense site—a deep surface—of complex and layered meaning, fusing (without quite confusing) rebellion and surrender, nobility and degradation, flesh and spirit, worldly and holy power. When "*their* mark" is read as "*God's* mark," it may also be reclaimed as "*my* mark"—a self-willed inscription, even a defiant self-writing, that nonetheless necessarily retains an ambivalent connection to submission, transgression, and shame. "Thus, markings, even the most horrendous, may be reversed into something positive, and patterns of social dependence symbolized by such markings, including slavery, may be transformed to represent ultimate authority—not despite, but because of their negative associations," notes Susanna Elm.[9] As Jane Caplan hints, the recent "tattoo renaissance" in Europe and America is perhaps as much the heir of the ancient (and medieval) Christian subversion and complication "of the status of bodily marking in European culture" as it is the effect of the modern colonial encounters with "other" cultures (most momentously in the South Pacific) in which tattooing is honorable and decorative.[10]

Yet this brief account, if admittedly already complex, is still not quite complicated enough. First, we should be careful not to overstress the uniqueness of Christianity in its ancient context. Practices of religious tattooing that marked and thereby exalted the devotee as the (priestly) slave of a god were widespread and well known in Mediterranean antiquity, if also consistently reviled by the Greek and Roman elite.[11] Further, the quintessentially "Roman" figure of the gladiator stands as a potent reminder of the intense desire (as well as the deep revulsion) broadly inspired by the body inscribed with the signs of slavery and punishment. The well-attested lure of the ambivalent performance of nobility-within-shame, power-within-submission, marks the gladiator as the double of the Christian martyr and thereby invokes the widespread troubling of discourses of domination and desire in the period of the early Roman empire.[12] In other words, Christians were not the only ones (though they may have been among the most flamboyant) who found themselves painfully interpellated as the passive subjects of empire, as "suffering selves,"[13] and responded by "talking back" from a position of paradoxically defiant acquiescence, metamorphizing the stigma of powerlessness into a source of empowered resistance.

Moreover, even non-Christian texts that at first seem simply to reinforce the association of tattooing with the shame of slavery and criminality also betray surprising complexity and ambivalence. The fifth *Mime* of Herodas (second or third century B.C.E.), turning on both an offer and a threat of tattooing that never in fact takes place, is instructive in this respect.[14] Here the tattoo serves rhetorically to negotiate the conflictual orders of gender and class that comically inflect the erotic exchange between one Bitinna and her male slave and lover Gastron. Enraged by the discovery of Gastron's faithlessness in love, his mistress has him stripped and bound in preparation for a cruel whipping (10–25). In a seeming attempt both to shift the terms and to defer the performance of punishment, the slave volunteers to subject himself to tattooing if he is ever again found to be unfaithful (28). Bitinna accepts the terms but chooses her own timing, sending immediately for the tattooer "with his needles and ink" (65–66). She remarks that Gastron will "know [himself] when he has this inscription on his forehead" (77–79). Eventually, however, Bitinna relents, neither whipping nor stigmatizing the slave after all: perhaps she is mastered as much by her desire to submit to the slave as by her desire to dominate him.

The humor of the scene (together with its implicit political critique) is finally located *both* in the hyperbolic performances of slavish abjection (when Gaston virtually requests a tattoo) and punishing power (when Bitinna summons the tattooer in defiant excess of his request) *and* in the failure of these performances (for Gastron has managed to get off scot free, in the end). In the course of events, the tattoo, rendered hypothetical, also becomes a remarkably unstable figure of contested knowledge and power. The proposed stigma, according to Bitinna herself, represents Gastron's self-knowledge, an ironic reference to the philosophical imperative to "know thyself"; as C. P. Jones remarks, "Bitinna clearly intends that Gastron will have one or more words inscribed on his forehead so that all may know his crime."[15] But if his mistress is the one who will inscribe that "knowledge," will she be able to control the interpretation of the sign? Indeed, the initiative for the tattoo is Gastron's own, and the knowledge returns to him as well: he will "know himself," but what precisely will he have learned? In this tale of two tricksters, the tattoo, all the more because in the end merely rhetorical and thus visible only to the eyes of the imagination, is layered with multiple, conflicting meanings.[16]

Similar ambiguity regarding the signification of the tattoo is produced in Petronius's *Satyricon*, the comic Latin novel of the first century C.E. Again, the theme is love and faithlessness: eros is the stage for the negotiation of relations of power and the contestation of claims of identity. The scene takes shape as one Encolpius (the narrator) and his lover Giton find themselves unexpectedly thrown together on a ship with two former, and apparently now hostile, lovers. Together with their comrade Eumolpus, Encolpius and Giton begin to concoct humorously melodramatic plans for their escape from impending exposure and punishment. The scheme upon which they finally settle involves taking on the disguise of slaves by having their foreheads inscribed with the condemnation of the runaway: "the letters will serve at the same time to divert the suspicions of your pursuers, and to hide your faces with mock punishment," suggests the poet Eumolpus. The "mockery" is satisfyingly subtle: the two men are indeed "runaways" from the enslavement of prior loves, and their spurned lovers are cast as both their rightful masters and their (erotic) "pursuers." Thus, the poetic inscription mimics—both reveals and disguises—the truth. The double-talk is materialized as a pseudo-tattoo. When the true identities of Encolpius and Giton are exposed, one of their "pursuers" is still half-tricked: "Tryphaena burst into tears, thinking that real tattoos had been imprinted on our captive foreheads." The other knows better: "You stupid female! As if these were wounds prepared with iron so as to absorb letters. . . . As it is, they have played a stage-trick on us, and fooled us with mere shadow-writing" (*Satyricon* 103–6).

These instances of merely rhetorical or "shadow" tattoos, hinting at doubled and contested interpretations and conveyed by the ambiguously subversive discourse of comedy, brings us, indirectly, to a second complication in the history of Christian tattooing. In resurfacing the Christian revalorization of the stigma as an ambivalent (because multivalent) mark of honor, we should not forget that there is also another story to be told. The christianization of the Roman Empire gave rise to shifts in its legal code, restricting, if not altogether outlawing, practices of tattooing even in the case of condemned criminals, on grounds both specifically scriptural (cf. Lev. 19:28) and more broadly theological, framed as a prohibition of the marring of a face that reflects the image of God.[17] On the surface at least, imperial Christianity historically represses the tattoo: it causes it to disappear, in perhaps more than one way. This observation leads to a question: Was the subversive appropriation of the tattoo by Christians as a sign of divinely granted self-knowledge and power not always at base a metaphorical affair? Were Christian tattoos (like Gastron's) hypothetical and thus invisible (like Encolpius's and Giton's), mere "shadow-writing," rhetorical figures rather than material inscriptions, performative signs of the body's disappearance rather than of its enhanced visibility? And, if so, what difference might this make?

In fact, scattered amongst the great number of seemingly "metaphorical" tattoos (like the apostle Paul's) or the perhaps rarer cases in which "literal" tattoos received involuntarily were given a new, metaphorical interpretation,[18] we also find instances of apparently literal, voluntary tattooing by Christians, particularly in regions that retained more ancient traditions of religious tattooing.[19] My own primary interest here, however, is with Macrina's tattoo—not least because it so effectively cuts across the boundaries of the "metaphorical" and the "literal," the body-of-writing and the body-as-text. It also, it must be said, marks the body of a *woman*.

Writing Macrina

The virginal body, opening itself to the prick of a needle, is a good place to write. It is also a shockingly transgressive place to publish. Unlike the facial stigmata of slaves or criminals (not to mention runaway lovers), Macrina's tattoo, as we have seen, is inscribed on a private part of her body, a part that remained carefully—indeed, almost obsessively—hidden during her life. Its exposure shortly after her death coincides with the writing of her *vita*: indeed, the two exposures are virtually one. The two indelible inscriptions are likewise closely linked. The *Life of Macrina* is the first full-length biography of a woman to be penned by an ancient writer, and Gregory (her brother) is well aware of his audacity in making public what might be thought best kept private.[20] The transgression entailed in the writing of a female saint's life is only partly mitigated by the sibling intimacy of the author and his subject.[21] It must also be underwritten—pre-scribed—by a divine author/ity. Gregory makes it clear that God has already pricked Macrina; indeed, he has made her his bride. Stung by the needle, Macrina is also stung by her mortality: for it is death that delivers the promise of the godly writing, as she rushes to meet her holy groom. "Truly, her race was toward the Beloved and nothing of

her's is not really a tattoo like the others talked a/b

the pleasure of life diverted her attention" (*Vita Mac.* 22). Macrina's tattoo presupposes, overtakes, and exceeds the martyr's stigma: it has made itself altogether innocent of worldly lordship; untouched by the executioner's sword, it issues miraculously from a purely divine affair. If it is barely visible, it is not quite invisible: it can be seen by the light of a lamp. Hagiography itself, I am suggesting, emerges as a kind of tattooing, and the tattoo becomes visible as the writing of holiness. Neither, however, is merely a metaphor for the other, because neither is merely metaphorical. The fleshly tattoo and the literary vita each lay claim to an irreducible materiality that is also the trace of divinity—more than that, of divine *desire*—in a woman's body.

If God has written on Macrina's body, God has done so in response to her own passionate—even imperious—desire. Like Gastron, she has asked for it, in a vigil of prayer. Unlike (and also like) Bitinna, God masterfully delivers what she commands. (In this *divine comedy*, the violence of eros, taken to hyperbolic extremes, not only repeatedly reverses active and passive roles, but also continuously intensifies pleasure.) Though God is Macrina's spiritual scribe, it is her mother's touch that actually places the holy seal on her bodily "part," and it is her companion Vetiana's keen eyes that perceive the meaning of the text. Female agency multiplies and fractures at the site of Macrina's stigmatization.

positive?

Gregory now holds the pen, but the *Life* itself—he is well aware—is also *Macrina's self-inscription.* Macrina's *Life* is her own partly because it is she who teaches Gregory how to write—even as Vetiana will teach him how to read. Indeed, Macrina embodies writing itself, in the very text that gives her body. In the opening lines of the *Life's* prologue, Gregory confesses that his writing, initially presented as a letter, has "extended itself into a lengthy narrative discourse" (*eis suggraphikēn makrēgorian*) (*Vita Mac.* 1). His "choice of words here is both significant and peculiar," notes Derek Krueger. The adjectival "narrative" derives from a noun designating a "(written) prose composition" (*suggraphē*), a term that Gregory uses elsewhere to designate not only his own written text but also Macrina's embedded autobiographical narrative, told "as if in prose composition" (*Vita Mac.* 20). The word for "a long (oral) discourse" (*makrēgoria*) is rare and "is surely here intended as a pun on the name Macrina," suggests Krueger. "Thus, Gregory calls his composition a 'written Macrina-speech,' its own genre, a history masquerading as a letter, written words imagining oral words. . . . Just as Macrina's speech is like writing, Gregory's writing is like speech."[22] The prologue thereby writes Macrina as a figure of speech, a mark that cuts across the borders of orality and literary inscription, while at the same time transgressing literary genres. But there is

wants to give female agency

more: Macrina's speech, delivered on her deathbed, is not only like writing; it is also like liturgy. She offers her words of self-memorialization as an act of "thanksgiving" (Vita Mac. 20). By equating Macrina's liturgical speech with his own hagiographical composition, Gregory makes his sister's discourse the model for his own practice of holy inscription as the performance of commemorative gratitude, argues Krueger.[23] Hagiography itself is a eucharistic (rather than a funereal) rite, in which joy finally eclipses mourning, thereby freeing desire from the paralyzing pain of loss, as memory continually resurrects the presence of the saint.[24]

Writing, as a sacred rite of remembering, an act of grateful commemoration, thus takes place in the midst of grief and desire, in the interplay of pain and joy. Writing, like love (or perhaps, as love), both sunders and joins past and present, self and other, life and death, creature and creator. It does not merely designate but continuously creates Macrina's sanctity. A fixed mark, the text is nonetheless a place of eternal becoming, where the pen cuts sharply between a recollected past and an anticipated future. As philosopher Karmen MacKendrick puts it, "This mark that both says and makes who I am—this mark by which the I is written—is a mark made by a brief and partial absence of the very body that I am, that becomes me. For a moment—for a time that may range from minutes to months—there was an opening in the surface, in my corporeal self-containment. . . . I carry the marks of my own rupture." MacKendrick continues, "We are who we are by virtue of these places in us that have been not-us, those marks that remind us that we can be broken, and that the I who is healed is not who I was."[25] The "written Macrina-speech" of the Life is, then, like Macrina's tattoo, the reminder of her broken "I." Marking and memorializing a part of a part, while also marking and thereby commemorating the constitutively transformative rupture of the borders of her "self," the Life—the mark—fragments and fetishizes her flesh, rendering her finally both less and more than "a body." The integrity of the subject is effectively shattered, as we draw close with Gregory and Vetiana to gaze at a small patch of skin under the light of a lamp. Reflecting the light, the stigma isolates itself: it is more particular than even a "part"; it does not mark anything even as whole as a "breast." Yet at the same time, it is "her"; it is where we recognize and how we remember "her." "It is the site of a locational memory."[26] The stigma—the text—is Macrina's "I," marking her ongoing dis/continuity.

The tattoo not only repeats and further condenses and materializes the figure of the "written Macrina-speech," but it also mediates between two other powerful images of Macrina's body—the one appearing in Gregory's prior dream, the other in his subsequent waking vision. In the dream, as he writes it, "I seemed to be carrying the relics of martyrs in my hand and a light seemed to come from them, as happens when the sun is reflected on a bright mirror so that the eye is dazzled by the brilliance of the beam" (*Vita Mac.* 15). This dream of relics, occurring as Gregory approaches what is to be his last meeting with his sister, anticipates Macrina's "martyrial" death: having finally understood that his sister is dying, Gregory remarks, "The vision in my dream seemed to have been explained by what I had seen" (*Vita Mac.* 19). "Thus the dream not only predicted her death but also showed her translation to heavenly status in a transformed body, fragmentary though it was," notes Patricia Cox Miller.[27] Gregory's intuition is confirmed when his view of her corpse—its bridal adornment protectively shrouded in her mother's dark mantle—is consciously refracted through the dream image: "Even in the dark, the body glowed, the divine power adding such grace to her body that, as in the vision of my dream, rays seemed to be shining forth from her loveliness" (*Vita Mac.* 32). Prior to viewing her well-dressed corpse, however, Gregory has already seen her naked tattoo. The dream thus not only explicitly anticipates the memorable luminosity of Macrina's publicly displayed corpse but also implicitly anticipates its "preview" in her memorializing fragmentation, glimpsed privately in the gleaming reflectivity of the modest little mark, exposed by both Vetiana's lamp and her interpretive words— words that in turn reveal the secret of a mother's transformative touch. Macrina is the mirror of God's brilliance. As such, she "is" her body; but "body" is no longer a reflection of wholeness, as the dream of relics, further interpreted by the sign of the tattoo, has taught. Gregory's view of his sister is partial, fragmentary, and indirect (mediated by the touch and eyes of women); it also thereby becomes a true witness. The tattoo, itself a relic of godly writing, fixes the gaze on the fragment that is not a part of a whole and is also not whole unto itself: for it exists in and as its marking, in and as its transgressed and transgressive edges, in and as divine stigma.

In the theology of incarnation conveyed by this vita, flesh is not transformed into spirit, it is not even redeemed by (or simply "married to") spirit. As Miller remarks, "Despite all of his metaphors of light, Gregory seems reluctant to let Macrina's body disappear in a blaze of glory. . . . The body is still there as a sign."[28] ("Tattooing represents the effort to mark the body at the very moment it is disappearing," notes Mark Taylor).[29] Flesh is itself the mirroring of spirit, the stigmatization of the spirit. By the same logic, spirit itself is the reflection, the mark (the sign), of the flesh. God writes (on) Macrina, and Macrina submits. (But Macrina also wills the mark, and God—

through the mediation of her mother—submits to her desire, according to Vetiana's commemorative recitation.) Macrina "becomes" in and as the divine writing itself, in and as the minute particularity of the transforming stigma. Infinite fragmentation is also infinite connectivity, a sublimely erotic communion (a *eucharist*) of creator and cosmos.

The *Life of Macrina* and the History of Women

What might it mean, in and for the history of women, to suggest that the tattoo is *Macrina's* tattoo, that the *Life* is her own? (Does Gregory in fact inscribe the *history of a woman*, or is his "sister" no more than the constructed virginal matrix of his own masculine self-conception?)[30] For scholars working "after the linguistic turn," argues Elizabeth Clark, the *Life of Macrina* cannot be approached simply as a passive repository yielding evidence of a woman's experience (still less of a generic "women's experience"). Bringing the challenge of poststructuralist critiques of "foundationalism" to bear on the history of ancient Christian women, Clark concludes that the day is gone when feminist historians could appeal confidently to "women's experience" or the "female body"—even "strategically"—in order to secure the object of study for "women's history." Rather, "historians must start with the processes of signification that stand prior to 'meaning' and 'significance,'" asking "how female subjectivity is produced, how agency is possible," she asserts. Furthermore, such processes must be located in the context of social interactions and power relations; even the historian working exclusively with literary sources must search for the "social logic" of a text.[31]

When Clark turns to apply these principles to the reading of the lives of female ascetics, her emphasis shifts, however, from the linguistic constructedness and complexity of all subjectivities to the androcentric bias of the surviving sources, reflective of the male-dominated society in which these texts were enmeshed. She stresses the impossibility of recovering "the voices of 'real' women in early Christian texts," even in sources as alluring as Gregory's *Life of Macrina*. Nonetheless, she affirms that the "woman" of Christian antiquity does enjoy a kind of "afterlife" in history, concluding: "she leaves her traces, through whose exploration, as they are embedded in a larger social-linguistic framework, she lives on."[32]

Macrina's tattoo is among those "traces." Following in the footprints—retracing the steps—of Clark's suggestive text, we may yet press the linguistic turn around another bend: might it be possible, *for one who so desires*, to read the tattoo—to read the vita—as a relic, a ritualized memory, of "how female subjectivity is produced, how agency is possible"? That Macrina's vita can be viewed as a positive resource for a postpositivist "women's history" is indeed the claim of this essay. Pursuing traces of difference produced within the ancient hagiographical text, we may discover an "other, woman" in the practices of history writing itself—Gregory's, and also our own. Earlier feminist historians (including Clark herself) have viewed woman's entry into the biographical genre as marking her attainment of a transcendental subjectivity—achievement of a virtual "maleness"—while also pointing out the lingering traces of her objectification, not least in her casting as a romantic heroine.[33] What I am suggesting here is something a bit different—namely, that the *Life of Macrina* inscribes feminine subjectivity as a stigma (marks the subject with and as difference) and, further, that "women's history" may be understood as a practice of reading and writing that continuously marks (and therein makes) a difference. In the process, it is not only the subject of history ("I, Macrina") but also the scholarly subject ("I, the historian") who is subtly transformed—stigmatized, even.

My Tattoo

My own tattoo is the work of Joshua Lord—for that, however unlikely, was the artist's name. (*I carry the marks of Lord Jesus on my body.*) I asked for it; I even paid for it; yet perhaps I got still more than I bargained for. The sign, a darkly radiant reflection (a doubly reflected moon, in fact), is inscribed on a part, a part of my chest (my breast), initiating change in the cut from the self I was to the self I am (ever) becoming. Indeed, it is an indelible mark of change that betrays the shifting tides of desire secreted in a female body, surfaced by an artist's needle. The stigma is received in suffering, recalling the intricate, intimate violence of all transition, of every transformation, alerting me to pain's exquisite variety (reverberating differently through muscle, bone, softer tissue). Needle's sting writes the mortality, the malleability, of flesh. It writes its improbable endurance as well. The delicate searing of steel on skin melds with the sustaining rhythms of breath and heartbeat, and the soul sings silently with the scarred joy of life (of a Life). Pain eventually withdraws, but not without leaving its trace: the mark of a Lord. I peer into the mirror's reflection, see reflection of bottomless reflection. *Jesus! It's beautiful, thank you,* I mumble inarticulately. Suddenly, I remember the Lord's words to the woman (whose name, Mary, I also bear, as it happens): *Don't touch me!* But I don't have to, I think, dazedly: for he has already touched me—breaking the surface, pricking open the borders, letting my blood run with his ink. He

why is this? here

touches me now: radiant, reflective smile, swift hug, light kiss of blessing. I am touched. I am marked by the divine grace of touch: my tattoo. Taken, given; offered, received: my tattoo, my body, my desire. And now, my memory. Mine: because the gift of another.[34] Mine: because read by you.

Notes

This essay is dedicated with admiration, gratitude, and love to Elizabeth Clark, whose scholarship has informed my own at every step along the way, and who has for nearly twenty years been a generous and inspiring model, mentor, and friend. I am also grateful to those who have read and commented critically on this text—David Brakke (who admonished me not to forget Vetiana), Karmen Mac-Kendrick (who helped me think better), and Stephen Moore (who helped me write better). As will become evident, I could not have conceived the essay without the insights gleaned from the published work of other friends in the field—most especially, Susanna Elm, Georgia Frank, Derek Krueger, and Patricia Cox Miller.

1. English translations of the *Vita Macrinae* generally follow Gregory of Nyssa, *Ascetical Works*, 163–91, hereafter cited in the text as *Vita Mac.* The Greek edition consulted is Maraval, *Grégoire de Nysse.*
2. Frank, "Macrina's Scar," 514.
3. Ibid., 528.
4. That the Greek term *stigma* typically refers in antiquity to a tattoo inscribed with needle and ink (and not, e.g., to a brand) is argued by C. P. Jones, "Stigma and Tattoo," in Caplan, ed., *Written on the Body*, 2–5. In the context of this common usage, "a stigma made by a small needle" can scarcely *not* refer to a tattoo.
5. See, e.g., the recent studies of Jones, "Stigma and Tattoo," and Gustafson, "Tattoo in the Later Roman Empire," both in Caplan, ed., *Written on the Body*, 17–31.
6. Jones, "Stigma and Tattoo," 2–4.
7. Gustafson, "Tattoo in the Later Roman Empire," 29–31. See also Gustafson, "*Inscripta in Fronte*," 98–101.
8. See Martin, *Slavery as Salvation*, 59–60.
9. Elm, " 'Pierced by Bronze Needles,' " 414.
10. Caplan, introduction to *Written on the Body*, xvi; see also Gustafson, "Tattoo in the Later Roman Empire," 31.
11. Elm, " 'Pierced by Bronze Needles,' " 417–22; Elm, " 'sklave Gottes,' " 354–55; Jones, "Stigma and Tattoo," 6.
12. See Barton, "Savage Miracles," as well as her *Sorrows of the Ancient Romans.*
13. See Perkins, *Suffering Self.*
14. The English translation and Greek text of Herodas's fifth *Mime* may be found in Cunningham, Knox, and Rusten, eds. and trans., *Theophrastus, Herodas, Cercidas.* Subsequent references are given in the text by line numbers.
15. Jones, "Stigma and Tattoo," 8; see also Gustafson, "Tattoo in the Later Roman

Empire and Beyond," 24. Note that my reading of the text's (and thus the tattoo's) ambivalence and instability is somewhat different from that of Jones and Gustafson.

16. Compare Gustafson, "Tattoo in the Later Roman Empire and Beyond," 29–31, on contested meanings in the case of Christian tattoos; he points out the analogy with the shifting interpretations of the "A" ("adultery"? "angel"? "able"?) with which Hester is stigmatized in Nathaniel Hawthorne's *The Scarlet Letter.*

17. Jones, "Stigma and Tattoo," 12–13; cf. Gustafson, "Tattoo in the Later Roman Empire and Beyond," 21–32, who emphasizes the continuousness of practices of penal tattooing in the late Roman empire and beyond, despite such "Christian" legislation.

18. Gustafson, "Tattoo in the Later Roman Empire and Beyond," 19–20.

19. Jones, "Stigma and Tattoo," 6; Gustafson, "Tattoo in the Later Roman Empire and Beyond," 29; Gustafson, "Inscripta in Fronte," 98–99. Elm, " 'Pierced by Bronze Needles,' " discusses the probability that Montanist Christians practiced tattooing, inspired by the prophetic traditions of the biblical book of Revelation (where references to bodily inscriptions are too numerous to list here). See also the intriguing exploration of the Christianization of insular Celtic traditions of tattooing by Charles W. MacQuarrie, "Insular Celtic Tattooing: History, Myth, and Metaphor," in Caplan, *Written on the Body,* 39–45.

20. Gregory's awareness of the novelty of a female biography—a transgression of both gender and genre—is thematized in his prologue. "We spoke of a woman, if indeed she was a woman; for I do not know if it is proper to name by her nature one who went beyond nature," he muses (*Vita Mac.* 1), recalling the initial conversation which has given rise to a work, the literary format of which cannot, seemingly, be clearly identified either by Gregory himself or by subsequent literary historians.

21. The authors of earliest vitae of women inevitably represent themselves as standing in a privileged relationship to their biographical subjects; the same is not the case for the writers of male saints' lives. See Giannarelli, "La biografia femminile," 231–35; and Giannarelli, "Women and Miracles in Christian Biography," 377. Momigliano's "The Life of St. Macrina by Gregory of Nyssa," 339, highlights the contrast. Gregory, even when composing a funeral oration on his brother Basil, elides rather than emphasizes his close relationship to his male subject: "While Macrina is brought near by a biography, Basil is made distant by a panegyric."

22. Krueger, "Writing and the Liturgy of Memory," 493–94.

23. Ibid., 497–510.

24. The contestation between thanksgiving and mourning is not, however, fully resolved. On the funereal context of Macrina's Life, see my *Begotten, not Made,* 120–22; and *Sex Lives of Saints,* 69–76.

25. MacKendrick, *Word Made Skin.*

26. Frank, "Macrina's Scar," 528.

27. Miller, *Dreams in Late Antiquity,* 237.

28. Ibid.

29. Taylor, Hiding, 129.

30. The latter possibility is explored in my Begotten, Not Made, 112–22. But see also my own counterreading, "Is Macrina a Woman?" 249–64.

31. Clark, "Lady Vanishes," 5–14.

32. Ibid., 31.

33. In an early work, The Life of Melania the Younger, 155, Clark critically interrogates the influence of the romance on female hagiography, in the face of the overwhelming maleness of the biographical genre: "Although the Vitae of early Christian women stress their overcoming of femaleness and subsequent incorporation into a world of "maleness," it is still dubious whether the classical bioi furnished any fitting models for these Lives. And if they did not, did any other form of ancient litera-ture, more focused on women, suggest itself as a more suitable model? Might not the Hellenistic romance, with its concentration on lively heroines, provide a better paradigm for a Vita like Melania's?" In the more recent essay discussed above, she returns to the question, reaffirming that "the Vitae of early Christian women saints share many features with the relatively new genre of novels or romances popular in this period rather than with classical biography that focused on the public activity of statesmen and generals: women did not operate in a public, political sphere." She also notes, however, the influence of the philosoph-ical biography, as measured by the fact that all ancient female hagiographical subjects are represented as teachers and purveyors of wisdom ("Lady Vanishes," 16, 22).

34. The gift of a "Lord" but also the gift of a woman: thanks for permission to relate this closing "autobiographical" narrative are owed not only to Josh but also to Karmen, who offered both friendly support and photographic commemoration of the event.

✣ GENDER

✣ **ASCETICISM**

✣ HISTORIOGRAPHY

✛ Rereading the Jovinianist Controversy:

Asceticism and Clerical Authority

in Late Ancient Christianity

DAVID G. HUNTER

Sometime early in the 390s Siricius, bishop of Rome, penned an anxious letter to his fellow Italian bishops. Reporting the results of a synod recently held at Rome, Siricius alerted his episcopal confreres that Jovinian and eight followers had been condemned as "the authors of a new heresy and blasphemy."[1] Siricius did not describe any of Jovinian's teachings in detail, although he noted Jovinian's view that married Christian women and consecrated virgins were equally deserving of honor (Ep. 7.5). Perhaps the most troubling feature of Jovinian's activity, from Siricius's point of view, was its impact on other Christians. Although the malice of heretics had afflicted the church ever since the time of the apostles, Siricius claimed, never before had they been so successful at undermining the church from within: "Wounding Catholics, perverting the continence of the Old and New Testaments, interpreting it in a diabolical sense, by their seductive and deceitful speech they have begun to destroy no small number of Christians and to make them allies of their own insanity" (Ep. 7.4).

Several features of this letter are noteworthy. Siricius's letter marked the first time in the history of Christianity that the superiority of celibacy over marriage was officially defined as doctrine, and, conversely, that its denial was labeled as "heresy." Certainly, many Christians, both in and out of the mainstream of the tradition, had long believed that celibacy was a higher or better way of life. Such a view seemed to many to be a reasonable interpretation of the apostle Paul's opinion that "he who marries his virgin does well, and he who refrains from marriage does better."[2] But despite this deeply rooted preference for celibacy in some quarters, such a view had never been regarded as the only Christian one.[3] Siricius's letter, therefore, marked a distinctive hardening of boundaries in the later fourth century, the moment at which a previously implicit Christian consensus about marriage and celibacy reached a consequential degree of explicitness.

And yet, it also is clear from Siricius's letter that Jovinian's teaching was regarded as dangerous precisely because so many Christians found it persuasive. In other words, Jovinian's success was a sign of the very fragility of the consensus that Siricius wished to define. Several other sources confirm this. Jerome, for example, expressed dismay that "clerics, monks, and others who lead celibate lives" had accepted Jovinian's view that marriage and celibacy were equally meritorious. "They cut themselves off from their wives in order to imitate the chastity of virgins," Jerome complained, "and yet they wish married people [to be considered] the same as virgins."[4] Augustine, likewise, observed that Jovinian's preaching had had the effect of leading many consecrated men and women at Rome to abandon the celibate life and to marry.[5] Jovinian's very popularity indicates that the consensus articulated by Siricius was not a consensus of the whole church.

This contrast between Siricius's effort to define Jovinian's views as a "new heresy" and Jovinian's evident success among Christians at Rome suggests the central theme of this essay. Since the late nineteenth century, only two major studies of the Jovinianist controversy have appeared, and both of these have been devoted to a consideration of Jovinian's theology.[6] Little attention has been paid to the responses of Jovinian's opponents and to their role in defining Jovinian as "heretic." Three Western churchmen—Siricius, Ambrose, and Jerome—engaged directly with Jovinian's views, but each one approached him from a different perspective. Each had different reasons for opposing Jovinian's teaching, and, to some extent, they seem to have been as hostile to each other as they were to Jovinian.

My aim here is to "reread" the controversy surrounding Jovinian by paying special attention to the tensions and differences among his three major opponents. In the later years of the fourth century, the status of ascetic behavior—celibacy, in particular—was still very much under negotiation in the Western church. Even those who were generally "pro-ascetic" could have rather different ways of conceiving the role of asceticism in defining ecclesiastical authority. Attention to the nontheological factors involved in the condemnation of Jovinian will enable us to view the Jovinianist controversy as a complex web of personal rivalries, clerical ambitions, and conflicting notions of asceticism and ecclesiastical authority in Western Christianity.[7]

Siricius

Let us begin with Pope Siricius. At first sight, Siricius was not the most likely candidate to lead the charge against the "heresy" of Jovinian. After succeeding Damasus in the papal office in December of 384, Siricius had responded in a decidedly lukewarm manner to the wave of ascetic enthusiasm sweeping through the Western church. For example, one of his first acts in office was to preside over the trial and expulsion of Jerome from the city of Rome in the spring of 385. In his Letter 45, composed shortly before he set sail from the port of Ostia, Jerome indicated that he had been the object of accusations of disreputable conduct, stemming from his relationship with the widow Paula.[8] A formal charge had been made, Jerome said, and the assembled clergy (whom Jerome contemptuously dismissed as a "senate of Pharisees") had unanimously passed judgment.[9]

Although it seems that the charge of immorality was not substantiated, Jerome apparently was compelled to sign a document agreeing to leave Rome immediately.[10] I will return below to the question of Siricius's relations with Jerome and Jerome's abiding grievances against him. For now it is sufficient to note that the official measures taken against Jerome by the Roman clergy, as J. N. D. Kelly has observed, "can scarcely have been taken without [Siricius's] cognizance and consent."[11]

A further example of Siricius's ambivalent attitude toward Western asceticism was his reluctance to admit monks into the ranks of the higher clergy. In the earliest document of his episcopate, a letter written in 385 to Himerius, bishop of Tarragona in Spain, Siricius had issued a series of canons pertaining to the ordination of monks. He noted that such ordinations were permissible, as long as the monastic candidates were "recommended by their sober bearing and the saintly character of their habits and beliefs."[12] Siricius insisted, however, that monks must follow the same course of preparation as other candidates: those under the age of thirty could be admitted only to the lower ranks of lector, acolyte, and subdeacon. After the age of thirty, one could become a deacon; after five years of acceptable service as deacon, one could advance to the presbyterate. Only after ten years as presbyter, Siricius declared, could a man advance to the "episcopal chair," as long as the integrity of his life and faith had been sufficiently demonstrated (Ep. 1.9.13).

The primary point of Siricius's legislation was to maintain that the normal sequence of clerical promotion should be respected. In other words, monastic profession was deemed essentially irrelevant to clerical office. As Siricius wrote in his letter to Himerius, monks "should not ascend to the lofty dignity of the episcopacy at a single leap."[13] It is important to view Siricius's legislation within its late fourth-century context. If his strictures on the recruitment of clerics had been carefully enforced, two of the most prominent ascetic bishops of his day—Ambrose of Milan and Martin of Tours—would have been ineligible for the episcopate![14] Clearly, Siricius was no friend of the newly emerging model of the monk-bishop. In his view, the practice of celibacy or other forms of ascetic renunciation was no substitute for working one's way through the ranks of the clerical hierarchy.[15]

If Siricius was decidedly unimpressed with monks as candidates for the clergy, he did view one form of ascetic behavior as essential to the clerical office, at least to the higher ranks of deacon, presbyter, and bishop. I refer to the requirement of clerical celibacy, of which Siricius was a prominent early proponent. Three encyclical letters of Siricius contain the earliest evidence of the Roman church's effort to extend the custom of clerical celibacy to other Western churches. Furthermore, these letters attest that Siricius encountered significant resistance to his initiative from the bishops of Spain, Gaul, and North Africa to whom he addressed his appeals. Siricius's commitment to the discipline of clerical celibacy, as well as his difficulty with its enforcement, does much to explain his role in the Jovinianist controversy.

A common theme is present in all of Siricius's letters. Siricius strongly emphasized the connection between the ritual or liturgical functions of clergy and the requirement of celibacy. In his letter to Himerius he asserted that Old Testament priests had to spend the entire year of their service in the Temple away from their wives "so they could offer an acceptable sacrifice to God." So, too, Siricius argued, Christian priests and levites (that is, bishops, presbyters, and deacons) were bound by an indissoluble law of celibacy: "From the day of our ordination we must surrender our hearts and bodies to sobriety and chastity, so that in every way we may be pleasing to God in those sacrifices which we offer each day" (Ep. 1.7.10). Similarly, in his letter to bishops in Africa, Siricius stated, "priests and levites must not have intercourse with their wives because they are concerned with the daily duties of ministry." If lay people are asked to be continent so that their prayers may be granted (cf. 1 Cor. 7:5), Siricius argued, so much more should a priest always be in a state of immaculate purity, ready to offer Eucharist or baptism (Ep. 5.3).[16]

Siricius's emphasis on the ritual purpose of clerical celibacy coheres well with his insistence that the order of clerical promotion be respected and that monks not be given preferred entry into the clergy. In both instances, Siricius's primary concern was to enhance the stature of the clerical office, especially in relation to the new monastic asceticism. As Peter Brown has observed, Siricius's effort to impose the discipline of "post-marital celibacy" on the higher clergy was an attempt to create a "middle party" in the Western church, somewhere "between the shrill ascetics and the new men of power, grossly stained by the world."[17] While clerical celibacy helped to elevate the clergy above the married laity, it also served to distinguish clerical asceticism from the less institutionalized asceticism of the monks.

Siricius's intense concern for the prerogatives of the clergy and his interest in celibacy as a means of enhancing clerical authority must have strongly influenced his zealous rejection of Jovinian. Siricius's letters indicate that his rules on clerical celibacy were being widely violated both in Gaul and North Africa. He even stated that his opponents offered arguments against the celibacy requirement that were grounded in the Scriptures. In several cases the texts cited against clerical celibacy were the same ones invoked by Jovinian in his arguments for the equality of marriage and celibacy.[18] Although we have no evidence that Jovinian attacked the practice of clerical celibacy in itself, his arguments for equating the merits of married and celibate Christians certainly would have undermined the papal arguments on behalf of clerical celibacy. Given the opposition that Siricius had already encountered in his efforts to enforce clerical celibacy, he probably would have seen in Jovinian's views a source of further damage to the dignity of the clergy.

Ambrose

This brings me to the second Western churchman involved in the Jovinianist controversy, Ambrose of Milan. Ambrose was alerted early on to the danger of Jovinian's views; he was one of several Italian bishops to receive a copy of Siricius's letter reporting the condemnation of Jovinian by the Roman synod. Ambrose responded by calling his own synod and by issuing his own condemnation of Jovinian, which he sent to Siricius. Ambrose's letter to Siricius is of great interest because it presented a position of Jovinian's that was mentioned by neither Siricius nor Jerome.[19] In his letter Ambrose spoke at length about Jovinian's view that Jesus could not have been born of a virgin, that is, his denial of Mary's *virginitas in partu*. Roughly half of Ambrose's letter was devoted to his defense of this doctrine and to a rebuttal of Jovinian's view of Mary. Clearly, the doctrine of Mary's *virginitas in partu* had a significance for Ambrose that was not shared by either Siricius or Jerome.

Another unique feature of Ambrose's letter was its accusation that Jovinian and his followers were "Manichaeans." This charge, which contradicts everything we know about Jovinian, was directly linked to Jovinian's denial of Mary's virginity. As Ambrose put it: "And they proved that they were Manichaeans in truth by not believing that [Christ] came forth from a virgin. . . .

If they do not believe that he came, neither do they believe that he took flesh. Thus, he was seen only as an illusion, and he was crucified as an illusion."[20] Ambrose even concluded his letter with an ominous reference to an imperial edict against the Manichees, implying that his action against Jovinian and his followers had been taken with the emperor's approval and that Jovinian had been condemned as a Manichee.[21]

The manner in which Ambrose focused on Jovinian's teaching about the virginity of Mary and his accusation of "Manichaeism" provide a key to understanding his role in the Jovinianist controversy. Ambrose's claim that Jovinian was a "Manichaean" was a rather obvious and deliberate distortion of Jovinian's teaching. The real Manichaean view, of course, was precisely the opposite. Manichees held a Docetic Christology; that is, they did not believe that Jesus could have taken on flesh at all.[22] Jovinian's point in questioning Mary's *virginitas in partu* had been a decidedly anti-Manichaean and anti-Docetic one. Jovinian had argued that the genuinely physical character of Jesus's birth meant that the Virgin Mary must have lost her physical integrity in the process of giving birth. As Ambrose himself noted earlier in the letter, Jovinian believed that Mary had conceived as a virgin, but that she had not given birth as a virgin: "Virgo concepit, sed non virgo generavit."[23]

Ambrose's attempt to tar Jovinian with the brush of Manichaeism was an extraordinarily clumsy maneuver, and it would be difficult to explain were it not for two salient facts. First, Ambrose himself was the one who had pioneered in the West the notion of Mary's *virginitas in partu*; second, Jovinian was the one who had first accused Ambrose of being a Manichee for holding the doctrine. Augustine affirmed both points many years later during the Pelagian controversy, when he was accused of Manichaeism by Julian of Eclanum. In De nuptiis et concupiscentia, Augustine noted that similar accusations against Ambrose had been made long ago by Jovinian: "Will you dare, O Pelagians and Caelestians, to call even this man [i.e., Ambrose] a Manichee? The heretic Jovinian called him that, when that holy man defended the perpetual virginity of holy Mary against Jovinian's impiety."[24]

If Augustine is correct—and I know of no reason to doubt his accuracy on the matter—Ambrose's condemnation of Jovinian as a heretic (and his odd distortion of Jovinian's views) would have been motivated, at least partially, by his desire to defend his own orthodoxy. The doctrine of the *virginitas in partu* was still something of a novelty in Western Christian theology at the end of the fourth century. It was certainly possible (perhaps even logical) to understand the idea as a Docetic denial of the reality of Jesus's body, and this was the basis of Jovinian's charge against Ambrose. The accusation of "Manichaean" directed against advocates of asceticism, of course, had become something of a commonplace by the late fourth century, and yet the charge could still have serious consequences.[25] One only has to recall the fate of Priscillian of Avila less than a decade earlier to realize that even bishops (especially ascetically minded ones) could be vulnerable to suspicion and imperial action on the grounds of such accusations. Ambrose's attack on Jovinian and his distorted portrait of his teaching surely must have been fueled by a concern to defend himself against the accusation of heresy.

But there was more to Ambrose's opposition than simply a defense of his personal orthodoxy. Ambrose's commitment to the ideal of virginity—and especially his defense of Mary's perpetual virginity—had deep roots in the very structure of his theology of Christ, salvation, and the church. In one of the more remarkable chapters of his magisterial volume *The Body and Society*, Peter Brown has argued that the notion of Mary's virginal integrity—before, during, and after the birth of Jesus—expressed Ambrose's abiding concern to maintain sharp boundaries between the church and the world. Ambrose's defense of the perpetual virginity of Mary, as Brown has put it, condensed "years of tense concern for boundaries, for the dangers of admixture, and for the absolute and perpetual nature of the antithesis between the Catholic Church and the formless, disruptive confusion of the *saeculum*."[26] If Brown is correct, then the ultimate source of Ambrose's conflict with Jovinian lay much deeper than personal rivalry. At root in their struggle were conflicting models of the church itself.

The ecclesial dimension of the Jovinianist controversy can be demonstrated on the basis of the alternative interpretations developed by Jovinian and Ambrose of that key biblical trope, the church as the Bride of Christ. For example, Jerome reported that one of the many biblical texts invoked by Jovinian was 2 Corinthians 11:2 ("I espoused you to one husband, that I might present you as a chaste virgin to Christ"). According to Jerome, Jovinian took the text to refer to "the whole church of believers" and claimed that this betrothal to Christ included all baptized Christians, all of whom share in the chastity of the church.[27] For Jovinian the image of the church as the Virgin Bride of Christ crystallized his view that all baptized Christians constituted one community of the redeemed, in which "God dwells in all alike" and where considerations of ascetic merit have become irrelevant.[28]

For Ambrose, by contrast, the image of the church as Virgin Bride had always been nearly indistinguishable from the idea of the consecrated virgin as bride, and both had been closely linked to the notion of Mary's perpetual virginity. In fact, the first time the idea of *virginitas in partu* is found in his writings—in his earliest work, the *De virginibus* of 377—it appears not in reference to Mary herself, but in reference to the church: "The church is unstained by sexual intercourse [*immaculata coitu*], and yet fruitful in child-birth. She is virgin because of her chastity and a mother because of her off-spring. She brought us into life, conceived not of man but of the Holy Spirit, in a birth free of bodily pain and full of the joy of angels."[29] Here, in Ambrose's earliest extant writing, the images of virginal conception and virginal birth were mobilized to portray the transcendent character of the church itself in its dual (and paradoxical) roles as Bride of Christ and Mother of Christians.

This tendency to identify the Virgin Mary as a "type" or model of the church became even more pronounced in Ambrose's later works. In his homilies on Luke from the mid-380s, Ambrose observed that it was fitting that Mary was both betrothed and virginal at the conception of Jesus: "For she is a type of the church, who is immaculate but married. A virgin has conceived us by the Spirit, a virgin has given birth to us without groaning."[30] The eccle-sial significance of Mary's *virginitas in partu* remained a theme dear to Am-brose. As late as his letter to the church at Vercelli, composed in 396 (shortly before his death) to counter the influence of Jovinian's followers, Ambrose described the church as Virgin in language drawn from the Song of Songs:

> We ought to recognize how much praise [of virginity] the prophet, or rather Christ in the prophet, has expressed in the brief verse, *A garden enclosed is my sister, my bride; a garden enclosed, a fountain sealed up* (Song 4:12). Christ says this to the Church, which he wishes to be a virgin, without stain, without wrinkle. Virginity is a good garden, which brings forth many fruits of good fragrance; virginity is a "garden en-closed" because on all sides it is fortified by the wall of chastity; vir-ginity is a "fountain sealed up" because it is the fountain and source of purity, which keeps the seals of integrity from being violated.[31]

By the time Ambrose composed his letter regarding Jovinian in 393, the doctrine of Mary's *virginitas in partu* had come to express much more than simply a conviction about Mary, the mother of Jesus. For Ambrose, Mary's perpetual virginity expressed the miraculous and admittedly supernatural character of the church itself.

While Ambrose's intense interest in female virginity may have been driven largely by theological concerns, it is likely that political interests were not wholly absent. By the later years of the fourth century, the notion that the consecrated Christian virgin was in some unique way married to Christ had already passed "from literary metaphor to liturgical reality."[32] The ritual of the *velatio*, the veiling of virgins, was a distinctively Western Christian development, and Ambrose himself seems to have been a prime mover behind the practice. The taking of the veil in a ceremony modeled after a Roman wedding established a new formal relationship between the consecrated virgin and Christ, one that was analogous in canon law to a regular human marriage.[33] What is significant for our purposes is the role of the bishop in the consecration and veiling of virgins, for the writings of Ambrose make it abundantly clear that the *velatio* was a decidedly *episcopal* event.

According to Ambrose it was the bishop's duty to decide at what age a girl should take the veil and whether or not she had the requisite virtues. The bishop customarily presided at the ceremony, bestowed the veil, pronounced the liturgical benediction, and delivered a sermon of exhortation. The bishop also continued to supervise the consecrated virgin after her veiling and sometimes took responsibility for her welfare after the death of her parents.[34] In essence, through the ritual of virginal consecration the bishop had assumed the traditional role of the *pater familias* by offering the virgin as his "daughter" to Christ as her "bridegroom." The analogy was not lost on Ambrose. In *De institutione virginis*, his sermon delivered at the veiling of the virgin Ambrosia, Ambrose referred to his namesake as "she, whom I present in my office as bishop [*sacerdotali munere*], whom I present with fatherly affection [*affectu patrio*]."[35]

It is clear that Jovinian's argument on behalf of the essential equality of all baptized Christians would have seriously undermined Ambrose's notion of the consecrated virgin as the bride of Christ. As we saw above, Jovinian applied the image of the virgin bride to "the whole church of believers" and included married persons as well as widows and celibates within the one Virgin Church. If indeed the ritual of virginal consecration did serve to enhance the authority of the bishop, as well as the stature of the consecrated virgin, then Ambrose had further reason to oppose the arguments of Jovinian. By challenging the status of consecrated virgins, Jovinian would have seemed (at least to Ambrose) to have undermined one of the central pillars of episcopal authority, namely, the bishop's role in consecrating the "bride of Christ" herself.

Jerome

The third and most prolific of the opponents of Jovinian was, of course, Jerome. To Jerome we owe most of what remains of Jovinian's writings, quoted in copious fragments in his two books, *Adversus Jovinianum*. In addition to this extensive polemic, we have three letters of Jerome written shortly afterward in response to criticism of his treatise. Jerome's literary presence in the Jovinianist controversy is so overwhelming that we tend to take it for granted. Whom else should we expect to rush to the defense of Christian celibacy than Jerome, the author of the ascetical Letter 22 to Eustochium, the polemical Contra Helvidium, and numerous ascetical vitae? Such an assumption, however, would be a mistake, for it would lead us to neglect the most obvious—though usually unasked—question: Why did Jerome insert himself into the controversy in the first place? Unlike Siricius and Ambrose, Jerome had no pastoral responsibilities in churches threatened by Jovinian's teaching; indeed, Jerome was far away in Bethlehem by the time Jovinian began to preach. And yet, of all the participants in the debate it was only Jerome who devoted time and effort in composing an extensive antiheretical treatise, the Adversus Jovinianum.

I would like to suggest that Jerome's engagement with Jovinian, though no doubt motivated by his sincere support for asceticism, also was strongly influenced by his own troubled history with the Roman clergy, Siricius among them, and with Ambrose of Milan as well. Jerome desperately needed to rehabilitate his own reputation, especially after his disgraceful exit from Rome eight years earlier.[36] What better way to reestablish himself than to enter Rome again in triumph in the persona of that powerful fiction of late antique Christian literature, the antiheretical writer? To put the matter another way, Jerome's Adversus Jovinianum served not only to portray Jovinian as a "heretic," but also to reinforce Jerome's own identity as an authoritative teacher of ascetic practice and interpreter of Scripture. Both his choice of genre and the shape of his argumentation attest to this program of self-representation.[37]

There can be no doubt that in the early 390s Jerome was deeply sensitive to the role that could be played in the Theodosian epoch by the Christian man of letters. As Mark Vessey has persuasively argued, already in the mid-380s Jerome had self-consciously fashioned for himself the literary persona of a Christian writer in the image of Origen, that is, as a master of biblical interpretation and ascetic practice.[38] Moreover, shortly before composing Adversus Jovinianum, Jerome had written De viris illustribus, a handbook of Christian biblical interpreters. The aim of this book had been to demonstrate, especially to pagan critics of Christianity, that the Church had produced its own men of learning. With characteristic immodesty, Jerome included himself prominently in the list of literary notables; his is the final (and lengthiest) entry among the contemporary authors.[39]

Even more telling is the fact that *De viris illustribus* included the following entry on Ambrose of Milan, which can only be explained as a sign of strained relations between the two men: "Ambrose, bishop of Milan, at the present time is still writing. I withhold my judgment of him, because he is still alive, fearing either to praise or to criticize him. If I praise him, I will be blamed for flattery, and, if I criticize him, I will be blamed for speaking the truth."[40] Jerome's hostile treatment of Ambrose indicates, at the very least, that relations between the two men were not entirely amicable at the time Jerome composed *Adversus Jovinianum*.[41]

Nor was this the first time that Jerome had spoken with disdain about Ambrose and his literary activity. In the preface to his translation of Origen's homilies on Luke, a work that Jerome seems to have undertaken around the year 391 primarily to expose Ambrose as a plagiarist, Jerome referred to the bishop as an ominous black crow who adorned himself with colored feathers pilfered from other birds.[42] Jerome had stated similar accusations a few years earlier in the preface to his translation of Didymus the Blind's book *On the Holy Spirit*, which likewise was undertaken to demonstrate Ambrose's wholesale and unacknowledged dependence on Didymus for his own *De spiritu sancto*.[43] It is true that Jerome sometimes acknowledged his admiration for (and even his debt to) Ambrose's ascetical writings.[44] Nevertheless, his treatment of Ambrose in *De viris illustribus* and in his translations of Origen and Didymus indicates that in some manner Jerome perceived Ambrose to be a rival, especially in the area of literary accomplishment.

But Jerome's rivalry with Ambrose existed on more than a strictly literary level. Ambrose's hasty rise to the episcopate from a position of secular leadership, although it had occurred nearly twenty years earlier, was still something of a sore point for Jerome at the time of the Jovinianist controversy. It represented the worst aspect of episcopal recruitment from Jerome's point of view, namely, the promotion of the rich and powerful into clerical office. Despite the fact that Ambrose eventually became a vigorous promoter of the ascetic life (or, more likely, because of Ambrose's prominence as an ascetic teacher), Jerome did not hesitate to continue to use Ambrose's secular past against him.

In Letter 69 to Oceanus, written two or three years after *Adversus Jovinianum*, Jerome described the elevation of a secular man to the clergy in terms that unmistakably pointed to Ambrose: "There is someone who yesterday was a catechumen and today is a bishop; yesterday in the amphitheatre, today in the church; in the evening at the circus, in the morning at the altar; just a little while ago the patron of actors, now the consecrator of virgins!"[45] Jerome's personal animosity toward Ambrose has here fused with his convictions about clerical office. Letter 69 suggests that Ambrose's accession to the episcopate was particularly vexing to Jerome. It placed Ambrose in a position of moral and intellectual leadership in the Western church to which Jerome continued to aspire, and to which he could only aspire.[46]

A similar point can be made about Jerome's relations with Siricius. As I noted earlier, Siricius was the Roman bishop who had presided over the trial and expulsion of Jerome from the city of Rome in 385. Obviously, this action (even if only approved, and not actually instigated, by Siricius) would have cast a lasting shadow over relations between the two men. But, again, their conflict was not merely a personal one. Even more fundamental were the differences between the two on the issue of asceticism and its place in the recruitment of the clergy. I have already spoken of Siricius's reluctance to accept professed ascetics immediately into the episcopate and his insistence that the sequence of clerical promotion should be respected. Jerome had a rather different view of the matter. For Jerome, the preference that many bishops showed in choosing married men for the clergy was a sign of the decadence of the church.

This argument is made explicitly in several chapters of *Adversus Jovinianum*, where Jerome shows an awareness both of Siricius's legislation on clerical celibacy and of its rationale.[47] When the apostle Paul prescribed that the bishop should be a "man of one wife," Jerome argued (citing 1 Tim. 3:2–4 and Titus 1:6), Paul was deliberately diluting the episcopal requirements for the new Gentile converts. "He made the rules for fresh believers somewhat lighter so that they might not shrink in alarm from keeping them." Since the new converts had just been told that they had to abstain from idolatry and fornication, "how much more would they have repudiated the obligation of perpetual chastity and continence." The fact that men of second- or third-rate character (that is, married men) continue to be elected to the episcopate, Jerome regarded as a regrettable necessity caused by the lack of virgins. That many congregations prefer to elect married clergy, Jerome complained, shows that these people just wish to approve themselves and, therefore, is further evidence of their inferiority to virgins.

Jerome went on to suggest—and this is the most telling point—that the fault for choosing married clerics often lay with the bishops themselves, and it is clear that he meant Siricius. "What I am about to say," Jerome wrote, "will perhaps offend many. Yet I will say it, and good men will not be angry with me, because they will not feel the sting of conscience." Jerome observed that bishops often choose clergy based on their wealth or education, or because they are relatives or friends, or (worst of all) because they receive flattery from these episcopal hopefuls. Jerome appears to have in mind a very specific case, that of Pammachius himself. In one of his letters to Pammachius, written in 394 in the aftermath of the disastrous reception of the *Adversus Jovinianum* at Rome, Jerome mentioned that Pammachius was considered a leading candidate for the episcopate, even though he was still a married layman and a senator. Moreover, Jerome identified Siricius as one of Pammachius's supporters: "I hear that the enthusiasm of the entire city is aroused on your behalf; I hear that the pontiff and the people are of one mind in this choice. To hold the priesthood is something less than to deserve it."[48]

It is difficult to read Jerome's comment as anything other than a rebuke, both of Pammachius and of Siricius himself. We know that in 394 Pammachius had not yet adopted the ascetic life, and his wife Paulina was still alive. Jerome himself had remarked in Letter 49 that Pammachius had yet to ascend from the third to the second place, that is, to move from the ranks of the married to that of the continent.[49] Siricius and the Roman church as a whole clearly preferred a different model of clerical celibacy and authority, what Peter Brown has described as the "post-marital" celibacy of the traditional married householder.[50] Jerome's opposition to Siricius, in the very pages of the *Adversus Jovinianum*, indicates that Jerome's entry into the debate did not involve simply an attack on Jovinian or even just an effort to rehabilitate his own reputation. The writing of *Adversus Jovinianum* also constituted an implicit challenge to the clerical leadership of the Roman and Milanese churches. For Jerome to trounce Jovinian as a "heretic" would have been a major step toward establishing himself as a giant in the competitive world of fourth-century ecclesiastical and literary politics.

✛ ✛ ✛

The condemnation of Jovinian was a turning point in the history of Western asceticism, although, as I have argued here, the leaders of the Western church did not speak with one voice on the matter. Each of Jovinian's opponents had his particular interests. For Siricius, concern for the status of the clergy was overriding; Ambrose was preoccupied with symbols of purity, such as the bodies of consecrated virgins and of that preeminent Virgin Mary (though concern for episcopal authority was not absent); for Jerome, a persistent effort at literary self-promotion was coupled with zeal to foster monastic asceticism. These differences reveal some of the diverse forms of ascetic piety in the West, as well as their potential for conflict. Ascetic behavior was a powerful source of social power in late antiquity and fertile ground for the production of diverse hierarchies. As Elizabeth Clark once observed, " 'distinction' is built into the fabric of ascetic theory and practice."[51] The "heresy" of Jovinian, if I may call it that, was to recognize and to resist the truth in this statement.

Notes

A version of this essay was presented in March 2001 at the Catholic University of America and Princeton University and in October 2001 at Duke University. I am grateful to Professors Philip Rousseau, Peter Brown, and Elizabeth Clark for the invitation to address their students and colleagues.

1. Siricius, *Epistolae* 7.6 (Corpus Scriptorum Ecclesiasticorum Latinorum [CSEL], vol. 82, pt. 3:301) (this and other collections of *epistolae* hereafter cited as Ep.): "auctores novae haeresis et blasphemiae." All translations of primary sources in the essay are my own. The most likely date of the Roman synod is spring of 393. See Aldama, "La condenación de Joviniano."

2. 1 Cor. 7:38; cf. 1 Cor. 7:9, 32–34. On the diverse ascetic interpretations of 1 Cor. 7, see Clark, *Reading Renunciation*, 259–329.

3. Clement of Alexandria, for example, had argued that celibate Christians are concerned only for their own salvation and are thus "in many respects untried." The married man, by contrast, who devotes himself to the care of the household, is a more faithful reflection of God's own providential care. See Clement, *Stromateis* 7.12.70; cf. 3.12.79.

4. Jerome, Ep. 49.2 (CSEL 54:352).

5. Augustine, *Retractationes* 2.22 (Corpus Christianorum, series latina [CCSL] 57:107–8); cf. Augustine, *De haeresibus* 82.

6. Haller, *Iovinianus;* Valli, *Gioviniano.* This volume was already in press when Duval's *L'affaire Jovinien* appeared.

7. The shift of focus from theological argument to social and political factors in the examination of early Christian controversies is a development in patristic studies that was signaled some time ago by Clark: "The State and Future of Historical Theology: Patristic Studies," in her *Ascetic Piety and Women's Faith,* 3–19.

8. Jerome, Ep. 45.2–3 (CSEL 54:324–25). For the version of events described in this paragraph, see Kelly, *Jerome,* 112–15; and Cavallera, *Saint Jérôme,* 86–88.

9. See Jerome, Ep. 45.6 (CSEL 54:328). The expression "senate of Pharisees" is found in the preface to Jerome's translation of Didymus of Alexandria, *De spiritu sancto* (Migne, *Patrologia Latina* [hereafter PL] 23:105). Cf. Ep. 33.5 (CSEL 54:259) and Ep. 127.9 (CSEL 56:152).

10. This information is inferred from Jerome, *Apologia contra Rufinum* 3.21 (PL 23:473), where Jerome reported that Rufinus had threatened to produce documents that revealed the circumstances of Jerome's departure from Rome.

11. Kelly, *Jerome,* 112.

12. Siricius, Ep. 1.13.17 (PL 13:1144–45); cf. Rousseau, *Ascetics, Authority, and the Church*, 129.

13. Siricius, Ep. 1.13.17 (PL 13:1144–45); cf. Ep. 10.5.15 (PL 13:1192), where Siricius repeats his strictures against ordaining laypersons and neophytes to the ranks of the higher clergy.

14. Ambrose refers to the irregular circumstances of his own ordination in Ep. 14.65 *extra collectionem* (CSEL 82/3:269).

15. Similar concerns are voiced in Siricius, Ep. 6.2.4–3.5 (PL 13:1165–66), although in this letter the issue seems to revolve around the problem of ordaining transient monks (*transeuntes, peregrini*).

16. In Ep. 10.6 (PL 13:1186), Siricius again cited the passage from 1 Cor. 7:5 and commented: "If intercourse is pollution [*si commixtio pollutio est*], it is obvious that the priest must stand ready to carry out his heavenly duty, since he must supplicate on behalf of the sins of others."

17. Brown, *Body and Society*, 358. For a somewhat different development of this theme, see my essay, "Clerical Celibacy and the Veiling of Virgins: New Boundaries in Late Ancient Christianity."

18. For example, Jovinian cited 1 Tim. 3:2 to argue that marriage did not exclude a man from the episcopacy; see Jerome, *Adversus Jovinianum* 1.34 (PL 23:268–69). Similarly, Siricius's opponents also invoked 1 Tim. 3:2 to argue on behalf of a married clergy; see Siricius, Ep. 5.8.3 (PL 13:1161). Both Jovinian and the opponents of clerical celibacy also invoked the example of married priests in the Old Testament. Cf. Siricius, Ep. 1.7.8 with Jerome, *Adversus Jovinianum* 1.23 (PL 23:253).

19. Later, however, in his apologetic letter to Pammachius, Jerome did refer to the notion of Mary's *virginitas in partu*, although he did not attack Jovinian explicitly on this point. See Ep. 49.21 (CSEL 54:386–87).

20. Ambrose, Ep. 15.12–13 *extra collectionem* (CSEL 82/3:310).

21. Ambrose, Ep. 15.13 *extra collectionem* (CSEL 82/3:310). Ambrose may be referring to *Codex Theodosianus* 16.5.18, the edict against the Manichees issued by Theodosius on 17 June 389.

22. See, e.g., the discussion in Augustine, *Confessiones* 5.10.20 (CCSL 27:69) and *Contra Faustum Manichaeum* 30.6 (CSEL 25:755).

23. Ambrose, Ep. 15.4 *extra collectionem* (CSEL 82/3:305). My arguments for the anti-Manichaean character of Jovinian's views can be found in my article "Resistance to the Virginal Ideal"; on the issue of Mary's virginity, see my "Helvidius, Jovinian, and the Virginity of Mary."

24. Augustine, *De nuptiis et concupiscentia* 2.5.15 (CSEL 42:267); cf. *Contra Iulianum* 1.2.4 (PL 44:643); *Contra Iulianum opus imperfectum* 4.121–22 (PL 45:1415–19).

25. Cf. Jerome's complaint in Ep. 22.13.3 (CSEL 54:161) that anyone who is pale and sad from fasting is liable to be called "Manichaean."

26. Brown, *Body and Society*, 355.

27. Jerome, *Adversus Jovinianum* 1.37 (PL 23:275–76).

28. Cf. Jovinian's comment on 1 Cor. 3:16 and 1 Cor. 6:19, cited in *Adversus Jovinianum*

2.19 (PL 23:328): "Nescitis quia corpora vestra templum est Spiritus sancti? Templum, inquit, est, non templa; ut similiter in omnibus habitatorem ostenderet Deum."

29. Ambrose, De virginibus 1.31; text in Sant'Ambrogio, ed. Gori, 1:132.

30. Ambrose, Expositio evangelii secundum Lucam 2.7 (Sources chrétiennes [SC] 45:74).

31. Ambrose, Ep. 14.36 extra collectionem (CSEL 82/3:253–54). Elsewhere I have explored the different readings of the image of the Virgin Bride in Ambrose, Jerome, and Augustine: "The Virgin, the Bride."

32. I borrow the phrase from Henry, "Song of Songs."

33. Cf. Siricius, Ep. 10.1.13 (PL 13:1182), who notes the canonical distinction between a virgo velata and a woman who has made merely a private profession of celibacy.

34. Cf. canon 31 of the Council of Hippo of 397 (CCSL 149:42).

35. Ambrose, De institutione virginis 107 (ed. Gori, 2:186). Cf. Pelagius, Epistula 1 ad Claudiam sororem de virginitate (CSEL 1:225), who also speaks of the presentation of the virgin at God's altar per summum sacerdotem.

36. Cf. Kelly, Jerome, 182.

37. I am unable in this space to give an adequate account of the Adversus Jovinianum itself as an antiheretical writing. I refer the reader to Benoît Jeanjean, who has recently demonstrated the extent to which Jerome's portraits of his adversaries as "heretics" were part of an effort to inscribe himself into a heresiological tradition: Saint Jérôme et l'hérésie.

38. Vessey, "Jerome's Origen" and "Forging of Orthodoxy."

39. Jerome, De viris illustribus 135; text in E. C. Richardson, Hieronymus: Liber de viris illustribus (Leipzig, 1896), 55. Pierre Nautin has suggested a date of 393 for both De viris illustribus and Adversus Jovinianum, with the former predating the latter: "Études de chronologie hiéronymienne."

40. Jerome, De viris illustribus 124 (ed. Richardson, 53).

41. The question of Jerome's troubled relations with Ambrose has received considerable attention in the scholarly literature. A good orientation can be found in Oberhelman, "Jerome's Earliest Attack on Ambrose"; and Adkin, "Ambrose and Jerome" (I gratefully acknowledge Mark Vessey for providing the latter reference).

42. Jerome, Praef. in omelias Origenis super Lucam evangelistam (SC 87:94); cf. Rufinus, Apologia contra Hieronymum 2.22–23, where he identifies Ambrose as the object of Jerome's attack. For a somewhat different reading of Jerome's remark, see Adkin, "Jerome on Ambrose."

43. See Jerome's preface to his translation of Didymus's treatise; also discussed by Rufinus, Apologia contra Hieronymum 2.24–25.

44. See, e.g., Jerome's Ep. 22.22.3 (CSEL 54:175), where he alluded to Ambrose's De virginibus; also Ep. 49.14 (CSEL 54:374–75), where Jerome quoted from Ambrose's De viduis and referred explicitly to De virginibus.

45. Jerome, Ep. 69.9 (CSEL 54:698).

46. Further discussion of Jerome's approach to Ambrose can be found in Wiesen, St. Jerome as a Satirist, 240–44.

47. See Adversus Jovinianum 1.34 (PL 23:268–69), where Jerome refers to the importance of ritual purity and cites several of the same biblical texts that Siricius had

invoked. The following quotations in this paragraph are taken from this chapter of *Adversus Jovinianum*.

48. Jerome, *Ep.* 48.4 (CSEL 54:349).
49. Jerome, *Ep.* 49.11 (CSEL 54:366–67).
50. See *Body and Society*, 377–78, where Brown used the term to describe the perspective of Ambrosiaster, the anonymous Roman cleric who, like Siricius, was an ardent defender of clerical prerogatives and avid critic of ascetic extremism.
51. Clark, *Reading Renunciation*, 263. Cf. Brown, in *Body and Society*, 360–61, who observes that Jovinian's views "threatened to undo all that the revolution of late antiquity had achieved for the Christian church. Hierarchy, and not community, had become the order of the day."

✛   The Dark Side of Landscape:

Ideology and Power in the

Christian Myth of the Desert

JAMES E. GOEHRING

In a fascinating study of English rustic landscape painting of the enclosure period (eighteenth to nineteenth centuries), art historian John Barrell uncovers what he identifies as "the dark side of landscape."[1] By this he means the hidden ideological agenda that informs the portrayal of the landscape, which in turn promotes the ideology. The paintings of the period fashioned an ideal image of rural life, suggesting a "stable, unified, almost egalitarian society."[2] When one examines the English society of the day, however, a disjuncture between the paintings and reality becomes immediately apparent. The enclosure period marked the stage in English society when new laws and practices led to the use of fences to divide and close off the common land. In the process, the traditional rights of the common people to the use of the land were extinguished. Barrell's interest lies in the disquieting fact that as English society was becoming more stratified and subdivided, English landscape painting was fashioning a version of rural life that concealed the harshness of the new social order. The paintings of the period offered a rural scene more acceptable in the drawing rooms of polite society, where they served the elite by lending ideological support to the new division of the land.[3]

Barrell writes in a tradition that views landscape painting as an ideological tool that promotes a particular view of reality among those who "see" it. In a reversal of creative power, the landscape, shaped by human ingenuity, in turn shapes the social and cultural world of its creators. It becomes not only "an object to be seen or a text to be read, but . . . a process by which social and subjective identities are formed."[4] English landscape painting of the enclosure period effectively promoted within the society "a set of socially and, finally, economically determined values to which the painted image gave cultural expression."[5] The artificial landscape impressed its vision of the world on those who viewed it. It filtered into and altered the cultural environment through a subtle process that conformed the cultural vision of the world to that of the painting. Its power as a cultural medium lay finally in its ability to "naturalize a cultural and social construction, representing an artificial world as if it were simply given and inevitable."[6] "The painting," Barrell writes,

> offers us a mythical unity and—in its increasing concern to present an apparently more and more actualized image of rural life—attempts to pass itself off as an image of the actual unity of an English countryside innocent of division. But by examining the process by which the illusion is achieved—by studying the imagery of the paintings, the constraints upon it, and upon its organization in the picture-space—we may come to see that the unity is artifice, as something made out of the actuality of division.[7]

The art historian's understanding of the painting lies not only in the description of its content, but also in the unraveling of its artifice so as to understand not only the ideology that lies behind it, but also "the process by which the illusion is achieved." "It is possible," Barrell contends, "to look beneath the surface of the painting and discover there evidence of the very conflict it seems to deny."[8]

These insights into the ideological function and power of landscape painting offer valuable tools for understanding the nature and enduring impact of the myth of the desert in late antiquity. Grounded in the ecological reality of the Egyptian desert and the experiences of actual individuals, the myth of the desert emerged in the writings of the Christian authors who told the stories of the desert saints. They fashioned, whether consciously or unconsciously, a spiritual landscape that transcended the everyday realities of desert life. The saints who populated the landscape came to embody the Christian theme of alienation from the world by reversing the classical conceptions of city and desert. They appear in the desert as the biblical saints, perfecting the demands of the Gospel, and in their perfection, prefiguring the world to come. In all of these ways and more, the myth of the desert served to naturalize the religious and social constructions of the church. Through the myth, readers transcended their own temporal limitations to communicate with the saints of the past and participate proleptically in the world to come.[9]

So, too, the ethical struggles and control of the passions witnessed in the desert saints served as evidence that one could fulfill the biblical injunctions. If the average Christian interpreted the demand of Luke 14:26 to hate one's father and mother as a warning not to put family before God, the ascetic perfected that path by refusing contact with her or his relatives. If the Christian in the world ate moderately and fasted occasionally, the ascetic embraced a higher standard. If the typical Christian moderated sexual desire and practice, the ascetic undertook perpetual continence and the elite among them overcame desire. If the average Christian gave alms to the poor, the ascetic sold all that he had so as to embrace a literal life of poverty. The myth of the desert held forth perfection as a worthy goal, encouraging imitation by those who would flee to the desert and even more importantly by those readers who remained in the world.[10] The near attainment of perfection by the ascetics of the desert landscape served to buttress more generally the Christian expectation of a virtuous life in the world.[11]

One must note, however, that while the individual stories and sayings of the desert saints participated in fashioning the myth, in the end, the myth transcends them all. It developed as a deeper and broader conception that captivated the late antique mind, and in which and from which all of the individual accounts drew their sustenance. The myth of the desert hung like a painting in the Christian consciousness, naturalizing Christian ideals in a world where ideals remained elusive. The power of the mythic landscape participated in the fashioning of new subjectivities and the creation of the new Christian culture.[12] It is the formation of this "artificial" desert landscape and its ideological power that I wish to begin to explore in this essay.

Central to the myth of the desert is, of course, the desert itself. The ideological power of the myth is exerted through its close association of ascetic authority with the desert landscape. "It was," as Peter Brown observed, "above all, a myth of liberating precision. It delimited the towering presence of 'the world,' from which the Christian must be set free, by emphasizing a clear ecological frontier."[13] While the Egyptian landscape with its visible, sharp separation of the black (fertile) and red (desert) land supplied the natural ingredients of the myth, the power of the myth is generated through the effective equation of this natural ecological divide with the spiritual separation of the ascetic and the world.

The equation gains further ideological power by creating the desert ascetic as an idealizing sign, the import of which is heightened through the erasure of alternative signs. The myth empowers the desert ascetic, for example, in part by fading the alternative urban ascetics, who remained a significant if not greater presence in the church, into the background of its ascetic landscape.[14] It is important to note that the illusion works precisely because it does not erase completely the alternative signs, in this case, the urban ascetics. By alluding to the actual conditions of the real landscape, the mythical landscape remains believable. As Anne Birmingham observed in the case of English rustic landscape painting, the created landscape "is ideological in that it presents an illusionary account of the real landscape while alluding to the actual conditions existing in it. Hence although it neither reflects nor directly mirrors reality, [it] does not altogether dispense with it."[15] So, too, the artificial landscape of the desert myth does not altogether dispense with the urban ascetics, though it certainly does not reflect or directly mirror their significance in the real world. The point is not that the myth purposefully ignores the urban ascetics, but rather that it finds in the desert ascetic a more fitting exemplar through which to promote its ideological goals. The near disappearance of the urban ascetics occurred naturally as a by-product of the process.

Athanasius's *Life of Antony*, which played a major role in the development and success of the desert myth, well illustrates this process.[16] In his storied account of the well-known anchorite, Athanasius draws a direct connection between his hero's increasing ascetic power and renown and his withdrawal from the inhabited world (*oikoumenê*) deeper and deeper into the desert. Antony's ascetic progress takes him from his own village, to the outskirts of the village, to nearby tombs, to a deserted fortress in the nearer desert, and finally to the further desert along the Red Sea. While his story begins in the world and he returns to it to contend against the Arians, his ascetic perfection is bound up with his withdrawal into the desert.

Urban ascetics appear in the *Life of Antony*, but as with the figures of the rural poor in the paintings of Constable, they "are so small as almost to escape our notice."[17] One meets them only at the very beginning of the text, where Antony entrusts his sister to village virgins before inaugurating his own ascetic career by turning to an elderly villager who had practiced the solitary life from his youth (*Vita Ant.* 3). Their appearance, however, is notably brief. For the typical reader of the *Life of Antony*, they disappear in the distance as Antony withdraws from their world to perfect the ascetic life in the desert. Unless one is specifically interested in urban forms of the ascetic life, they are soon forgotten. Landscape theory would argue, however, that their brief appearance helps to facilitate the working of the illusion. Their presence lends credibility to the myth by connecting it with the real ascetic landscape in Egypt. Whether intentional or not, the difference between the artificial landscape of the *Life of Antony* and the actual ascetic landscape of early Christian Egypt underscores the ideological nature of the text that empowers the myth of the desert.[18]

In a similar fashion, the *Life of Antony* portrays an ascetic landscape innocent of the ecclesiastical and theological divisions that divided the church. Antony himself, of course, is rigorously Athanasian in his ecclesiastical and ascetic orientation. He "honored greatly the rule of the church . . . bowing his head to the bishops and priests" (*Vita Ant.* 67). "In things having to do with the faith, he was truly wonderful and pious" (*Vita Ant.* 68). He perceived the wickedness of Melitian schismatics and Manichaean and Arian heretics from the outset and refused to interact with them (*Vita Ant.* 68, 89). He returned to Alexandria from his ascetic withdrawal to dispute the Arian teachings and rally the crowds against them (*Vita Ant.* 69–70; cf. 86).

In addition to his explicit condemnation of the Arians, Antony's ascetic performance supports his Nicene faith. Contrary to the Arian emphasis on the ascetic's achievement of holiness through the imitation of Christ, Athanasius's Antony attains perfection through the working of Christ in him. His conquering of the passions and redemption of the flesh required the power and grace of a fully divine logos.[19] In Athanasius's portrayal, the unity of the church around the Nicene faith becomes a central concern of the perfected saint.

The reader presumes that the remaining ascetics who appear in the *Life of Antony*—the trusted virgins, the old village ascetic, and the disciples of Antony—conform to the Athanasian model. The text fosters this assumption by never explicitly linking any of the Arians that it mentions with the ascetic movement. They are never identified as monks or virgins. While monks and Arians both visit Antony at his ascetic retreat (*Vita Ant.* 55, 68), for example, the two are never equated. The Arians appear in the text more closely related with the rejected Melitian schismatics and refuted Greek philosophers (*Vita Ant.* 68, 73–80). In the *Life of Antony*, asceticism has become not only a desert phenomenon, but also a performance innocent of the ideological divisions that plagued the broader church within the world.

Other sources, including texts penned by Athanasius, belie the artificial nature of the ascetic landscape constructed in the *Life of Antony*. The Arians and Melitians also had their monks and virgins, who, like their Athanasian counterparts, were active in both the cities and the deserts. Various papyrological archives, for example, have revealed an active Melitian monastic presence in both the village of Hipponon and in the nearby desert monastery of Hathor in the vicinity of Arsinoë.[20] The leader of this ascetic community, in fact, a certain Pageus, was summoned to the Synod of Caesarea in 334 C.E.[21] A further document indicates that Melitian ascetics were active in Alexandria as well and suffered persecution at the hands of Athanasius and his followers.[22] In the myth of the desert that is taking form in the *Life of Antony*, however, the unorthodox and schismatic ascetics have all but disappeared.

The text offers the reader a mythical unity, which it passes off as the actual unity of an ascetic movement innocent of division. One can detect, however, within the "illusionary accounts of the real landscape," allusions to the actual situation existing within it.[23] Athanasius, for example, reports "the Arian claim that 'he [Antony] held the same view as they.' "[24] "In this single remark," observed Gregg and Groh, "Athanasius provides a reason for wondering whether Antony himself was the (or a) symbolic figure in whom this battle centered, each party claiming the monk's allegiance, or each attempting to win the followers by co-opting the life and teaching of the prestigious hero."[25] Only a careful reader, however, would consider from this the possibility that both sides were seeking (and undoubtedly had) monastic support. Since no actual Arian or Melitian ascetics appear in the text, the casual reader is more likely to assume that they did not exist. Therein lies the ideological power of the text. It fosters assumptions as part of a process that fashions social and subjective identities that conform to its particular Christian vision.

It is interesting to note further that in the ascetic landscape of the *Life of Antony*, the only "false" monks to appear are relegated to the realm of phantasm and dream. "It is possible," Athanasius writes, "when they [demons] model themselves after the form of monks, for them to pretend to speak like the devout, so that by means of the similarity of form they deceive, and then drag those whom they have beguiled wherever they wish."[26] While he proceeds to link the beguiling with ascetic practice rather than belief or ecclesiastical order, it seems significant that these "unreal" or demonic monks are the only monastic figures that appear in the text in opposition to the monks who are aligned with Athanasius's ascetic ideology. The underlying message is that "real" monks are Athanasian in their orientation. The landscape of the desert myth fashions an artificial unity that it in turn passes off as the actual unity of the ascetic desert.

The process of fashioning this illusionary, mythic landscape witnessed in the *Life of Antony* developed its own momentum as the desert myth grew by naturalizing its image of reality in the emerging Christian culture. Subsequent authors built on existing patterns, and readers interpreted existing sources in terms of the desert myth.[27] The association of ascetic power with the distance of the saint's withdrawal into the desert, for example, an association begun in the *Life of Antony*, led to a sort of hagiographic competition that resulted in accounts of desert saints whose remoteness from the inhabited world became truly mythic. In the process, the desert myth linked up with the themes of the edges of the earth so common to ancient geography.[28]

Jerome, for example, in an apparent effort to "outdistance" Athanasius, fashioned the story of the monk Paul, who lived deep in the desert beyond Antony's own withdrawn cell.[29] According to Jerome, Paul's existence was revealed to the ninety-year-old Antony in a dream after he had considered himself the most righteous monk in the desert (Vita Pauli 7). Instructed by the revelation to seek out the superior monk Paul, Antony left his cell and journeyed deeper into the desert past a hippocentaur and a dwarf with horns and the legs and feet of a goat (Vita Pauli 7–8), sure signs that he was approaching the edges of the earth. Beyond them, he found Paul, whose more remote location, following the logic of the desert myth, confirmed his superior status (Vita Pauli 9–12). Paul's perfection, of course, assumes his ideological unity with the great tradition, a fact that Jerome establishes by reporting Paul's request to be buried in a cloak that Athanasius had given to Antony (Vita Pauli 12).

The Coptic Life of Onnophrius offers a second example.[30] It presents itself as the personal account of a certain Paphnutius's miraculous journey in search of "any brother monks in the farthest reaches of the desert" (Vita Onnoph. 2). The author reports that he walked for four days and four nights into the desert without food or drink. He then continued walking for a number of days until he found a deceased monk in a cave whose clothing and body disintegrated at his touch (Vita Onnoph. 2). Clearly no one had been there before him to bury the long-deceased ascetic. After burying the remains, he walked on into the desert to another cave, where he found the anchorite Timothy, an ascetic whose nakedness and acceptance by wild animals under-scored his complete withdrawal from civilization (Vita Onnoph. 3). After a brief stay with Timothy, Paphnutius continued his journey deeper into the desert. With miraculous help, he traveled an additional eight days until he found the naked Onnophrius (Vita Onnoph. 10).

Paphnutius's return to the world is no less amazing. After Onnophrius died, Paphnutius traveled for some days until he arrived at an oasis where he found four brothers living the ascetic life (Vita Onnoph. 28). He listened to their story and then traveled with them for six miles back in the direction of Egypt (Vita Onnoph. 35). When they left him to return to their oasis, Paphnutius continued on his way for another three days until he arrived at Scetis (Vita Onnoph. 36–37). His long return trip thus brings him back not to the inhabited world, but to the outer edges of the historical penetration of the desert by monks. There is no room for urban ascetics here. In the Life of

Onnophrius, the reader discovers an imaginary ascetic community of distant anchorites whose caves and cells lie forever beyond the reach of disciples, visitors, and pilgrims. The story seals off the towering presence of the world that had, in reality, followed the early ascetics into the desert. Onnophrius has become an angel on earth, and his withdrawn landscape a reflection of heaven. As such, ideological unity is assumed; no schismatic or heretic appears in the text, even as a foil for the saint.

The imaginary nature of such accounts cuts the concept of withdrawal free from the historical or physical practice, revealing its function as an idealized sign in the myth of the desert. The increasing impact of the desert landscape on the Christian consciousness is evident as well in the way it shapes subsequent readings of the early sources. An intriguing example can be seen in the descriptive shift that occurs between the earlier authentic prologue of Palladius of Helenopolis's *Lausiac History* and the later proem or foreword attached to it.[31] The *Lausiac History*, which includes considerable evidence of urban asceticism, is in fact less focused on the connection between the desert and asceticism. Palladius emphasizes this very point at the end of his prologue. As he turns to begin the narrative proper, he writes: "I shall leave unmentioned no one in the cities, or in the villages, or in the desert. For we are concerned not with the place where they settled, but rather it is their way of life that we seek" (*Hist. laus.* prologue 16).

Palladius's point, however, seems to have been lost on the later author of the foreword. He prepares the reader to embark on a literary journey into the desert. "In this book," he writes, "is recorded the wonderfully virtuous and ascetic lives of the holy fathers, monks, and anchorites of the desert" (*Hist. laus.* foreword 1). There is no indication here that various of these "unconquered athletes" lived in towns, cities, and villages. While he does note later in the foreword that he has "recorded only a few of their lesser contests, and in most cases [has] added the family, the town, and the place of the monastic abode" (*Hist. laus.* foreword 5), the reference to the town surely points to the place of the monk's origin, since the location of his ascetic abode is mentioned separately. Indeed, earlier in the section that contains this reference, the author claims that he had "traveled on foot and looked into every cave and cabin in the desert with all accuracy and pious motive" (*Hist. laus.* foreword 5). The reader whose copy of the *Lausiac History* begins with this foreword is prepared by it to read the entire text as an account of desert ascetics. While urban ascetics had begun to fade into the background in the original version of the *Lausiac History*, in the mind of the author of the later foreword, they have all but disappeared. The enduring process of erasure evident here, whether applied consciously or unconsciously, underscores the creative power of the myth of the desert to conform individual and social subjectivities to its own vision of the ascetic world. It works by naturalizing the artificial world that it creates. The desert becomes the assumed location of ascetic perfection.[32]

Early Christian sources abound with evidence of this naturalization process. When Gregory of Nazianzus, for example, responded to Basil's description of his new tranquil retreat in a steep, wooded valley at Annisa, he framed his friend's experience in terms of the desert. Basil had described his new abode in the positive language of cultured retirement (otium liberale).[33] His was an Eden-like retreat against which Kalypso's isle so admired by Homer for its beauty paled in comparison. A thick forest, deep ravines, and an encircling river closed out "the disturbances of the city [tôn astikôn thorubôn]. Cool breezes off the river nourished the sense of tranquility, and flowers and singing birds were abundant. The human need for food, too, was easily met. Fruit of every kind was abundant, fish filled the river, and game filled the forests. Dangerous predators like bears and wolves, on the other hand, were notable by their absence. In the best classical sense of otium liberale, he had freed himself from the bustle and cares of civic life to focus on his spiritual progress in a pleasant and safe withdrawn location.

In his response, Gregory employed mythical and wilderness themes to shift the focus from the pleasures of retirement to the spiritual dangers inherent in ascetic withdrawal.[34] He asks whether he should falsely call it Eden, or rather the dry and waterless desert (tên xêran kai anydron erêmian) that Moses tamed (Ep. 4.5). He brings the wild beasts back into the picture as tests of Basil's faith (Ep. 4.3) and compares his life to that of Tantalus (Ep. 4.11), whom Homer described as suffering thirst and hunger while standing in a lake with water up to his chin unable to drink or eat the fruit that hung from the boughs over his head (Odyssey 11.582–92). In Gregory's view, Basil's "musical birds sing, but only of famine, and they fly about, but only about the desert [tên erêmian]" (Ep. 4.12).[35] Gregory recognized that the verdant nature of Basil's retreat threatened his ascesis by its appeal to the senses. To avoid the attack, to keep the retreat as a place of exile rather than of leisurely retirement, Basil must mentally frame the external reality of the forest with myth, the myth of Tantalus and the myth of the desert. The desert landscape must inform Basil's subjective experience of the woods. The warblers singing in the forest must become desert birds singing of famine. In Gregory's response, one can see the myth of the desert moving in on and replacing the older classical concept of cultured retirement.[36]

The popularity and power of the desert myth over time and across geographical boundaries depended finally on its successful equation of the Near Eastern desert landscape with the spiritual interpretation of Christian withdrawal from the world. As the Coptic word for mountain (*toou*) came to be associated with monastery and desert, so the meaning of "desert" itself came to equate less with the nature of the land than with the general concept of ascetic withdrawal.[37] In the spiritual and literary world of the anonymous sixth-century author of the *Lives of the Jura Fathers*, for example, Romanus's journey into the forested wilderness of the Jura Mountains northeast of Lyon corresponded perfectly with the journey of the fourth-century Egyptian ascetics into the desert.[38] According to the text, the thirty-five-year-old bachelor Romanus left the estate of his well-to-do family around 435 C.E. and withdrew from the world (*Jura Fathers* 4–5), seeking solitude in the wilderness of the Jura Mountains. No paths or roads eased his journey through dense forests littered with fallen trees and abounding with stags and broad-horned deer. He traveled for miles, crossing three mountain ridges, until he found a small fertile meadow watered by two streams. There, beneath a dense fir tree on its eastern edge, he set up his monastic camp. The thick branches that spread above him in a dense circle offered a green roof against both the summer's heat and the freezing rains of winter. He drank from the cold water of the mountain streams and ate berries that grew wild in the meadow (*Jura Fathers* 6–9).

The author, in fact, has drawn from the desert sources to model Romanus's withdrawal. The dense fir beneath which he found protection at the edge of the isolated meadow served to equate him with the hermit Paul, who found shelter in the remote desert beneath a palm tree (*Jura Fathers* 7). In the author's own words, Romanus had in fact left his estate because he had been "attracted by the solitudes of the desert" (*secretis heremi delectatus*) (*Jura Fathers* 5). Romanus's successor, Lupicinus, confirms the equation. Speaking to a crowd of lay people who arrived at the monastery during a famine, he says: " 'Come my dear children, let us go into our granary here, where only a few handfuls of grain remain, and let us pray; we too, who have left our towns, follow the Savior into the desert [*in deserto*] in order to listen to him' " (*Jura Fathers* 68).

In this text, the term "desert" has simply become a cipher for separation from the world. The ideological power of the myth has developed so as to impose itself on and take power from any form of physical withdrawal. This same usage is evident in the writing of Eucherius of Lyon, whose *In Praise of the Desert*[39] offers perhaps the finest Western equation of the monastery and the desert.[40] The text glories in the love of solitary places. Through the workings of God, "the material desert becomes a paradise of the spirit," "a delightful meadow for the interior soul" (De laude heremi 39). It is, in fact, "a temple of our God without walls," a God who prefers "the solitudes of heaven and of the desert," and who "prepared the desert for the saints to come" (De laude heremi 3, 5). Eucherius traces the role of the desert in Christian history from Moses to the desert monks, "whose way of life was like that of heaven, . . . [who] drew as close to God as divine law permits" (De laude heremi 7). The desert becomes, in fact, a heaven on earth, a place that "holds [the saints] as in their mothers' laps," that protects them from satan as a strong-walled sheepfold guards the sheep, that dispenses with the need of civil laws because "the obligations of eternal life are observed more exactly," where "no sound is heard . . . save the voice of God" (De laude heremi 34–37).

The desert for Eucherius, however, is the desert of Lérins, a Mediterranean island monastery situated off the coast of Provence. We learn from John Cassian that Eucherius had intended to visit the monks in Egypt, but his desire was never fulfilled.[41] Nonetheless, his familiarity with the desert myth shapes his understanding of the ascetic life. He transforms the landscape of Lérins so that the spiritual, ascetic experience of the monks becomes the experience of the desert. The myth works through the text to fashion a new Christian subjectivity in its readers, and more generally to participate in the creation of the new Christian culture. In Eucherius's words, the monks of Lérins "desire to live in the desert, and in their hearts they do" (uitam heremi adipisci gestiunt coram adipiscuntar) (De laude heremi 43).

In Eucherius's In Praise of the Desert, one can see the myth of the desert working its magic. The hidden ideological agenda that shaped the landscape of the myth here promotes the ideology that shaped it. By representing its artificial landscape as given or natural, the myth fashioned an attainable ideal toward which the reader and the culture could strive. In naturalizing its construction of ascetic reality, it supplied Eucherius with the perfect tool to shape his readers' ascetic world. While the hidden nature of the ideology behind the myth defines the dark side of landscape in landscape theory, there is nothing unusual in the process. In working its illusion, the myth of the desert does nothing more or less than any cultural myth. It "naturalize[s] a cultural and social construction, representing an artificial world as if it were simply given or inevitable."[42] To the extent that it succeeds, the artificial world comes to shape a new cultural identity. It is as such that the myth of the desert played a major role in the Christian transformation of late antiquity.

Notes

Earlier versions of this paper were presented at the Claremont Graduate University (Feb. 2000), the Catholic University of America (Mar. 2001), and the Annual Meeting of the American Academy of Religion and Society of Biblical Literature in Denver, Colorado (Nov. 2001). I have benefited from the comments and support of many in attendance on those occasions.

1. Barrell, *Dark Side of Landscape*.
2. Ibid., 5.
3. Ibid.
4. Mitchell, *Landscape and Power*, 1.
5. Bermingham, *Landscape and Ideology*, 3.
6. Mitchell, *Landscape and Power*, 2.
7. Barrell, *Dark Side of Landscape*, 5.
8. Ibid.
9. See the excellent study by Frank, *Memory of the Eyes*, esp. 32–33, 168–70.
10. The stories of the desert fathers are, of course, replete with the trials and temptations of desert life. Failures were undoubtedly common. While the heroes of the desert myth warn of and even value continuing temptations, their success against the passions and the miraculous rewards that frequently follow set them well apart from the average Christian reader.
11. Brakke, *Athanasius and the Power of Asceticism*, 237–38.
12. While others have explored the role played by ascetic performance in the inauguration of new subjectivities and a new Christian culture, I want to address the role played by the broader myth of the desert in those same inauguration processes. See Richard Valantasis, "A Theory of the Social Function of Asceticism," in Wimbush and Valantasis, eds., *Asceticism*, 544–52.
13. Brown, *Body and Society*, 216.
14. Goehring, "Encroaching Desert."
15. Bermingham, *Landscape and Ideology*, 3.
16. The significance of the desert in Christianity drew much of its sustenance, of course, from biblical themes. See Louth, *Wilderness of God*; and Mauser, *Christ in the Wilderness*. For Athanasius's *Vita Antonii*, I have consulted *Athanase d'Alexandrie: Vie d'Antoine*, ed. and trans. Bartelink; Migne, *Patrologia Graeca* 26:823–976; St. Athanasius: *The Life of Saint Antony*, trans. Meyer; and *Athanasius: The Life of Antony and the Letter to Marcellinus*, trans. Gregg. Citations of the *Vita Antonii* are to chapter numbers and are given parenthetically in the text, using the abbreviation *Vita Ant.* Translations are my own unless otherwise noted.
17. Barrell, *Dark Side of Landscape*, 6.
18. The fact that Athanasius was well acquainted with urban ascetics, many of whom supported his cause (see Brakke, *Athanasius and the Politics of Asceticism*), cannot be used to argue for his intentional downplaying of the role of urban ascetics in the *Life of Antony*. The focus on Antony, who had in fact withdrawn to the desert, simply worked against their greater inclusion. It is, however, ironic that Athanasius may have composed the *Life of Antony* while hiding as a fugitive in the

homes of urban ascetics. One tradition has him hiding in the home of an Alexandrian virgin following his escape from the Arian attack on the Church of St. Theonas in 356 C.E. (Palladius of Helenopolis, *Historia lausiaca* 63; *Chronicon Athanasianum* 32). See Badger, "New Man Created in God," 209–11.

19. Gregg and Groh, *Early Arianism*, 135; Gregg, *Athanasius*, 11–12.

20. Greek papyri in the British Museum, *P. Lond.* 1913–22. They are edited and translated in Bell, *Jews and Christians in Egypt*; Goehring, "Monastic Diversity and Ideological Boundaries"; see also Kramer and Shelton, *Das Archiv des Nepheros*.

21. *P. Lond.* 1913.

22. *P. Lond.* 1914.

23. Bermingham, *Landscape and Ideology*, 3; Barrell, *Dark Side of Landscape*, 5.

24. Gregg and Groh, *Early Arianism*, 138; quoting *Vita Antonii* 69.

25. Gregg and Groh, *Early Arianism*, 138.

26. *Vita Ant.* 25; trans. Gregg, *Athanasius*, 50.

27. This process can still be seen today in the often unchallenged assumption of an ascetic's "orthodox" orientation when in fact no evidence of her or his ideology is known. See Goehring, "Melitian Monastic Organization," 188–89.

28. Romm, *Edges of the Earth*; Hartog, *Mirror of Herodotus*; Frank, *Memory of the Eyes*, esp. chap. 2.

29. The *Vita Pauli* is in W. Oldfather et al., *Studies in the Text Tradition of St. Jerome's Vitae Patrum*; Migne, *Patrologia Latina* 23:17–60; Paul B. Harvey Jr., "Jerome: Life of Paul, the First Hermit," in Wimbush, ed., *Ascetic Behavior in Greco-Roman Antiquity*, 357–69. Hereafter citations of the *Vita Pauli* are given parenthetically in the text.

30. The Coptic *Life of Onnophrius* is edited by Budge, in *Coptic Martyrdoms*, 205–24; and translated by Vivian in *Histories of the Monks of Upper Egypt and the Life of Onnophrius* (Kalamazoo, Mich.: Cistercian Publications, 1993), 145–66. Further citations are given parenthetically in the text, abbreviated to *Vita Onnoph.* Translations are Vivian's.

31. Palladius, *Hist. laus.* Further citations are to *Hist. laus.* by paragraph number in the prologue and foreword, according to *Palladius: The Lausiac History*, the translation by Meyer. On the inauthenticity of the *proemium*, see *Lausiac History*, ed. Butler, 184; Draguet, "L'inauthenticité du proemium" and "Un nouveau témoin du texte G," 303.

32. The tendency to assume or associate ascetic figures with the desert continues today. See Goehring, "Encroaching Desert," "Hieracas of Leontopolis," and "Withdrawing to the Desert."

33. Basil of Caesarea, *Epistula* 14, in *Saint Basile: Letters*, ed. and trans. Courtonne, 1:42–45.

34. Gregory of Nazianzus, *Epistula* 4, in *Saint Grégoire de Nazianze: Lettres*, ed. and trans. Gallay, 1:3–5; and *Gregor von Nazianz: Briefe*, ed. Gallay, 4–6. Further citations of *Epistula* 4 (hereafter *Ep.* 4) are to Gallay's edition and translation unless otherwise noted. On the complex issue of the relationship between Basil's *Epistula* 14 and Gregory's *Epistulae* 4–6, see Rousseau, *Basil of Caesarea*, 65–67.

35. Translation from Browne and Swallow, *S. Cyril of Jerusalem; S. Gregory Nazianzen*, 447.

36. The date of these letters, 357–59 C.E. (Rousseau, *Basil of Caesarea*, 66–67), underscores the early and pervasive nature of the desert imagery. While Gregory knew Athanasius's *Life of Antony* (*Oration* 21.5), we cannot know if he had read it before he wrote his *Epistle* 4 to Basil. Since the letter was written shortly after Antony's death in 356 C.E., Gregory would have had to obtain a copy of the *Life of Antony* very shortly after its composition.

37. Cadell and Rémondon, "Sens et emplois de *to oros*"; Vivian, *Histories of the Monks*, 18–26.

38. Martine, *Vie des pères du Jura*; Vivian et al., *Lives of the Jura Fathers*. Further citations are to this edition. Translations are Vivian's.

39. Eucherius of Lyon's *De laude heremi* (*In Praise of Deserts*) is in *Sancti Eucherii Lugdunensis Epistula de laude heremi*, ed. Wotke, 178–94; *Eucherii De laudeeremi*, ed. Pricoco; and translated by Cummings, "In Praise of the Desert." A copy of Cummings's translation revised by Jeffrey Burton Russell appears in Vivian, *Lives of the Jura Fathers*, 197–215. Translations are Cummings's, as revised by Russell.

40. Markus, *End of Ancient Christianity*, 160.

41. Cassian, *Conlationes*, 2 Praefatio 1, in *Johannis Cassiani Opera: Conlationes* XXIIII, ed. Petschenig; *John Cassian: The Conferences*, trans. Ramsey, 399.

42. Mitchell, *Landscape and Power*, 2.

✛   Monks and Other Animals

BLAKE LEYERLE

The deserts of late antiquity were a prime location for ascetics intent on transforming their souls by confronting their bodies.[1] But not every body was human. Animals also inhabited the landscape of Egypt and Palestine, and the stories of the earliest monks feature animals with surprising frequency. Yet the topic of monks and animals has received scant scholarly attention. Not only have we been busy considering other aspects of asceticism, but the topic itself commands little respect. As Steve Baker has observed, "[T]he animal is the sign of all that is taken not-very-seriously in contemporary culture; the sign of that which doesn't really matter."[2] Such easy dismissal overlooks not only the fact that animals are, in Keith Tester's words, "a historical object," but also their undeniably important semiotic function.[3] It has been, for example, a commonplace to observe that late antiquity was a society obsessed with rank and status, a time when hierarchy informed, if not controlled, every aspect of life. Hierarchy, in turn, implies that the strong are right, simply because of their strength, to make use of the weak as they see fit. Animals figure in this pattern, allowing Aristotle, when thinking schematically, to consider a slave the same as an ox.[4]

Fables, moreover, of which Aesop's collection is the best known, had long made use of animals as a medium for ethical instruction. Despite the apparent artlessness of talking animals, the message borne by these creatures is not a simple one; rather, it shares in the equivocal nature of the genre itself as one of challenge as well as comfort.

Yet it will not do to regard animals as though they were only cultural signs. For to focus only on the literary construct of the animal is to discount the reality of labor and collude in society's desire to render its exploitation of (various) others invisible.[5] On the other hand, to regard our early monastic texts as transparent witnesses to reality is to fall into the error of accepting a constructed value assigned to "animals" as natural. That being said, the line between these two categories is often impossible to draw because the symbolic controls the experience of real animals and traces of real animals are only available to us through the symbolic mode of the text. Like the important work already done on women in the early Christian period, by Elizabeth A. Clark among others, we must first retrieve evidence about beasts before complicating the value of the sign of their bodies. To this large project, this essay makes a preliminary contribution by considering the role of animals within some of the monastic communities of Egypt and Palestine from the fourth through the sixth centuries.[6] To do so effectively, however, we must first locate ourselves within the wider Greco-Roman view of animals, both actual and imaginary.

Greco-Roman View of Animals

Whereas our own experience of animals in the urbanized Western world is largely limited to interactions with family pets and to purchases of meat, in late antiquity, as J. M. C. Toynbee long ago observed, "[t]here were, indeed, few aspects of human activity, either in work or in leisure, in which beasts did not share."[7] Animals provided transport, food, dress, and adornment; they facilitated agriculture, hunting, war, and religion. They were kept as pets, studied for scientific knowledge, and captured for public entertainment. Underlying this impressive variety of function, however, was a common context of domination. This is nowhere clearer than in the games celebrated throughout the Roman Empire. Libanius tells us that the beast shows were so attractive in fourth-century Syria that people were willing to wait outside all night for seats, preferring the hard pavement to their soft beds.[8] Particularly popular were the *venationes*, or wild beast hunts.

Artistic renditions joined in celebrating blood sport. Consider, for example, the Honolulu Hunt Mosaic, dating from late fifth or early sixth century, and found in Daphne, the wealthy suburb of Antioch.[9] Four groups of animals in combat are arranged around a central striding lion. Under the lion's stomach, a hare runs to the left, but turns its head back and raises its ears, as if in alarm. Farther below, a tigress with a cub under her belly is about to attack a stag and doe that flee before her. To the left, a leopard pounces on the rump of a huge ostrich; the collapsing ostrich turns its head backward to defend itself with its sharp bill. Directly above the lion, a lioness chases two rams. On the right, a zebu[10] charges a bear with its head lowered, hindquarters squared and tail lashing the air.[11] The animals depicted in this mosaic are typical of those featured in the venationes, and for this reason, Christine Kondoleon has seen in the popularity of such mosaics, "a vivid testimony to the passion with which the ancient world pursued hunting as entertainment and leisure activity."[12]

An even more popular artistic subject was the scene of humans triumphing over beasts.[13] Another sixth-century mosaic from Daphne, entitled the Worcester Hunt, applauds the successful hunter.[14] The outer field of this mosaic is divided into four sections by trees, placed on the diagonal; in each section, hunters, both on foot and mounted, are shown in victorious poses. Although some of the animals on the interior are depicted fleeing or even quietly grazing, most of them are either dead or wounded. A bear, for example, wounded in the side by an arrow, is shown moving to the right of the central figure; its head, with its lolling tongue, already seems to be falling between its paws. And on the right-hand side, where a lioness has succeeded in throwing down a swordsman, a horseman has already speared her side, causing a stream of blood to spill from the wound.[15]

While the passion with which antiquity embraced the venationes and other animal shows[16] may well strike us as rather alien, it cannot be entirely divorced from certain culinary choices in which we ourselves may share. Beasts slain in the arena were offered to the spectators to take home as meat. And meat was a much desired, luxury product in late antiquity.[17]

We must begin, then, with animals in their most inert form, and ask why early Christian ascetics repudiated meat in favor of a vegetarian diet.[18]

Meat Eating

While generally abstinent in matters of food, the desert monks were especially known for their scrupulous avoidance of meat. Nowhere is this proclivity more patent than in its breach: several stories describe monks in the awkward social position of either being offered meat or of discovering that a dish they had already eaten contained meat.[19] Whether they eat it out of respect for hospitality, or reject it on principle, the clear message is that monks differ from other people in their choice of vegetarianism. Thus when the biological brother of Abba Stephen came to visit him and discovered him eating meat, he took grave offense. Only a divinely sent trance could reassure him that Stephen had not abandoned his calling but was eating out of necessity and obedience.[20]

If we ask why the monks opted for a vegetarian diet, our texts point us to various answers.

DIFFERENTIATION

Among the solitaries, the repudiation of meat eating undoubtedly served as one way, among many, of distancing themselves from village life. Unlike secular people, the solitary ascetics of Scetis refused to engage in agriculture or animal husbandry. While not all could be as untainted as John of Lycopolis, who received bread directly from heaven, his way of life encapsulated the ideal: "he did not cultivate the soil; he did not worry about what he had to eat; he did not seek to satisfy his bodily needs with plants, not even with grass; and he did not go hunting for birds or any other animals."[21] Others, like Abba Or, held body and soul together by foraging for herbs and edible roots.[22]

Meat eating was a rare event in late antiquity, limited to those few festive occasions when cautious private restraint was dropped in favor of communal celebration. Precisely because of its rarity, it served to celebrate group bondedness. Any refusal to participate marked a pointed rejection not only of the festivities themselves but also of the ties that joined together those gathered at the feast. Vegetarianism thus served an important boundary-marking function; in Bourdieu's terms, it gave ascetics "the body for the job": a body, as Teresa Shaw notes, "that communicates social identity and establishes distance by each one of its practices."[23] By rejecting meat, the desert solitaries emphasized their separation from surrounding society, while at the same time strengthening their own shared identity.

A different picture emerges when we turn to examine the food eaten in the Pachomian monasteries. We immediately discover that it was far more plentiful and varied than that consumed by the solitaries—as apparently everyone knew. A saying attributed to the solitary Poemen records his conversation with the head of a monastery who came asking how he could acquire "the fear of God." Abba Poemen replied laconically, "How can we acquire the fear of God when our belly is full of cheese and preserved foods?"[24] In the cenobium, a typical midday meal might consist of "pickled greens, olives, cheese made of cow's milk, . . . and small vegetables."[25] The mention of cheese is striking. Clearly the Pachomian monasteries were willing to accept animal products into their diet. Even more provocative is the witness of Palladius on animal husbandry. He writes: "They even raise swine. When I criticized this practice, they told me, 'It is a custom we have received

in the tradition, to raise them with the winnowings and the vegetable par-
ings and all that is left over and thrown out, that it not be wasted. The swine
are to be killed and the meat sold, but their feet must be given to the sick and
the old' "[26] For this reason, Palladius includes "animal's feet" among the
typical fare of a midday meal.[27] If true, they were, in all likelihood, pigs' feet,
pickled and served cold.

In considering why the Pachomian monks were less strict in matters of
diet, we must register compelling differences in their relationship to outsiders. With their walls,[28] distinctive clothing, and rules, the monks of the
Koinonia had little need to underscore their separation from secular society
through their diet. A visibly different mode of life freed them to pursue the
same tasks as their neighbors. Palladius observes their labor: "One works
the land as a farmer, another the garden, another in the carpenter's shop,
another in the fuller's, another weaving the big baskets, another in the
tannery, another in the shoe-shop, another at calligraphy, another weaving
the soft baskets."[29]

The distinctions that set the common life apart from society cannot, then,
obscure important continuities, of which none is more striking than the
commitment to hierarchy. The tasks of a monk, his seat at table, or his place
in the assembly, were all assigned by seniority. Rituals of punishment and
demotion are carefully spelled out in the *Rules*. The spiritual goals of this
lifestyle are achieved primarily through the creation of disciplined bodies.
Thus while it is far from clear whether we should accept the unsupported
testimony of Palladius,[30] the possibility that Pachomian monks raised pigs
for slaughter and tolerated at least some meat eating would cohere with their
deep acceptance of hierarchy.

In Palestine, John Moschus attests to the practice of tending swine in the
communal monasteries.[31] Indeed, beasts of burden were such a recognized
part of cenobitic life that when Theodosius set out to found a cenobium, his
first act was to buy "two little asses" to fetch what was needed.[32] Mules were
used for transporting water, vegetables, and other food, and donkeys for
riding. Routine maintenance work as well as new construction also required
beasts of burden.[33] As part of the community, such animals were protected as
well as exploited. When a muleteer killed one of them, he was promptly
expelled for thirty years.[34] As we shall see in greater detail below, the particular blend of communal and solitary elements that constituted the Palestinian
laura made animals an especially inflected symbol.

If we turn back, now, from this cenobitic material to reexamine the *Sayings*, it is scarcely surprising to find an explicit rejection of all forms of overt

discipline. Even in the most provocative situations, the old men seldom allow themselves more than a terse, "Watch yourself."[35] They prefer to teach indirectly, through example.[36] Some disciples found this lack of explicit instruction extremely frustrating:

> Abba Isaac said, "When I was younger, I lived with Abba Cronius. He would never tell me to do any work, although he was old and tremulous; but he himself got up and offered food to me and to everyone. Then I lived with Abba Theodore of Pherme and he did not tell me to do anything either, but he himself set the table and said to me, 'Brother, if you want to, come and eat.' I replied, 'I have come to you to help you, why do you never tell me to do anything?' But the old man gave me no reply whatever. So I sent to tell the old men. They came and said to him, 'Abba, the brother has come to your holiness in order to help you. Why do you never tell him to do anything?' The old man said to them, '*Am I a cenobite that I should give him orders?* As far as I am concerned, I do not tell him anything, but if he wishes he can do what he sees me doing.' From that moment I took the initiative and did what the old man was about to do."[37]

Theodore forthrightly rejects any hierarchy in which some command and others obey. Like other disciplinary forms, overt instruction belongs to the communal way of life. Among the solitaries the ethic was strictly herbivore.[38]

MORALITY: PASSIONS

The morality of meat was, furthermore, an elaborated topic in late antiquity. While it may initially strike us as an odd preoccupation, late antiquity was attuned to the moral qualities of certain foodstuffs. The anonymous Jewish author of the *Letter of Aristeas*, living in Alexandria in the first century before our era, expatiated at some length upon the moral qualities of animals. Whoever ate a weasel, he averred, was ingesting the very essence of malicious, backbiting slander.[39] Those who ate foxes, dogs, lions or donkeys, were likely to become like them, according to Galen.[40] And Philo opined that Moses had forbidden the eating of carnivorous animals lest "the savage passion of anger should turn [people] unawares into beasts." Sea creatures without fins and scales were similarly disallowed lest those who ate them find themselves passive when caught in the undertow of pleasure.[41] Such prohibitions mark the boundaries of civilized society. To eat beyond the pale is, quite literally, to out oneself: to be exiled from one's social group and to share the animal's alien nature.

Beyond these specific associations, the very act of eating meat was inevitably and indissolubly connected with violence.[42] To eat meat was to participate in this violence, as Abba Hilarion knew when he refused some chicken with the words, "Forgive me, but since I received the habit, I have not eaten meat that has been killed." Epiphanius, however, quickly countered, "Since I took the habit, I have not allowed anyone to go to sleep with a complaint against me, and I have not gone to rest with a complaint against anyone."[43] The effectiveness of his point, which Hilarion acknowledged, stems from the way it extends the concept of oral violence: Epiphanius's mouth is innocent of causing harm not only to animals but also to humans. The fathers knew that no mortification was more difficult than "to get up from the table when still hungry, and to do our hearts violence so as not to say a disagreeable word to a brother."[44]

Hurtful words could even be seen as a kind of cannibalism, as in Abba Hyperechius's striking advice that it is "better to eat meat . . . [than] to eat the flesh of one's brothers through slander."[45] When Achilles was found spitting blood out of his mouth, we discover that its source lay in an angry word against a brother that "became like blood" in his mouth.[46] The avoidance of meat was thus in service of a wider formation in nonviolent behavior.[47] In its origin, meat was connected with violence, and as a foodstuff, it was understood to fuel aggression.

Nor was this the only passion fostered by meat eating. Following the lead of philosophers and doctors,[48] ascetic theoreticians labored the intimate and direct connection between eating meat and experiencing sexual desire. As a heavy food that increased bodily "heat," meat was guaranteed to exacerbate desire.[49] For a typical, if extreme, example of this linkage, we may turn to Jerome. Writing to widow Salvina in 400 C.E., he admonishes: "Let them eat flesh who serve the flesh, whose heat is worked off in sexual intercourse."[50] Thus the most obdurately corporeal connection with animals, namely the eating of their bodies, came to bear a heavy symbolic charge.

But it was not only through meat-eating that animals figured in moral reflection. Fables had long made use of animals as a medium for general ethical instruction. At the end of every story, a maxim provided an improving lesson as well as the lens through which the tale should be read. Since these summaries appear to endorse the ethical codes of the ruling class, fables are frequently regarded as yet another "mechanism of ideological repression."[51] But Annabel Patterson has noted, to the contrary, that they can also be viewed as a means of political analysis and communication "in the form of a communication from or on behalf of the politically powerless."[52] For if those without power wish to comment upon unequal power relations, they must do so in code. Consider, in this context, the Aesopian tale of *The Lion, the Ass, and the Fox*:

> A lion, an ass, and a fox, having entered into partnership, went off hunting together. After they had seized a lot of game, the lion ordered the ass to divide the spoils. The ass made three equal portions and invited the lion to choose. The lion became enraged, pounced on the ass and devoured him. Then he ordered the fox to apportion the spoils. The fox gathered everything together into one share, keeping in reserve only a small amount for himself, and invited the lion to choose. The lion then asked the fox who had taught him to divide thus. The fox replied, "The calamity of the ass."[53]

Stripped of the anodyne (and patently false) moral, supplied by the compiler of the Augustana Collection, that "the misfortunes of others make people wise,"[54] this tale is unsurpassed as a survival manual for those yoked in unequal partnerships. As Caxton summarized in the late fifteenth century, "[T]his fable techeth to al folk that the poure ought not to hold felawship with the myghty. For the myghty man is never feythfull to the poure."[55] We must not, then, make the mistake of dismissing stories about animals, no matter how unnatural, as simply naive. Their naiveté may be a political strategy. Nor must we assume that the overtly prescribed message is the only possible reading.

The main effect of fables, however, was to underscore the widespread association of specific creatures with certain psychological tendencies. Echoing Aelian, Basil averred that each animal had its own distinctive trait: "the ox is calm, the ass is slow, the horse is ardent in desire for the mare, the wolf is savage, the fox is crafty, the deer is timid, the ant industrious, the dog is grateful and mindful of friendship."[56] Thus it was clear to Origen that, when God told Adam to have dominion over all the creatures in the sea and in the air and on the earth, these beasts were, in fact, interior dispositions or desires.[57]

This language of dominion allows us to return to the mosaic of the Worcester Hunt and consider the figure in the middle. Dressed as a hunter, he stands in the attitude of triumph, his left arm resting on the staff of his spear. At his feet, a slaughtered boar lies supine. Unlike the dynamism of the surrounding figures, this hunter seems absent-minded, even indifferent to the carnage swirling all about him. His legs are crossed in a position of full rest. He is, as Doro Levi noted, "a symbol of triumph in its abstraction."[58]

However faithful its representation of antiquity's passion for the hunt, the mosaic must be read semiotically as an indirect, but powerful, expression of the virtue of the noble person.[59]

In support of this interpretation, consider the contemporary mosaic of Megalopsychia. We see an almost identical stylization of trees placed on the diagonal.[60] But instead of a triumphant hunter, the center is filled with a medallion of the great-souled person. It is this image that provides the interpretive gloss for the whole. The dangerous beasts are to be read allegorically; they represent vices such as intemperance, ignorance, and error.[61] The victorious hunter represents the great-souled person gaining victory over irrational elements in the human soul.

It is this close connection between certain animals and maleficent forces that informs the relatively rare stories of Abbas destroying creatures. Snakes, serpents, and vipers lent themselves particularly readily to this kind of moral baggage. Thus to illustrate Abba Paul's purity, it was enough to relate how "he used to take various kinds of snakes in his hands and cut them through the middle."[62] Particular features of Egyptian culture were, no doubt, responsible for strengthening the association between demons and animals. Where the indigenous gods were worshipped in creaturely form, live animals were all too readily associated with idolatry.[63] Domination of them became, accordingly, the demonstration of a more public virtue: the triumphalist spread of Christianity—or of a particular brand of Christianity.[64] The reliance upon creatures in late antique ethical discourse reveals how the meaning of an animal is inseparable from its cultural representation; in Steve Baker's words, it is "necessarily a construction, a representation, and not an accessible essence or reality."[65]

Peaceable Kingdom

Not all mosaics featuring animals portray scenes of domination and carnage. While Hesiod and Vergil had both dreamed of a golden age, when "oxen will not fear the mighty lions" and "the timid deer will drink beside the hounds,"[66] the first visual depictions of a peaceable kingdom occur in Christian mosaics from the eastern provinces in the fifth and sixth centuries, that is, at exactly the time of most interest to us.[67] The most famous of these images comes from Ma'in.[68] Unfortunately, the mosaic was badly damaged by the iconoclasts and later patched during a restoration, probably in the early eighth century. But from the remaining fragments, we can reconstruct the scene of a lion and zebu facing each other on either side of a bush. The meaning is clear, thanks to an inscription, still largely intact, running across the top. Taken from Isaiah 11:7, it reads, *kai leôn kai bous hama phagontai achura*, "And the lion shall eat straw like the ox." In this context, vegetarianism is an eschatological act.[69]

The most remarkable example of this allegorical theme comes from the house of Farïd el-Masri at Madaba.[70] Previously interpreted as merely ornamental decoration for a dining room, this image is divided into four panels by means of large pomegranate trees placed on the diagonal. A small head lies at the center of the composition. Between the trees, pairs of animals face each other. In addition to the lion and zebu, there are two hares, two lambs, and two quails. The choice of precisely these animals seems to be the result of some care, as each represents the most timid of species. Yet here they feed together in, seemingly, complete safety.

This mosaic is especially fascinating when we realize that it copies the standard Greco-Roman hunt composition that appears, on its surface, to bear the completely opposite meaning of conquest and domination. Those mosaics were also divided by trees placed on the diagonal. There we also saw animals grouped in pairs. If not implacable enemies, they were typically a wild beast and a herbivore that would usually be its victim; the herbivore was always either running away in fright or being torn apart. Where animals were linked together in action, they were positioned in hierarchical relation, with the dominant beast attacking its victim.[71]

If pagan iconography has left no trace of the dream of a golden age, the allegory seems to have been widespread in Christian circles in Palestine and Syria.[72] And it is from this same region that come the most elaborated tales of monks and animals. To assess why this should be so, we must examine one of these stories in some detail.

GERASIMOS AND THE LION

Among the many tales of desert Christians befriending or securing the aid of wild beasts, the most striking concern lions. Of these, none is more provocative than the story of Abba Gerasimos as told by John Moschus.

The story begins with a lion approaching the monk as he was walking beside the river Jordan. The lion was "roaring mightily" because of an inflamed paw. The elder promptly sat down, lanced the infected paw, extracted the reed point that had caused the suppuration, cleaned and bandaged the wound, and told the beast to leave. So far, the tale is far from unique.[73] But it develops along extraordinary lines as the lion becomes a quasi-postulant. For despite the Abba's dismissal, he refuses to leave, instead following the old man wherever he goes like "a noble disciple." Amazed at its gentle disposition, Gerasimos begins feeding it a monastic diet of bread and boiled vegetables. A period of testing or probation follows in which the lion is given the task of supervising the daily collection of water. When the lion's fidelity has been fully proven, he is given a new name and accepted as a fellow disciple by the other monks. The vicissitudes of this probation deserve retelling in full. John Moschus writes:

> Now the lavra [or monastic community] had an ass which was used to fetch water for the needs of the elders, for they drink the water of the holy Jordan; the river is about a mile from the lavra. The fathers used to hand the ass over to the lion, to pasture it on the banks of the Jordan. One day when the ass was being pastured by the lion, it went away some distance from <its keeper>. Some camel-drivers on their way from Arabia found the ass and took it away to their country. Having lost the ass, the lion came back to the lavra and approached Abba Gerasimos, very downcast and dismayed. The Abba thought that the lion had devoured the ass. He said to it: "Where is the ass?" The beast stood silent, hanging its head, very much like a man. The elder said to it: "Have you eaten it? Blessed be God! From henceforth you are going to perform whatever duties the ass performed." From that time on, at the elder's command, the lion used to carry the saddlepack containing four earthenware vessels and bring water.
>
> One day an officer came to ask the elder for his prayers; and he saw the lion bringing water. When he heard the explanation, he had pity on the beast. He took out three pieces of gold and gave them to the leaders, so that they could purchase an ass to ensure their water supply, and that the lion might be relieved of this menial service. Sometime after the release of the lion, the camel-driver who had taken the ass came back to the Holy City to sell grain and he had the ass with him. Having crossed the holy Jordan, he chanced to find himself face to face with the lion. When he saw <the beast> he left his camels and took to his heels. Recognising the ass, the lion ran to it, seized its leading rein in its mouth (as it had been accustomed to do) and led away, not only the ass, but also the camels. It brought them to the elder, rejoicing and roaring at having found the ass which it had lost. The elder had thought that the lion had eaten the ass, but now he realised that the lion had been falsely accused. He named the beast Jordanes and it lived with the elder in the lavra, never leaving his side, for five years.[74]

This story is particularly fascinating for its account of behavioral modification. The lion becomes, in effect, a monk: he abandons flesh eating in favor of a monastic diet of bread and boiled vegetables; he humbles his proud and fierce nature first to tend to an ass and then actually to do its work; when falsely accused, he accepts his punishment meekly.[75] And when Gerasimos dies, Jordanes refuses to outlive his master. He lives, in short, the exemplary life of a devoted disciple.

What, then, is the meaning of this tale? For while it is certainly possible that a Palestinian monastery had a tame lion that was known to pasture the community's donkey,[76] this story, with its "narrative luxury,"[77] appears to function semiotically every bit as much as Aesop's fables. Its purpose is undoubtedly theological—to provide a "living example" of how monasticism is even now instantiating the peaceable kingdom[78]—and protreptic—to shame prideful monks with the example of an obedient lion.[79] But there is more—always more—as we can see when we read this account against two other tales from *The Spiritual Meadow*.

In the first story, a visitor to Abba Paul's cell hears a knocking at the door. He assumes that another human visitor has arrived, but when he looks out, he is surprised to see first a lion and then Abba Paul opening the door and setting before it bread and soaked peas. When asked to explain his actions, the old man said, "I have required of [the lion] that it harm neither man nor beast; and I have told it to come here each day and I will give it its food. It has come twice a day now for seven months—and I feed it." Some days later, when asked how the lion fared, Abba Paul replied dejectedly: "Badly." When pressed, he admitted that the lion's muzzle had been blood-stained when it had come the day before to be fed. His reaction had been immediate: "What is this? You have disobeyed me and eaten flesh. Blessed Lord! Never again will I feed you the food of the fathers, carnivore! Get away from here." When the lion would not go away, Abba Paul took a rope, folded it into thirds and struck it until it finally left.[80]

Like Jordanes, this lion obtained its daily food without labor. But, like creatures in a modern zoo, maintenance came at the expense of nature: the lion had to live like a herbivore.[81] The lesson of the tale also resembles that of zoos in that it is primarily visual.[82] The lion's daily visits to Abba Paul, like the regular submission of Jordanes, must surely impress the spectator with the colonizing prowess of the monks: their ability to tame the savage desert. That the moral is indeed partly about the spread of "civilization" is made clear by a parallel story featuring not a lion but a prostitute. When a prostitute came to the cell of Abba Sisinios to ply her trade, he asked her why she followed such a way of life. "Because I am hungry," she replied. His response, like Abba Paul's above, was to invite her to give up prostitution and come to him each day for food.[83] The price of monastic rations—for humans as for animals—remains the same: the restraint of passions understood to be "natural."[84] Whether the story figures a lion or a prostitute, the true hero is the monk who tames them both. In the status negotiation of the desert, animals also played their part.[85]

The second story is a variant of the lion and ass tale. Cyril of Scythopolis tells us that a monk named Flavius was accustomed to place his ass in the care of a lion whenever Sabas sent him away on a commission. He describes how every morning, "the lion went off with the halter of the ass in its mouth, pastured it the whole day and, when it was late, watered it and brought it back." All was well until Flavius fell first into presumption and then into fornication. The result was immediate. "On the very same day the lion ripped the ass apart and made it his food. On discovering this, Flavius realized that his own sin was the cause of the ass's being eaten."[86] Here the lion—and for that matter the ass as well—image, quite transparently, aspects of the monk's soul. When the monk loses control of his passions, all restraint is lifted from the lion. The resulting carnage resembles the mosaics of the hunt.

As if to underscore this ethical message, John Moschus ends the story of Gerasimos and Jordanes with an explicit warning: "This happened, not because the lion had a rational soul, but rather . . . to show how subordinate the beasts were to Adam before he misunderstood the commandment and fell from the luxury of paradise."[87] We are not to think that the story is about an unusual lion. Like the fables of Aesop, it is about power relations. But its moral is the very opposite of Aesop's fable of *The Lion, the Ass, and the Fox* where the strong exercises its right to make use of the weak simply because of its strength. The story of Jordanes is, above all, a tale of voluntary restraint.

The mosaics of the Peaceable Kingdom, then, like those of the hunt, have as their subject ethical formation. But unlike the hierarchical dynamism of the hunt, the animals pictured in the Madaba mosaic seem notably static. Instead of domination, the ideal is restraint.[88] And this is an important inflection. For when elite males were encouraged to dominate over their passions, they were both trained and entitled to exercise dominion over subordinate others such as women, slaves, barbarians, and, of course, animals.[89] Early Christian monastics, to the contrary, were encouraged to restrain themselves. And it is this formation that explains the remarkably consistent hesitation of monastics to eat meat, to assume positions of leadership, or even to give advice. In Greco-Roman terms, such behavior was servile, appropriate only for the dominated fractions, for, if you will, the donkeys.[90] The tale of Jordanes asserts, to the contrary, that it is leonine. Thus the animal stories from the desert, like those of Aesop, can sustain a reading that challenges the status quo.

Conclusion

In conclusion, then, the complex relationship of early Christian ascetics to animals is fundamentally determined by an ethic of restraint rather than of domination.

Among the solitaries, the deliberate choice of vegetarianism announced their separation from a culture that endorsed the right of the strong to make use of the weak in whatever manner they saw fit. They refused to live by the categories of their contemporaries (which are also largely our own) that relegate animals under the heading of essentially other and therefore suitable for human use and, indeed, exploitation.[91] For these monks, animals, like secular people, were different but not other. Explicitly they tied meat eating to other forms of oral violence. As they would not place the product of domination in their mouths, so they spoke against savaging another person with words; even overt instruction was eschewed as yet another insidious form of domination.

In the literature of the great cenobitic monasteries of Egypt, animals were a less elaborated topic. This absence is hardly surprising when we appreciate the extent to which Pachomius founded his communal life on the principles of obedience and subordination. Keeping animals for purposes of labor, and perhaps even for food, was in accord with this deep acceptance of hierarchy. With their distinctive dress and customs, moreover, Pachomian monks had far less need of characteristic practices by which to mark themselves off from their surrounding society.

It is in Palestine that we find the most elaborated tales where the line between monk and beast becomes blurred if not completely erased and lions seem no different from prostitutes. Animals were a powerful way in which monks thought and spoke about the encounter with the body—their own as well as that of others. The ethical instruction they offered, like that of Aesop's fables, was on a deliberately "low" plane.[92] For animal stories command little respect; in our own day, as Steve Baker notes, their presumed audience is, "women, children, 'unruly men,' and—if they could only understand—animals too," in short, those constituencies "with something to gain from seeing the values of the dominant culture undermined."[93]

Like evidence for real Early Christian women after "the linguistic turn,"[94] the bodies of animals have all but disappeared under the weight of the symbolic. Yet, by their traces, we know they were there, populating the desert as well as the villages, and exploited for their labor as well as for their utility in the production of elaborated codes.

Notes

1. A point made expertly by Brown, *Body and Society*, 213–40.
2. Steve Baker, *Picturing the Beast*, 174.
3. Berger suggests, following up on Rousseau (*Essay on the Origins of Languages*), that "[i]f the first metaphor was animal, it was because the essential relation between man and animal was metaphoric" ("Why Look at Animals?," 5). The classic study remains Lévi-Strauss, *Savage Mind*.
4. Aristotle, *Politics* 1252b 13.
5. Rosemary Radford Ruether suggests that "early urban states linked together four phenomena in close relation: organized warfare, domination of women, of conquered people and of animals. Ownership and control became the model of relationship to all of these 'other' groups, which also accounts for the tendency to equate the three groups symbolically; i.e. to equate women and slaves with 'beasts' and to equate conquered men with women" ("Men, Women and Beasts: Relations to Animals in Western Culture," in Pinches and McDaniel, eds., *Good News for Animals?*, 14).
6. Texts for Egypt include the various collections of *Sayings* collated in the fifth to sixth centuries, although many of the individual stories would have circulated earlier in oral form, the Pachomian material dating from the second generation of monks (mid- to late fourth century), Athanasius, *Life of Antony* (357 C.E.), Palladius, *Lausiac History* (late fourth century), and the *History of the Monks in Egypt*, written before 400 C.E. Sources for Palestine include the *Lives* of Cyril of Scythopolis; and John Moschus, *Spiritual Meadow* (dated to about 600 C.E.).
7. Toynbee, *Animals in Roman Life and Art*, 15. Berger writes: "In the last two centuries, animals have gradually disappeared. Today we live without them" ("Why Look at Animals?," 9).
8. Libanius, *Epistula* 1399.3 (*Opera*, ed. Foerster, 11.441).
9. House of the Worcester Hunt, room 3. The overall dimensions of the mosaic, dated to ca. 450–520 C.E., measure 9 ft. 6 in. x 9 ft. 3 in. (Kondoleon, *Antioch*, 158–60, cat. no. 43).
10. According to the Suda, the Greeks called the zebu the *bous kamêlites*. It is mentioned by Aristotle (*Historia Animalium* 8.28. 606a) as well as by Pliny (*Naturalis Historia* 8.70.179). It is included in lists of exotic animals for menageries and wild beast fights (Levi, *Antioch Mosaic Pavements*, 1.319).

11. A fuller description may be found in Levi, *Antioch Mosaic Pavements*, 1.365, to which this summary is indebted.

12. Kondoleon, *Antioch*, 160; cf. Levi, *Antioch Mosaic Pavements*, 1.237.

13. Toynbee, *Animals in Roman Life*, 25–31.

14. House of the Worcester Hunt, Daphne, sixth century. The pavement measures 20 ft. 6 in. x 23 ft. 4 in. (Kondoleon, *Antioch*, 66, fig. 2).

15. A full description may be found in Levi, *Antioch Mosaic Pavements*, 1.364, to which this summary is indebted.

16. In most Greek cities, existing theaters were converted to accommodate the taste for Roman spectacles, gladiatorial games, and staged hunts. Antioch also had an authentic Roman amphitheater. See the comments of Malalas (*Chronicle* 9.5) and Libanius (collated in Liebeschuetz, *Antioch*, 141–42).

17. Hamel, *Poverty and Charity*, 9, 19–21; cf. Mireille Corbier, "Ambiguous Status of Meat," esp. 224–34; Meggitt, "Meat Consumption and Social Conflict," 137–41.

18. For a more detailed discussion of monastic food practices, see my essay, "Monastic Formation and Christian Practice."

19. *Apophthegmata Patrum* (hereafter *Apoph. Patr.*), Epiphanius 4 (Migne, *Patrologia Graeca* [hereafter PG] 65.164), trans. Ward, *Sayings of the Desert Fathers*, 57; *Apoph. Patr.*, Theophilus 3 (PG 65.200); ibid., Poemen 170 (PG 65.364). While rejecting meat, they might occasionally eat fish (ibid., Gelasius 3 [PG 65.148–49]; ibid., Pistus 1 [PG 65.372–73]).

20. John Moschos, *Pratum Spirituale* (hereafter *Prat. Spir.*) 65 (PG 87iii.2916), trans. Wortley, *Spiritual Meadow*, 49.

21. *Historia monachorum in Aegypto* 1.45 (ed. Festugière, 27; trans. Russell, *Lives of the Desert Fathers*, 59). Hereafter cited as *Hist. monach.*, by chapter and paragraph, followed by the page number in Festugière's edition. For other holy men being fed by angels, see *Hist. monach.* 10.8, 11.5, 12.4, 12.14, ed. Festugière, 78, 91, 93, 96.

22. *Hist. monach.* 2.4, ed. Festugière, 36; cf. ibid., 7.2, ed. Festugière, 45–46. A whole class of ascetics was known simply as "the grazers" (e.g., *Apoph. Patr.*, Bessarion 12 [PG 65.141–43]; *Prat. Spir.* 19, 167 [PG 87iii.2865, 3034]); Cyril of Scythopolis, *Vita sancti Sabae* (hereafter *V. Sab.*) 15 (ed. Schwartz, *Kyrillos von Skythopolis*, 98.3–6, trans. Price, *Lives of the Monks of Palestine*, 107]). These were solitaries who, having abandoned clothing, housing, and the use of fire, roved from place to place, sheltering in caves or hollow trees, and foraging for their food. Brown views these stories as the temptation to *adiaphora*, in which "the boundaries of man and desert, human and beast collapsed in chilling confusion" (*Body and Society*, 220). Miller, following Page DuBois and Hayden White, suggests that "the wild man held in tensive balance two contrary views of the relation of the human to nature and the animal: on the one hand, identifying with the wild man signified a regressive return to the bestiality, while on the other, sympathizing with him signaled a radical rejection of the values, norms, and institutions of a civilization now viewed as cramping and corrupt" ("Jerome's Centaur," esp. 80–84, 87–89).

23. Bourdieu, *Distinction*, 191; Bourdieu, *Logic of Practice*, 58, in general, 52–79. Shaw, "Askêsis and the Appearance of Holiness," 493; Shaw, *Burden of the Flesh*, 233. Cf. Goody, *Cooking, Cuisine and Class*, 2.

24. *Apoph. Patr.*, Poemen 181 (PG 65.365), trans. Ward, *Sayings of the Desert Fathers*, 192. When the solitary Macarius tried to join the *koinonia*, he was initially rebuffed by Pachomius, who thought he was too old to practice ascesis. But when the brothers saw his way of life, they complained to their superior that Macarius's austerity was making them look bad (Palladius of Helenopolis, *Historia lausiaca* (hereafter Hist. laus.) 19 [PG 34.1057d–1058a]).

25. *Hist. laus.* 39 (PG 34.1105a–b), accepting Russell's emendation of "pickled" for "mixed" (Russell, *Lives of the Desert Fathers*, 128 n. 3). Cf. Pachomius, *The Bohairic Life* 59, *The First Greek Life* 55, *The Tenth Sahidic Life*, fragment 3, in *Pachomian Koinonia*, trans. Veilleux, 1.78, 335, 452. The brothers typically ate two meals a day, though some voluntarily reduced their intake to one meal (*Jerome's Preface to the Rules of Saint Pachomius* 5, in *Pachomian Koinonia*, trans. Veilleux, 2.143).

26. *Hist. laus.* 39 (PG 34.1105a); also in *Pachomian Koinonia*, trans. Veilleux, 2.128; Veilleux notes, however, that there is no trace of swine keeping in either the *Rules* or the *Life* (*Hist. laus.* 134).

27. *Hist. laus.* 39 (PG 34.1105b).

28. Torp, "Les murs d'enceinte des monastères coptes primitifs," 173–200.

29. *Hist. laus.* 32.12, in *Pachomian Koinonia*, trans. Veilleux, 2.129.

30. Of the seventh-century monastery at Thebes, Crum writes: "The *Synaxarium* speaks of meat as not eaten by ascetes and when we find a deed of gift presenting the monastery of Saint Phoebammon with a *prosphora* of 31 sheep and 14 goats, or letters in the Pesenthian dossier relating to cattle belonging to a monastery, we may conclude either that in those days the fare of coenobites differed from that of the hermits, or else that the monasteries owned flocks without using them for food" (in Winlock and Crum, *Monastery of Epiphanius*, 149).

31. *Prat. Spir.* 92 (PG 87iii.2949).

32. Cyril of Scythopolis, *Vita sancti Theodosii* 3, ed. Schwartz, 238.18–19, trans. Price, *Lives of the Monks of Palestine*, 265. For texts mentioning mules and muleteers, see *Vita sancti Euthymii* 18, 44, 59, ed. Schwartz, 28.16, 65.21–23, 81.27–82.2; *V. Sab.* 8, 18, 26, 27, 36, 44, ed. Schwartz, 92.12–16, 102.9–12, 109.18–23, 112.7–9, 123.11–14, 134.8–16. For mules in the Sinai, see *Prat. Spir.* 125, 158 (PG 87iii.2988, 3025). For goatherds and guard dogs, and a camel that was used to work the winch of the monastery's well, see Theodor Nissen, "Unbekannte Erzählungen aus dem *Pratum Spirituale*," *Byzantinische Zeitschrift* 38 (1938): 358–59; and *Prat. Spir.*, trans. Wortley, *Spiritual Meadow*, no. 6, 201–2. For evidence for beasts and leather work in the communal monasteries of seventh-century Egypt, see Winlock and Crum, *Monastery of Epiphanius*, 1.67, 75–78, 165.

33. Patrich, *Sabas, Leader of Palestinian Monasticism*, 183.

34. *V. Sab.* 44, ed. Schwartz, 134.8–135.28.

35. *Apoph. Patr.*, Ammonas 10 (PG 65.121–24), trans. Ward, *Sayings of the Desert Fathers*, 28; *The Systematic Collection* 10.44, trans. Helen Waddell, *The Desert Fathers* (Ann Arbor: University of Michigan Press, 1977), 103; *Anonymous Sayings* 5.43, in Guy, *Apophtegmes des pères* (Sources chrétiennes [hereafter SC] 387.288.48–50).

36. "To instruct your neighbor is the same thing as reproving him" (*Apoph. Patr.*,

Poemen 157 [PG 65.360], trans. Ward, *Sayings of the Desert Fathers*, 189; "Be their example, not their legislator" (ibid., Poemen 174 [PG 65.364], trans. Ward, *Sayings of the Desert Fathers*, 191). Compare the description of Pachomius (*First Greek Life* 25, *Pachomian Koinonia* 1.312). Reciting scripture also implied authority (*Apoph.-Patr.*, Poemen 109 [PG 65.348–49]; *First Greek Life* 118, *Pachomian Koinonia* 1.380). Nagel, "Action-Parables." See also the comments of Frank, *Memory of the Eyes*, 134–70; Rapp, "Story-Telling as Spiritual Communication."

37. *Apophg. Patr.*, Isaac, Priest of the Cells 2 (PG 65.224), trans. Ward, *Sayings of the Desert Fathers*, 99–100, emphasis added.

38. A further illustration of this ethic is provided by the accounts of animals eating the stores or ravaging the gardens of the solitary ascetics. When Antony was finally persuaded to cultivate a small plot of land around his cell in the Inner Mountain so that the brothers would not have to bring him provisions, his agricultural labors were damaged by the incursions of wild beasts. He solved the problem, Athanasius tells us, by reasoning gently with them (*Vita Antonii* 50.8–9 [SC 400.272]; ed. Nau, *Revue de l'orient chrétien* 17 [1912]: 210, no. 333).

39. *Letter of Aristeas*, 165–66.

40. Galen, *De alimentorum facultatibus* 3, in *Claudii Galeni Opera Omnia*, ed. Kühn, 6.664). Nutton, "Galen and the Traveller's Fare." Socrates suggested that after death the souls of "those who have cultivated gluttony or selfishness or drunkenness . . . are likely to assume the form of donkeys and other perverse animals" (Plato, *Phaedo* 81e–82a).

41. *De specialibus legibus.* 4.103, 110–12 (Loeb Classical Library 8.71, 75–77). When monks use their mouths appropriately to speak of spiritual matters, they are surrounded by angels; but when they indulge themselves in idle chatter, pigs, the bestiary symbol of gluttony, attend them (*Apoph. patr.* 359, ed. Nau, *Revue de l'orient chrétien* 18 [1913]: 137; trans. Regnault, *Les Sentences des pères*, 123).

42. This, of course, remains the case. See Peter Singer, "Becoming Vegetarian . . . ," in *Cooking, Eating, Thinking: Transformative Philosophies of Food*, ed. Deane W. Curtin and Lisa M. Heldke (Bloomington: Indiana University Press, 1992), 172–93; Julia Twigg, "Vegetarianism and the Meanings of Meat," in *The Sociology of Food and Eating: Essays on the Sociological Significance of Food*, ed. Anne Murcott (Aldershot: Gower Press, 1985), 18–30; Catherine Osborne, "Ancient Vegetarianism," in Wilkins, Harvey, and Dobson, *Food in Antiquity*, 214–24.

43. *Apoph. Patr.*, Epiphanius 4 (PG 65.164), trans. Ward, *Sayings of the Desert Fathers*, 57. Real fasting is to cease slandering or condemning others (J 741, trans. Regnault, *Les sentences des pères*, 317).

44. Epiphanius, *Ethiopian Collection* 14.17, trans. Regnault, *Sentences des pères du désert: Nouveau recueil*, 317.

45. *Apoph. Patr.*, Hyperechius 4 (PG 65.429), trans. Ward, *Sayings of the Desert Fathers*, 238. It is better to eat meat than to be inflated with pride (ibid., Isidore 4 [PG 65.236], trans. Ward, 106–7; *Anonymous Sayings* 8.26 [SC 387.416]). Also described as "smoke" (*Apoph. patr.* 372, ed. Nau, *Revue de l'orient chrétien* 18 [1913]: 140). Taking advantage of another brother's labor could be described as eating "his blood" (*Apoph. patr.* 348, ed. Nau, *Revue de l'orient chrétien* 17 [1912]: 298). In

Artemidorus's second-century dreambook, analysis of dreams of meat-eating merges imperceptibly into dreams of cannibalism (*Oneirocritica* 1.70, trans. White, *Interpretation of Dreams*, 52–53).

46. *Apoph. Patr.*, Achilles 4 (PG 65.125).

47. Fasting is thus related to silence (*Prat. Spir.* 67 [PG 87iii.2917], trans. Wortley, *Spiritual Meadow*, 50).

48. For philosophic condemnations of meat-eating, see Plutarch, *De tuenda sanitate praecepta* 18, 131f–132a, *De usu carnium* 6, 995d–996a; Musonius Rufus, *Discourses* 18A; Porphyry, *De abstinentia* 1.27; Shaw, *Burden of the Flesh*, 37, 44, 167. For medical condemnations, see Rufus of Ephesus, *Oeuvres de Rufus d'Ephèse* (ed. C. Dremberg and C. E. Ruelle [Paris, 1897, reprint, Amsterdam: Adolf M. Kakkert, 1963], 64–84, 318–23, 429–31, 508–9); Galen, *Quod animi* (in *Claudii Galeni Opera Omnia*, ed. C. G. Kühn [Hildesheim: G. Olms, 1965], 4.767–822); Shaw, *Burden of the Flesh*, 47–48, 59, 61.

49. Porphyry, *De abstinentia* 1.31–38; Clement of Alexandria, *Stromata* 2.20.105 (in *Clément d'Alexandrie*, ed. Mondésert, SC 38.114); Shaw, *Burden of the Flesh*, 105.

50. Jerome, *Epistulae* 79.7 (in *Eusebius Hieronymi Epistulae*, ed. Hilberg, CSEL 55.96); cf. Jerome, *Adversus Jovinianum* 2.37 (Migne, *Patrologia Latina* 23.351A), quoted in Shaw, *Burden of the Flesh*, 102.

51. Christos A. Zafiropoulos, *Ethics in Aesop's Fables: The Augustana Collection* (Leiden: Brill, 2001), 26–44, esp. 31–32.

52. Annabel Patterson, *Fables of Power: Aesopian Writing and Political History* (Durham: Duke University Press, 1991), 2.

53. Aesop, *Aesopi Fabulae* 2.347–48 (ed. Aemilius Chambry [Paris: Belles Lettres, 1926], 2.347–48).

54. Dated to the first or second century C.E., the Augustana Collection is the oldest complete collection of Aesop's fables (Zafiropoulos, *Ethics in Aesop's Fables*, 66).

55. Patterson, *Fables of Power*, 84.

56. *Hexameron* 9.3 (149,11), trans. Robert M. Grant, *Early Christians and Animals*, 101. See also Patricia Cox Miller's comments on the *Physiologus* ("The *Physiologus*: A Poesis of Nature," in her *Poetry of Thought*, 61–73). Gillian Clark observes that "the use of animal behaviour as moral example was also well established" for the early Christian period ("The Fathers and the Animals: The Rule of Reason?," in *Animals on the Agenda: Questions about Animals for Theology and Ethics*, ed. Andrew Linzey and Dorothy Yamamoto [Chicago: University of Illinois Press, 1998], 70).

57. Origen, *Homilia in Genesim* 1.16 [SC 7bis.69]. Cf. Aristotle, *Historia Animalium* 71.588a. Patricia Cox Miller, "Origen on the Bestial Soul: A Poetics of Nature," and "Adam Ate from the Animal Tree: A Bestial Poetry of Soul," in her *Poetry of Thought*, 35–59, 23–25.

58. Levi, *Antioch Mosaic Pavements*, 1.344.

59. Ibid.,1.340–45, cf. 243. See the remarks of Michel Foucault on the essentially agonistic conception of virtue in the classical world (*The History of Sexuality*, vol. 2, *The Use of Pleasure* [New York: Random House, 1986], 63–77).

60. From the Yakto village near Daphne, fifth century (Kondoleon, *Antioch*, 8 fig. 6);

cf. Levi, *Antioch Mosaic Pavements*, 1.337. See also the description in my *Theatrical Shows and Ascetic Lives: John Chrysostom's Attack on Spiritual Marriage* (Berkeley: University of California Press, 2001), 1–3.

61. In Cebes (late first to early second century C.E.), the struggle against vice is compared to a victorious fight against every kind of wild animal (*Pinax* 22; Levi, *Antioch Mosaic Pavements*, 1.341).

62. *Apoph. Patr.*, Paul 1 (PG 65.380–81), trans. Ward, *Sayings of the Desert Fathers*, 204; cf. *Hist. Monach.*, Prologus 9, 9.8–10, 20.12, ed. Festugière, 8, 71, 73–74, 122; Cyril of Scythopolis, *Vita sancti Euthymii* 48, ed. Schwartz, 69.31–70.5; *Vita sancti Sabae* 12, 27, ed. Schwartz, 95.19–96.11, 110.17–25; cf. *Vita sancti Euthymii* 8, ed. Schwartz, 15.19–22; true also of crocodiles (*Hist. Monach.* 12.6, Epilogue 11–13, ed. Festugière, 94, 137–38). See also the comments of John Binns about "cleansing" the desert of "devils, wild beasts and Saracen tribes" (*Ascetics and Ambassadors of Christ: The Monasteries of Palestine, 314–631* [Oxford: Clarendon, 1994], 166–67, 170, 226–27, 229–32).

63. *Hist. monach.* 8.21–23, ed. Festugière, 54–56.

64. Antony's premonition of the Arian schism was foreshadowed by a vision of a pack of mules trampling on the altar of the Lord. For the teaching of the Arians, Athanasius declares, "is infertile, irrational, and incorrect in understanding, like the senselessness of mules" (*Vita Antonii* 82.6–13, in *Athanase d'Alexandrie*, ed. Bartelink, SC 400.346–50, and in Gregg, *Athanasius*, 91). The military governor of Palestine was prevented from entering the church of the Holy Sepulcher by a vision of a ram charging at him as though to impale him on its horns, because he was in communion with Severus (*Prat. Spir.* 49 [PG 87iii.2904–5]; cf. ibid., 105, 106 [PG 87iii.2964–65]).

65. Baker, *Picturing the Beast*, 4.

66. Vergil, *Eclogues* 4.22, 8.27–28; Horace, *Epodes* 16.33–64. Cf. Hesiod, *Opera et dies*, 110–20; Shaw, *The Burden of the Flesh*, 165–68. Such wishful imagery also had the effect of underscoring current reality as a time of brutality.

67. Weitzmann, *Late Antique and Early Christian Book Illumination*, 285.

68. Piccirillo, *Chiese e Mosaici di Madaba*, 332. A similar mosaic was found in the town of Nebo (Saller and Bagatti, *The Town of Nebo*, plate 29.3).

69. Compare Basil of Caesarea, *De ieunio hominis* 1.5 (PG 31.169B), and *De hominis structura* 2.6–7 (SC 160.238–46); Jerome, *Adversus Joviniam* 1.18 (PL 23.247B–248A); Shaw, *The Burden of the Flesh*, 177–78, 197. See also the comments of Stanley Hauerwas and John Berkman, "A Trinitarian Theology of the 'Chief End' of 'All Flesh,' " in *Good News for Animals?*," 72.

70. Piccirillo, *Chiese e Mosaici di Madaba*, 133.

71. In all likelihood the animals in the synagogue of Beth Alpha, dated to 518–27 C.E., have the same meaning. The mosaic of the Seasons of Dair Solaid in Syria seems also influenced by the allegory of the golden age (Levi, *Antioch Mosaic Pavements*, 1.318–319); cf. Piccirillo and Alliata, *Mount Nebo*, 345–46.

72. Levi, *Antioch Mosaic Pavements*, 1.318.

73. Robert M. Grant writes: "Stories about lions and their humane relations with human beings were not uncommon in the first century" (*Early Christians and*

Animals, 18). Particularly common were variants on the tale of Androcles and the lion (Pliny, *Naturalis Historia* 8.21.56–58; Seneca, *De beneficiis* 2.19.1).

74. *Prat. Spir.* 107 (PG 87iii.2968), trans. Wortley, *Spiritual Meadow*, 86–87.

75. Even as Macarius humbly set about supporting his "wife" when falsely accused of impregnating a village girl (*Apoph. Patr.*, Macarius 1 [PG 65.257–60]).

76. Variants of this story occur in the *Life of Sabas* (49, Schwartz, 138,19–139,19, trans. Price, *Lives of the Monks of Palestine*, 148–49) and the *Itinerary* of the Piacenza pilgrim (*Antonini Placenti Itinerarium* 34, in *Itineraria et Alia Geographica*, ed. P. Geyer, Corpus Christianorum series latina 175 [Turnholt: Brepols, 1965], 146). Peter Brown observes that, in late antiquity, "wild beasts roamed the desert in far greater numbers than they do today" (*Body and Society*, 218, citing S. Sauneron and J. Jacquet, *Les ermitages chrétiens du désert d'Esna*, vol. 1, *Archéologie et inscriptions* [Cairo: Institut Français d'Archéologie Orientale du Caire, 1972], 25–26); cf. Patrich, *Sabas*, 161; Binns, *Ascetics and Ambassadors*, 229–30.

77. Elizabeth A. Clark, discussing Roland Barthes on "the effect of the real" ("Holy Women, Holy Words," 420).

78. As Teresa Shaw notes, "the ideal ascetic body is a visible sign or representation of both the original, pure human body of paradise and the incorruptible condition of the paradise to come" (*Burden of the Flesh*, 163).

79. The lion was, of course, proverbially proud. "Courage is innate for the lion, as well as its solitary life and unsocial attitude towards its species. Like a tyrant over the irrational animals, it is proud by nature and rejects equal treatment with others in the crowd" (Basil, *Hexameron* 9.3 [149,11], trans. Grant, *Early Christians and Animals*, 101). Donkeys, on the other hand, were decidedly low status. If wild, they were valued only as sources of meat; if domesticated, of wretched labor (ibid., 193–96).

80. Perhaps a kind of ritual excommunication? (*Prat. Spir.* 163 [PG 87iii.3029–32], trans. Wortley, *Spiritual Meadow*, 134). Another elder was known for welcoming lions who came into his cave and feeding them at his lap (*Prat. Spir.* 2 [PG 87iii.2853], trans. Wortley, *Spiritual Meadow*, 5).

81. Berger, *About Looking*, 19–26.

82. The message of fables is also often visual: in response to the lion's question, the fox said that it was seeing the calamity of the ass that taught him how to divide the spoils.

83. *Prat. Spir.* 136 (PG 87iii.3000], trans. Wortley, *Spiritual Meadow*, 111–12; cf. Cyril of Scythopolis, *Vita sancti Euthymii* 15, ed. Schwartz, 24.20–22.

84. Abba Sergios warded off a lion from the monastery's mules by taking a holy bread-ration (*eulogia*) out of his pack and saying to the lion, "Take the eulogia of the fathers and get out of the path, so that we can go by." The lion took the bread ration and left (*Prat. Spir.* 125 [PG 87iii.2988]).

85. For this preoccupation among ascetics, see Gleason, "Visiting and News," 501–21.

86. *V. Sab.* 49, ed. Schwartz, 139.1–139.12. Similarly, Abba Poemen predicted that he would be torn apart by wild beasts because, as a young man, he had not restrained his hostility (*Prat. Spir.* 167 [PG 87iii.3033]).

87. *Prat. Spir.* 107 (PG 87iii.2969); cf. ibid., 18 (PG 87iii.2865); *Apoph. Patr.*, Paul 1 (PG 65.380–81); Cyril of Scythopolis, *Vita sancti Euthymii* 13, ed. Schwartz, 23.4–10; *V. Sab.* 23, 35, ed. Schwartz, 107.8–22, 121.2–12.

88. Michel Foucault claims that *enkrateia* "is located on the axis of struggle, resistance and combat" and "seems to refer in general to the dynamics of domination of oneself by oneself and to the effort that this demands" (*Use of Pleasure*, 65, and generally, 63–77). In Christianity, he thought, "the ethical subject was to be characterized not so much by the perfect rule of the self by the self in the exercise of a virile type of activity, as by self-renunciation and a purity whose model was to be sought in virginity" (ibid., 92, 82). To the contrary, Elizabeth Clark insists that "[s]elf-domination was perhaps even more important for them [i.e. Christian monks] than for the Greek males to whom Foucault appeals" ("Foucault, The Fathers, and Sex," *Journal of the American Academy of Religion* 56 [1988]: 632). I would agree with Foucault that there was an important shift in ethic, but align myself with Clark that it was not to a "feminine" virtue of passivity.

89. Foucault, *Use of Pleasure*, 215–17, 75–76. In this way ethical formation plays a central role in cultural reproduction.

90. Later scoffers mocked Shenoute's monks for being "harnessed like asses" with the leather straps of their *schêma* (Winlock and Crum, *Monastery of Epiphanius at Thebes*, 1.151). John Moschus tells a remarkable story of a monk who took on a donkey's work in the service of travelers on the road from Jericho to Jerusalem (*Prat. Spir.* 24 [PG 87iii.2869]).

91. Deane W. Curtin, "Food/Body/Person," in *Cooking, Eating, Thinking*, 13–14.

92. The Aesopian ethical tradition, according to Patterson, was an alternative to the elitist Platonic tradition (*Fables of Power*, 11). In early Christian asceticism, as Clark has observed, "a democratizing of opportunity existed in tandem with an elitism based on choice and achievement" ("Foucault, The Fathers, and Sex," 636).

93. Baker, *Picturing the Beast*, 156.

94. Clark, "Holy Women, Holy Words," 413–30.

✛ GENDER

✛ ASCETICISM

✛ **HISTORIOGRAPHY**

✣ Archives in the Fiction: Rabbinic Historiography and Church History

DANIEL BOYARIN

Not long ago, unless there were very good reasons, in advance, for suspecting witnesses or narrators of falsehood, three fourths of all facts stated were facts accepted.

—Marc Bloch, *The Historian's Craft*

The historiography of Judaism in the rabbinic period, together with its implications for history of Christianity, has been, until quite recently, founded on the assumption that the kind of historical information rabbinic legends could yield was somehow directly related to the narrative contents they displayed, which were understood as more or less reliable, depending on the critical sensibility of the scholar. This scholarship was not, of course, generally naive or pious in its aims or methods, merely very old-fashioned. It asked the critical questions that Marc Bloch ascribed to an earlier generation of historians: "The documents most frequently dealt with by the early scholars either represented themselves or were traditionally represented as belonging to a given author or a given period, and deliberately narrated such and such events. Did they speak the truth?"[1] As Bloch shows, such historians did not take the narrations of such documents as the "truth," and the same goes for the historians of the rabbinic period who have followed them. More often than not, in fact, they concluded that the rabbinic narratives did not speak the truth. Despite this very critical stance, however, the assumption is that once the impossible or contradicted has been excised, the texts do, indeed, speak truth.[2]

One of the central questions in rabbinic historiography has been evaluating the ubiquitous rabbinic legends about the founding of Judaism, or, if you will, the refounding of Judaism, at Yavneh in the late first century. A recurring question within the quest of the historical Yavneh had to do with the question of the credibility of a given text or passage of rabbinic literature or the recovery of its "historical kernel." Even when such recovery is successful and convincing, however, this leaves us with very slim and thin bits of historical knowledge. As long as we are engaged in the process of extracting the fact from the fiction in rabbinic legend, we shall learn precious little about the history of the rabbinic group and even less about the histories of those other Jewish groups it is seeking to control and suppress. This question has, of course, enormous implications for the study of early Christianity, as well. Centrally important scholarly interventions in church history have been dependent on Christian scholars' acceptance of naively positivistic accounts of Yavneh by Jewish scholars.[3]

Reading Gedaliah Alon's classic essay, "Rabban Joḥanan B. Zakkai's Removal to Jabneh,"[4] will illustrate these points. Alon begins by citing what is truly the remarkably naive historiography of the nineteenth century, by Jews and Christians, on this issue. These were apparently, to a man(!), prepared simply to accept the Talmud's narrative as "fact" and thus to discuss in all seriousness the contents of Rabbi Yoḥanan's negotiations with Vespasian over the founding of Yavneh.[5] In the end, Alon concludes that the rabbinic historiographical sources are virtually valueless, and he comes to the plausible conclusion that Yavneh was a Roman internment camp and Rabban Yoḥanan a political prisoner and not much more than that.[6]

I am prepared to grant that Alon's reconstruction is plausible in this instance, but essentially all we end up knowing from this is why the later tradition fixed at all on Yavneh as its privileged site of origin, that is, simply because Rabban Yoḥanan was there. To adopt language of Neusner's, what I want to know is: What do we know if we do not know anything significant about Yavneh beyond that it was one of the places in Palestine where Jewish refugees, peacemakers, and "deserters" were interred and that arguably (even plausibly) Rabban Yoḥanan ended up there? What sort of historical work can we do if the kernel of truth proves so dry and fruitless?[7] If—I would suggest by way of answer—the object of research is the motives for the construction of a narrative that is taken to attest to the political context of its telling or retelling, rather than the "historical kernel" or truth contained in the diegesis of the narrative, then all texts are by definition equally credible (which is not to say, of course, that they are all equally intelligible). This point—hardly "postmodern"—can be seconded via reference to Marc Bloch. Bloch distinguishes between two kinds of documents that a historian may use. On the one hand there are what he calls "intentional" texts, citing as his example the *History* of Herodotus; on the other hand there are texts that are not intentional and, in Bloch's view, are precisely therefore all the more valuable for the historian: "Now, the narrative sources—to use a rather baroque but hallowed phrase—that is, the accounts which are consciously intended to inform their readers, still continue to provide valuable assistance to the scholar. . . . Nevertheless, there can be no doubt that, in the course of its development, historical research has gradually been led to place more and more confidence in the second category of evidence, in the evidence of witnesses in spite of themselves."[8] However, as Bloch states clearly, even the most intentional of texts, and the rabbinic narratives of Yavneh are nothing if not intentional in his sense, also teach us that which they did not want us to know; they "permit us to overhear what was never intended to be said."[9] In this sense, we can have equal "confidence" in all texts.[10] The question of the "narrative source" versus the "witnesses in spite of themselves" can be seen, now, as a distinction between protocols of reading texts and not as an essential difference between the texts themselves. As Bloch concludes: "Everything that a man says or writes, everything that he makes, everything he touches can and ought to teach us about him."[11] Whatever else rabbinic narratives might be, they are certainly something that someone has said and written, and even when we don't know who said or wrote them "originally," we can frequently determine at what historical period someone has "touched them." I seek to learn, then, about those who have touched the stories, those who have passed on and inscribed and reformulated the anecdotes within the rabbinic documents they have produced, teaching us, perhaps, what they never intended to say.

All texts inscribe willy-nilly the social practices within which they originate,[12] and many also seek to locate the genealogy of those social practices in a narrative of origins, producing a reversal of cause and effect. This reversal is a mode of narration that is particularly germane to the project of replacing traditional patterns of belief and behavior ("We have always done it this way") with new ones that wish, nevertheless, to claim the authority of hoary antiquity. In short, narratives of origin are particularly useful in the invention of orthodoxies, and thus are particularly useful texts in which to study their invention.

All of the institutions of rabbinic Judaism are projected in rabbinic narrative to an origin called "Yavneh."[13] "Yavneh," seen in this way, is the effect, not the cause, of the institutions and discursive practices that it is said to "originate" in the myth: rabbinic Judaism and its primary institutions and discursive practices, "Torah," the Study House, and orthodoxy.[14] Demystifying the rabbinic narrative of the origins of these practices and of their hegemony allows us to inquire into their "causes" somewhere else, namely, in the complex interactions and negotiations that produced rabbinic Judaism itself as one of the two successfully competing forms of postbiblical religion to emerge from late antiquity, the other being, of course, orthodox Christianity. Thus, although traditional scholarly historiography refers to Yavneh—however characterized in detail—as a founding council that "restored" Judaism and established the rabbinic form as hegemonic following the disaster of the destruction of the Temple, if we want to study how people conceived of themselves as belonging to a group, it is more useful to approach Yavneh as an effect of a narrative whose purpose is to shore up—even this may be presuming too much—the attempt at predominance on the part of the rabbis in the wake of the greater debacle following the fall of Betar in 135.[15] That which the rabbis wished to enshrine as authoritative, they ascribed to events and utterances that took place at Yavneh, and sometimes even to divine voices that proclaimed themselves at that hallowed site. As Seth Schwartz has recently characterized the post-Neusner historiographical project in general: "It was Neusner who first argued consistently that rabbinic documents were not simply repositories of tradition but careful selections of material, shaped by the interests, including the self-interest, of tradents and redactors. In his view the documents did not simply reflect reality but constituted attempts to construct it, that is, they are statements of ideology. Finally, they are the writings of a collectivity of would-be leaders, scholars who aspired to but never in antiquity attained widespread authority over the Jews. In sum, Neusner's work historicized rabbinic literature and reduced it to an artifact of a society in which it was in fact marginal."[16] It is without exaggeration that I would say that, notwithstanding important criticisms that I have at particular moments of Neusner's writings, this is the program out of which my present work is generated.

Anecdotal Evidence; or, Thinking outside the Books

Any focus on the historical and diachronic development of the institutions and discursive practices of rabbinic Judaism raises some serious historiographical problems. Rabbinic literature presents us with no historical documents and virtually no extended historical narratives. It would not be unfair to say that classical rabbinic literature (by which I mean the texts produced between the third and sixth centuries) has no historical writing at all. What we do have are myriad anecdotes, most of them in several widely varying versions, about the important founding "events" of the rabbinic school tradition and its primary actors, the rabbis. In addition, this literature contains extensive discussions of points of ritual and civil law based to greater or lesser extent (depending on genre) on a particular method of interpretation of the Bible—midrash.

How, then, can we "learn Torah" to speak history? In my previous projects on this literature, and especially in *Carnal Israel*, I "finessed" this problem by working in an essentially synchronic version of cultural poetics, treating the whole of rabbinic literature as one ideologically differentiated and contested cultural territory.[17] The method permitted me to avoid the problem of historical referentiality and instead to analyze the texts as sites of struggle and cultural problematic without reference to a "real" outside. This approach is, however, limited, for it prevents precisely what my present project attempts, namely to tell a story of diachronic development, both of and within rabbinic Judaism, as but one particular institution and set of religious ideas among Jews in late antiquity. A referential "outside" to the text has to be invoked, therefore. Accordingly, great attention needs to be paid to the procedures by which such hypotheses can be generated and justified without falling into the traps of either naive positivism or "postmodern" nihilist constructivism "It's all made up anyway, so I can make it up too."

Even the most trenchant versions of a "postmodern" historiography, such as that of Hayden White, presuppose some access to knowledge of "facts" or "events": "The events are *made* into a story by the suppression or subordination of certain of them and the highlighting of others, by characterization, motific repetition, variation of tone and point of view, alternative descriptive strategies, and the like—in short, all of the techniques that we would normally expect to find in the emplotment of a novel or a play. . . . The same set of events can serve as components of a story that is tragic or comic, as the case may be, depending on the historian's choice of the plot structure."[18] White's characterization of historical narratives explicitly assumes that some knowledge of the "events" is granted, common among historians as different in their interpretations of the French Revolution as Michelet, Toqueville, and Taine.[19] However, because of the extraordinary problems of evidence in regard to rabbinic history, it is not only historical interpretation that is at issue but the very events themselves that are put into question, according to different theoretical protocols for reading rabbinic literature.[20] Interestingly the questions about evidence in and from rabbinical texts seem strikingly alike for "modernist" and "postmodernist" historians. Rabbinic literature provides particular problems of evidence, owing to its complexly generated, redacted, anecdotal literary character, rendering the question of context itself—in its most brutally literal form—a matter of selection, interpretation, and analysis. Moreover, rabbinic literature does not come associated with "authors" to whom intentions could, even problematically, be ascribed. If poststructuralism has declared the death of the author,[21] the rabbis produce their literature in a world in which the author has not yet been born, as it were. It follows that even when a general theoretical stance toward historiography has been adopted, questions of method specific to the task of a talmudic history yet remain, since much if not nearly all of our evidence for this historiography consists of already emplotted narratives, either themselves historiographical or history-like in their rhetoric. Whether or not we accept Hayden White's notion of historiography as being fiction-like, the materials upon which rabbinic history must be based are for the most part fictions indeed. With rabbinic narratives we have neither an author about whom we can know anything, nor even a sure historical or social context (as we frequently do when studying the texts of other cultures including contemporaneous Christian texts), and, having largely abandoned attributions to named rabbis as a reliable method of dating,[22] we have only a roughly established time of redaction to go on.[23] By "roughly established time of redaction" I mean two things: a first cut, as it were, between the tannaitic texts of the Mishna and the Tosefta—which are plausibly datable to the third century, with the Mishna seemingly a generation or so earlier than the Tosefta for time of redaction—and the amoraic Talmuds, which belong to the fourth and later centuries, with the Palestinian somewhat earlier (conventionally a century or two earlier) than the Babylonian. This puts the two sets of texts on two sides of the watershed in Roman history known as Christianization, as well as sometimes allowing for a time-line approach to discursive developments. But it does not allow for a specific or precise historical contextualization, nor even an association with specific figures and their oeuvres, as we find for many literatures, including much early Christian.

On the other hand, one could say that it is this very characteristic of rabbinic textuality that provides the material for the work of historiography; not a problem, then, but the very object of our investigations. A formulation of Jonathan Hall's will serve me well: "The present objective is to attempt an identification of the social groups who thought themselves through these genealogies. Because, however, the field of myth is relatively autonomous, it is necessary to treat mythical episodes as phenomena rather than as epiphenomena, and this dictates that any approach should initially be conducted independently 'from within.' "[24] I am not writing, then, the biography of an individual, or even the history of an institution, so much as the history of a text, including its ostensible motivations and effects (and these, one hopes, implicate some kind of history of institutions, competing groups, or at any rate sites of power/knowledge).

The problem of dating developments within rabbinic Judaism remains fraught with difficulty even after (or especially after) Neusner's interventions. First occurrence in the literature, even when we can reasonably project a date for that first occurrence, constitutes only a *terminus ante quem* (latest possible date) for the ideologeme at issue; the question is, of course, to what extent the silence of prior sources where one might expect the term or concept to appear constitutes a *terminus post quem* (earliest possible date). Any given statement in the Mishna might very well reflect any earlier tradition. However, in spite of the advances of recent research strategies, we cannot ever be certain that a given text existed in the precise form in which we find it in the Mishna prior (or much prior) to the redaction of that text. To a certain extent, it seems to me, the debate on "attributions" has been misfocused.[25] The alternatives are not either believing simply that the text as we have it represents the *ipsissima verba* of the tannaim or the amoraim or holding that the editors of the rabbinic texts made them up out of whole cloth, although it might appear that this is the question from the rhetoric of some of the participants in the discussion. Let us grant that attributions to named authorities are meaningful, that is, that there is something in the tradition that associates a given statement with a given authority or at the very least the generation or circle of scholars around that authority. The question yet remains of the verbal form of that statement and its context, both critical for any historical evaluation of its import. I would submit that if Rabbi Akiva is cited, for example, as having held a given opinion, whether theological or halakhic (legal), we still do not know what he said and how he said it and in what context. Just to take one palpably—to me at least—credible instance: the given proposition may have been uttered in the context of an interpretative discourse on Torah (midrash), and then couched in the language of abstract law (Mishna), and then placed into the context of a given dispute on the law and into a tractate dealing with a given topic in the law. This is a particularly strong point when we pay attention to the extremely stylized, almost formulaic nature of these sayings. All of the rephrasings and recontextualizations would be highly significant and simply do not allow us to reconstruct, I would submit, an ancient position as held by Rabbi Akiva. We can, however, read that statement as a contextualized verbal utterance in its present context and interpret it as such. This does not allow me to deny the earlier existence of a given idea or representation, but it does allow examination of a particular "later" context as an ideological system. In other words, I suggest that we slightly shift our perspective on these texts from seeing them either as anthologies or as documents to seeing them as texts that are largely composed of citations. Since citation is always out of context, by definition, it becomes very difficult to imagine how we might think about interpreting the citations by themselves.

We can be certain, I suppose, that the cited passage was current and deemed significant at the time of the editing of the Mishna and that it has a semantic function within the present context.[26] In any case, what should be clear is that we can hardly credit the semimythical narratives of Yavneh that we find in the Mishna (even less so in the later texts) with bearing any positivistic probative weight. I am searching for the historicist matrix of a narrative now, not for the historical reality that it is deemed to convey in its content.[27] I would not dare to write a "canonical history of ideas" based on this method,[28] but I would hold, with Jacob Neusner, that the burden of proof, at least, is on those who wish to assert the utility of late legends and texts in the reconstruction of much earlier events.[29] Rather, assuming that which we can know, namely that the traditions in question were in existence at the presumed time of the redaction of the rabbinic texts and that they were apparently significant at that time, we can hypothesize connections and nexuses. The kind of historical work that I do here involves primarily the placing of textual "events" into a contextual and intertextual context, implying a discursive (and thus, social) world, and not so much the charting of the development of particular phenomena (ideas, institutions) through time. My claim is that contextualizing the fragments of narrative within rabbinica in the time of their narration (and not the time of their narrative contents) is the stronger, more intuitive, and even methodologically more conservative position.

A good-sense approach to the dating of traditions within rabbinic texts in the postneusnerian era is that of Alan Segal: "Since we are dealing with a culture which distinguished various levels of antiquity of traditions in order to formulate legal precedents and valued older traditions more highly, we must rule out the earlier dating by methodological premise *unless and until* other evidence warrants it."[30] It should be noted that, given the consideration Segal raises here, this will be just as much the case, or even more so, with halakhic materials as with aggadic (narrative). At the same time, however, I wish to emphasize the contingent force of these reconstructions. They are dependent on taking a defensible, but certainly not provable, position on dating of the documents and on the use of the documentary context as a way of thinking about the dating of developments within rabbinic religion. Other, perhaps equally defensible, ways of thinking about these questions would produce other, very different, and necessarily also defensible narratives. That seems to me to be just as it should be.

Comparison with a roughly analogous (but also interestingly different) historiographical situation may be helpful. Jonathan M. Hall has undertaken a detailed study of the traditions relating to the origins and movements of the various "ethnic" groups that made up the Greek people in early antiquity. These narratives, which have reached us in written texts produced sometimes a millennium or more later than the events, have been taken by many scholars to be the records of memories of the historical movements and divisions of original ethnic groupings, notably the Dorians in archaic Greece. In a character sketch of these "historically positivist" approaches, which could be applied as well, mutatis mutandis, to the procedures of most historians of rabbinic Judaism as well, Hall writes:

> The series of somewhat contradictory variants in which such myths exist are then understood as pathological aberrations from a "real" historical memory—a collective amnesia, or even polymnesia, resulting from the passage of time. The task of the historical positivist is to reconcile these contradictory variants within a single, rationalising work of synthesis in order to reveal "what actually happened" . . . The problem with the historically positivist approach is that it views myths of ethnic origins as the passive trace-elements of groups whose "objective" existence is deemed to stand independently of those same myths.[31]

In contrast, Hall suggests that if we do not accept ethnicity as a "primordial given" but rather as an ongoing project of construction of identity "that is repeatedly and actively structured through discursive strategies," then the very narratives, the myths of origins, can be understood as elements in discursive strategies, as at least some of the "media through which such strategies operate . . . as cognitive artefacts which both circumscribe and actively structure corporate identity, so that whenever the relationships between groups change, then so do the accompanying genealogies." According to Hall, the mythical variants—instead of being the problem for historiography, in which guise they appear in traditional positivist historiographies—become now instead a resource for history writing, as these very variants indicate "specific stages in the discursive construction of ethnicity."[32] The analogy to my project should be apparent. Similarly, abandoning positivist historiography that considers the aggadot (legends) of Yavneh as more or less corrupted memories and traces of the actual events that took place there, with the concomitant necessity to extract the historical kernel out of the variants and corruptions of the legendary texts, I too am investigating how the shifting and varying legends themselves indicate specific stages in the discursive construction of religious identity as seen by the rabbis. This enables the work to take up a position between the positivist historiography most excellently represented by Gedaliah Alon and an opposite extreme that would see absolutely no historical value in the legends of the rabbis. The work is not, however, positivist, in that it recognizes the inevitable textuality of this very historical record. Not an attestation to something outside of themselves that we can discover (or reconstruct, or even construct) in order to hypothesize things "as they really were," these literary artefacts are the very stuff of the history themselves, and their interpretation as historical objects can be no more "objective" than could any interpretation of any literary text as such. It is just that in this case the interpretation itself takes as part of its interpretative goal the interpretation of the "outside" reality to which the text can be explained as alluding by indirection.

The variations in the traditions about Yavneh, once an obstacle to be removed, now become the very matter of the history, especially when they contradict one other. Accordingly, I make no attempt to reconstruct from them events of that century, but rather attempt to read them in the context of the time of their production, as evidence for the ideological work that they are doing within the cultural and social context in which they have been produced. This involves a shift from the utterance and its referent to the act of uttering as the focus of inquiry, that is, adopting the language of Dominick LaCapra, shifting from a research paradigm to a reading paradigm of historiography.[33] The modes of interpretation employed are, accordingly, seemingly more similar to the modes of interpretation of fictions[34] than of historical documents, still less of historical facts.[35] The mode of interpretation that is formative for me is that called the New Historicism.[36] Although this is not the place to rehearse the assumptions and practices of this mode of reading, suffice it to say for the moment that it issues from the postulate that literature is not produced out of the free-will act of an "author" but rather that language/discourse speaks through authors and their texts. The literary text is, then, no less historically concrete and accessible than is the document:

Nor is it unusual for literary theorists, when they are speaking about the 'context' of a literary work, to suppose that this context—the 'historical milieu'—has a concreteness and an accessibility that the work itself can never have, as if it were easier to perceive the reality of a past world put together from a thousand historical documents than it is to probe the depths of a single literary work that is present to the critic studying it. But the presumed concreteness and accessibility of historical milieux, these contexts of the texts that literary scholars study, are themselves products of the fictive capability of the historians who have studied those contexts. The historical documents are not less opaque than the texts studied by literary critics.[37]

The historian's task is, then, to reconstruct a discourse, a regime of power/knowledge through contextualized examination of some of the products of that discourse read as symptoms. In other words, the dominant cognitive strategy of my work is that of synecdoche.[38] And frequently enough, "probing the depths" of a single text before us may well prove more illuminating than the concatenation of a thousand texts treated as documents—that is, at any rate, the belief upon which this work of historical writing is predicated.

In reading rabbinic anecdotal narrative, I attempt to construe the anecdote in a field of other anecdotes, reading it both closely and contextually (inspired by the New Historicism).[39] This method of interpreting anecdotal evidence has seemed to me a highly productive mode of reading the stories of the past, enabling the description/redescription/construction of the complex ideological texture of the moment: "The historian's task is not so much to collect facts as to relate signifiers."[40] Relating sign to sign synchronically, I thus attempt to build a description of a semiotic (and therefore discursive) state of the cultural system. I am describing, then, signs, interpreting texts. There is an implicit claim that these texts and systems of texts amount to something real "out there" but no claim that we can predict or even ever know how they do: "A linguistic characteristic, a point of law embodied in a text, a rite as defined by a book of ceremonial or represented on a stele, are realities just as much as the flint, hewn of yore by the artisan of the stone age—realities which we ourselves apprehend and elaborate by a strictly personal effort of the intelligence."[41] Rabbinic texts, for all their anecdotal form are, then, flint-like realities, requiring no more, but no less, interpretative effort than any other artefacts. This is the point most richly elaborated in my experience in the writings of the New Historicists.

However, I seek to extend the New Historicist synchronic construction of discursive moments by plotting two such synchronic states on a timeline, by contextually reading narrative (aggadic) and legal (halakhic) texts from a given document or documentary group together, attempting to describe certain differences between these synchronic moments, then providing some hypotheses having to do with the multiple overdeterminations of those differences. I'm interested in the ways that certain shifts seem to cohere with each other in a manner that makes sense of them. I am thus not only describing synchronic systems of signs, but also attempting to narrate the shift from one such system to a later one and thus to write some kind of a history. The next step (or sometimes a heuristically prior step) involves an attempt to site the suggested historicized interpretation in a still broader textual/contextual field, including primarily patristic and other Christian textual materials, in order to develop a broader understanding of socio-cultural processes producing and being produced by the rabbinic texts. I am trying to identify various textual artefacts as belonging to a single stratum of the remains of rabbinic religious culture, to reconstruct and interpret the assemblage, and then to relate the different assemblages so reconstructed one to another.

Before Foucault, Marc Bloch had already mobilized the language of archaeology, to be sure in a somewhat different sense from Foucault's, in thinking about the historiographical project. In his now classic *The Historian's Craft*,[42] Bloch begins his remarkable chapter on historical observation by explicitly invoking archaeological evidence against the notion that all historical evidence is "indirect," that is, filtered through another's intentions before reaching the historian. His example regards the bones of children immured in very ancient Syrian fortresses and the inference that these are the remains of human sacrifice.[43] Bloch argues that the inferences from these data, fully "historical" in nature, are at least as reliable as the up-to-the-minute reports of lieutenants that Napoleon had to deal with in making his strategic adjustments during the battle of Austerlitz. Had Bloch remained, however, at that level of argument, he would not be helping me very much here, for I make little enough use, not knowing quite how, of archaeological evidence in the strict sense.[44] Bloch, however, takes us a vital step further, writing:

> Now, a great many vestiges of the past are equally as accessible [as those Syrian bones]. Such is the case not only with almost all the vast bulk of the unwritten evidence, but also with a good part of that which

is written. If the best-known theorists of our methods had not shown such an astonishing and arrogant indifference toward the techniques of archaeology, if they had not been as obsessed with narrative in the category of documents as they were with incident in the category of actions, they would doubtless have been less ready to throw us back upon an eternally dependent method of observation.[45]

Let me here mobilize but one aspect of "the techniques of archaeology": stratification. Archaeologists, it is well known, infer much from the ways that artefacts are found in particular strata of their excavations, building up more complete pictures of the world of those artefacts by coordinating the remains from a particular stratum. Similarly, by piecing together the different relics of discourse that we find within a given stratum of rabbinic literature, we can begin to reconstruct richer pictures of that stratum.[46] The process remains not only speculative but to a great extent a work of the imagination—but that is, I would suggest, the natural condition of historiography.

I have further modified the synchronic approach by supposing that the rabbinic narratives not only give us insight into the static or synchronic moment of their own production but also record some form of historical memory of broad shifts and conflicts that have taken place and are taking place.[47] For example, I would now read a biographical narrative that tells the story of the death of a rabbi after a particularly bitter dialectical contest and the regret of his opponent at having "caused his death" and lost his intellectual partner as possibly teaching us something about the abandonment of certain types of dialectic within the rabbinic movement in fourth- or fifth-century Babylonia (where the story was told), while teaching us next to nothing, of course, about the lives of those individual rabbis (Palestinians of the third century).[48] I do, moreover, believe that there is some (limited) historical depth to be afforded by the gap between the sources and redactional level of the major rabbinic texts (not equal to the gap between time of redaction and the ostensible time of the "speakers" of the sources, however). These are, after all, texts composed out of the found objects of earlier texts and traditions, suggesting that a gap between the redactional deployment of these objects in this narrative and some earlier partly reconstructable deployments can be discerned. Once again, in Hall's words:

> Faced with both the totality, or system, of the genealogies and the individual genealogemes, one is able to discern how the latter are hierarchically clustered to constitute the former. Yet within the overall system one will also be able to recognise "fracture points"—that is, nodes which

contradict or challenge the internal logic. Sometimes these fracture points will occur *between* variant versions and reflect both authorial and sociopolitical intention, but sometimes they will arise *within* individual accounts which may betray originally diverse social applications.[49]

This also gives us some possibility of discerning a dynamism, a diachrony within the documents, a kind of internal variation within the document, particularly when we can grasp tension between the "redactor" and the "source" or when we can perceive a diachronic shift between them analogous in kind to the variations taken to indicate diachronic shifts and tensions between the different documents as well.[50]

Notes

1. Bloch, *The Historian's Craft*, 89. The epigraph to this chapter quotes ibid., 134.
2. The work of Gedaliah Alon discussed immediately below is an excellent example of this. After decisively showing that nearly nothing of the legend of Rabban Yohanan ben Zakkai's removal to Yavneh can be sustained, he, nevertheless, continues to believe that the event itself took place and even busies himself with the question of whether Vespasian or Titus was the real emperor who met and negotiated with Rabban Yohanan.
3. I refer most notably to the classic works of Davies, *Setting of the Sermon on the Mount*, and Martyn, *History and Theology in the Fourth Gospel*. Elsewhere (in "A Tale of Two Synods" and "Justin Martyr Invents Judaism") I have tried to show how thoroughly their respective accounts of Matthew and John would have to be revised in the light of a more critical rabbinic historiography. See also Le Boulluec, *La notion d'hérésie*, and my strictures in "Diadoche of the Rabbis."
4. Alon, "Rabban Johanan B. Zakkai's Removal."
5. Ibid., 269. In spite of his overall critical stance to the material, it must be said that Alon is remarkably, by our standards, credulous as well. Thus he can deliver himself of a statement such as the following: "Thus the fact, recorded in *Avot de-R. Nathan*, that they signalled with arrows that Rabban Johanan was 'a friend of Caesar,' testifies that the Romans were at this juncture close to the gates," ibid., 276, a simply astonishing statement given that the rabbinic text cited is one of the latest of all classical rabbinic texts and that there is no reason whatsoever to imagine that it preserves anything like eye-witness accounts from hundreds of years—as much as seven hundred—earlier (nor that it wished to!). Truly oddly, from my (and I think more than my) perspective is Alon's treatment of the late midrash and Josephus as roughly equivalently valuable historical sources for the first century. (Truth to tell, he is sometimes more critical with respect to Josephus than with rabbinic legends, ibid., 279). My point here is not to attack Alon, who was a great scholar and whose work necessarily informs our own at every turn, but to point out the enormous epistemic differences between his time and ours.

6. Ibid., 294.
7. Neusner's original formulation for a slightly different instance was: "What do we know if we do not know that Rabbi X really said what is attributed to him? What sort of historical work can we do if we cannot do what Frankel, Graetz, and Krochmal thought we could do?," Neusner, *Reading and Believing*, 33.
8. Bloch, *Historian's Craft*, 60–61.
9. Ibid., 63.
10. I have heard this point made thirty years ago by my teacher, Prof. Saul Liberman, OBM.
11. Bloch, *Historian's Craft*, 66.
12. This is the fundamental insight of the New Historicism. See most recently Gallagher and Greenblatt, *Practicing New Historicism*.
13. See Stemberger, *Jews and Christians in the Holy Land*, 275.
14. Cf. Neusner, *Reading and Believing*, 37.
15. See, making a closely related point, Neusner, "Judaism after the Destruction of the Temple." For the impact that this revisionist work has already had on New Testament studies, see, e.g., Motyer, *Your Father the Devil?*, 75. Motyer, however, seems too readily to assume that Neusner's conclusions have been generally accepted, not noticing that the very example he gives of work done under the "old paradigm" was published quite a bit after Neusner's. Moreover, at least in his "Formation of Rabbinic Judaism," Neusner seemed prepared to ascribe a much greater role to a real, historical Yavneh than I would. See on this point, discussion in Gafni, *Land, Center and Diaspora*, 64.
16. Schwartz, *Imperialism and Jewish Society*, 8.
17. Boyarin, *Carnal Israel*.
18. Hayden White, "The Historical Text as Literary Artifact," in Pomper and Vann, eds., *History and Theory*, 18.
19. "The different kinds of historical interpretations that we have of the same set of events such as the French revolution as interpreted by Michelet, Tocqueville, Taine, and others," White, "Historical Text," 28.
20. In a sense then, we need to go beyond White and assert that at least for rabbinic history, the very description or articulation of the events is always already implied by the plot structure assumed by the historian. What might substitute for White's "events" in this instance, again at least in this instance, are the texts themselves, and then we could rewrite the sentence quoted in note 20 above as "The different kinds of historical interpretations that we have of the same set of texts such as the Talmuds as interpreted by Graetz, Lieberman, Alon, and others."
21. Foucault, "What Is an Author?"
22. It is to Jacob Neusner's lasting credit that he overturned attribution in rabbinic texts as a reliable dating tool. See also Green, "What's in a Name?"
23. For a helpful articulation of these special problems of writing history with rabbinic texts, see Neusner, *Documentary Foundation of Rabbinic Culture*, 8–13. To prevent confusion I would add that I do not associate myself with all of the specific critiques of scholars, nor with the general character of the field as given in that book.

24. Hall, *Ethnic Identity in Greek Antiquity*, 86.

25. A classic statement of the "Neusnerian" position remains that of Green, "What's in a Name?"

26. "Materials designated 'traditional' are . . . always a selection from those that could be so designated. The ones selected are those that figure centrally in the organization of Christian materials favored by the party that puts them forward: therefore, what is labeled 'tradition' always has links to a preferred course of Christian behaviors now," Tanner, *Theories of Culture*, 163. This does not necessarily mean, with respect to the Mishna, for instance, that every statement included or story told represented literally the halakhic practice of the redactors, but it does mean that these statements and their meanings were deemed a significant part of the discursive practice of their time and place and thus are relevant for the description of the religious discourse thereof. I thus disagree with Goldenberg, "Is 'the Talmud' a Document?," 9, who writes that the Mishna, Tosefta, and Talmuds are "anthologies," comparing them to modern anthologies and claiming, therefore, that the compilers were not necessarily "always careful to include only those materials that reflected their own views or ways of thinking." If even texts that surely did not originate among the Qumran sectaries but are found there are deemed useful evidence of their religious stance, because "[they were] read and preserved by the Qumran community" (Boccaccini, *Beyond the Essene Hypothesis*, 105), shall we not say the same for the surely much tighter reading and preserving involved in the production of the rabbinic texts? Of course, it is palpably the case that the redactors of these texts cannot always have included material that they "agreed" with, since the texts are rife with disagreement and self-contradiction. The issue is not whether a particular specific idea or practice "reflected" in a text was or was not characteristic of the redactors of the text but rather of the overall ideological stance of the text, including the ideology of its very practices of redaction. The fact that the Mishna is a different kind of text from the Talmud now becomes the stuff of history rather than an obstacle on the way to doing history.

27. Cf. Moore and Graham, "Quest of the New Historicist Jesus."

28. *Pace* Neusner, *Canonical History of Ideas*.

29. A whole generation of younger scholars of rabbinic Judaism, either trained by Neusner or under his tutelage in more metaphorical senses, have been pursuing his method for the last three decades. For an excellent example, see Goodblatt, "From History to Story to History." The results of Goodblatt's excellent critical analysis are curiously thin however. I think that the addition of a discourse analysis perspective would have served him well in achieving more positive results. This does not by itself, however, provide as much methodological stability as one would wish, for while we can assume, with Neusner, that the presence of a textual element within a document of, say, the fifth century attests to its significance, in some shape or form, at that time, we cannot, *pace* Neusner, presume that this moment marks the appearance of the emergence of that significance within rabbinic culture. At best this would be an argument *e silentio*; at worst an argument against the very palpable fact that rabbinic texts do have historical

depth; they are anthological (although not in the sense, I think, discussed by Goldenberg, "Is 'the Talmud' a Document?"), and many of the pieces can be shown to be older than the contexts in which they first appear to us (Kalmin, *Sages, Stories, Authors, and Editors*). The Talmud presents itself as a layered and diachronic production, i.e., qua document, it is a document with historical depth. We cannot, in short, in my opinion write a "documentary" or "canonical" history of rabbinic ideas. (See Neusner, *Canonical History*; Boyarin, "On the Status of the Tannaitic Midrashim.") What we can do, I think, modifying somewhat Neusner's original and productive insight, is attempt a supple diachronic study of the growth, development, shift within discursive elements by observing their appearance within the overall contextual structure of different rabbinic texts historically (that is in both time and space) contextualized. Thus the function of a signifier such as "Yavneh" or "Beruriah" (Goodblatt, "Beruriah Traditions") can be studied within the context of the third-century Palestinian Mishna and the fifth-century Babylonian Talmud and the results usefully compared to yield historical data upon which the historian may construct her narratives. See on these methodological issues as well Schwartz, *Jewish Society*, 8, who takes a position that I think is quite close to the one I have independently arrived at.

30. Segal, *Two Powers in Heaven*, 27. See too Neusner, *Reading and Believing*, 78 on where the burden of proof ought to lie.

31. Hall, *Ethnic Identity*, 41.

32. Ibid., 42–43.

33. LaCapra, *History and Reading Tocqueville*, 24–29. I would argue (and frequently will) that the fractures and ruptures within the narratives as well as their other intertextual dimensions provide access (at least in theory) to realities that are not only ideal. I believe that by searching hard for what the rabbinic texts are not telling us, indeed what they are telling us not, what they seek to conceal from us, we can find intimations of a social and cultural world beyond the confines of the Beth Hamidrash itself. One of the biggest inspirations for my specific historicist method, then, is the work of Macherey, *Theory of Literary Production*. And see perhaps closer to home Hasan-Rokem, *Web of Life*.

34. Hopkins, "Novel Evidence for Roman Slavery."

35. This proposed paradigm shift is much wider than late ancient Jewish history, of course. As Dominick LaCapra has written, "A relatively self-sufficient research paradigm was in certain ways important for the professionalization of history as a discipline, and attacks on tendencies that question it may be taken as one indication of the extent to which it is still understood (perhaps misleadingly) as essential to the discipline even today. This paradigm enjoins gathering and analyzing (preferably archival) information about an object of study in contrast to reading and interpreting texts or textualized phenomena. (In this exclusionary sense, reading a text, especially a published text, is *not* doing research.)," LaCapra, "History, Language, and Reading: Waiting for Crillon," in Pomper and Vann, eds., *History and Theory*, 94. LaCapra's essay makes many of the points that I am making here.

36. Gallagher and Greenblatt, *Practicing New Historicism*.

37. White, "Historical Text," 23.

38. Cf. ibid., 27.

39. Gallagher and Greenblatt, *Practicing New Historicism*.

40. Vann, "Turning Linguistic," 57, paraphrasing Barthes.

41. Bloch, *Historian's Craft*, 55.

42. Ibid. This is, not incidentally, a book that has brought me much comfort for its explicit permission to the "non-historian" to write history (ibid., 21).

43. Ibid., 52.

44. For examples of effective use of archaeological material in investigations of Roman period Jewish history, see Peskowitz, *Spinning Fantasies*; Schwartz, *Jewish Society*; and Baker, *Rebuilding the House of Israel*. None of these scholars, however, is trying to do the same kind of history that I am (Schwartz comes closest), so I am not sure how to adopt their methods or results (again with the exception of Schwartz's results).

45. Bloch, *Historian's Craft*, 53.

46. It will be seen that this is a less severe application than Neusner's documentary history of what is, otherwise, a similar notion.

47. Another way of saying this would be to suggest that the use of these narratives is analogous to the use of "oral traditions" in historiography; on which see Graham, *Beyond the Written Word*, 14.

48. This example was suggested by my friend, Dr. Dina Stein.

49. Hall, *Ethnic Identity*, 87.

50. This is, hopefully, a way of reconciling the powerful insights of Neusner's documentary hypothesis with the equally compelling insights of such scholars as Kalmin, *Sages*, who have focused on the manifest indications of historical depth within the documents. Thus we could assume that there might be plausibly reconstructible earlier texts within the texts of rabbinic literature without abandoning the notion that the redacted form of the texts as we have it are also texts. This is not all too different from the approach to other literary works, for instance Shakespeare's histories. Even when we discover his "sources" in Hollingshead, we hardly feel tempted to abandon the analysis of the Shakespearian text. See too now Goldenberg, "Is 'the Talmud' a Document?," 10.

✛ How to Read Heresiology

AVERIL CAMERON

If, as has been suggested, literature is the Cinderella of Byzantine studies, then heresiology is still the Cinderella of late antique and Byzantine literature.[1] Whether writings against heresy can be considered literature at all is of course a wider question; this essay starts from a lower level of inquiry and sets more basic questions. Our starting point, it must be emphasized, is the almost total lack of rhetorical or literary interest shown for this type of writing in late antiquity and Byzantium; indeed, one might even say that it is usually treated with a degree of repugnance and embarrassment. This may be hard to understand, given the huge interest in heresy in the later medieval West and the sophistication of some recent discussion, and the recent growing interest in heresy in late antiquity. I would like to demonstrate the centrality of the topic for Byzantium as well as the West, and to raise the question of how heresiological texts should be approached.

Baroque in its variations and its ornament, Christian heresiology did not of course begin in late antiquity with the extraordinarily inventive, even fictive, catalogues contained in the *Panarion*, or "Medicine-Chest," of Epiphanius of Salamis in the 370s, but from that moment on it never looked back.[2] Theodoret of Cyrrhus, another neglected writer, this time of the fifth century,[3] countered with works including a *Compendium of Heretical Fables* and a "Remedy" for the *Affections* of the "Greeks," or pagans—for, as I shall suggest, these writers operated with a capacious definition of what constituted error. Judaism was regarded a heresy by Epiphanius; Islam, by no less a person than John of Damascus. A certain Timothy wrote on the reception of repentant heretics into the church perhaps in the seventh century, and the patriarch Nicephorus in the ninth carried on the same enthusiastic listing and (mis)naming of both historical and contemporary beliefs.[4] They were succeeded in later centuries by a host of others. As part of the process, and at the same time to cash in on it, iconoclasm, not a heresy in modern eyes, was presented as such by its opponents, and the ending of the long controversy over the status of religious images (or better, over the representation of the divine) stimulated the production of the so-called *Synodikon of Orthodoxy*. This crucial document could be progressively updated to meet new conditions, offering to the imaginative flights of heresiology an official and prominent place within the Lenten liturgy.[5]

Tracing the existence and the nature of Byzantine heresy as an objective entity is notoriously difficult. We tend to have only the version of the orthodox or of the persecutors, and they themselves irritatingly call their subjects by a variety of anachronistic or otherwise inappropriate names. In contrast, the study of medieval heresy in the West profits from a wholly different level of documentation.[6] Those who work on the East, or indeed on heresy in late antiquity, have much to learn from the huge amount of scholarship that now exists on medieval heresy, but in the absence of such documentary records for the East we shall probably never know whether ordinary people in Byzantine villages really harbored heretical ideas, or how their allegiances affected their lives and their families. Nevertheless, the heresiologies have a poetics of their own that has yet to be studied. A reviewer commented on my *Christianity and the Rhetoric of Empire* that heresiology was not there included, and that had it been, a different, and darker, Foucauldian analysis might have emerged, the story of Byzantine power relations.[7] Perhaps so, but that may take too literal a view of the literature. There may be other agendas that heresiology also served, and I believe that it is well worth looking at this prolific, and to us not very attractive, genre in order to find out what these agendas might have been.

It seemed appropriate that an essay in a volume dedicated to Elizabeth A. Clark should continue her own extremely welcome exploration of the rhetorical techniques and the discourses adopted by early Christian writers. If I concentrate on a period somewhat later than the one Clark has made her own, it is with a lively consciousness both that the period covered by what we often call "the early church" needs to be generously defined in order to understand it properly, and that the patterns set in late antique and Byzantine heresiological discourse form a coherent and easily traceable trajectory from the earliest centuries of Christianity through to the medieval world. In addressing this topic, moreover, I am able to build on Clark's work on Epiphanius and others in *The Origenist Controversy*, a book that set the doctrinal quarrels of the late fourth century firmly in the context not only of personal rivalries but also of polemical writings.[8]

Heresiology is an embarrassment to modern scholars. It began early and never lost its appeal. But our modern liberal prejudices make us highly resistant to the idea that there can be much imaginative content in such writing, still less that anyone can have found it interesting. Is heresiology therefore merely utilitarian, or worse, a kind of scholastic exercise? For whom was it written, and did anyone bother to read it? Was it the equivalent of publishing a note in a learned journal, whose main claim to fame will be the number of entries in a future citation index? One suspects that this last purpose was indeed the case with John of Damascus's *De haeresibus*, a hundred chapters refuting wrong beliefs, which drew the first eighty on Epiphanius, but with further additions including a controversial and tantalizing final chapter on Islam, the "heresy of the Saracens."[9] Why bother, except as one more addition to the encyclopedism already evident in theological writing in the period?

This modern feeling is a major barrier to appreciation. Jean Gouillard, the editor of such a classic heresiological text as the *Synodikon of Orthodoxy*, is only one of many scholars in describing the portrayal of heretics in the Greek texts as somewhat "mechanical."[10] Writing of Epiphanius, he describes him as marking by common agreement the apogee of heresiology.[11] The tendency to encyclopedism noted by Gouillard led, at a later date, to anthologies or *panoplia* of heresies, like that commissioned from Euthymius Zigabenus (fl. ca. 1100) by Alexios I,[12] or the *Treasury* of Nicetas Choniates (d. 1217),[13] or to monographs on specific examples.[14] In Gouillard's view the genre led to stylized, defensive, and limited ways of describing heresy; to a lack of originality; and to a superficiality that impedes accurate description. The latter point is certainly true: nowhere is it more apparent than in the sources relating to the Paulicians and later the Bogomils (dualist heretics who appear in the texts from the early medieval period onward), if one is trying to reconstruct the extent and nature of these beliefs themselves.[15] Nor is this distaste for heresiology an uncommon general reaction, if, for example, we judge from the scholarly consensus, discussed below, on Epiphanius of Salamis.

I suggest that the very nature of these writings is the first problem to be addressed.[16] Scholars frequently complain that writing about heresy is made the more difficult because we have to depend so heavily on the versions of the winning side, those who successfully appropriated for themselves the term "orthodox"; this bias is reinforced by the representations of heretics in Byzantine art, which again naturally stem from the "orthodox" side and tend equally to reduce their subjects to caricatures and stereotypes.[17] So Byzantine heresy is doubly difficult for the historian. On the one hand, the cataloguing of heresy itself is a subject with which most of us in the post-Enlightenment West have little sympathy and which we are apt to dismiss with disparaging remarks about superficiality and stereotyping, and on the other hand, the texts themselves, with few exceptions, present heresy and heretics from only one side, as the realm of the "other," or even the demonic. All these reactions, let it be noted, start from the premise that heresiologies are there as sources of information, rather than as performative or functional texts.

Such reactions have of course fuelled the idea of Byzantium as a repressive and unenlightened society. Scholars have in the main read heresiologies and other writings on heresy as indicative of real situations. Within the field of Byzantine studies, orthodox theology is generally regarded as a special technical area, and therefore, when it comes to heresiology, historians have rarely been willing to take the theological content seriously. A well-known article by Robert Browning, for example, describes what he saw as the "emasculation" of Hellenism, in the form of education, in Byzantium in the twelfth century.[18] John Italos, the successor of Psellos as consul of the philosophers, and others like him were in his view the victims of a repressive atmosphere in which genuine questioning was stifled. Many scholars have refused to take the actual charges on their own terms; rather, the victims were tried for "intellectual" heresy, to be distinguished from allegedly "popular" heresies, such as Bogomilism is said to have been.[19] Real religious motives are discounted, and on this reductionist view it is the state that leads the attack; the fact that the charges against John form part of the catalogue in the *Synodikon of Orthodoxy* is noted rather than discussed.[20] Written some twenty-five years ago now, Browning's article still illustrates how extremely hard it is for modern historians to approach either the topic of heresy or heresiological material as such. More recently, Michael Angold has adopted an essentially similar approach, seeing the trials as "political" and the charges as at least partly "trumped up."[21] Indeed, refusal to take them on their own terms is rather the norm than the exception, and I think we must recognize that it is a response arising from the assumption, familiar enough, that the appropriate explanation must be both rationalizing and reductionist.[22] Perhaps, however, it is precisely here where the inspection of heresiological texts as texts can help.

Attempting to write the history of late antique and Byzantine heresy does indeed involve treading a very slippery path. In the first place, evidence is often scanty and, particularly for the Byzantine period, surviving texts may lack modern editions. In the second, contemporaries continued to use old names for new ideas: Arians, Manichaeans, Montanists, Messalians—all these labels are applied to "heretics" in later centuries, whether these were iconoclasts, Paulicians, or Bogomils. Timothy of Constantinople in the seventh century and John of Damascus in the eighth repeat as though still current lists of "Messalians," which some argue went back to the fifth-century councils.[23] Heretics and Jews are mentioned in one breath, as though tarred with the same brush even if not quite identical, and the accusation of being a "Judaizer" is standard.[24] Like the heresiologist Timothy, the canons of the Quinisext Council in the late seventh century distinguish between types of heresy in relation to the procedures for admitting them into orthodox communion, dividing them into heresies of ancient standing, whose adherents are to be treated on a par with pagans and baptized, and christological heresy, which they divided into two types and whose followers are to be required to produce libelli or to anathematize Nestorians and Monophysites.[25] But in general, it is distressingly difficult to deduce from heresiological texts what was really happening, as scholars of later medieval heresy have also found. It is not surprising, then, if many scholars give up the quest, leaving the field to others keen to trace a new Manichaean diaspora or to recover their own national and religious identity, a quest in which the Bogomils become symbolic of national struggle against an oppressive feudalism, or of nostalgia for a pre-Ottoman past.[26]

We can at once blame and credit Epiphanius and his predecessors for the (to us) irritating traits of their successors in the genre. Epiphanius's Panarion, or "Medicine Chest," is one of the most elaborate, yet also the most classical, of heresiologies, which with its lists of rare and exotic groups and practices continues to be searched by many scholars for evidence of unknown sects or female cults.[27] Yet writing as he did in the 370s, Epiphanius already came at the end of a line of earlier writers, and he himself depended heavily on the mainly lost Syntagma of heresies by Hippolytus (ca. 170–236) and on the five books of Irenaeus's Adversus haereseis (late second century).[28] The notion of heresies as serpents whose bites required the remedy of truth was not original to Epiphanius, and he may have derived his awareness of classical treatises on remedies from a handbook.[29] Nor has he received a sympathetic reception among modern scholars. Frances Young writes of him that "few would claim that Epiphanius was an original thinker or an attractive personality," and others have described his style as difficult and his language as clumsy and contorted.[30] The use of the Panarion as a reliable guide to the geography of heresy is at once undermined by Epiphanius's proud revelation that he has modeled his list of heresies on the number of concubines in the Song of Songs, reaching the number of eighty by listing seventy-five heresies and five "mothers of heresies."[31] Even more disconcerting, he illustrates the numerology of the Song of Songs by counting the generations of the faithful before Christ, and the line of philosophers from Thales to Epicurus. Thus Epiphanius poses an interpretative challenge to the modern reader. For Young, this is all part of Epiphanius's deficiencies of intellect, which included "fanatical animosities," and which are also revealed in the slightly earlier *Ancoratus* by the formulaic statements which she sees as replacing real argument.[32] To quote another modern writer on Epiphanius, "Indignant historians have formulated harsh judgements on his person and style; his unfairness has been punished by a lack of attentive study of his heresiology."[33] Quite.

A less hostile view might be willing to recognize a degree of literary skill in the ways in which Epiphanius modeled the *Panarion* both on the Song of Songs and on scientific treatises on snake bites and poisons.[34] It is an ambitious work, in other words, if also a pretentious one. It is also interesting, and important for understanding later writings on heresy, that it begins with classifications that in modern terms would not be relevant to Christian heresy at all, namely, the five "mothers of all the sects": barbarism, Scythianism, Hellenism, Judaism, and Samaritanism. From this seemingly odd and even incoherent group, according to Epiphanius, flowed every other sect.[35] With a logic that, on this point at least, cannot be challenged, we are told that only after the coming of Christ and the establishment of orthodoxy did heresies in the common sense break away.[36] In fact, if we wonder where the first four of the "mothers of heresies" are to be found, we have only to look to Colossians 3:11, "In Christ Jesus there is neither barbarian, Scythian, Hellene nor Jew, but a new creation," cited explicitly later in the *Panarion* (*Anacephaleosis* 1.4.2, 1.9, 8.2). Yet the work is predicated on classical models, including Nicander. It also competes with them: for while the Greek authors, the poets and chroniclers, invoke the Muse, says Epiphanius, he will invoke the Lord of all (Praefatio 2.1.3).

Epiphanius shares the Eusebian view of the evolution of mankind through the centuries from barbarism to Christianity;[37] his treatise on heresies is part of a broader vision of the history and development of mankind according to the dispensation of God. It is, in other words, an apologetic vision, like that of Eusebius, whose work was well known to Epiphanius. At the same time, while following on from the work of his predecessors, Epiphanius set a definitive pattern for the rhetorical treatment of heretics in Byzantine literature. Aline Pourkier describes the technique as twofold: first exposition and then refutation.[38] The first involved the notion of a genealogy or family tree of heresies, their naming and classification, the delineation of a type of a typical heresiarch, and the attribution of ideas (not necessarily actually held), and the assimilation of one heresy to groups of others, so that all could be tarred with the same brush.[39] At the same time, the notion of a "genealogy" or family tree of heresies goes far toward explaining why Epiphanius and the later Byzantine heresiologists thought it important to record historical as well as contemporary heresies; their aim was to produce a traditio haereticorum, the perfect antithesis of the traditio legis.[40] The result of this maneuver has unfortunately been confusion and puzzlement for generations of scholars trying to understand the origins of later heresies that are described in terms applicable to earlier centuries, but the thinking behind it is understandable enough. Once the heresy or heresies had been caricatured in this way, the heresiologist would move on to the formal refutation, which might take one or more of several approaches: refutation by apparently rational argument, refutation from Scripture, refutation from tradition, and finally straightforward polemic: the resort to abuse, wordplay, rhetorical questions, exclamations, and so on—in many ways the direct antithesis of the rhetorical style and techniques that might be employed by the same writer in his homilies, but the close relative of contemporary writing directed against Jews.

What then did Epiphanius's Panarion establish about the writing of heresiology? Baroque though it may seem, this work enshrines certain fundamentals about heresiological literature. For example, it names the many heresies it wishes to condemn; in so doing it differentiates them from a stated norm and thereby defines the nature of that norm; it classifies, that is, it imposes an ordering on things according to the principles of the writer; it lays down a virtual hierarchy of heresies according to their origins; and finally it prescribes their nature, and thereby defines and lays down the structure of knowledge. As conceived in late antiquity, Christianity implied a structured system of explanation, covering everything from the natural world and the nature of history to anthropology and the nature of man. We can also see from the work of Epiphanius that the point of heresiology was not simply to record (and condemn) Christian sects. It was also intended to demonstrate the superiority of Christianity over paganism and Judaism, and to express the truth of orthodoxy. As we have seen, it was not enough to condemn; one had also to state the correct dogma. Thus the third part of the Panarion consists of an Expositio of the orthodox faith, and this is also what Theodoret of Cyrrhus does in his late Compendium, which illustrates the easy step, not quite yet taken by Epiphanius, from heresiology to producing what was effectively an encyclopedia of orthodoxy. John of Damascus's Fount of Knowledge is perhaps the best known and most conspicuous example of the genre, comprising both heresiology and a conspectus of orthodoxy—the negative and the positive, synthesis of what is allowed going hand in hand with condemnation of the aberrant.

Theodoret, writing in the fifth century, illustrates these developments very well. The *Compendium*, strictly the "Compendium of Heretical Myths," and still awaiting a critical edition, comprises five books on sects and heresies.[41] It cites the names of earlier heresiologists—Justin, Irenaeus, and so on—but takes its own line, and appropriately to the period, its emphasis is christological. Furthermore, Theodoret turns from the genealogical model to a synthetic one, classifying heresies by types.[42] As Ian Tompkins has argued, the first book contains an account of Marcionism (and this may be typical) that is allusive at best but more likely extremely distorted.[43] But the last book turns from heresiology to synthesis, from the listing of heresy to the statement of orthodoxy. Theodoret had his own line to pursue, and as a bishop he was also an energetic seeker out of heretics himself.[44] But that does not in itself explain his output in this field; by now, it is clear, heresiology has become a major enterprise, and it is no surprise when we find Theodoret sending a copy of Epiphanius's *Panarion* to Naukratios.[45] He lists his own antiheretical works as including writings against Arius, Eunomius, Apollinarius, and Marcion, against Jews and gentiles, a *Curatio* in twelve books against pagan beliefs, and the *Eranistes*, an extraordinary work consisting of three dialogues between an orthodox and an opponent expressing a variety of heretical positions, each dialogue with a *florilegium* attached of passages adduced to support the orthodox position.[46] Scholars have naturally been interested in the nature and source of the citations in the *florilegia*, but they ought to be equally curious about the work's very interesting form, one that was to be taken up by others in later centuries and that has close parallels with the dialogues in the *Adversus Iudaeos* tradition.

Scholars have noted a change over time in heresiology toward a more encyclopedic and less argumentative presentation, in which familiar positions are rehearsed rather than new arguments produced.[47] As I have suggested already, John of Damascus's treatise had many precedents, including the *Synodical Letter* of Sophronius, patriarch of Jerusalem in the 630s, with its attached list of heresies to be anathematized, or the patriarch Germanus's work on heresies and councils in the early eighth century, to name only two surviving examples.[48] It is facile, however, to see this tendency of merely copying out an existing model as a symptom of a genre that was running out of steam.[49] In the first place, writing against heresy took many forms, among which heresiology in the narrow sense of listings was only one. Even the latter still had a long life ahead of it. Further, the perceived need to combat error in whatever form, and indeed to label it as heresy, by no means came to an end in late antiquity with the supposed establishment of orthodoxy; on the contrary, it was to remain a fundamental and urgent aim in Christian writing throughout the Byzantine period. The notion that the genre was somehow becoming less necessary equally fails to take into account the many complex issues surrounding the legal and conciliar processes against heresy, which became so prominent a feature from late antiquity onward, and which indicate a lively interest in the matter.[50] Finally, like writing against Judaism, arguments against and condemnation of heresy can be found as an integral part of almost every type of Byzantine religious literature.[51] Our challenge is to understand why this was so, and what form it took.

Other factors encouraged this tendency toward listing rather than argument. Chief among them was the search for authoritative proof texts and their collection in specialized lists (florilegia), a process that can be seen from the fifth century onward. By the early iconoclastic period, when John of Damascus was writing, these were a major component in doctrinal argument.[52] Indeed, one can hardly exaggerate the importance attached in the large Byzantine literature dealing with heresy to the citation of earlier precedent. Substantial parts of the literary attack on heresy always depended on listing authorities and the repetition of orthodox definitions. We can see the same process in works on the councils such as that by Germanus of Constantinople (which also draws on Epiphanius but is now entitled, significantly, "On Heresies and Synods") and in their depiction in visual art.[53] At the conclusion of the Second Council of Nicaea in A.D. 787, the victorious iconophiles had a strong interest in endorsing their council as the seventh and culminating representative of a series already formally recognized.[54] They wanted to have it all ways: thus Tarasius termed the iconoclasts "Jews and Saracens, Hellenes and Samaritans, Manichaeans and phantasiasts, equal to Theopaschites."[55] Naming was all important, for it was far from clear that the iconoclasts were in fact heretics. The same drive to categorize had arisen in an earlier period in relation to the Donatists in late Roman North Africa, and Brent Shaw opens a recent study with the observation that one of the important texts for understanding the progress and the procedures of Catholic dealings with Donatists is in fact *Alice in Wonderland*.[56] "Who are you?" asks the Caterpillar when he sees Alice. And Alice replies, "I—I hardly know, Sir, just at present." Like Alice, the Donatists, and others considered to be heterodox, would be told by the dominant group just where they belonged in the pecking order.

The repetition of standard accusations and standard authorities is itself an important rhetorical technique. Polemical lists, of which there are many from late antiquity onward, are an obvious candidate for explanation in terms of labeling theory, as a technique whereby deviance is identified and embedded.[57] But the dismissal of works like that of John of Damascus as wholly academic and static fails to take into account the fact that they too were constantly being adapted to changed conditions. Thus the additional chapter on the "heresy" of Islam added to the part of the *Fount of Knowledge* dealing with heresies makes some attempt to describe the actual beliefs of Muslims, and is in fact the earliest attempt from the Byzantine side to do so. Overall, John's voluminous writings illustrate the actual flexibility of heresiology, its connections with the *Adversus Iudaeos* texts and its tendency to inform other types of writing and to spill over into other genres.

The claim that iconoclasm was a heresy and therefore fell within the realm of the techniques of heresiology was something that needed to be argued. The justification may not indeed fit well with modern ideas of what heresy is: thus, according to the ninth-century *Life of Niketas of Medikion*, iconoclasm is undoubtedly a heresy of the worst kind, both because it strikes at the very *oikonomia* of Christ and because it originated suddenly and in the very bosom of imperial power.[58] Neither argument is very convincing. Yet the assimilation was vital to the iconophile case. A useful example of official attitudes toward heretics had been given by the decrees of capital punishment issued against Montanists and "Manichaeans" by the iconoclast emperors Leo III and Constantine V and their attempted enforcement by Michael I.[59] Guilt by association was implied in the use of these and other classic labels. If iconoclasts could be consigned to the same category, the iconophile case was made.[60] Similarly, if Peter of Sicily in the ninth century could make a plausible case for classifying the Paulicians as Manichaeans, they too would fall within the scope of the laws just mentioned.[61] All that a heresiologist had to do was to draw on an established tradition and on well-established existing arguments against Manichaeanism.[62]

Few heresiologists were as inventive in amassing a vocabulary of denigration as the patriarch Nicephorus (patriarch 806–15), whose *Apologeticus* and *Antirrhetici* against the iconoclasts enabled their French translator to compile a whole lexicon of terms of abuse.[63] Again Nicephorus's aim is twofold—to set out the correct (orthodox) doctrine of images and to attack and disparage that of the iconoclasts. In order to achieve the latter part of his aim, he produced a three-pronged attack: iconoclasts are enemies of the holy, they are irrational, and they are the antithesis of culture and *oikonomia*. The Jews and Hellenes, like the familiar triad of Arius, Apollinarius, and Eutyches, are cited for comparison: the iconoclasts are like them, or worse. The language of heresiology, like the language commonly employed about Jews, easily turns into the language of scorn and the vocabulary of abuse.[64] Similarly, in ninth-century illuminated psalters, iconoclasts are directly equated with heretics. Thus in the Chludov and Pantokrator psalters, John the Grammarian is likened to Simon Magus, the head and leader of all heresies, according to the Acts of the Second Council of Nicaea and many earlier texts.[65] Not surprisingly, heretics are also, and even more frequently, equated with Jews, in an elision of anti-Jewish, antiheretical and anti-iconoclast rhetoric.[66]

As I have argued, heresiology has much in common with the *Adversus Iudaeos* literature, but it has not shared in the interest that the latter has recently aroused, nor has it stimulated the same speculation as to its relation to "reality" or its implications for Byzantine attitudes.[67] Why so many dialogues against Jews continued to be written through the Byzantine period, and the nature of their relation to the actual situation of Christians and Jews—for instance in connection with the decrees of forced baptism of Jews issued by Heraclius, Leo III, and Basil I—remain difficult questions.[68] It tends to be forgotten that heresiologies also continued, and at times overlapped with the anti-Jewish texts. How and why the two types of writing interact is a story yet to be fully told.

At least in its written culture, Byzantium was a debating society. Richard Lim has drawn attention to the importance of debate in late antiquity, whether in the form of public disputation or in writing.[69] Much of the most striking late antique evidence concerns Manichaeans, in whose case a precedent had been set in 302 by Diocletian, a pagan emperor, who ordered their condemnation and the burning of their books,[70] and it is clear that dealings with the Manichaeans provided ample instruction for the development of process against heretics. In the well-known case of Augustine, written treatises and actual debate worked together in the formulation of Augustine's arguments against Manichaeans and Donatists. Augustine was caught by the "burning zeal for disputations" through his experience of them when he was a Manichee himself,[71] and undoubtedly the treatment of Manichaeans set many examples for the future; even repeated and ferocious imperial legislation was not enough in itself to suppress the heresy, and had to be accompanied by an astonishing amount of anti-Manichaean writing and argument.[72] Manichaeism also provided a label; how useful that was can be seen from the fact that the later Augustine could still be attacked as "a new Manichaean."[73] In this way Manichaeism provided both the exemplar and vocabulary for later antiheretical works.

In general, internal Christian disputes, beginning in the earliest centuries, intensified in late antiquity and continued throughout the Byzantine period. The disputes led to a large literature of debate, which could be both apologetic and polemical. Indeed, it would not be an exaggeration to say that this huge literature, of which heresiology forms a part, is one of the features that characterize late antique and Byzantine Christian culture. I have argued elsewhere that it formed an important element in Christian pedagogy, that is, in the formation of a Christian intellectual system.[74] Confrontation, labeling, and the listing of authorities can all be seen as part of this process. In the *Adversus Iudaeos* texts of late antiquity we tend to find confrontations, real or fictive, between Jews and Christians, or even, as in the so-called *Trophies of Damascus*, a text from the seventh century, between "Hellenes, Saracens, Samaritans, many Jews and Christians, in a word, a large number of spectators."[75] The end of this dialogue contains an obviously fictionalized "narrative" of the discomfiture of the Jews after their debate and their recognition that the Christian had won the argument. Significantly, the same author also composed a listing of all heresies from Arius onward as part of a refutation of the Monophysites.[76] Thus, while there is a connection apparent from the earliest stages between Christian heresiology and anti-Jewish writing (which certainly needs more exploration), both belong to this culture of debate and dispute that became so embedded in early Christian and later in Byzantine discourse.[77] Both, again, raise profound and difficult issues about the level of intolerance within early Christianity.[78]

It has often been remarked that real persecution—and, in particular, execution—for heresy was relatively rare in Byzantium, especially in comparison with persecution in the medieval West. This is worth remarking, in view of the increased severity of legal penalties in late antiquity, and the topic certainly needs more study.[79] But over the centuries the denunciation of heresy in Byzantium became both shriller and more thoroughly ritualized. It was also made visible. The removal of names from the patriarchal diptychs, on the pattern of the Roman *damnatio memoriae*, is one example, and it began at an early stage. It was a visible and public act, which at the same time underlined the degree to which the official denial of orthodoxy was a matter of real power and competition. Justinian decreed that his edicts should be posted in churches,[80] and the battles over heresy, as happened in the course of the Monothelete controversy of the seventh century, were often conducted by literally pinning manifestoes to the doors of S. Sophia in Constantinople. Another manifestation of this public visibility lay in the records of councils, which involved not only complex matters of procedure and verification but also the control of attendance lists and the carefully structured control of the *acta*, or in essence, the minutes, a procedure highly familiar to anyone who is concerned in our own day with getting decisions through committees and making sure they have any chance of being carried out afterward.[81] It has even been shown that the acta of later councils were commonly composed before the meeting actually took place, and that spaces were simply left for signatures to be appropriately filled in. There were complex legal issues involved, and the proceedings of councils have been likened to senatorial precedent, condemnation of heretics being like the Roman trials for treason.[82] The formal reading of the *Synodikon of Orthodoxy* (the defeat of iconoclasm having been significantly, if inaccurately, defined in terms of the establishment of orthodoxy) during the Lenten liturgy is another example of this ritualization, and no one apparently thought it odd that it should be revised as new heretics came along. This was done even as late as the Palamite controversy in the fourteenth century, and was accompanied in typically Byzantine manner by the depiction of the reading of the anathemas as a scene in visual art.

The liturgical character of the *Synodikon* is apparent from many details in the textual tradition, and it was read from the ambo like the Gospel and the homily.[83] Like the epigraphic recording of imperial edicts, it was also engraved on tablets in S. Sophia.[84] Above all, it became, even if it did not originate as such, a public and a political document. Even its earliest form listed a roll call of orthodox, that is, iconophile, clerics, the purpose of which was the exclusion of the opposite side from the approved record. The list of four orthodox (iconophile) patriarchs is followed, predictably, by anathemas on heretics; thus we see again in this document, as in the literary heresiologies, orthodox exposition juxtaposed with condemnation of heresy.[85] The *Synodikon* is only the most conspicuous example.[86]

There are many and deep questions to be asked about Byzantine attitudes to heresy: Was there a gap between language and practice, and if so, how did this come about? Who in fact read all these treatises? What is the relation of Byzantine discourses about heresy to the condemnation of pagans and Jews? Why was such a premium placed on the seemingly unachievable ideal of a pure orthodoxy? What does this tell us about the nature of Byzantine culture and society? None of these questions can be answered without first analyzing the texts, especially in terms of their rhetorical techniques, a prerequisite urged indeed by Elizabeth Clark for the writing of church history. This essay cannot answer these questions; rather, it simply seeks to raise the issue of heresiological discourse as something that needs to be addressed rather urgently.

How then—to return to my title—should one learn to read heresiology? I am aware, first of all, that we have not yet even defined what it is that we are "reading": even allowing for their derivativeness and repetitiveness (in some cases), heresiological treatises in fact come in many different shapes and forms. Dismissing heresiology as sterile or boring, as a mere scholastic exercise, therefore misses several points at the same time. To explain it as the product of insecurity and ascetic closure—both explanations favored by me in the past—now seems too reductionist in the first case, and too ready to take Byzantium on its own terms in the second.[87] We can of course read these contests as a power game between individuals or groups, or as the politics of the early Christian world. It remains the case that many modern critics, both of late antiquity and Byzantium, remain uncomfortable with the idea that theological argument needs to be taken seriously as a historical factor; but in this they could learn much from the historiography of other periods, such as Reformation history. Whether we like it or not as historians, writing heresy, in all its various forms, did occupy a major place in Byzantium—so much so indeed that a full treatment would in its way constitute a new history of Byzantium. This is far from having been written as yet.[88] But meanwhile, at the very least, I suggest that one ought to read these compositions, so strange to our minds, as part of Byzantine pedagogy and the Byzantine sociology of knowledge, as self-perpetuating constructions that helped to formulate thought and underpin social norms in the Christian society of Byzantium.[89]

Notes

1. Hence one is grateful for the collection edited by Elm, Rebillard, and Romano, *Orthodoxie, christianisme, histoire*. I take the reference to literature as a "Cinderella" from Margaret Mullett, a notable pioneer in the effort to change the situation.
2. For Epiphanius, see further below; for earlier heresiology, which was already well established by the late second century, see in the first place Le Boulluec, *La notion d'hérésie*. For heresiology as a genre, and a list of examples in Greek and Latin up to ca. 430, see Inglebert, "L'histoire des hérésies."
3. See, however, Sillet, "Culture of Controversy"; Tompkins, "The Relations between Theodoret of Cyrrhus and His City"; Urbainczyk, *Theodoret of Cyrrhus*; and see below.

4. Timothy of Constantinople, *De receptione haereticorum*, in Migne, *Patrologia Graeca* (hereafter PG) 86:1.13–68; Nicephorus, see further below. A work on "sects" with similar listings, also beginning with Hebrews and Samaritans (PG 86:1.1194–1265), is ascribed in the manuscripts to Leontius of Byzantium (sixth century); see van Esbroek, "La date et l'auteur."

5. Gouillard, ed., "Le Synodikon d'orthodoxie."

6. There is a vast literature, constantly increasing. A classic is Moore, *Formation of a Persecuting Society*; Merlo, ed., *Eretici e eresia medievali*, contains substantial bibliographical surveys; and see Le Goff, ed., *Hérésies et sociétés*. But there is almost always a gap where Byzantium should be.

7. Woolf, review of Cameron, *Christianity and the Rhetoric of Empire*.

8. Clark, *Origenist Controversy*. This essay builds on lectures and seminars delivered in a number of places, including the Oxford Patristic Conference, the conference of the Australian Association of Byzantine Studies held at Macquarie University in July 1999, and at Reading and Lund Universities and elsewhere in Sweden. I am grateful for all those invitations and opportunities for discussion.

9. See R. Le Coz, *Jean Damascène*, with discussion of authenticity and numbering. The number of heresies gradually accumulated between Epiphanius and John of Damascus: see McClure, "Handbooks against Heresy." Another who drew on Epiphanius was Augustine, in his unfinished *De haeresibus*.

10. Gouillard, "L'hérésie dans l'empire," 301–2. It is perhaps indicative that, as Gouillard points out, there is as yet no book which attempts to address the place of heresy in Byzantine culture as a whole. But the very title he has chosen for his article (heresy, not heresiology) is revealing of an attitude which is looking for the real heresy behind the texts. Gouillard's view of heresy is also limited on the whole to the dogmatic, whereas even contemporaries debated whether heresy extended to ritual and behavior as well as doctrine. For good discussion, see Kolbaba, *Byzantine Lists*, 88–101.

11. Ibid., 301.

12. Euthymius Zigabenus, PG 130. This *panoplia*, too, began early with Epicureanism and took the listing up to the Paulicians and Bogomils of Euthymius's own day.

13. Nicetas Choniates, *Treasury*, PG 139–40. Again we find the notion of collecting all heresies together.

14. PG 301.

15. Paulician texts are edited by C. Astruc, W. Conus-Wolska, J. Gouillard, P. Lemerle, D. Papachryssanthou, and J. Paramelle in *Travaux et Mémoires* 4 (1970): 2–227; see also the translations of texts on the Paulicians and Bogomils in Hamilton and Hamilton, *Christian Dualist Heresies*. Not trusting the texts they present, the editors frequently refer to "alleged" Paulicians and the like. Following this line of argument, see also C. Ludwig, "The Paulicians and Ninth-Century Byzantine Thought," 23–35. Studies of dualist beliefs include Garsoian, *Paulician Heresy*; Lemerle, "L'histoire des Pauliciens"; Loos, *Dualist Heresy*; Obolensky, *Bogomils*; Stoyanov, *Hidden Tradition*. Against social, regional, and dualist interpretations of the Paulicians, see Garsoian, "Byzantine Heresy."

16. Gouillard, "L'hérésie," 324, rightly calls for more critical editions: "l'austère

critique des sources sans laquelle il n'est pas de synthèse qui vaille"; my point here is rather one of methodological approach.

17. See Walter, "Heretics in Byzantine Art."

18. Browning, "Enlightenment and Repression"; cf. Smythe, "Alexios I and the Heretics"; also Smythe, "Outsiders by Taxis."

19. Ibid., 14–19. Admittedly, Alexios himself made this into a state affair.

20. Ibid., 14. For the dossier of documents surrounding the trial, see, however, Gouillard, "Le procès officiel de Jean l'Italien." The dossier does not include the synodal Semeiosis, but it was these anathemas which were included in the Synodikon. The matter is admittedly more complex than I suggest here, and Gouillard underlines the extent to which the emperor did seek to control and direct the synod, though he concludes that "la nature réelle de l'enjeu nous échappe" (169).

21. Angold, Church and Society. According to Angold, Emperor Alexios's synchronization of John Italos's trial with the celebration of the Feast of Orthodoxy was the emperor's "most brilliant stroke" (51). Of course a rhetorical analysis of the texts in no way precludes recognition of political manipulation. See also Agapitos, "Teachers, Pupils and Imperial Power," 184–87. To adapt Kolbaba, Byzantine Lists, 171, "religion is not all theology"; but equally, neither is it all politics.

22. For discussion see Kolbaba, Byzantine Lists, introduction.

23. See Stewart, Working the Earth, 33.

24. See Cameron, "Jews and Heretics"; and on the accusation of being a Judaizer in the seventh century, Dagron, "Judaïser," though the accusation is ubiquitous.

25. Abjuration formulae were prescribed for repentent heretics and some survive, both from the anti-Manichaean context and from later periods. Cf. Timothy of Constantinople, De receptione haereticorum; also canons 71 and 95 of the Quinisext Council of 691, following a precedent set already in the canons of Nicaea in 325 (cf. canon 8). For a later period, see the important article by Patlagean, "Aveux et désaveux," which points to the intensification of the evidence for trials and abjuration procedures from the eleventh century on, and likewise to the production of yet more encyclopedic heresiological works.

26. See Stoyanov, Hidden Tradition in Europe, 129, 131, 209.

27. Epiphanius's Panarion is edited by K. Holl, in Ancoratus und Panarion, hereafter cited parenthetically in the text; English translation by Williams, Panarion; partial translation also by Amidon, Panarion of St. Epiphanius. See Pourkier, L'hérésiologie chez Epiphane; Lyman, "Making of a Heretic" and "Origen as Ascetic Theologian"; also Lyman, "Ascetics and Bishops: Epiphanius and Orthodoxy," in Elm, Rebillard, and Romano, eds., Orthodoxie, christianisme, histoire, 149–61. See also Cameron, "Jews and Heretics."

28. See Pourkier, L'hérésiologie chez Epiphane, 81–82, 93–114; Vallée, Study in Anti-Gnostic Polemics, 63–69.

29. See Dummer, "Ein naturwissenschaftliches Handbuch."

30. Young, From Nicaea to Chalcedon, 133; cf. Young, "Did Epiphanius Know What He Meant by 'Heresy'?"

31. See, however, Pourkier, L'hérésiologie chez Epiphane, for detailed discussion of Epiphanius's sources.

32. Young, *From Nicaea to Chalcedon*, 134, 138.
33. Vallée, *Study in Anti-Gnostic Polemics*, 74.
34. Epiphanius, *Panarion*, Praefatio 2.1.3, ed. Holl; cf. Dummer, "Ein naturwissenschaftliches Handbuch."
35. Samaritanism being a Jewish heresy, not a Christian one. However, Epiphanius was not the first in this: see Cameron, "Jews and Heretics."
36. Much has been written on the development of the term "heresy" in the Christian sense. Epiphanius uses it in the pejorative sense, to include schism (a disagreement about matters other than doctrine).
37. The inverse, as it happens, of the view held by Tatian and Clement of Alexandria of Christianity as the "barbarian philosophy" in contrast to Greek *paideia*. See Stroumsa, *Barbarian Philosophy*.
38. Pourkier, *L'hérésiologie chez Epiphane*, 486–95; Vallée, *Study in Anti-Gnostic Polemics*, 68–69, 73: "E. has no equal in the history of heresiology for the art of insulting."
39. On the genealogical approach in heresiology, see Le Boulluec, *La notion d'hérésie*; Burrus, *Making of a Heretic*; Elm, "Polemical Use of Genealogies"; Buell, *Making Christians*.
40. Vallée, *Study of Anti-Gnostic Polemics*, 70.
41. Theodoret's *Compendium* may be found in PG 83:335–556.
42. See Helen Sillet, "Orthodoxy and Heresy in Theodoret of Cyrus's Compendium of Heresies," in Elm, Rebillard, and Romano, eds., *Orthodoxie, christianisme, histoire*, 261–73, esp. 263–67.
43. See note 3. Admittedly there is room for argument as to why this should be so, i.e., what sources Theodoret was using.
44. For Theodoret the bishop and his agenda in the *Historia Religiosa*, see Urbainczyk, *Theodoret of Cyrrhus*.
45. Theodoret of Cyrrhus, *Epistula* 4.22–25, ed. Azéma.
46. Theodoret lists antiheretical works in *Epistula* 146. Theodoret, *Curatio*, ed. Canivet; see Canivet, *Histoire d'une entreprise*; Theodoret, *Eranistes*, ed. Ettlinger. The date of the work is probably 447, and Eutyches was condemned in 448 (3–4).
47. See Sillet, "Orthodoxy and Heresy," 262–63. Kolbaba, *Byzantine Lists*, emphasizes that the texts she discusses take a similar or even more stereotyped form, but also that they were by no means the only heresiological works directed against the Latins in Middle Byzantium.
48. For the anathemas, see Sophronius, PG 87:3.3189–92, 3193, also included in the documents of the Sixth Ecumenical Council: Germanus, *De haeresibus et synodis*, PG 98:40–88, again without critical edition. Gouillard, "Le Synodikon," 306–7, comments that Germanus was not original, but again that is because Gouillard is looking for historical evidence about actual heresy. For other examples see Munitiz, "Synoptic Greek Accounts." Munitiz comments that "the [later] synoptic accounts of the Councils offer little attraction at first sight" (177). But they make their own contribution to the persuasive power of the sheer repetition of orthodox doctrine. Moreover, the anathemas of the councils themselves provided the subject matter for heresiology and constituted the official and legal record.

49. Vallée, *Study of Anti-Gnostic Polemics*, 5–6. On John of Damascus, see Louth, *St. John Damascene*.

50. For the incorporation of legal arguments in the literature, see Caroline Humfress, "Roman Law, Forensic Argument and the Formation of Christian Orthodoxy (III–VI Centuries)," in Elm, Rebillard, and Romano, eds., *Christianisme, orthodoxie, histoire*, 125–47. Lists of anathemas were also attached to conciliar documents. For the later standing court which acted in such matters, see Hajjar, *Le synode permanente*.

51. For this tendency in relation to Judaism, see Cameron, "Blaming the Jews."

52. See Cameron, "Texts as Weapons." For this development as shown in the evidence of the sixth- to eighth-century councils, see Alexakis, *Codes Parisinus Graecus* 1115.

53. Walter, *L'iconographie des conciles*. Walter makes a striking connection between the iconography of councils and the emphasis in early Christian art on scenes of teaching and instruction (187–98).

54. Munitiz, "Synoptic Greek Accounts," 175.

55. Mansi 157 E, cited by Speck, *Ich bin's nicht* 25. Speck's book memorably traces the blackening of the name of the iconoclast Constantine V in the "orthodox" sources. In the thirteenth-century *Treasury* of Theognostos, for example, we find the anathemas of II Nicaea against the leaders of the "impious" Council of 754 (ed. J. Munitiz, Corpus Christianorum series graeca 5 [Turnhout-Leuven: Peeters, 1979], 203–22).

56. Shaw, "African Christianity."

57. For this and other theories of deviance, see Sanders, *Schismatics, Sectarians*, 129–51; Mullett, "The 'Other' in Byzantium." Byzantines were also famously snobbish about the superiority of their own culture and society when compared to those of any others; see also Kolbaba, *Byzantine Lists*, 133–36.

58. *Acta Sanctorum*, April I.23.

59. Gouillard, "Le Synodikon," 308–10. On Michael I, see Theophanes Confessor, *Chronographia*, 1:494–95; with Alexander, "Religious Persecution and Resistance," 239. The extent of the actual persecution under iconoclasm is open to question, but is beyond the scope of this study.

60. Marie-France Auzépy has recently underlined the sticky ground on which the Seventh Council found itself in condemning a particular form of worship rather than deviation from dogma: "Manifestations de la propagande en faveur de l'orthodoxie," in Brubaker, ed., *Byzantium in the Ninth Century*, 85–99, esp. 87, 93.

61. See Ludwig, "Paulicians and Ninth-Century Byzantine Thought," 29–34.

62. For the argument that there was a revival of concern about Manichaeanism in the early Islamic period, in response to a real encounter on the Islamic side, see Stroumsa, "Aspects de la polémique antimanichéenne," 376–77; cf. Riggi, *Epifanio contro Mani*. Manichaeanism continued to provide a model for many centuries; for example, Augustine's anti-Manichaean arguments were known to Western writers on the Cathars.

63. See Mondzain-Baudinet, *Nicephore*; cf. Speck, *Ich bin's nicht*.

64. Cameron, "Texts as Weapons."

65. See Corrigan, *Visual Polemics*, 27–28.
66. Ibid., 30–37 and chap. 3.
67. For the anti-Jewish literature, see Stroumsa and Limor, eds., *Contra Iudaeos*; Cameron, "Blaming the Jews," with further bibliography.
68. See particularly the contributions by Dagron and Déroche in *Travaux et Mémoires* 11 (1991).
69. Lim, *Public Disputation, Power, and Social Order* and "Christian Triumph and Controversy."
70. See Lieu, *Manichaeism*, 97, 157.
71. Augustine, *De duabus animabus* 11, cited by Lim, *Public Disputation*, 90.
72. See Lieu, *Manichaeism in the Later Roman Empire* and *Manichaeism in Mesopotamia*; Lim, *Public Disputation*, chap. 3. On laws against Manichaeans, see Lim, *Public Disputation*, 104; and on anti-Manichaean writings, see the list in Lieu, *Manichaeism in Mesopotamia*, 197–202.
73. Lieu, *Manichaeism in the Later Roman Empire*, chap. 6. Technically, Manichaeism remained on the books until an amazingly late date, as even did Donatism. Lieu believes that Justinian's persecution of Manichaeans resulted in the extermination of the sect, and sees the continued use of the term by heresiologists as a useful rhetorical feature adopted by them (215). Lim accepts that Manichaeism ceased to be a force in the Byzantine empire after the sixth century and argues for a general closure on religious debate (*Public Disputation*, chap. 7); but this is not borne out by the later Byzantine evidence.
74. Cameron, "Education and Literary Culture," in Cameron and Garnsey, eds., *Cambridge Ancient History* 13:665–707, esp. 702–4. For both heretical and antiheretical writings as pedagogy in the medieval West, see, e.g., Copeland, *Pedagogy, Intellectuals, and Dissent*.
75. Bardy, ed., *Les trophées de Damas*, 233–34.
76. Ibid., 277ff.
77. See Cameron, "Jews and Heretics"; and Cameron, "Apologetics."
78. See Cameron, "Apologetics."
79. For the *summa supplicia* in relation to heretics (only once in the Theodosian Code, when there is an association with Manichaeans), see D. Grodzynski, "Tortures mortelles et categories sociales," 380; J. Callu, "Le jardin des supplices au Bas-Empire," ibid., 313–59, at 344–45.
80. Justinian, *Novellae* 6.1.
81. See Alexakis, *Codex Parisinus Graecus* 1115, chap. 1. For a vivid exposition of the lengths to which this process could go, see Brandes, "Orthodoxy and Heresy"; and cf. Chrysos, *He ekklesiastike politike tou Ioustinianou* and "Konzilsakten und Konzilsprotokolle."
82. See Walter, *L'iconographie des conciles*, 125–26, 151–55.
83. Gouillard, "Le Synodikon," 12–13.
84. Walter, *L'iconographie des conciles*, 161.
85. On the origins of the Synodikon, see Gouillard, "Le Synodikon," 141ff.
86. Cf., for instance, the *Synaxarion* or the *Menologion* of Basil II; see Walter, "Heretics in Byzantine Art," 159–60.

87. Cf. Averil Cameron, "Ascetic Closure and the End of Antiquity," in Wimbush and Valantasis, eds., *Asceticism*, 147–61.
88. But Dagron, *Emperor and Priest*, presents a powerful case for the competition and uncertainty which (contrary to popular impressions) were characteristic of Byzantine political life. Likewise Kolbaba, *The Byzantine Lists*, 102–23 argues for the complexity of Byzantine religion, which left room for "gray areas between doctrine and ritual."
89. See Douglas, *How Institutions Think*; Douglas and Hull, eds., *How Classification Works*; Goodman, *Ways of Worldmaking*.

✝ Ascetic Practice and the Genealogy of Heresy:

Problems in Modern Scholarship and

Ancient Textual Representation

TERESA M. SHAW

In the past twenty-five years, analysis of the ancient and modern categories of orthodoxy and heresy has figured prominently in late ancient historical study. This interest and activity have been stimulated in no small part by the publication of Alain Le Boulluec's study on the "notion of heresy" in early Christian discourse.[1] Influenced by contemporary theory and new textual resources as well as the pioneering work of Walter Bauer, Le Boulluec shifted the discussion of heresy away from questions of chronological priority and geographical distinctions to the "representation" of heresy in early Christian texts. He traced the ways that authors such as Justin and Irenaeus used the concept of hairesis to create rhetorical categories of difference and deviance in behavior and belief that could be identified and traced back through a genealogical succession of teachers and disciples, and thus could be used to justify exclusion. Le Boulluec argued that "heresy," as well as "orthodoxy," far from being the stable and consistent entities that these and other representations suggest, are "contingent" constructions and the products "of the historical process." Moreover, he observed that modern scholars continually face the challenge of interpreting ancient texts, which both assume and perpetuate these constructions, without "reproducing the discourse" in our own analyses.[2]

Le Boulluec's study is both representative of and influential in a larger body of research that seeks to recast the study of "orthodoxy" and "heresy" with sensitivity to the dangers of historically contingent categories and the problems of reading ancient texts, as well as attention to gender, sexuality, constructions of deviance, and other social and political factors that may have influenced ancient debate. Thus recent studies have challenged scholars to "rethink" previous understandings of "heretical" individuals and groups, understandings that in many ways relied on ancient genealogies and labels developed in the agonistic context of theological dispute and its aftermath.[3] Moreover, recent scholarship has questioned the facile association of "heresy" as a static category with certain forms of ascetic behavior and ascetic groups or communities. Here the focus of work by scholars such as Elizabeth Clark, James Goehring, Samuel Rubenson, Susanna Elm, and Daniel Caner has been to challenge previous conceptions of uniformity and consensus in both early Christian ascetic practice itself and in the interpretation of "legitimate" ascetic motivations and theological justifications. In particular, these scholars question the historical reliability of the hagiographical and heresiological images of earliest monasticism, its institutions and practices, its famous leaders (such as Antony and Pachomius), and its famous deviants and heretical extremists (such as Eustathius of Sebaste, Evagrius of Pontus, Hieracas of Egypt, the "Messalians," or the "Melitians").[4]

With this essay I hope to contribute to the ongoing discussion of the construction of heresy, especially as related to ascetic behavior, by analyzing a Greek treatise on the virginal life attributed to Athanasius of Alexandria and by discussing its interpretation in modern scholarship. In particular, I will consider how ancient and modern categories of heretical asceticism have influenced the scholarly reception of the text. Edited by Eduard von der Goltz in 1905, the text is preserved in manuscripts dating only as early as the tenth century, and there is no definitive attestation regarding the treatise prior to the eighth century.[5] Two different titles appear in the manuscripts: "Discourse on Salvation to a Virgin" (*Logos sôtêrias pros tên parthenon*) and "On Virginity, or On Asceticism" (*Peri parthenias êtoi peri askêseôs*). Of these, the former title is generally regarded as earlier, and I will use it in this essay.[6] While the majority of authors who have discussed the *Discourse on Salvation* agree that its content and themes are consistent with a fourth-century date, they have tended to reject the claim to Athanasian authorship on a number of grounds that I will discuss below, one of which is the type and intensity of ascetic discipline.

I will make no argument for or against authenticity; rather, I will focus on the scholarly and historical assumptions concerning the asceticism advocated and represented by the author.[7] After describing the contents of the text briefly, I will discuss in more detail those features of the text that strike scholars as evidence that Athanasius did not write the *Discourse* or, further, that the text represents a suspect or heretical tendency to extremism in early Christian asceticism. The *Discourse* presents us with another challenge to both ancient and received schemes for classifying behavior and belief and to the literary ideal of Egyptian monasticism that developed in part, as it happens, in relation to the events and conflicts of Athanasius's career. Although Ferdinand Cavallera, in his brief discussion, describes the *Discourse on Salva-*

tion to a Virgin as "a true jewel of ascetic literature,"[8] the text has not been prominent in recent discussions of late ancient asceticism and female virginity. I will argue that because the text has been studied only in relation to questions of Athanasian authorship, Athanasius becomes normative for evaluating ascetic ideology and ascetic practice, Athanasian views become representative of "orthodox" monasticism, and thus the behavior in the treatise becomes problematic. I will suggest that we should instead consider the ascetic ethic of the text apart from questions of authorship and focus on the specific behaviors described in order to contribute to our understanding of late ancient ascetic piety. In this way, my study is influenced by recent scholarship and discussion on the topics of asceticism, heresy, and identity.

The treatise exhibits all of the features we have come to expect in the genre of the *de virginitate*, including the praise of virginity and its superior status, the portrayal of the virgin as the bride of Christ, warnings about associating with certain people, and specific instructions about daily lifestyle, appearance, and ascetic practices.[9] Particular emphasis on the hours of prayer, the recitation of psalms, the endurance of suffering and hardship in this world and the rewards of the kingdom, the importance of a rule for the ascetic life, the value of fasting, and the struggle against wicked thoughts (*logismoi*) distinguish the work.[10] But it is also distinguished by what it does *not* have. While it begins with an account of the creation of the world and the first humans, an affirmation of trinitarian faith, and a comparison of earthly marriage and marriage to Christ the heavenly bridegroom, the discourse develops no extended theological treatment of virginity and its role in creation and salvation, such as we find in Gregory of Nyssa or Basil of Ancyra. Further, the author makes no warning against specific theological opponents or heretical teachers of the type we find in works on virginity by Athanasius, John Chrysostom, Jerome, and others. Instead we find only very general condemnations of worldly and foolish people and the traps of Satan or "the enemy." If there is any defensive posture in the text, it is found in the author's repeated emphasis on keeping the commandments and enduring suffering in this world in imitation of Christ. The author reinforces this by encouraging the virgin to keep to her rule and her ascetic discipline in the face of those who, provoked by "the enemy," want to see her fail and so encourage her either to slacken or intensify her *askêsis* (3–4, 6, 8, 12, 18–19, 22–23). While this defense of ascetic discipline is pronounced in the text, it is not unique, and again there are no particular individuals or groups who appear to be in conflict with the author or recipients.

The virgin addressed in the text lives at home or in a small group of virgin "soul mates" under a rule and under the watchful and experienced authority of a female elder (*presbytis*).[11] The instructions on prayer, meals, and psalmody assume private rituals or very small groups (9–10, 12–13, 20, 22). The virgin should observe her *askêsis*, pray, sing psalms, and read in private for fear of vainglory, yet she may reveal her life and share her ascetic piety with a few virgins whose souls are in harmony with hers (9–10, 20). Likewise the text describes private meals and prayers at meals, noting the presence of others as an alternative, for example, "*if* two or three virgins are present with you, let them give thanks for the bread lying before you and join you in prayer" or "*if* you should sit at table with other virgins" (13, 22, emphasis added). In addition to private and small group ritual, the virgin attends church, where she should keep silent and avoid laughter, giving her attention only to the reading, psalms, and prayers, and banishing the idle thoughts (*logismoi*) that try to enter her heart (23). The author does not mention male clergy, but instructs the virgin to remember the "slaves of God" and keep them in her heart. Further, he tells her that if a "holy man" should come to her home she should receive him as if he were the son of God, and if a "righteous man" should visit, she is to prostrate herself before him, wash his feet, and listen to his words reverently (22).

Modern discussions of the *Discourse on Salvation* have focused exclusively on the question of authorship, especially Athanasian authorship, and have tended (with the principal exception of Eduard von der Goltz's discussion, published with his 1905 edition of the text) to reject Athanasian origins on several grounds, including textual attestation, style and vocabulary, theological formulae, use of scripture, evidence for the role of the church and its clergy, and the ascetic regimen and understanding of virginity described and advocated in the text. While this essay will focus in particular on the questions related to ascetic practice, it will be useful first to review some of the other arguments. Doubts concerning the manuscripts' claim of Athanasian authorship date as early as Erasmus, who translated the work into Latin in the sixteenth century,[12] but the modern discussion was stimulated primarily by Pierre Batiffol's 1893 essay arguing against attribution to Athanasius and von der Goltz's 1905 argument for authenticity.[13] Regarding textual history and attestation, the facts that the earliest extant manuscript for the *Discourse on Salvation* dates to the tenth century and that the earliest known witness to the text is a late eight-century letter from Hadrian to Charlemagne do not inspire scholars' confidence in Athanasian authorship.[14] In addition, some argue that the author's style and vocabulary are not compatible with what is found in sources accepted as genuinely Athanasian. The writing style and character, in contrast to what one expects from a "great bishop,"[15] seem to the modern scholar "primitive," "flat," and full of "vulgarisms."[16] Batiffol observes, "the general tone of the writer gives the impression that he speaks not with the authority of a bishop of Alexandria, but only with the zeal of a very fervent ascetic."[17] The author's vocabulary, likewise, is suspicious: Michel Aubineau counted 121 words in the treatise that are not found in the vocabulary of the Athanasian writings generally regarded as authentic.[18]

The *Discourse on Salvation* begins with an exhortation to trinitarian faith in Father, Son, and Holy Spirit, "three hypostases, one divinity, one power, one baptism" (1). Brakke and others note that while Athanasius did not criticize the phrase "three hypostases, one divinity" as unorthodox or problematic, neither did he use the phrase himself in any of his undisputed writings. Brakke concludes that it is "doubtful that Athanasius spoke of God as having 'three hypostases,' " and that "the presence of the phrase in the present work is suspicious, though perhaps not decisive."[19] In addition to the theological formula, scholars have questioned the author's use of some noncanonical texts as authoritative, arguing that this could not be the same person who set down the accepted canon of scripture in his thirty-ninth *Festal Letter.*[20] Finally, some have observed that the lack of emphasis on ecclesiastical authority or the role of clergy (a topic to which I will return in more depth below) is not compatible with an author who wields episcopal authority and struggles to assert that authority over ascetic men and women.[21]

These arguments demonstrate that, in the effort to identify or define the authoritative list of authentic Athanasian writings on asceticism in the face of a bewildering array of manuscripts claiming legitimacy,[22] a key criterion is the resonance of textual elements and themes with the Athanasius we think we already know from a more or less recognized textual corpus. This is of course a reasonable and careful approach, but in the case of a dominant and weighty personality such as Athanasius, who is the subject of a long tradition of scholarship with its own heavy stakes, the momentum of that scholarship tends to be toward the establishment of consistency and conformity both in texts and in historical personalities. Thus if scholars read and interpret a text such as the *Discourse on Salvation* primarily in comparison to one who, like Athanasius, is already so closely related in scholarly discourse to a historical category of "orthodoxy," they risk forcing that text to represent suspect or heretical views to the extent that it does not fit the Athanasian mold.[23] In this way, ancient heresiological and modern scholarly constructions of both Athanasian "orthodoxy" *and* ascetic "heresy" are adopted and perpetuated through research and analysis of historical evidence. The analysis of the

Discourse on Salvation illustrates J. Rebecca Lyman's point that "when historians accept the self-definition of orthodoxy, other conflicting facets of belief or institution are marginalized."[24]

Regarding the ascetic lifestyle advocated and represented in the *Discourse on Salvation*, which will be the focus of the remainder of this essay, several features of the author's instructions and the virgin's regimen strike modern interpreters as suspiciously enthusiastic (and therefore non-Athanasian) or even heretical. In the following pages, I will describe in some detail the features of the text most relevant to these issues, and outline the response of scholars who argue against Athanasian authorship. In this way I hope to provide the reader with a good sense of the ascetic tone and content of the treatise as well as the points on which scholars reject authenticity. I will also describe relevant comparisons to other Athanasian and Pseudo-Athanasian writings on virginity in the notes. Pierre Batiffol's 1893 argument against attribution to the bishop of Alexandria is built primarily around issues of the theory and interpretation of *askêsis* and virginity as well as the ascetic practice itself, and several subsequent discussions have included an evaluation of the ascetic vision, usually as compared to an Athanasian standard.[25] Some scholars point to the interpretation of virginity and its relationship to marriage and to "the world." As presented in the *Discourse on Salvation*, the path for the "slave of Christ and all who wish to be saved" (*doulê tou Christou kai pantes, hosoi thelousi sôthênai*) is found through the rejection of attachments to this world and through betrothal to Christ (2–4). The author encourages his reader to maintain a strict separation from the world's folly and the world's concerns, recognizing that the kingdom of heaven is for those who endure "in great affliction and constraint." He further urges her to fulfill all of God's commandments, and not to assume that they are too difficult (18–19, 23).

While the treatise does not condemn marriage as evil, and indeed the first chapter describes the beauty of God's creation and the joining of Adam and Eve, neither is marriage the subject of particular praise or additional affirmation. For example, the author does not make use of the argument, common in ascetic literature, that marriage is good while virginity is better, but other than the claim that marriage distracts one from "the things of the Lord" (1 Cor. 7:34), there is no explicit critique of marriage, not even the fairly common ascetic *topos* of the "woes of marriage." Yet there is one passage, elaborating on the theme of distraction by the concerns of the world (1 Cor. 7:32–35), that implies that marital intercourse is defiling: "every virgin or widow who practices abstinence, if she has her concern in this world, that concern is her husband. Even if she has possessions or property, this preoccupation defiles [*molynei*] her thoughts. For just as the body is defiled [*molynetai*] by a man [or a husband], so also worldly habits defile [*miainousi*] the soul and the body of the one who keeps abstinence, and she is not holy in body and in spirit" (2). The passage is difficult to interpret, and it may be read either as an outright condemnation of all marital intercourse, or as a more rhetorical argument within the monastic context, namely that the one who has dedicated herself to virginity or sexual chastity and yet becomes caught up in worldly affairs violates her abstinence and becomes defiled as surely as if she were having sexual relations.

In any event, this passage as well as the lack of explicit arguments for the goodness of marriage (which can be found in some of the writings on virginity more widely accepted as genuinely Athanasian),[26] and the emphasis on strict separation from the world as *the* way of salvation, together constitute for some scholars at least a point of clear distinction from Athanasian thought if not an indication of a dangerous tendency or heretical ascetic enthusiasm.[27] Batiffol writes, "[T]he *Discourse on Salvation* . . . does not condemn marriage: but it lays down the principle of salvation by virginity, and it does not leave any hope for those who live 'a dishonorable life.' "[28] On this basis and others, discussed below, Batiffol characterizes the *Discourse* as excessive in its advocacy of the ascetic life, exclusivist in its vision of salvation, and therefore unorthodox.

Specific elements of the virgin's daily *askêsis* are likewise unsettling to those who argue against Athanasian authorship. Batiffol, whose 1893 article provided a vehement condemnation of the ascetic ethic of the *Discourse*, was clearly scandalized. He argued that while the "formula of faith" is orthodox, the "mystical tendencies and the asceticism" are not, and that the ascetic view of the author and recipients is "closely related" to that of the followers of Eustathius condemned at Gangra in the mid-fourth century.[29] Batiffol and others since him have characterized the *askêsis* represented in our treatise as "rigorous" and elitist,[30] "unorthodox," "mystical" and "enthusiastic,"[31] "troubling,"[32] and lacking in moderation.[33] They point in particular to the virgin's clothing and short hair, the emphasis on rigorous daily fasting, the virgin's relations with male visitors, the private prayers and *synaxes*, as well as what appears to be a private eucharistic prayer, and the author's minimal emphasis on the church. In the next few pages I will discuss these features in some detail.

To be sure, as noted above, the *Discourse* gives considerable attention to the virgin's daily regimen of prayer, psalmody, vigils, fasting, and eating, as well as to her clothing, bathing, decorum, and behavior around others. The prominence of this type of instruction is, in itself, enough to raise doubts about Athanasian authorship for Aimé Puech, who writes that the author "is preoccupied with precise and detailed rules (on clothing, hours of prayer, etc.). One would expect from Athanasius higher insights and a more penetrating eloquence."[34] Regarding bodily renunciations, our author encourages virgins to observe *askêsis* according to a rule and under the authority of an elder, maintaining their regimen in the face of external criticism yet moderating its harshness in the case of illness or in response to temptation to excess and vainglory (6–8, 12, 14). Like many texts describing the lifestyle appropriate for ascetics, the *Discourse* warns that the bath is no place for the one whose body is sanctified for God. Not even the virgin herself should see her naked body unless absolutely necessary. If she washes, therefore, it is only her face, hands, and feet that enter the basin, and even then she should not rub vigorously or add any herbs or salts to the water (11).[35]

This concern to protect the privacy of the virginal body as the dedicated, sanctified temple of God continues in the discussion of appropriate clothing. The virgin's garb should be modest and simple: "Your outer garment should be black, . . . and your veil should be without fringe . . . and your sleeves wool, covering your arms up to the fingers. The hairs on your head [should be] shorn all around and your little headband woolen, with the head bound tight and the hood and cape without fringe. If you should by chance meet someone, let your face be veiled, covered up, bent down, and do not lift your face toward a person, but only toward your God." Even while covered and veiled, the virgin must take care that no one gets a peek under her garment at her feet (11). Discussing this description of clothing, Batiffol again makes a connection to the ascetic behaviors targeted at Gangra, which anathematized those who criticize others for wearing common clothing as well as any woman who cuts her hair "under the impression that this annuls the ordinance of subjection."[36]

The prominent discussion of the benefits of fasting (*nêsteia*) and the specific instructions on diet distinguish the *Discourse* and draw scrutiny from modern readers. The author confidently praises the physical and spiritual benefits of fasting as a virtue and tool of great power. Fasting is a protection or "safeguard" (*phylaktêrion*) that, together with almsgiving and prayer, "delivers a person from death." It has physical and spiritual powers, by which it "heals diseases, dries up the bodily fluids, casts out demons, chases away wicked thoughts, makes the mind clearer, the heart pure, and the body sanctified, and places the person before the throne of God." Obedient fasting returns one to paradise, just as through disobedient eating Adam was cast out. Indeed, by fasting one lives the angelic life and "has angelic status." Finally, fasting adorns the virgin's body and pleases her bridegroom Christ, just as perfume and expensive jewelry beautify a worldly woman's body and delight earthly men. The heavenly bridegroom does not look for earthly adornment and the artifices of beauty, "but only a pure heart and an undefiled body mortified by fasting" (6–7).[37]

Thus fasting is not only an integral part of the virgin's daily *askêsis*, it is woven into the fabric of the ascetic ethic and vision of the *Discourse*. In their analyses of the text and their consideration of the question of authorship, scholars have identified the overall emphasis on fasting and some passages in particular as too rigorist in tone for the bishop of Alexandria. For example, the author warns the virgin not to listen to those who suggest that she should not fast so often because she will become physically weak, and to steel her resolve by remembering that Daniel and the three youths ate vegetable food rather than the food from King Nebuchadnezzar's table and still remained healthy (6; Dan. 1:3–16). Moreover, the author encourages continual fasting and specifies a vegetarian diet. He writes, "[F]ast for the entire period [or fast all year], except in case of great necessity. But in the ninth hour of the day, continuing in hymns and prayers, take your bread and vegetables prepared with oil. Everything is pure as long as it is nonanimal [*panta hagna hosa apsycha*]" (8).[38] While ascetic literature is full of examples of vegetarian diets and the expectation of life-long fasting, the use here of purity language and the bluntness of the instruction imply to some readers at least a solid distinction from the accepted ascetic writings of Athanasius,[39] if not evidence of an unorthodox exclusivism. Here again Batiffol points to the canons of the Council of Gangra, which anathematize those ascetics who condemn others for eating meat and who fast on Sunday.[40] He argues that the instruction above to "fast for the entire period" as well as the later instruction to "continue all of the years of your life in fasting, prayer, and almsgiving" (12) show that these ascetic women fasted constantly, in disregard for the church's rules on days for fasting.[41]

Two features of the text have raised further doubts about its attribution to Athanasius and further questions about the orthodoxy of its ascetic views, namely, the relationship of virgins with male ascetics and the role of the church and clergy. As mentioned earlier, the virgins addressed in the *Discourse on Salvation* live either at home or in a community with other virgins. It is apparent that the community would not be a large one, and may even consist of as few as two virgins, but the author recommends that young virgins should live with the strong guidance of a female elder: "It is not good for a young virgin [or a new virgin, neôteran] to live with another young virgin; at any rate they accomplish no good, for the one disobeys the other and the other one despises the other. But a young virgin under the authority of an elder woman [hypo presbytida] is good. For the elder will not submit to the will of the young one." In addition, the virgins should live according to a rule: "Woe to the virgin who is not under a rule [hypo kanona]. For she is like a ship that has no captain. . . . Blessed is the virgin who is under a rule. For she is like a fertile vine in paradise" (14).[42] Thus while the community advocated in the text does not resemble the later enclosed, organized monasteries, nevertheless it functions according to a rule and understandings of authority. Further, the author recommends private meals, private prayer, and private askêsis (9, 16, 20, 22), but the situation is flexible and the virgin does interact with other women—including other virgins, female elders, catechumens, poor women, and wealthy women—at meals, in church, in prayer, and in spiritual instruction (9, 13, 16, 22–23).[43]

Moreover, the Discourse describes the proper behavior for a virgin who receives a male visitor. Recall that in his description of clothing and veiling, the author notes that if the virgin should meet anyone, she should keep her face veiled and lowered. Later in the text, he tells the virgin how to behave if a "holy man" (hagios) or "righteous man" (anêr dikaios) should come to the house. He tells her to receive him as she would the son of God, with "fear and trembling." He writes, "[Y]ou shall prostrate yourself on the ground at his feet. For you do not prostrate yourself to him but to God who sent him. You shall take water and wash his feet and you shall listen to his words with all reverence. Do not feel confident in your self-control [sôphrosynê], lest you fall. But be fearful, for to the extent that you are fearful, you do not fall" (22). This is the extent of the discussion, and the author moves on in the next sentence to the topic of eating with others. The virgin receives a holy man with acts of reverence and listens attentively to his words, taking care to maintain her self-control and her fearful vigilance.

Commentators have noted that the male visitors do not appear to be clergy and further, as this is the only example in the text of interaction with male authority and spiritual instruction by a male, that the official clergy of the church, priests and bishops, have no place in the text.[44] Further, the provisions for visits between female and male ascetics strike some as unusual, in comparison with the common ascetic concern for separating men and women. Brakke observes that "the usual Athanasian warnings against interactions with men, especially false teachers, do not appear here," and that it is "hard to imagine" Athanasius instructing virgins to welcome visiting holy men and even wash their feet.[45] Not surprisingly, Batiffol goes further than the question of Athanasian authorship to characterize the behavior, and concludes that the relations between the ascetic woman and an ascetic male visitor show an astonishing "boldness" uncharacteristic of "orthodox asceticism."[46]

The absence of direct reference to priests, male presbyters, or bishops relates to the question of the role of the organized church in the lives of the virgins. It should be noted first that the author seems to assume that the virgin attends church regularly, for he tells her to be silent in church, avoid laughter, pay attention to the reading, and keep her thoughts from wandering dangerously (23). Other than this one passage, however, the lengthy discussions of prayer, *synaxes*, the recitation of psalms, and vigils indicate either a private or small group setting and make no mention of clerical participation or oversight. The cycle of *synaxes* is described in some detail, and the symbolism of the third, sixth, ninth, and twelfth hour elaborated according to the events of the passion of Christ. Each *synaxis* consists of prayer, psalms, hymns, and tears (12–13, 16, 20). The author specifies, "[I]f the twelfth hour arrives, you shall celebrate a greater and longer *synaxis*, with your virgin soul mates [*meta tôn homopsychôn*]. But if you have no soul mates with you, complete it by yourself, with God who is with you and hears you." He also gives instructions for prayer and psalmody in the middle of the night, and makes provision for either private or group observance (16, 20). This seems to indicate, by the exceptions specified, that most of the *synaxes* during the day and evening would normally be observed as a group, while individual private prayer and psalmody would not be unusual, especially during the night.

One of the features of the *Discourse* that has stimulated significant discussion is the style of the prayers offered at meals and, in particular, the character of the prayer offered over bread before the meal at the ninth hour. We read:

> And when you sit at the table and start to break bread, giving thanks in this way, say: "We give thanks to you our father for your holy resurrection, for through Jesus your son you have made it known to us; and just as this bread which is at first scattered becomes one when it is gathered together on this table, in this way may your church be gathered together from the ends of the earth into your kingdom, for yours is the power and the glory unto ages of ages, amen." (13)

What strikes some scholars is that this prayer, which is paralleled in *Didache* 9 in a eucharistic context, is recited by the virgins themselves daily at the ninth hour, before the main meal of the day. This may suggest that the virgins observed private daily eucharist, again seemingly without clerical presence.[47] For Batiffol, the use of this prayer "transforms the meal of the ninth hour into a sort of mystical communion," represents "a strange secularization of the sacerdotal office," and further links the asceticism of our text with those anathematized at Gangra. In a later essay responding to von der Goltz's commentary on the text and his analysis of this issue, however, Batiffol identified several sources of evidence not only for daily eucharist and eucharist before meals among the Egyptian ascetics, but also for the practice of communicating at home before the meal with consecrated bread brought from the church, and suggests that this may be the situation represented in the *Discourse*.[48]

These, then, are the principle points on which scholars have challenged the claim to Athanasian authorship. In the more than one hundred years since Batiffol's argument, very few (other than von der Goltz) have supported authenticity, and even these assent to von der Goltz's conclusions without substantial independent argumentation.[49] And while Batiffol attempted to identify a historical connection to a specific group, the followers of Eustathius, others since have analyzed the text primarily in relation to the Athanasian connection. (One exception is Buonaiuti's 1923 study in which he identified a possible connection to Evagrius of Pontus and discussed textual parallels with Evagrius's *Sentences to a Virgin*).[50] Yet the general aura of mystery, if not suspicion, remains around the ascetic commitments of the author and the ascetic practitioners.

In a lengthy 1905 commentary on his edition of the text, and responding to Batiffol's 1893 essay, Eduard von der Goltz made what remains the fullest defense of Athanasian authorship. In relation to our current focus on the practical life of the ascetic, von der Goltz demonstrated, effectively I think, that the ascetic practice in the text and the behaviors Batiffol regarded as hyperascetic and unorthodox were in fact common in fourth-century Egyptian monasticism, including the specific hours of prayer as well as the practice of consuming blessed bread before the daily meal, the style of dress and hair, the living arrangements, and of course the practice of regular fasting and vegetarianism. His argument is built on the comparison of ideas and practices recorded in the *Discourse* with other sources for early Egyptian monasticism, particularly Palladius's *Lausiac History* and the *History of the Monks in Egypt*, but also the *Life of Antony*, the *Life of Syncletica*, Evagrius's *Sentences to a Virgin*, and others.[51]

Moreover, he argued that the very idea of a *logos sôtêrias* or "word of salvation," along with the references to "all those who wish to be saved" (2, 4, 7), should be interpreted not as an indication of mere exclusivity and elitism, but rather as locating our text firmly within a monastic setting and a tradition of spiritual guidance.[52] To cite just two examples, he points to an account in the *History of the Monks in Egypt* in which monks receive John of Lycopolis, wash his feet, and ask him for "a word of salvation" (*logos sôtêrias*) concerning how to avoid the devil's traps and shameful thoughts, and another in which brothers "wishing to be saved" (*sôthênai thelontes*) approach the monk Ammonius.[53] Thus in the text's title, which could be more appropriately translated as "Word of Salvation," in the several references to those who "desire to be saved," and in the author's expressions of concern for the virgin's soul, von der Goltz argues, the connection to Egyptian monastic piety and spiritual guidance becomes clear.[54]

While he demonstrated persuasively that the *Discourse on Salvation* is perfectly at home in the context of fourth-century Egyptian monasticism, von der Goltz, like others before him and since, remained primarily focused on the question of Athanasian authorship. Yet I would argue that if we approach the treatise only in the context of whether or not Athanasius wrote it, it will always be found lacking and will remain on the margins of the scholarly assessment of early Christian ascetic practice and monastic formation. In the case of the *Discourse*, comparison with the Athanasian norm of orthodox ascetic formation constructs the text as problematic and suspect. The ascetic discipline in the text appears extreme only because the text does not repeat the often politicized and contextualized conditions expressed in so many other ascetic texts, including several that are more widely accepted as Athanasian, such as the *Life of Antony* and the *Letters* to virgins. There are here no Arians, no Melitians, and no followers of Hieracas against whom the author needs to define the boundaries of the ascetic life;[55] nor on the other hand is there a defense of the ascetic life against identifiable detractors. It is perfectly fair, in a debate over authorship, to compare the representation of asceticism in the text and the author's concerns or lack of concerns to the representation of asceticism in Athanasius's other writings and Athanasius's concerns and preoccupations. The problem arises with the additional attempt to fit the text and the ascetic practice advocated in it into contentious categories ("encratite," "Eustathian"), when the text itself gives no justification for this move.

Indeed, when we try to read the *Discourse* without reference to particular personalities or debates, the essentially *moderate* position of the text appears in high relief. Features and emphases of the text that were ignored or passed over in previous scholarship now may be seen in a different perspective. With regard to fasting, for example, it is true that the author manifests almost giddy enthusiasm for the physical and spiritual benefits of regular fasting and encourages the ascetic woman to maintain her discipline in the face of warnings from others about bodily weakness. Yet he also observes that "the enemy" provokes *both* slackening of discipline *and* greater *askêsis* to the point of weakening the body. He also notes that it is the enemy who leads the virgin to the sin of pride by suggesting that she "have contempt for those who eat." Indeed, her fast should have "due measure" (*metron*), and fasting from food alone is useless if not accompanied by a fast from vices such as anger, slander, love of money, and vainglory (6–8).

Further, throughout the *Discourse* every instruction concerning bodily discipline carries an exception in the case of illness or some other "necessity." Consider, for example: "Fast for the entire period, except in case of absolute necessity [*chôris pasês anankês*]" (8); "Not even another female should see your naked body, except in absolute necessity [*aneu pasês anankês*]" (11); "If you are healthy you shall not go to the bath except in absolute necessity [*aneu pasês anankês*]" (11); "If your body should become weaker, take a little wine for your stomach. But if, God forbid, you should fall ill, take care of yourself; do not give an occasion for people to say, 'This illness befell her because of asceticism' " (12); "[Do not] eat your morsel with careless women or buffoons, except when necessary [*aneu anankês*]" (13); "It is not good for you to go out, except in great necessity [*chôris anankês megalês*]" (22).[56]

It must also be noted that the prominence of fasting in the treatise is matched by the prominence of meals, eating, and behavior at the table. The author recommends regular fasting and a vegetarian diet and suggests that "it is best for the abstinent one to eat her bread in private." But he also describes meals with other virgins (8, 13). In one passage he explicitly instructs the virgin to eat and drink in spite of her normal discipline, if she would otherwise cause offense: "If you should sit at table with [other] virgins, eat with them everything that they have set out; for if you do not eat, you appear as if you are judging them. And if they are drinking wine, and you do not [normally] drink, drink a little for their sakes. But if they are eminent elder women and they urge you to drink more, do not listen to them, but say to them: 'You have spent your youth in great *askêsis*, but I have not yet advanced even to the first degree' " (22). Here we see a rather remarkable balance between the commitment to progress in asceticism, the dangers of appearing contemptuous, and the needs of hospitality, humility, and community.

Finally, as von der Goltz has argued, the instruction to "fast for the entire period [or all year]" is so generally stated that it should not be taken to indicate resistance to the traditional practice of breaking one's fast on Sundays, which the author may simply assume. And the so-called vegetarian rule ("everything nonanimal is pure") should not surprise anyone, since a vegetarian diet is standard in ascetic sources.[57] It is a mistake to read either the lack of overt praise of marriage, or the presence of an overt claim to vegetarianism, as condemnation or contempt for those nonascetics who do marry and eat meat. This is, after all, a text addressed to those dedicated to lifelong chastity and an ascetic regimen. Batiffol's attempt to link the ascetics of the *Discourse* with the so-called Eustathians or encratites and with the anathemas of the bishops at Gangra represents a tendency, in both ancient heresiology and modern scholarship, to use labels such as "encratism" as lump categories. Daniel Caner, in his recent study of the Messalians, describes this tendency: "groups totally unrelated in time or place become assimilated under specific heretical labels (e.g., Apotactites, Encratites) simply because their ascetic practices appear similar, or they become linked to specific heretical leaders (e.g., the 'heresiarchs' Tatian, Mani), despite the lack of any demonstrable connection."[58]

Clearly, many of the "heretical" behaviors and understandings of asceticism that were criticized at the Council of Gangra were shared widely among Christian ascetics, including those who would be idealized as holy and orthodox as well as those who would be marginalized as extreme and heretical. It would be the task of Athanasius, as well as others such as Jerome and Basil of Caesarea, to make the arguments for the fine distinctions in interpretation (of marriage, virginity, and fasting) or to effect structural or institutional adjustments that would allow some Christians to continue in their *askêsis* without heretical taint and without threat to either lay sensibilities or episcopal authority. But the *Discourse* does not seem to be engaged in that debate. Thus the absence, for example, of a long argument for the goodness of marriage may simply reflect the absence of polemical context or self-defensive posture. After all, the elaboration of the arguments for the goodness of marriage happened in large part in the midst of debate and conflict.

In short, the ascetic behavior addressed in this text is a far cry from the heresiological construction of an "unorthodox" *askêsis*, whether that construction is the product of an ancient debate or council or a modern scholarly framework. This same conclusion may be drawn concerning another feature of the text singled out by Batiffol and others as suspicious, namely the relations with men and with the church and clerical authority. Batiffol was particularly scandalized by what seemed to him to be an unacceptable "bold-ness" in the virgin's way of greeting the visiting "holy man" by prostrating herself before him, washing his feet, and listening to his teaching. But von der Goltz has demonstrated that the same behavior is recorded in the *History of the Monks in Egypt*, where monks greet each other with prostration and feet washing before spiritual discussion.[59] That the passage in the *Discourse* refers to a virgin greeting a male visitor and teacher is perhaps notable, but it is no more than that. More important, this passage in our text in no way implies an easy familiarity or intimacy between the virgin and the holy man. On the contrary, it is full of a sense of the danger of contact between men and women and warnings about protecting the virtue of self-control. Likewise regarding the virgin's relationship to the church: if the text does not contain any instructions to submit to clerical authority, it *does* assume that the virgin attends church and benefits from it. So what if her presence in church is only mentioned once? While the lack of any insistence on ecclesiastical authority may be an indication that the bishop of Alexandria was probably not its author,[60] nothing in the text justifies Batiffol's characterization of anticlerical arrogance.

I do not mean to overemphasize Batiffol or to suggest that his two essays on the text, written one hundred years ago, have forever cast their shadow over scholarship. But I do want to highlight some of the problems with analyzing a text or a practice with preexisting genealogies and categories of interpretation framing that analysis. In the case of the scholarship on the Greek *logos sôtêrias*, it has been evaluated only against standards of Athana-sian authenticity or heresiological types. If, then, there is nothing that is particularly extreme or polemical in the text, and since the ascetic practices themselves are not unusual, I would suggest that it be considered apart from the Athanasian question and in light of new approaches to questions of heresy and identity. While nineteenth- and twentieth-century efforts to es-tablish the canon of Athanasian works are of course important in their own right, and the manuscripts' assertion of Athanasian authorship needs to be assessed, this bibliographic context has become the only filter through which the treatise has been discussed and evaluated. Thus the studies dis-cuss the treatise only against the norms and standards of a personality and a tradition that may or may not have been important to the author or to those whom he addresses. As James Goehring has noted with reference to the Egyptian "Melitian" controversy, as Susanna Elm has argued regarding the changes in the practice and ideology of female asceticism in Egypt and Asia Minor, and as Daniel Caner has observed concerning the so-called Messalians of Asia Minor, the categories and labels developed in the context of early debates that are "not inherently ascetic"[61] and in the pages of ancient heresiologies, when they are adopted in modern scholarship, may in fundamental ways not only limit our ability to see commonalities in practice and ascetic formation, but also force our ancient subjects into interpretive boxes of orthodoxy and heresy that may not have held meaning for them.[62]

Indeed, the processes not only of ideological debate or heresiological definition, but also literary idealization of proper ascetic heroes such as we see in many of the sources on Egyptian monasticism in particular, result in orthodoxy (in this case, an "orthodoxy" constructed as Athanasian) becoming "a constituent element in the definition of early Christian asceticism."[63] In relation to such a process, texts such as the *Discourse* may be problematic for readers because they do not show *enough* of what we have come to expect as "orthodox" revision, enough of an overt theological agenda articulated against identifiable opponents or in agreement with identifiable and authoritative figures with familiar names and genealogies. (Ironically, the most overt move in our text was made by whoever added the name "Athanasius" to the manuscript title.) In contrast, texts such as the *Life of Antony*, the Pachomian *Lives*, or the *Sayings of the Desert Fathers*, for which political motivations or orthodox revisions may be clear (as Goehring and others have argued),[64] are in some ways (deceptively) easier for modern readers to approach, because we have, in fact, already inherited the analytical tools, categories, and judgments from both ancient and modern readers. Thus, in Alain Le Boulluec's words, as historians we risk "reproducing the discourse arising from theological, ecclesiological, and confessional controversies"[65] in our own readings of normative orthodoxy and orthodox ascetic behavior.

Perhaps, finally, behavior does not always express doctrine or ideology. Perhaps the "ideological boundaries" of theological debate that continue to shape the contours of our approach to ancient texts were not as clear to the ascetic practitioners as they are to us.[66] Perhaps ascetic practices were not always or even usually distinctive enough by group and affiliation that we should expect to reclaim this text's association with a particular "movement" or person. This is not to deny the suggestive elements in the text that *are* distinctive and on their own call for additional research, such as the trinitarian formula or the parallels with Evagrian themes and with the *Sentences to a Virgin*, but it is to allow for the historical ambiguities *and* particularities of our treatise. Paradoxically, it seems, the *Discourse on Salvation to a Virgin*, a "true jewel of ascetic literature,"[67] remains on the margins of our reconstruction of early Christian ascetic history precisely because it does not "name names" in the fashion of heresiological discourse or other controversial literature.[68] In this and other ways it does not function as a "literary enactment"[69] of either orthodox or heretical asceticism, nor does it betray the kind of textual clues to political motivation that we have come to expect from other, more well-known texts and their more prominent authors.

Notes

I would like to thank David Brakke, James Goehring, J. Rebecca Lyman, Dale Martin, and Patricia Cox Miller for reading and commenting on earlier versions of this essay.

1. Le Boulluec, *La notion d'hérésie*.
2. Ibid., 13, 19; Le Boulluec, "Orthodoxie et hérésie aux premiers siècles dans l'historiographie récente," in Elm, Rebillard, and Romano, eds., *Orthodoxie, christianisme, histoire*, 303, 308. Translations from ancient and modern languages are my own unless another English translation is cited in the notes.
3. Representative works include Burrus, *Making of a Heretic*; Clark, *Origenist Controversy*; Lyman, "Topography of Heresy"; Lyman, "Historical Methodologies"; and Williams, *Rethinking Gnosticism*. See also the essays in two recent collections on the theme, the special issue "The Markings of Heresy: Body, Text, and Community in Late Ancient Christianity" of *Journal of Early Christian Studies* 4 (1996): 403–513; and Elm, Rebillard, and Romano, eds., *Orthodoxie, christianisme, histoire*.
4. See especially Clark, *Origenist Controversy*; Goehring, "Monastic Diversity and Ideological Boundaries"; the essays in Goehring, ed., *Ascetics, Society, and the Desert*; Rubenson, *Letters of St. Antony*; Elm, "*Virgins of God*"; Caner, *Wandering, Begging Monks*. For an analysis of the strategies of reading, in particular reading scripture, employed in the early Christian interpretation of asceticism, see also Clark, *Reading Renunciation*.
5. Pseudo-Athanasius, *De virginitate* (in *Logos sôtêrias pros tên parthenon*, ed. von der Goltz); also in Migne, *Patrologia Graeca* 28.252A–282B. French translation by Bouvet, *Discours de salut à une vierge*; English translation by Shaw, "Pseudo-Athanasius: Discourse on Salvation to a Virgin."
6. In the note citations, I will use the traditional Latin title of *De virginitate*, in keeping with previous convention. In quotations from the text, numbers in parentheses indicate chapters.
7. The identification of the authentic list of ascetic writings by Athanasius has been the topic of a significant amount of research during the twentieth century and into the twenty-first. The process has been complicated because much of the ascetic material, including writings on the topic of virginity and addressed to virgins, is preserved only in Syriac, Coptic, Arabic, and Armenian. Several texts have been edited and published, not only making this material more accessible but also encouraging scholars to question the prioritizing of texts preserved in Greek. Recently David Brakke has been particularly active in the discussion and in the translation of texts. See especially Brakke, "Authenticity"; see also Brakke,

Athanasius. Prior to Brakke the fullest discussion of the texts and issues relating to authorship is Aubineau, "Les écrits de saint Athanase." Aubineau has a full discussion of the earlier reception of von der Goltz's argument for authenticity (144–50). Several Athanasian texts on virginity have been edited and published since von der Goltz published his edition of the Pseudo-Athanasian *logos sôtêrias*. These include (1) a "Letter to Virgins" preserved in Coptic (in *S. Athanase*, ed. Lefort; English translation by Brakke, in Brakke, *Athanasius*, 274–91; (2) a "Letter to Virgins Who Went and Prayed at Jerusalem and Returned" preserved in Syriac ("Athanasiana Syriaca II," ed. Lebon, 169–216; English translation by Brakke, in Brakke, *Athanasius*, 292–302; (3) a treatise "On Virginity" preserved in Syriac and Armenian ("Athanasiana Syriaca I," ed. Lebon, 205–48; English translation by Brakke, in Brakke, *Athanasius*, 303–9. Brakke has recently edited and translated another treatise, (4) "On Virginity," preserved in Syriac, which is attributed to Athanasius. Brakke argues that the treatise is not an authentic writing of Athanasius (*Pseudo-Athanasius*, ed. Brakke).

8. Cavallera, *Saint Athanase*, 329.

9. For general discussions of the genre of the *de virginitate* and the common themes and elements, see especially Camelot, "Les traités 'de virginitate'"; and Aubineau, *Grégoire de Nysse*. On virginity and early Christianity recent studies include Elm, "*Virgins of God*"; Cooper, *The Virgin and the Bride*; Brown, *Body and Society*; Brakke, *Athanasius*; Shaw, *Burden of the Flesh* and "Askêsis and the Appearance of Holiness."

10. The attention to the dangers of *logismoi* (wicked thoughts or vices) also suggests the influence of ascetic thought associated with Evagrius of Pontus. For this it is useful to compare the text to Evagrius's *Sententiae ad virginem*, as von der Goltz has done, as well as to the Pseudo-Athanasian hagiographical treatise on Syncletica (Evagrius of Pontus, *Sententiae ad virginem*, 146–51; von der Goltz, *Logos sôtêrias*, 72–75; Pseudo-Athanasius, *Vita et gesta Sanctae beataeque magistrae Syncleticae* [Migne, *Patrologia Graeca* 28:1488–1557]). For a discussion of these three texts together see Shaw, "Virgin Charioteer."

11. The author mentions the virgin's relatives in chap. 9. For references to other virgins and elder women see chaps. 9–10, 13–14, and 22.

12. Batiffol, "Le *peri parthenias*," 275–76; Aubineau, "Les écrits," 144.

13. Batiffol, "Le *peri parthenias*"; Von der Goltz, *Logos sôtêrias*. Responses to von der Goltz and reviews of his edition and commentary include, in addition to Batiffol and Aubineau, Bardy, "Athanase"; Batiffol, "Recension"; Buonaiuti, "Evagrio Pontico"; Burch, "Early Witness"; Cavallera, *Saint Athanase*, 326–30; H. Delehaye, review of von der Goltz, *Analecta Bollandiana* 25 (1906): 180–81; G. Krüger, review of von der Goltz, *Theologische Literaturzeitung* 31 (1906): 352–55; Lebon, "Pour une édition critique," 527; Lefort, "Athanase, Ambroise, et Chenoute," 60–61; J. Leipoldt, review of von der Goltz, *Zeitschrift für Kirchengeschichte* 27 (1906): 225–56; Puech, *Histoire de la littérature*, 3:116–18; Roldanus, *Le Christ et l'homme*, 396–99; A. Souter, review of von der Goltz, *Journal of Theological Studies* 9 (1908): 140–41; Zucchetti, "Il sinodo di Gangra," 548–51.

14. Aubineau, "Les écrits," 146; Brakke, "Authenticity," 44–45; Burch, "Early Wit-

ness," 740–41. For a discussion of the manuscripts see von der Goltz, *Logos sôtêrias*, 3–35, and the update and corrections in Lake and Casey, "Text of the *De Virginitate*."

15. Lebon, "Athanasiana Syriaca I," 239.
16. Puech, *Histoire*, 118.
17. Batiffol, "Recension," 296; Aubineau, "Les écrits," 148–49; c.f. von der Goltz, *Logos sôtêrias*, 120–22.
18. Aubineau, "Les écrits," 149.
19. Brakke, "Authenticity," 45–46. On the question of the trinitarian formula, see also Batiffol, "Le peri parthenias," 277; Batiffol, "Recension," 296; Lebon, "Pour une édition critique," 527; Lebon, ed., "Athanasiana Syriaca I," 239; Burch, "An Early Witness," 740; Leipoldt, review of von der Goltz, 226; Aubineau, "Les écrits," 146–47; Roldanus, *Le Christ et l'homme*, 386, 396–97. Von der Goltz's argument that the appearance of the formula in the *Discourse* must be the result of a textual interpolation (*Logos sôtêrias*, 118–19) has not proven persuasive.
20. Leipoldt, review of von der Goltz, 226. The argument that Athanasius would not treat noncanonical texts as authoritative is not exactly clear-cut, as Aubineau notes ("Les écrits," 146).
21. Batiffol, "Le peri parthenias," 278–86; Roldanus, *Le Christ et l'homme*, 398; Brakke "Authenticity," 46.
22. On the difficulties and challenges of the ascetic texts in particular, see Brakke, "Authenticity"; Aubineau, "Les écrits"; and Lebon, "Pour une édition critique."
23. On the scholarly categories of orthodoxy and heresy see Lyman, "Historical Methodologies," 77–82. As will become clear, in the case of our text I believe that Brakke's approach is the more reasonable and fair, by focusing on the evidence of the text itself and well-defined criteria for authorship, whereas others, particularly Pierre Batiffol, have relied on heresiological stereotypes.
24. See ibid., 78. I am grateful to Lyman for her thoughts on these issues.
25. See especially Batiffol, "Le peri parthenias"; von der Goltz, *Logos sôtêrias*, 60–85; Aubineau, "Les écrits," 148; Brakke, "Authenticity," 46–47; and Roldanus, *Le Christ et l'homme*, 397–98.
26. On Athanasius's arguments for the goodness of marriage in the context of his opposition to Hieracas see especially Brakke, *Athanasius*, 44–57; Brakke, "Authenticity," 46–47; also on Hieracas see Elm, "*Virgins of God*," 338–42, 346–47; and Goehring, "Hieracas of Leontopolis," in *Ascetics, Society, and the Desert*, 110–33. For Athanasius's argument on marriage and virginity (and against Hieracas), see Athanasius, "Letter to Virgins," 1–3, 18–30 (Lefort, ed. and trans., *S. Athanase*, 50:73–74, 80–88 [Coptic] / 51:55–56, 62–69 [French]; English translation Brakke, *Athanasius*, 274–75, 279–84). See also the Syriac "On Virginity," 10 (Lebon, ed. and trans., "Athanasiana Syriaca I," 213 [Syriac] / 222 [French]; English translation Brakke, *Athanasius*, 306). But note also that the "Letter to Virgins Who Went and Prayed at Jerusalem and Return," which Brakke and others consider authentic, includes a discussion of 1 Cor. 7:32–35 similar to that in the *Discourse on Salvation*. In the context of his arguments against male and female ascetics cohabiting in spiritual marriage, Athanasius writes: "But perhaps

you will say, 'I guard my virginity and holiness.' But it is fitting for the perfect virgin to be 'holy in body and in soul' (1 Cor. 7:34), to escape from the defilement of spirit and flesh, and—for the sake of him who came to collect human thoughts, for the sake of him who knew the secrets of the heart—to be undistracted and undividedly attentive (1 Cor. 7:35)" ("Letter to Virgins Who Went and Prayed," 25 [Lebon, ed. and trans., "Athanasiana Syriaca II," 184 [Syriac] / 225 [French]; English translation Brakke, *Athanasius*, 300]). While the defilement here is not explicitly defined as related to sexual intercourse, it may be implied by the context of the discussion.

27. Brakke "Authenticity," 46–47; Batiffol, "Le peri parthenias," 278–79, 283; Aubineau, "Les écrits," 148; Roldanus, *Le Christ et l'homme*, 397–98.

28. Batiffol, "Le peri parthenias," 283.

29. Ibid., 277, 286; and Batiffol, "Recension," 296–97. Zucchetti, writing in 1925, also connects the text to those anathematized at Gangra ("Il sinodo di Gangra"). On the Council of Gangra and Eustathius see, e.g., Elm, "*Virgins of God*," 106–12, 124–36; Caner, *Wandering, Begging Monks*, 100–101 and passim; Gribomont, "Le monachisme au IVe s."; Gribomont, "Eustathe de Sébaste"; Gribomont, "Eustathe de Sébaste"; Dagron, "Les moines et la ville"; Rousseau, *Basil of Caesarea*, 23–22, 73–76, 239–45, and passim. For the canons, see the English translation by Yarbrough, "Canons from the Council of Gangra," in Wimbush, ed., *Ascetic Behavior*, 449–54.

30. Roldanus, *Le Christ et l'homme*, 398.

31. Batiffol, "Le peri parthenias," 277–78.

32. Aubineau, "Les écrits," 148. Aubineau discusses Batiffol's arguments for the connection to the Eustathian ascetics and concludes: "The convergence of all the traits, of which none constitutes a proof, is troubling nevertheless."

33. Brakke, "Authenticity," 47.

34. Puech, *Histoire*, 118.

35. There are numerous examples of prohibitions to the bath in ascetic literature; for this essay the most relevant text is Athanasius's "Letter to Virgins Who Went and Prayed in Jerusalem and Returned," in which Athanasius instructs the virgin to wash like a dove in a basin, without taking off her clothing or showing her naked body. He also gives biblical examples of modest bathing and ascetic avoidance of bathing (Sarah, Rachel, Miriam, and the apostles) as well as the immodest bathing (Bathsheba and Susannah) that caused others to fall into sin and defilement ("Letter to Virgins Who Went and Prayed," 15–17 [Lebon, ed. and trans., "Athanasiana Syriaca II," 179–80 (Syriac) / 196–97 (French); English translation Brakke, *Athanasius*, 297–98]).

36. *Canons* 12, 17 (English translation Yarbrough, "Canons from the Council," 452–53). Batiffol, "Le peri parthenias," 283.

37. For a discussion of the relationship between fasting and sexual renunciation in early Christian ascetic theory, see Shaw, *The Burden of the Flesh*. On fasting in the Pseudo-Athanasian *Discourse on Salvation*, see especially 1–2, 8–9, 225–26, 249–50.

38. The phrase "except in great necessity [*chôris pasês anankês*]" could also mean "without any compulsion," so that the sentence would read "fast for the entire

period, without any compulsion." But in each of several other instances of the same phrase or almost the same phrase, the meaning is clearly "except in necessity" (see the discussion below). Because this sentence is analogous to the others, I have chosen to translate it in the same sense.

39. Brakke, "Authenticity," 47. Surveying just some of the texts focusing on asceticism and widely accepted as genuinely Athanasian, we find several references to the ascetic avoidance of meat and to vegetarian regimens. Of course Antony followed a simple diet of bread and water, eating once a day. Athanasius notes that Antony avoided meat and wine, and that none of the other zealous ascetics ate meat (Vita Antonii 7 [Migne, Patrologia Graeca 26.853A]). In the "Letter to Virgins Who Went and Prayed," Athanasius uses the dove as the model for proper virginal lifestyle and decorum. In the context of this description he notes that the dove does not "rejoice . . . in eating flesh" ("Letter to Virgins Who Went and Prayed," 14 ["Athanasiana Syriaca II," 179 (Syriac) / 196 (French), ed. Lebon; English translation in Brakke, Athanasius, 297]). A more intriguing passage is in the "Fragments on the Moral Life," which is addressed to both lay and ascetic Christians and distinguishes moral and ascetic criteria between the two groups. Here Athanasius describes the life of "those who walk angelically according to their free will," live with discipline "in the life of the angels," and separate themselves from the things of the flesh. He notes that "vegetables replace meats for such people, and water replaces wine" (Fragments, 2 [English translation Brakke, Athanasius, 314]). Of course the difference in genres of these texts (hagiography, instructional letter, and homily) in part affects how Athanasius frames the topic, and what Athanasius presents as an elite ideal in the case of Antony or those who lead the angelic life is not held up as the only legitimate lifestyle for faithful Christians. For additional discussion of Athanasius and fasting, see especially Brakke, Athanasius, 186–89, 230–33. It is also worth noting here that the Canons attributed to Athanasius but generally regarded as inauthentic specify that virgins and male monks do not eat any meat or fish (Canons 92, 98; English translation in Canons of Athanasius, ed. Lebon, 59, 62).

40. Canons 2, 18 (English translation Yarbrough, "Canons from the Council," 451, 453). On the Canons of Gangra and ascetic fasting, see Shaw, The Burden of the Flesh, 231–35; on vegetarianism or the rejection of meat in ascetic renunciation see ibid., passim.

41. Batiffol, "Le peri parthenias," 283–84.

42. On the authority of the elder or more experienced ascetics, see also chap. 23: "Do everything with the counsel of your elders [meta boulês meizoterôn]." That the virgin might live with her family is suggested by the instruction in chap. 9: "let no one observe your askêsis, not even your own relatives." Of course this may refer to a situation in which two or more members of the same family lived in an ascetic community with others.

43. The wealthy woman and poor woman appear to be other virgins in the community, but it is not completely clear (13).

44. Brakke, "Authenticity," 46; Roldanus, Le Christ et l'homme, 398; Batiffol, "Le peri parthenias," 280, 285.

45. Brakke, "Authenticity," 46. This is supported by comparison to Athanasian texts on virginity that are accepted as genuine; we observe that there is no parallel to the prostration and washing of feet, although there are some similarities to the situation and advice in the *Discourse* in the "Letter to Virgins Who Went and Prayed." Here, in the context of vehement warnings about the attraction between the sexes, Athanasius observes that the "perfect virgin," protecting her virginity, "does not speak to men, except to be instructed or to receive some spiritual profit. For when a teaching is divine or a word penitent, it is recognized (as such) because it is without laughter or levity or any desires of the flesh." Here Athanasius appears to allow for visits between virgins and male spiritual guides, although these could be clergy (18–19 ["Athanasiana Syriaca II," ed. Lebon, 181 (Syriac) / 197 (French); English translation Brakke, *Athanasius*, 298]). The treatise on virginity preserved in Syriac, however, is less confident and fairly blunt in its warning: "Therefore, watch yourself, O virgin, lest lascivious men seduce you with words of 'God's love.' Revere the words, but scorn the man. Do not be led astray by a human being; let him serve for you (only) as a minister of the Word. It is fitting, if possible, not to speak to a man at all, not to observe one, not to frequent one, not to remain with one, not to have acquaintance with him" (Athanasius, "On Virginity," 5 ["Athanasiana Syriaca I," 210–11 (Syriac) / 220 (French), ed. Lebon; English translation in Brakke, *Athanasius*, 304]). In the "Letter to Virgins" preserved in Coptic, where the Virgin Mary is the model for the life of virgins, Athanasius notes that the young Mary lived so separately from men that she was afraid when she heard the angel Gabriel's male voice ("Letter to Virgins," 17 [*S. Athanase*, 94–95 (Coptic) / 246 (French), ed. Lefort; English translation in Brakke, *Athanasius*, 279]). Also worthy of note is the Pseudo-Athanasian *Canons*, which specify that no priest may enter the virgin's convent unless he is elderly and unless his wife is with him. Further, a young presbyter may enter the convent if he has, by means of fasting, developed a continence that will both protect him and keep him from being a stumbling block to the virgins (48 [English translation in *Canons of Athanasius*, ed. Riedel and Crum, 35–36]).

46. Batiffol, "Le *peri parthenias*," 285.

47. Ibid., 281–82, 286; Batiffol, "Recension," 299; Roldanus, *Le Christ et l'homme*, 398. See also Burch, who argues in general that the language of the doxologies in chaps. 12–14 is more Syrian in character, as part of his broader argument that the *Discourse* is of Syrian or Cappadocian, rather than Egyptian, origin ("Early Witness," 742).

48. Batiffol, "Le *peri parthenias*," 282, 286; Batiffol, "Recension," 297–99.

49. Aubineau, "Les écrits," 145, 149. For sympathetic discussions of Athanasian authorship and von der Goltz's arguments see, e.g., Lefort, "Athanase, Ambroise, at Chenoute," 60–61; Cavallera, *Saint Athanase*, 329; Krüger, review of von der Goltz. Note that in the period prior to Batiffol's essay both Harnack and Eichorn also accepted Athanasius as the author (Aubineau, "Les écrits," 144).

50. Buonaiuti, "Evagrio Pontico." See also Zucchetti, "Il sinodo di Gangra," 551. Von der Goltz had also earlier identified parallels to the *Sentences*, some of which are

striking, as well as similarities with the teachings of Evagrius (*Logos sôtêrias*, ed. von der Goltz, 73–75).

51. See *Logos sôtêrias*, ed. von der Goltz, esp. 61–85.

52. Ibid., 63–64, 79–85, 119–20.

53. Ibid., 63–64; *Historia monachorum in Aegypto*, 1.55, 20.9–10 (ed. Festugière, 31, 121). Burton-Christie has demonstrated the importance of receiving a "word" among the monks of Egypt (*Word in the Desert*).

54. Von der Goltz also points out that the sermon of Syncletica recorded in her *Vita* is in essence a *logos sôtêrias pros tên parthenon*. Syncletica begins her discourse by noting that while "we all know how to be saved," many neglect the path to salvation (Pseudo-Athanasius, *Vita et gesta* 22 [Migne, *Patrologia Graeca* 28.1500B]). The discussion of Syncletica is significant moreover because the text has much in common with the *Discourse* and with Evagrius of Pontus's *Sentences to a Virgin*. See Shaw, "Virgin Charioteer."

55. On these issues see especially Elm, "*Virgins of God*," 330–72; and Brakke, *Athanasius*.

56. In fact these exceptions are so regular and formulaic that one wonders if the author or a later editor included them specifically to claim a moderate *askêsis* and avoid the rigorist label.

57. *Logos sôtêrias*, ed. von der Goltz, 82, 119–20. On the monastic diet and fasting in sources on early monasticism and for further discussion of the rejection of meat in an ascetic diet, see Shaw, *Burden of the Flesh*, 10–17 and passim.

58. Caner, *Wandering, Begging Monks*, 85.

59. *Historia monachorum* 2.7, 8.55 (ed. Festugière, 37, 68).

60. Brakke, "Authenticity," 46.

61. Goehring, "Monastic Diversity," 71. The passage concerns three archives of documentary papyri that suggest that Melitian and non-Melitian monks interacted regularly, and thus call into question the role and importance of ideological difference in comparison to shared ascetic practice. It reads, "Would Paphnouthios have identified himself as a Melitian, or simply as a monk? Would he have been concerned whether or not those with whom he interacted, both monastics and laity, were Melitian? Or do we, by identifying the three archives of Paieous, Paphnouthios and Nepheros as Melitian, foster a bipolar construction of ascetic history in terms of a debate that is not inherently ascetic."

62. Ibid., 64, 71, 82–83; Elm, "*Virgins of God*," 384–85; Caner, *Wandering, Begging Monks*, 12–13, 83–86.

63. Goehring, "Monastic Diversity," 83–84.

64. Ibid., 73–78; Brakke, *Athanasius*, 201–65; Rubenson, *Letters of St. Antony*.

65. Le Boulluec, "Orthodoxie et hérésie," 303.

66. Goehring, *Ascetics, Society, and the Desert*, 10.

67. Cavallera, *Saint Athanase*, 329.

68. Cameron, "On Naming"; Cameron, "How to Read Heresiology," in this volume.

69. Goehring, "Monastic Diversity," 73.

✢ History, Fiction, and Figuralism
in Book 8 of Augustine's *Confessions*

MARK VESSEY

To begin with, an often told tale. Book 8 of the *Confessions* tells three "conversion" stories. The first is of Marius Victorinus, an acclaimed rhetorician whose public profession of Christianity at Rome in the 350s caused a stir at the time. Augustine says he heard about Victorinus from the priest Simplicianus at Milan, when he was wrestling with his own religious doubts in the mid-eighties. The second story, also told to him at Milan, is of two imperial officials (*agentes in rebus*) who were led to adopt the monastic life by a chance reading of the *Life* of Antony the Egyptian hermit, while on service at Trier, near the northern frontier. Finally, Augustine relates how he and his friend Alypius were set on their spiritual course by a providential encounter with texts of the apostle Paul in a garden at Milan in the summer of 386.

As one commentator remarks, this eighth book is unique in the *Confessions* in "consist[ing] almost entirely of a series of specific recalled episodes."[1] Enlarging upon the point, another observes that, from around Book 6 onward, "distant persons and remote models of virtue are gradually replaced by those nearer at hand, that is, by individuals whose stories are recorded within the living memory of Augustine's own time. The climax of this development is the introduction of the life of St. Anthony in Book 8."[2] These episodes of recent history are linked together in ways manifestly designed to make the fullest possible sense of the event of Augustine's own "conversion," as we are used to calling it. The overall effect is of a kind of extrabiblical *figuralism* or typological exegesis, in which "foreshadowing and fulfilment take place not between historical events, figures, or stories in the Bible, but between secular figures."[3] The figures, in this case, are at once objects of exegesis and its practitioners or subjects. Like Augustine (and Alypius), Victorinus and the two imperial agents are decisively affected by their *reading* of particular Christian texts, biblical or hagiographic. Likewise, the dramatic narrative of their "conversions" not only prefigures Augustine's own but also prospectively implicates his readers, down to and including ourselves, in the situational logic of the sequence.

The process becomes transparent in Augustine's account of the impact of the story of the two *agentes in rebus* on his former self:

> Ponticianus went on with his story; but, Lord, even while he spoke you were wrenching me back toward myself, pulling me round from that standpoint behind my back which I had taken to avoid looking at myself [*retorquebas me ad me ipsum, auferens me a dorso meo, ubi me posueram, dum nollem me adtendere*]. You set me down before my face [*constituebas me ante faciem meam*], forcing me to mark how despicable I was, how misshapen and begrimed, filthy and festering. I saw and shuddered, and there was no way of escaping from myself. If I tried to turn my gaze away from myself, he went on relentlessly telling his tale [*narrabat quod narrabat*], and you set me before myself once more, thrusting me into my sight [*tu me rursus opponebas mihi et impingebas me in oculos meos*] so that I might perceive my sin and hate it. (8.7.16)[4]

We recall that earlier in the *Confessions* Augustine has pilloried himself for weeping over Dido and sympathizing with the heroes of tragedy. Such outpourings are a form of self-abandonment, to be counted among the dissipations that he collectively calls *concupiscentia* or disordered desire: ambition for glory, lusts of the flesh (including love of spectacle), appetite for knowledge without reference to the love of God (*curiositas*). By contrast, the kind of self-alienation that he describes in this passage of Book 8 is evidently meant to mark a crucial stage in the reintegration of the human being as one whose loves of self, God, and fellow human beings are properly adjusted. To force the distinction a little: the Augustine of circa 386 who appears in the narrative constructed by Augustine (circa 397–400) of the narration by Ponticianus of the "conversion" of the two imperial agents suffers neither with nor for those characters. Instead, under the stress of their narrative, a narrative of which "they" are now only objects, he becomes a narrative-dramatic character to himself, and by seeing himself from the outside—an object of narrative in his turn, even before he writes a word of the narrative we are now reading—he achieves the inward sense of self that the *Confessions* makes inseparable from the sense of God. It is a complex narrative dramatology or dramatic narratology. It is the central literary device of the *Confessions*. Augustine in the late 390s *characterizes* himself in order to reexperience the self-integrative alienation effect that inspires his praise of God, and in the hope of inducing the same effect and hence the same outpouring of praise in his reader. "My *Confessions*," he would state toward the end of his life, "were written to excite knowledge and love of God. With respect to myself, I can say that they had that effect when I was writing them and still do when I hear them read. What others feel, I leave for them to say."[5] Augustine could no more speak for his readers than he could usefully feel for Dido. He could only present himself, as relentlessly as Ponticianus kept presenting those two officials at Trier, in a light that would exhibit them to themselves, God willing.

How did Augustine come to write this way?

One possible answer, perhaps the best, would be: by reading the Psalms.[6] The purpose of this essay is to suggest another. Its argument consists of two parts with an interlude.

Confession and Chronicle

In Book 7 of the *Confessions* Augustine describes how the reading of certain "books of the Platonists" (*libri Platonicorum*) convinced him of the existence of a truth beyond the material realm and disposed him to return to the Christian beliefs in which he had been brought up. Uncertain of his ability to live by the Gospel commandments, he went to see Simplicianus. In conversation, he mentioned having read certain neo-Platonic texts in a Latin version by one Marius Victorinus, a rhetorician at Rome (*quondam rhetor urbis Romae*) who, he had heard, had died a Christian (*Christianum defunctum esse*).

Modern scholarship allows Victorinus a period of several years in the 350s and 360s in which to research and compose his ample works of Christian theology and exegesis. There is no certainty that Augustine knew much about these even by the time he wrote the *Confessions*. He would, however, have read the entry on Victorinus in Jerome's catalogue of Christian writers, the *De viris illustribus*, where the rhetorician is said to have become a Christian at an advanced age (*in extrema senectute Christi se tradens fidei*).[7] It is possible that Augustine heard about Victorinus's Christianity while at Milan, as he seems to say he did, if not at Rome a few years earlier. His account of the latter's "conversion" was likely in any case to be shaped by his subsequent reading and reflection. Whatever figure Victorinus may have cut in his own time, by the late 390s he had a character part to play in Augustine's *Confessions*. Most obviously, he had been a famous rhetorician at Rome and could thus be made to stand for all that the young Augustine (of the *Confessions*) once aspired to and was about to give up in 386.

While still a teacher at Carthage, Augustine had dedicated his first published work, a treatise in aesthetics, to Hierius, another well-known orator at Rome (*Romanae urbis oratorem*).[8] Not long afterward he made his own way to the city on the Tiber, and did his best to attract the attention of those best placed to advance his career. We do not know how he came to the notice of Quintus Aurelius Symmachus, prefect of the city, who in 384 recommended him for the prestigious post of public orator in the imperial capital of Milan.[9] Did he give performances (*declamationes*) at senatorial salons? Symmachus's correspondence from this period contains more than one account of men from faraway places who impressed by their oratorical virtuosity.[10] If the name of Victorinus signified anything to Augustine in 383 or 384, it would most probably have stood for a fellow professional, and African, who had won favor with the rich and powerful at Rome a generation or so earlier.

"Of this Victorinus," he would write, "Simplicianus told me a story which I will not pass over in silence. . . . Thoroughly versed in all the liberal arts, [he] had also read widely and discriminatingly in philosophy" (*Conf*. 8.2.3). With due allowance for the eulogistic genre, this description would fit the Augustine who came to Italy as well as it does the Victorinus whose works we read today. But the hero of Simplicianus's tale had additional titles of fame: "He had taught many a noble senator, and in recognition of his distinction as a teacher a statue had been erected to him in the Roman forum." Let us mark the place of this statue. The rest of the story can be briefly retold. Victorinus was a notable worshipper of the pagan gods and defender of their ancient cults. He was converted to Christianity by reading. When Simplicianus, then at Rome, asked why he did not come to church, he joked: "Is it the walls of buildings, then, that make Christians?" At length he agreed to be baptized and to make his baptismal profession publicly before a Roman congregation. It was a great spectacle, the crowd rapturously chanting "Victorinus! Victorinus!" as he went up to recite the Creed. Later on, when the emperor Julian passed a law prohibiting Christians from teaching, Victorinus distinguished himself by resigning his post, "preferring to abandon the babbling school than [God's] word" (8.5.10). At least that is how Augustine puts it, partly no doubt for the sake of the precedent thereby provided for his own, less heroic resignation from the chair of rhetoric at Milan in the fall of 386.

Back now to that statue in the forum.

We are well informed about such honors, at Rome and elsewhere. In the first "Roman" digression in (the extant part of) his history, Ammianus Marcellinus satirizes the vanity of those in the city who "set their hearts upon statues, believing that in this way their fame will be secured for ever, as if there were more satisfaction to be gained from senseless bronze figures than from the consciousness of a well-spent life."[11] Ammianus's late fourth-century city of Rome is of course also Augustine's. Their times there over-lapped. Both were provincial outsiders in the old capital. Both craved the same senatorial patronage. Both presumably saw many of the same sights of the ancient and modern city. Presumably. For to come to the *Confessions* after reading Ammianus is to experience a sudden sensory deprivation. Where Ammianus's narrative is full of vibrant and sharply etched scenes of city life, scenes whose graphic and often theatrical quality has struck literary and social historians alike,[12] Augustine gives the impression of one who walked around Rome, as he did Carthage and Milan, with his eyes wide shut, like Alypius in the famous gladiatorial scene (or "antiscene") at the Flavian am-phitheater, only with far better success. After that episode in the Colosseum, the one of Marius Victorinus in a Roman basilica is the second and last big Roman spectacle in Augustine's book, not counting the famous "vision" (in which nothing was seen) at Ostia. Just like the first, it is devoid of to-pographical or other visually circumstantial detail. Even if, ritually and so-ciologically speaking, walls did indeed make Christians—the walls of a church or baptistery that defined the space of the liturgy, crammed with images or "figures" from the sacred history daily reactualized in the sacra-ments—Augustine makes no attempt to delineate them in his text. All the more imposing, in the absence of any other public monumental fabric, is the statue of Marius Victorinus that briefly looms in his text. Not even the tomb of his mother Monica, solemnly edified in the poetic prose of Book 9, will have that much plastic reality.

It does not take much ingenuity to see what the statue is doing here. As satirical as Ammianus but with a more urgent purpose, Augustine sacrifices the pagan Victorinus's frail claim to immortality on the altar of the One Eternal God. The statue is a sign of the honor in which the rhetorician was held by the "citizens of this world" (*cives huius mundi*), a monument of vain ambition, vain show, and vain cult. In place of it Augustine substitutes another kind of figure, less plastic and mimetic, crafted to catch the inner rather than the outer eye, no longer mute but speaking: that of a "professor" of Christianity raised above a crowd of faithful men and women who reach out to clasp him to their hearts (*Conf.* 8.2.5).

If the thirty-year-old Augustine ever had looked up from his book while walking in the *centro storico*, he would have seen the statue of Marius Vic-torinus. To know of its existence and location, even if he never set eyes on it, the forty-something writer of the *Confessions* needed only to consult Jerome's adaptation of Eusebius's *Chronicle*, a copy of which had been obtained for him (from Jerome's literary agent in Rome) by Paulinus, the Christian aristocrat, *littérateur*, and ascetic who had recently settled at Nola in Campania,[13] and whose request for details of the life of Alypius is thought by some to have given a vital stimulus to the narrative that became the *Confessions*.[14] As all commentators on this passage duly note, a statue of Marius Victorinus is also mentioned in a notice in the *Chronicle* for the year 354. From this we learn that it stood in the Forum of Trajan, where Jerome, who was the kind of man who noticed such things, must often have gazed enviously upon it.[15]

Among Jerome's additions to the *Chronicle* is a series of entries on famous men of learning. For the period already covered by Eusebius, these insertions refer mainly to Latin figures and are probably based for the most part on information derived from the *De viris illustribus* of Suetonius.[16] Apart from a few Latin Christian writers unknown to Eusebius, Jerome has little to add for the period between the early second century and the beginning of the fourth. Thereafter he reels off a series of names, Latin rhetoricians or orators in most cases, many of them Gallic, several of them associated with the city of Rome.[17] Although Victorinus's is the only statue mentioned, Jerome makes a point of marking the tombs of such earlier writers as Ennius, Caecilius, and Vergil.[18] Those may be purely "literary" references, but they reflect the author's more general interest in the civic-monumental landscape. Here is the material part of his entry for the year 354: "Victorinus rhetor et Donatus grammaticus praeceptor meus Romae insignes habentur. E quibus Victorinus etiam statuam in foro Traiani meruit." (Victorinus the rhetorician and Donatus the grammarian, my teacher, are held in great repute at Rome. Indeed, the latter was granted a statue in the Forum of Trajan.) Augustine (8.2.3) describes Victorinus as the "teacher of many noble senators," "qui etiam ob insigne praeclari magisterii . . . statuam Romano foro meruerat et acceperat" (who, indeed, on account of the high reputation of his teaching, had been granted and had accepted a statue in the Roman Forum). Coincidences of vocabulary may slightly exceed what the common object dictates. The imprecision of Augustine's *Romano foro*, compared with Jerome's *in foro Traiani*, is in keeping with the generic, figuralizing style of evocations of place in the *Confessions*.[19]

Whenever Augustine read of Victorinus's fame in the *Chronicle*, he then also found Jerome's reference to the Roman grammarian Donatus as *praeceptor meus*. This first overtly autobiographical intrusion by Jerome into the annals of his own time is quickly followed by another for the year 356, where we read that "the monk Antony died in the desert in the one hundred and fifth year of his age, who used to tell his many visitors about a certain Paul of Thebes, a man of remarkable sanctity, on whose death we have composed a short book."[20] Not only is Jerome the sole preserver for us of basic chronographical data for Latin authors of the classical period, he is also the first Christian author to annalize himself. The *Chronicle* is among the first works he is known to have published. A big book in an awkward format, requiring exceptional scribal labor, it was clearly intended for an elite readership. It would make, or so Jerome must have hoped, a desirable Christian counterpart to the deluxe volumes that we know were favored by the senatorial class of the late empire, books like the *Codex Calendar of 354*, the illustrated Vergils, and other codices of classical authors attested by *subscriptiones* copied in later manuscripts.[21] The *brevis libellus* cross-referenced in the *Chronicle* under the death of St. Antony, while less physically impressive, may have been directed in the first instance to the same clientele, if Ammianus's censorious remarks on the literary tastes of the urban artistocracy can be trusted.[22] The *Life of Paul* begins in most unholy fashion, with a gratuitous scene of the attempted rape of a young male ascetic by a demon disguised as a beautiful woman.[23] Aroused despite himself, pinned naked beneath his lissom assailant, our would-be hero has no visible means of escape. . . . Now read on! Jerome makes his literary debut with a Christian *fabula Milesiaca*, a grotesquely racy tale whose nearest extant Latin equivalents are in the *Golden Ass* of Apuleius.[24]

We do not know whether Augustine ever read the *Life of Paul*, nor even for sure that he ever read the Athanasian *Life of Antony*.[25] But we can be certain that he was shrewd enough to realize, if only on the strength of this cross-reference in the *Chronicle*, that Jerome had made a clever bid for the now twice-reflected glory of Athanasius's no less cleverly constructed protomonk by inventing an early competitor for him in the shape of the entirely mythical Paul of Thebes. Is it significant, or merely another coincidence, that the metaphorical toppling of the statue of Marius Victorinus in Book 8 of the *Confessions* is followed almost immediately by Augustine's own narrative appropriation of the example of Antony? To Jerome's telling of the story of Paul, as once told by Antony, a contemporary reader would now be able to juxtapose Augustine's telling of the story of the two readers of the *Life of Antony*, as once told to him and his friends at Milan by Ponticianus. Athanasius and Jerome were not the only writers skilled at "backing into the limelight" of the holy men they staged in their texts.[26] If that maneuver sounds too self-serving for Augustine, we may still allow that the theatrics of the *Confessions* share something with the new hagiodramaturgy of his time.

Marius Victorinus would never be canonized, yet Augustine gives him all the honors of a confessor of the faith. First, his baptismal profession is somewhat implausibly presented as an act of dangerous defiance. Then he becomes a white martyr of the Julianic "persecution." Augustine is our only source for the story of Victorinus's professorial resignation. (He would have been in his seventies by that time.) More than one teacher may have lost his job because of Julian's edict. It is therefore interesting to note how closely Augustine's claims for Victorinus echo the language of Jerome's report in the Chronicle (a. 363) on the case of Prohaeresius, an Athenian sophist. "When your servant Simplicianus narrated these things concerning Victorinus," says the narrator in the Confessions, "I was fired to imitate him; and indeed it was to that end that he had related them. But he added a further point." And Augustine (8.5.10) adds in his turn: "quod imperatoris Iuliani temporibus lege data prohibiti sunt Christiani docere litteraturam et oratoriam—quam legem ille amplexus loquacem scholam deserere maluit quam verbum tuum" [when a law was passed in the reign of the emperor Julian which forbade Christians to teach literature and oratory, Victorinus willingly complied, for he preferred to abandon the babbling school than your word]. Jerome (Chron. a. 363) had written: "Prohaeresius sofista Atheniensis lege data, ne Christiani liberalium artium doctores essent, cum sibi specialiter Iulianus concederet, ut Christianus doceret, scholam sponte deseruit." [When a law was passed which prevented Christian from being teachers of the liberal arts, the Athenian sophist Prohaeresius, despite receiving special permission from Julian to teach as a Christian, of his own accord abandoned his school.] Again, the language of the two passages is no more similar than we might expect if the author of the Confessions had used the Chronicle for a guide.

Among Christians, the idea that a Christian should give up a traditional cultivation or profession of the liberal arts for the sake of his religious faith is a (Latin) novelty of the post-Julianic era, promoted by the translator of Eusebius's Chronicle. Its classic or canonical instantiation is Jerome's "vision" or fantasy of being haled before Christ the examining magistrate on a charge of Ciceronianity, related in one of several purposeful digressions in the epistolary booklet on "How to Stay a Virgin," addressed by him to the young Julia Eustochium.[27] That story travesties the acts of martyrs of a bygone age, for whom the profession "Christianus sum" might mean death. The notice on Prohaeresius in the Chronicle is a thumbnail sketch for the pseudo-martyrdom of St. Jerome. Augustine must have known "How to Stay a Virgin." In the Confessions he plots his own changing relation to Cicero, Vergil, and the rest of classical literary culture partly in response to Jerome's radical prescriptions. The story of the "conversion" of Marius Victorinus belongs in that context.[28]

Modern scholars have difficulty deciding when Victorinus became a Christian, whether his statue in Trajan's Forum went up before or after his "conversion," and which of his translations or more original works (if any) Augustine actually knew.[29] These problems are surely related. To attempt to construct a biography of Victorinus on the basis of Augustine's narrative is wasted labor. The Victorinus of the *Confessions* is no near likeness of the Roman rhetorician and Christian theologian, no statue or *signum* in that mimetic sense. This Victorinus stands in for someone else, is a sign or signifier of the kind of literary professional Augustine once was and the kind of Christian he was once about to become. In the language of Book 3 of his treatise on biblical hermeneutics, the *De doctrina christiana* or "On Christian Teaching," a work broken off in its first recension around the time he began the *Confessions*, Victorinus is an "ambiguous sign."

Signa Imaginaria

"Angels and demons are notably absent in the *Confessions*," it has been said.[30] That is true, at least for the main autobiographical narrative. But they are not entirely absent even there. To speak for the demons there is Marius Victorinus. "Until this period of his life," writes Augustine, after mentioning the statue, "he had been a worshipper of idols and shared the abominable superstitions which at that time blew like an ill wind through almost the whole of the Roman nobility" (8.2.3). The next phrase is corrupt in our text but introduces lines from Book 8 of the *Aeneid* that refer to the cults of Anubis and other foreign gods worshipped at Rome. In resolving to profess his Christian faith openly, we are told, Victorinus reflected on his former readiness to speak on behalf of the "profane rites of the proud demons" (*sacris sacrilegis superborum daemoniorum*).

The theory that traditional Greco-Roman religion in all its forms, civic and mythic, was a traffic between human beings and demons masquerading as gods was one that Augustine would develop at length in the *City of God*. Many of its tenets are already set out in the unfinished *De doctrina christiana* of 396–97. Coming in Book 2 of that treatise to a general discussion of the types of disciplinary knowledge present in contemporary "pagan" culture (*apud gentes*), he first marks off a realm of superstitious observance. The apostle Paul had warned against idol worship and sacrifice as ways of associating with demons. Augustine amplifies: "What the apostle said about idols and sacrifices made in their honour must guide our attitude to all those fanciful signs [imaginariis signis] which draw people to the worship of idols or to the worship of the created order or any parts of it as if they were God."[31]

"Fanciful signs" is a possible rendering of imaginariis signis, but another sense may also be intended here: that of "artistic signs" or "signs made by a process of art."[32] Augustine is extending the Mosaic ban on idols or "graven images" to embrace a wider range of visual and other representations capable of being mistaken for, or of distracting attention from, the One True God. His use a few sentences later of the word curiositas, which is linked in other contexts with concupiscentia oculorum, points in the same direction. We are close to the roots of Augustinian iconophobia. Having dismissed all such "imaginary signs" as media of intercourse with demons, Augustine makes a further distinction between superfluous and useful forms of human communication (2.25.38). His inventory of superfluous signs is complicated by an attempt to distinguish strictly conventional signs from others that depend on a measure of visible similitude between signifier and signified. Signs used by actors in the theater, pictorial representations, and statues are mentioned in quick succession: "This whole category should be classed among superfluous human institutions," Augustine asserts. Then he adds, almost as an afterthought: "Finally, the thousands of fictional stories and falsehoods, which through their lies give people pleasure, are human institutions" and likewise to be shunned.[33]

For anyone who would credit Augustine with a positive theory of the role of the visual, plastic, and other "imaginative" arts in a Christian society, this passage is a huge stumbling block. Theatrical representations are only implicitly ruled out, not yet explicitly branded as superstitious practices, as they would be in the City of God.[34] Even so, when these stipulations are combined with the critique of drama and literary fictions in the Confessions, they already restrict the potential modes of approved artistic mimesis to a very narrow span. The Augustine who walked through the centro storico of Rome with a bag (or book) over his head is recognizably the same one who prospectively exiles poets, fiction writers, painters, sculptors, and other artificers of imagines or simulacra from the new Christian republic of the De doctrina christiana.

Augustine's teaching on images, signs, and artistic representations remains staggeringly difficult to grasp in its entirety,[35] and it is another task to relate it to his own practice as a maker of texts. One of the more productive lines of modern inquiry was opened half a century ago in a book called Mimesis.[36] Early in that book's chronological progress, its author protests against what he sees as the grossly exaggerated, "sinister" or "silly" realism of such later Latin prose-writers as Apuleius, Ammianus, and Jerome. Of a Roman crowd scene in Ammianus, which revolves around the figure of a tall, red-haired man named Peter Valvomeres, he writes: "it is the gestural, the graphically imaged, which predominates. . . . We are forced to picture the scene." Augustine releases us from this somber tyranny of the hyperreal; the discussion in *Mimesis* takes off from the passage describing Alypius's trials in the Flavian amphitheatre. Augustine's narrative is said to present a more human, less "spectral" reality. He pioneers a distinctive "Christian realism," a style that is both down-to-earth and capable of the sublime, like Christ himself. The new *sermo humilis* can be aligned with another specifically Christian phenomenon, namely the *figural* interpretation of one event or person in history as "signif[ying] not only itself but also [a] second [event or person], while the second involves or fulfills the first." Such events are held to be "vertically linked to Divine Providence, which alone is able to devise . . . a plan of history and supply the key to its understanding."[37]

This chapter of *Mimesis* is one of the densest in the book. Its value for the study of late ancient Christian texts is far from having been exhausted. The argument combines analysis of a mode of highly graphic or "glaringly pictorial" realism in later Latin literature, in regard to which Augustine appears as a major exception, with a compressed account of the emergence of a figural (or typological) mode of Christian exegesis, of which he is taken to be a leading exponent. How is the relation between Augustine the *antipictorialist* and Augustine the *figuralist* worked out in his own texts? We have noted the pivotal role in the "conversion" story of the *Confessions* played by a deiconized figure of Marius Victorinus. Augustine's narrative may also conceal—or displace—the likeness of another celebrated Latin rhetorician, already discovered in *Mimesis* in company with Ammianus and Jerome: Apuleius.

Asinus in Fabula

By most accounts, Augustine's recourse to Apuleius appears mainly in his *City of God* and is primarily to the latter's philosophical works.[38] One of these, the *De mundo*, is cited at *De civitate dei* 4.2 as Augustine addresses himself to Roman religion, a subject for which his main source is Varro, solemnly touted as "a man of the highest reputation for learning among the Romans and of most weighty authority" (4.1). The use of Varro as an engine of antipagan polemic is one of the supreme dialectical sleights of the *City of God*; Apuleius serves a similar turn without the fanfare.[39] Book 8 introduces him as "Apuleius the Platonist from Madauros" (8.14) and mines his treatise *De deo Socratis* for its demonology. By now Augustine is ready to let the demons bear full responsibility for the fictions and performances of traditional Roman religious culture. Their role as patrons of the Roman theater is evoked at length in earlier books. Augustine's reprise of Plato's expulsion of the poets from his republic seems to have been inspired directly by Apuleius's *On the God of Socrates*, which he claims should have been called "On the Demon of Socrates" (8.14).

In view of his confessed enthusiasm for *libri Platonicorum*, we could imagine Augustine devouring Apuleius's philosophical works as early as the 380s. The absence of any clear association of demons with literary fictions and stage-plays in Book 2 of the *De doctrina christiana* tells against such a hypothesis. Augustine's serious attention to the Apuleian corpus seems to have come later. Letter 138, addressed to the imperial tribune and *notarius* Marcellinus in 412, suggests a context. Marcellinus had raised questions about the power and purposes of the Christian God that would soon be dealt with at length in the *City of God*, dedicated to him. He also related an anti-Christian sentiment that does not reappear in that work: the claim that Apollonius of Tyana and Apuleius were greater magicians than Jesus Christ.[40] In response, Augustine gives a capsule version of a theory of the demonic inspiration of stage plays and other literary fictions (4.18). He then launches an ad hominem attack on Apuleius, arguing that a man as hungry for renown as this one from Madauros would have used his magical powers to obtain high office, had they been sufficient. As evidence of Apuleius's vaingloriousness, he cites a speech made by the latter in support of a proposal to raise a statue to him at Oea (4.19). Remarks in the same breath indicate that Augustine also knew something of Apuleius's defense against charges of magic in the *Apologia*, another text connecting him with Oea.

No oration of Apuleius *pro statua sibi apud Oeenses locanda* survives, but we do have one in which he agitates for such an honor at Carthage.[41] Hence, unless Augustine confused Oea with Carthage, which seems unlikely, we know that Apuleius spoke at least twice in favor of the erection of a monument to himself. In the speech at Carthage he refers to other cities where he had been honored in this way. A statue base dug up in his native Madauros, bearing an inscription to a *philosophus Platonicus*, is assumed to come from such a memorial.[42]

The statues of Apuleius at Oea and of Marius Victorinus at Rome may be the only monuments of their kind to appear in Augustine's works.[43] Both references are profoundly negative. As seen by Augustine, or rather as not seen by him but reported from texts read by him, these artifacts witness to a vicious self-love. They belong to the expanded class of idols as *signa imaginaria*, human creations pleasing to demons because they draw people "to the worship of the created order or parts of it as if they were God." Apuleius appears to have contributed to the elaboration of this Augustinian anti-iconism both substantially as a demonologist and incidentally as a man fond of seeing images of himself. In the latter respect, he provided the late antique reader with a striking counterexample to another Platonist philosopher, Plotinus, whose refusal to be the physical object of mimesis had to be circumvented by his disciples.[44] Such resistance was to be expected in a man of his profession. Apuleius, however, had more professions than *philosophus Platonicus*. Like Victorinus and Augustine after him, he was a rhetorician. And he had as rare an instinct as any man of his time for what we now call the "performative" aspect of social identity, especially its more pathetic registers.[45]

An example. In his speech to the senate of Carthage urging public funding and a good location for his statue, Apuleius fancifully compares his situation with that in which a famous writer of Greek comic drama once found himself, or was found.[46] Rain had stopped Philemon's public reading of his new play. The next day the crowd assembled again, eager for the sequel. Apuleius describes the packed theater and the audience's anticipation. They wait and wait. Still the star does not appear. Finally someone goes to look for him at home and finds him stone dead on his bed, frozen in the posture of one meditating what he has just read. So might the present speaker have been found, says Apuleius, after spraining his ankle in the *palaestra* a few days earlier! The city fathers should be relieved that he is not restaging the last act of Philemon's drama, and see to it that he is cast in bronze before becoming any more rigid in his own body. "Epideictic" does not quite capture this performance. It is a brilliant instance of what we might call the Apuleian *genus se-monstrativum* or "autodeictic" oration, a style of tragicomic recitation heavily reliant on ecphrasis.

The device is familiar to readers of the *Golden Ass*, even without the author to recite it. The day after the night in which he slays the "robbers" at Milo's gate, Lucius is hauled into the theater at Hypata to stand trial.[47] The place is packed, the atmosphere tense with excitement and an odd sense of barely suppressed laughter. An indictment is read, Lucius offers his defense, then suddenly the bereaved mother and widow of one of his victims come forward and make a piteous appeal for the bodies to be uncovered. Lucius is ordered to lift the pall and does so, to reveal . . . three punctured wineskins. The crowd explodes: "Some were hooting wildly with glee, others were clasping their stomachs in silent agony. All of them were in an ecstasy of joy, and kept turning to look at me as they made their way out of theatre [*meque respectantes theatro facessunt*]. And all this while," says Lucius the narrator, "I had stood like one of the statues or columns in the theatre as if congealed to stone."[48] Going one better, the citizens vote him a statue in bronze to commemorate his performance of the rites of the god of laughter. Covered in shame, Lucius implores them to keep their statues and images for some more worthy object.

The device is just as familiar to readers of the *Confessions*, though there are fewer laughs in that text: "Ponticianus went on with his story; but, Lord, even while he spoke you were wrenching me back toward myself, pulling me round from that standpoint behind my back which I had taken to avoid looking at myself [*retorquebas me ad me ipsum*]. You set me down before my face, forcing me to mark how despicable I was, how misshapen and begrimed, filthy and festering. I saw and shuddered, and there was no way of escaping from myself" (8.7.16).

The idea that the *Confessions* could owe something to the *Golden Ass* is not new,[49] and has lately been encouraged by a trend-setting study of Apuleius's novel.[50] What is to be considered now is the extent to which the distinctive and original narrative figuralism of the middle books of the *Confessions* could be the product of a recasting of Apuleian autodeictic in the mould of a "conversion" history provided by Jerome's *Chronicle* and related texts.

In Book 18 of the *City of God* Augustine refers in passing to a work of Apuleius that he has not previously quoted. The context is a sweeping narrative of the fortunes of the earthly city from the time of the Assyrian and Babylonian empires to the rise of Rome. For chronology Augustine relies (again) on Jerome's adaptation of Eusebius's *Chronicle*. His treatment of the material is based closely on Varro. Chapters 13 to 15 are an account of the emergence of pagan myths of gods and heroes and of the "theological" poets. The fall of Troy ushers in a further class of stories, many involving marvelous transformations like those of Odysseus's companions at the hands of Circe. Varro had tried to win credence for such tales. Augustine, though more sceptical, does not pronounce them definitively false. They may, he suggests, be truthful accounts of demonic contrivances. Or there could be some other mechanism at work. During his time in Italy, he had heard stories of unwary travelers being turned into pack animals by female innkeepers who fed them drugged cheese. "Afterwards," he recalls, "they were restored to their original selves. . . . This is what Apuleius, in the work which he entitled *The Golden Ass*, related or feigned as happening to him, that after taking a magic potion he became an ass, while retaining his human mind" (18.18).

"Sicut Apuleius . . . sibi ipsi accidisse . . . aut indicavit aut finxit." The *Golden Ass*, otherwise known as the *Metamorphoses of Lucius*, is the story of the trials and adventures of a man accidentally transformed into a donkey. His human shape is finally restored to him by the goddess Isis, into whose cult he is then initiated, emerging at the end of the process "like a statue [*in vicem simulacri*] while the curtains were suddenly pulled back and the people crowded in to gaze at me" (11.24).[51] Although the plot of Apuleius's narrative largely depends on a Greek source, the Isiac finale is apparently his own invention, as are a number of other episodes and inserted tales. The identification of Lucius the narrator-hero with Apuleius the author hangs by a single phrase in the last book, in which Lucius, on proceeding to initiation in the cult of Osiris, is described as "a man from Madauros," *Madaurensem* (11.27). For readers with no prior inclination to construe the *Metamorphoses* as Apuleian autobiography, this description comes as a shock, one of several in the final book which invite us to think more carefully about the relations between different plot lines and episodes, thus contributing to a sense of the whole work as a "hermeneutic entertainment."[52]

Augustine was surely not the first reader to collapse the persons of Lucius and Apuleius into one. He may not have remembered the story very well, since he mistakenly ascribes the initial transformation of the hero to a magic potion rather than an ointment. Alternatively, this minor alteration and the conflation of authorial and narratorial personae may have been actuated by the need to make the Apuleian case-history fit the syndrome of out-of-body experience that he is attempting to explain.[53] These concessions made, it remains a notable fact that our first recorded reader's response to the *Golden Ass* is one that makes of it a species of autobiography, and is offered by a writer whose own first-person narrative of serial misadventure and religious transformation is generally taken for a major generic innovation.

There is more at stake here than the history of literary genres. After Paul's on the road to Damascus, Augustine's "conversion" as narrated in the *Confessions* is the paradigm case of a type of religious experience to which the cultures of western Christianity have attributed enormous significance. It is not even obvious that Paul's "conversion" necessarily occurred before Augustine's, since the common understanding of what happened to Paul seems to have become all but inextricable in Christian tradition from Augustine's rendering of it. Augustine read Paul's life into his own by reading a "Life of Paul" out of Pauline texts whose original reference is not always as self-evidently autobiographical as Augustine makes it.[54] There is good reason to think that he read Apuleius the same way, even that adolescent enjoyment of the raciest work of this man of Madauros may have disposed him to read Paul as he eventually did.

✦ ✦ ✦

To call a work like the *Golden Ass* a "hermeneutic" entertainment is already to acknowledge the impact of professedly Christian-biblical modes of textual encounter on Western ideas of readerly engagement. The importance of Augustine in the longer history of Western hermeneutics is not in doubt. Among his more remarkable experiments is the technique of *reflexive figuralism* contrived for the *Confessions* and wrought to its highest point at the beginning of the narrative sequence that we think of as his "conversion." While there is finally no accounting for literary effects as eventful as these, one of the historian's jobs is to make them less completely mysterious.[55] This essay has been an attempt, after many others, to clarify the narrative-dramatic resources and devices of one of the best-known tales in western Christendom.[56]

If its main argument is sound, the objectification of "Augustine" as a hermeneutical figure in Book 8 of the *Confessions* can now be seen as the product of a fusion of two literary models that were readily available to the author: the annalistic self-dramatization of Jerome, his coadjutor and rival in Latin Christian exegesis, and the novelizing autodeixis of Apuleius, Africa's most celebrated philosopher-rhetorician. Eye-catching as it was likely to be, the resultant discursive strategy also carried the risk of making Augustine seem, if not simply self-regarding, then at best a sculptor of his own statue in the style of other "men of the Muses."[57] That this is not finally the impression most readers receive from the *Confessions* may be put down to two reasons. First, unlike Lucius-Apuleius, Augustine never restores himself to any visible shape more glorious than that of the ugly sinner exposed in the light of another man's tale. Secondly, by a stroke explicable only in terms of his imaginative response to Scripture, he denies the *signum* "Augustine" any mimetic function, encoding it instead within the totality of a divine text, beyond history and narration: "And is there anyone, Lord, who is not sometimes dragged a little beyond the bounds of what is needful? If there is such a man, he is a great man, so let him tell out the greatness of your name. I am not he, for I am a sinful man [*quia peccator homo sum*]; yet I will tell out the greatness of your name nonetheless; and may he who has overcome the world intercede for my sins, and count me among the frailer members of his body, because your eyes rest upon my imperfections and in your book everyone will be written [*et in libro tuo omnes scribentur*]."[58]

Notes

1. James J. O'Donnell, in Augustine, *Confessions*, ed. O'Donnell, 3.3.
2. Stock, *After Augustine*, chap. 3 ("Later Ancient Literary Realism"), 44.
3. Ibid., ("Reading and Conversion"), 77. On Christian figural exegesis, see now Dawson, *Christian Figural Reading*, building on the seminal work of Auerbach, notably his essay "Figura," in *Scenes from the Drama*, 11–77.
4. Translations from the *Confessions* follow the version by Maria Boulding, modified in places. Other translations are my own, unless credited. Latin text is found in *Confessiones*, ed. M. Skutella et al.
5. Augustine, *Retractationes* 2.6 (CCSL 37).
6. One might begin by tracking his citations of Psalm 138 (139): "O Lord, thou hast searched me, and known me." See already Knauer, *Psalmenzitate in Augustins Konfessionen*.
7. Jerome, *De viris illustribus* 101 (ed. Richardson). Augustine's initial reception of this work is recorded in his Letter 40, datable ca. 397–99, the period during which he wrote the main narrative of the *Confessions*.
8. Augustine, *Confessiones* 4.14.23: "ille rhetor ex eo erat genere, quem sic ambabam, ut vellem esse me talem."
9. McLynn, "Augustine's Roman Empire," 32–33.
10. Cf. the case of Palladius, an Athenian orator who captivated audiences at Rome in the 370s and was later summoned to the imperial court: Symmachus, *Epistulae* (hereafter Epp.) 1.15, 94.
11. Ammianus Marcellinus 14.6.8, trans. Hamilton, 46.
12. After Auerbach, *Mimesis*, chap. 3 ("The Arrest of Peter Valvomeres"): MacMullen, "Some Pictures in Ammianus Marcellinus"; Matthews, "Peter Valvomeres, Re-arrested"; Barnes, *Ammianus Marcellinus*, 11–19; Stock, "Later Ancient Literary Realism" (above, note 2).
13. The transaction is recorded by Paulinus, *Epistula* (hereafter Ep.) 3.3, to Alypius, ed. G. Hartel (CSEL 29), which also appears in the correspondence of Augustine, Ep. 24.3, ed. A. Goldbacher (CSEL 34).
14. Paulinus to Alypius, ibid. 4: "Specialiter autem hoc a te peto . . . ut pro hac historia temporum [sc. Eusebii] referas mihi omnem tuae sanctitatis historiam." Courcelle, "La correspondance avec Paulin de Nole"; Augustine, *Confessions*, ed. O'Donnell, 2.360–62; Trout, *Paulinus of Nola*, 202–5. Further signs of the implication of Paulinus in Augustine's literary and spiritual projects of the later 390s: Conybeare, *Paulinus Noster*, passim.
15. Marrou, "La vie intellectuelle," 109 n. 3; Packer, *Forum of Trajan in Rome*, 1:5–10, surveys the epigraphic and other evidence for the later imperial period but misses these references.
16. Helm, "Hieronymus' Zusätze."

17. Jerome, *Chronicon* (hereafter *Chron.*), anno 327 C.E. (Nazarius), a. 336 (Pater, Nazarii filia [!], Tiberianus), a. 353 (Gennadius, Minervius), a. 354 (Victorinus, Donatus), a. 355 (Alcimus, Delfidius) (ed. R. Helm, CGS 33).
18. Ibid., a. 240 B.C.E. (Ennius; also a. 168), a. 179 (Caecilius), a. 18 (Vergil).
19. Cf. Courcelle, *Les Confessionse*, 558: "S'il substitue à la donnée topographique exacte de Jérôme, la formule vague 'Romano foro,' c'est parce qu'il écrit à l'usage de lecteurs africains."
20. Jerome, *Chron.*, a. 356.
21. Caltabiano, *Litterarum Lumen*, esp. 63–73. On the implied readership of Jerome's *Chronicle*, see Inglebert, *Les Romains chrétiens*, 276–77. Rebenich, "Asceticism, Orthodoxy and Patronage: Jerome in Constantinople," situates this work and the *Life of Paul* in Jerome's early career as a publishing Christian writer.
22. Ammianus Marcellinus, *Res Gestae* 28.4.14 mentions their fondness for the third-century biographer Marius Maximus, who, according to the *Scriptor(es) Historiae Augustae* (Firmus 1.2), "dabbled in fabulous histories" (Magie, ed.).
23. Jerome, *Vita Pauli* 3 (Migne, *Patrologia Latina* [PL] 23).
24. Bauer, "Novellistisches bei Hieronymus Vita Pauli"; Weingarten, "Jerome and the *Golden Ass*"; Huber-Rebenich, "Hagiographic Fiction as Entertainment," 199–200.
25. Apart from the highly mediated account in the *Confessions*, the only reference to Antony in Augustine's writings is *De doctrina christiana*, praefatio 8, which makes a claim for him that is not directly borne out by the *Life*. Monceaux, "Saint Augustin et saint Antoine," assumes no direct encounter of Augustine with the Athanasian text; but cf. Frank, "Antonius Aegyptius Monachus."
26. The phrase is Peter Brown's.
27. Jerome, *Epistulae* 22.29–30: "Referam tibi meae infelicitatis historiam" (ed. Hilberg, CSEL 54). The letter, entitled "De virginitate servanda" at *De viris illustribus* 135 and in the manuscript tradition, dates from Jerome's final period in Rome, 381–84.
28. Having read Jerome's commentary on Galatians (Ep. 40.3–4.), Augustine would also have noted the negative judgment delivered there on Victorinus's scriptural culture, which reinforces the theory of literary "conversion" dramatized in the letter to Eustochium: "Non quod ignorem Caium Marium Victorinum, qui Romae me puero rhetoricam docuit, edidisse commentarios in Apostolum, sed quod occupatus ille eruditione saecularium litterarum scripturas omnino sanctas ignoraverit, et nemo possit, quamvis eloquens, de eo bene disputare quod nesciat" (*Commentarius in epistulam Pauli ad Galatas.*, prol. [PL 26]). This was a challenge Augustine himself had to meet: Vessey, "Conference and Confession."
29. Following Hadot, *Marius Victorinus*, 27ff., 302ff., state of the question in Augustine, *Confessions*, ed. O'Donnell, 2.13–15. See also Courcelle, *Les Confessions*, 557–58, and Nello Cipriani, "Marius Victorinus," in Fitzgerald, ed., *Augustine through the Ages*, 533–35.
30. Peter Brown, "Asceticism: Pagan and Christian," in Cameron and Garnsey, eds., *The Cambridge Ancient History*, 13:628. "Augustine's *Confessions*," Brown writes in the same paragraph, "was a book strikingly different from any work that came out of the exprinces of the Egyptian desert." This important point is somewhat

blurred by the (perhaps unnecessary) concession that Augustine "had been converted to continence ten years earlier by the story of Antony."

31. Augustine, De doctrina christiana 2.23.36, ed. and trans. Green, Augustine, 99. Augustine's Pauline reference (1 Cor. 10:19–20) is the same as Jerome's at the
moment of introducing the "story" of his near martyrdom at Ep. 22.29 (above,
note 28).

32. The Thesaurus Linguae Latinae 7.402 gives the primary sense of imaginarius as "ad
imaginem arte factam pertinens," citing Diocletian's Edict on Prices with its pay
rate for pictores imaginarii, and a handful of other late classical texts, including this
one from the De doctrina christiana.

33. De doctrina christiana 2.24.39: "In picturis vero et statuis ceterisque huiusmodi
simulatis operibus, maxime peritorum artificum, nemo errat, cum similia viderit,
ut agnoscat, quibus sint rebus similia. Et hoc tantum genus inter superflua
hominum instituta numerandum est, nisi cum interest, quid eorum, qua de causa et ubi
et quando et cuius auctoritate fiat. Milia denique fictarum fabularum et falsitatum,
quarum mendaciis homines delectantur, humana instituta sunt." The exclusion
clause (here in italics) is apparently designed to take account of the practical
utility, even for Christians, of being able to read the social significance of such
forms of representation. At this point, the ideal Christian subject becomes a
reader of signs rather than a viewer of art objects. Mimesis yields to semiosis. For the
importance of that distinction in Augustine's thought, and its relation to ancient
philosophy and literary theory, see Pollmann, Doctrina christiana; Pollmann, "Zwei
Konzepte," esp. 275–76. Pollmann's work is fundamental for the present inquiry. Among the key Augustinian texts she quotes is one from the Quaestiones
evangeliorum (ca. 399) on biblical signification through images: "cum autem fictio
nostra refertur ad aliquam significationem, non est mendacium, sed aliqua figura
veritatis" (2.5.1). Pagan statues appear again at De doctrina christiana 2.17.27 ("simulacra Musarum") and 3.7.11 ("simulacra manufacta deos hab[ita]").

34. For evidence of a hardening in Augustine's attitude toward pagan spectacles after
399, see Markus, End of Ancient Christianity, 107–23.

35. Pollmann, Doctrina christiana, and Markus, Signs and Wonders, break new ground.
See also Brown, "Images as a Substitute for Writing."

36. Above, note 12.

37. Auerbach, Mimesis, chap. 3, here 54, 58, 66–67, 73–74. Discussion by Dawson,
Christian Figural Reading, 83–113; White, Figural Realism, 87–100.

38. Hagendahl, Augustine and the Latin Classics, 1.17–33; O'Donnell, "Augustine's Classical Readings," 149–50; O'Daly, Augustine's "City of God," 253. Citations of the
City of God follow the edition of Dombart and Kalb, Sancti Aurelii Augustini episcopi
de civitate Dei.

39. See now O'Daly, Augustine's "City of God," chaps. 6–7.

40. Cf. Augustine, Epp. 102.32 (redated 412 by O'Donnell, "Augustine's Classical
Readings," 149 n. 15), 136.1, 137.13 (to Volusianus) (ed. Goldbacher, CSEL 44).
O'Donnell makes an attractive argument for seeing the circle of Volusianus and
fellow refugees from Italy as the source for a codex of Apuleius's philosophical
works that came into Augustine's hands at this time.

41. Apuleius, *Florida* 16 (ed. Vallette).

42. Gsell, *Inscriptions latines de l'Algérie*, no. 2115. "Philosophus Platonicus" is the title used consistently by Apuleius of himself and by later writers in reference to him; Harrison, *Apuleius*, 19 n. 5. The "image" of Apuleius in his own fashioning and later tradition is the subject of a forthcoming study by Julia Haig Gaisser.

43. It is not certain that the statue at Madauros was still visible when Augustine was a student there. For restoration of public works in that town in the mid-fourth century, see Lepelley, *Les cités de l'Afrique romaine*, 2.128–33.

44. Porphyry, *On the Life of Plotinus and the Order of His Books* 1, discussed in this context by Stock, *After Augustine* 40–41, who concludes: "it would appear that a set of literary works is replacing a portrait based on memory as the symbolic icon of the master. This is an indirect connection with the method brought to perfection in Augustine" (43). Cf. Cox, *Biography in Late Antiquity*, 108–10; O'Donnell, "Authority of Augustine," 8.

45. For his peers, see Gleason, *Making Men*; Whitmarsh, *Greek Literature and the Roman Empire*, chap. 2; Goldhill, ed., *Being Greek under Rome*.

46. Apuleius, *Florida* 16, analyzed by Harrison, *Apuleius*, 116–20, as "a good example of [the author's] high epideictic style" (118).

47. Apuleius, *Metamorphoses* 3.1–11 (ed. Hanson).

48. Ibid., 3.10–12, trans. E. J. Kenney (London: Penguin, 1998), 45–46.

49. See, e.g., Courcelle, *Les Confessionse*, 101–109 ("Le péché de 'curiosité': Augustin et Apulée"), a line of argument previously suggested by H. J. Mette in an article of 1956, extended by Walsh, "The Rights and Wrongs of Curiosity," and retrojected on Apuleius by Shumate, *Crisis and Conversion*; Martin, "Apulée, Virgile, Augustin"; Burrus and Keller, "Confessing Monica."

50. Winkler, *Auctor and Actor*. For Winkler, Apuleius is a fabulist "fascinated by problems of resignification, of revealing new meanings at the end that were in a sense already there." Such a perspective, he argues, "may start fruitful lines of thought about resignification as both a narratological and a theological process" (98). For explicit comparisons with Augustine's *Confessions*, see 141–42, 194.

51. This passage is appositely cited by McLynn, "Seeing and Believing," 248, in a discussion of the civic-monumental ostentation of Christian "conversion" from the time of Constantine. On the *Golden Ass* as novelistic epideixis, see Harrison, *Apuleius*, 226–35.

52. Winkler's formula. Harrison, *Apuleius*, concurs in seeing Apuleius's novel as fundamentally a work of "literary entertainment and cultural display, rather than ideological commitment" (259).

53. According to Winkler, *Auctor and Actor*, 297, "Augustine seems pleased to have caught Apuleius in a dilemma: either he was an ass or he was a novelist—in either case his contemptibility is self-proclaimed." This reading may make too light of Augustine's own dilemmas.

54. As demonstrated by Fredriksen, "Paul and Augustine." "The New Testament canon . . . serves as a sort of chamber for [a] mythic feed-back system, where Augustine the convert interprets Paul's conversion through his own, and his own through what he sees as Paul's . . . He . . . sees in Paul . . . the charter for the

introspective self as the premier theological category, the setting for the drama of human will and divine grace" (27). For Apuleius between Paul and Augustine, see now Smith, "Apuleius and Luke," 88–99.

55. For a model, see Clark, "Rewriting Early Christian History."

56. A first draft was aired before the Late Ancient Studies Forum at Duke University in November 2000, at the kind invitation of Elizabeth Clark.

57. Marrou, *History of Education in Antiquity*, 44, 98, citing Plotinus, *Enneads* 1.6.9: "Be always at work carving your own statue." Cf. the same writer's *Mousikos aner*; and Brown, *World of Late Antiquity*, 32.

58. Augustine, *Confessiones* 10.31.47, closing on a citation of Ps. 138:16. See O'Donnell, in Augustine, *Confessions* 3.216–17; Knauer, *Psalmenzitate*, 94–95; and, for God's book as a "totality of the signifier," Derrida, *Of Grammatology*, 18, discussed further in my "Reading like Angels."

✣   Hellenism and Historiography: Gregory
of Nazianzus and Julian in Dialogue

SUSANNA ELM

On 25 June 363 the emperor Julian met his death on the Persian battlefields
near Ctesiphon, after little more than two years as sole ruler. A few months
earlier a young Cappadocian from Diocaesarea—Nazianzus in the native
tongue—had announced his decision to lead "the true philosophical life," at
first to his city, and then to friends in Constantinople and elsewhere. Though
he had received advanced training in Athens, his decision came as a surprise
to many, who had expected him to embark on the more customary as well as
lucrative career of a provincial rhetor.

But why should this have anything to do with Julian? Julian the emperor
and Gregory the Theologian are almost never mentioned in the same breath.
If we are to trust the impression given by the scholarly literature, they might
as well have inhabited different planets—even though they were contemporaries, spent much of their youth in relative proximity in Cappadocia, and
overlapped for some time at Athens. The historiographic Julian and the
historiographic Gregory have remained separated, not so much because one
was an emperor and the other merely one of his subjects. Rather, what
crucially sets them apart is that one was a pagan and the other a Christian.

But, what happens if we suspend the "pagan" and "Christian" aspect of
their respective personae for a while, and instead bring these two men into
dialogue? If we permit them to talk to each other, we might, I would like to

propose, actually gain new insights and a new understanding of the emergence of Byzantine culture and society. This is because Gregory's oeuvre, with its "marriage between Christianity and classical culture," became fundamental for "Byzantine civilization."[1]

But—and this is the most significant aspect for our present purpose—Gregory's oeuvre and the central themes he addressed and developed in all the literary genres of the time were a direct response to Julian and the characteristics of his reign. Julian was the catalyst that spurred Gregory into action. Julian's thoughts and actions significantly influenced Gregory's response, which in its turn became foundational for many aspects of later Byzantine thought and institutions.

What, then, were the themes and issues that Julian raised to which Gregory felt compelled to respond? If we listen to these two men talk, four interrelated topics, or questions, emerge most clearly. First, what was the nature of the true philosophical life? Second (and here both agreed), given that the true philosophical life is divinely inspired, in what language did the divine communicate? Further (and here, too, both agreed), given that the divine was one and universal, was that universality best embodied by the words of the ancient gods of the Greeks and the Romans, or by the Word of the Christian God? Fourth and finally, who could lay claim to the true, divinely created universality of Greekness within the Roman *oikoumene*? In other words, who was the true heir of Greekness within Rome, and who could claim to represent true Hellenism?

Barely a generation after Constantine made Christianity legal, it was not at all clear what "being Christian" meant for members of the Greco-Roman elite. Therefore, instead of presupposing, as a scholar of the period, that there was a clear dividing line between being "pagan" or "Christian," and instead of proceeding accordingly in two diverging directions, one might more fruitfully explore another question. Namely, how did members of the elite discuss and articulate the subject of differing religious belief prior to the stabilizing reign of Theodosius I? In this context, *Greekness* (a term I will use rather than "Hellenism" because of the historiographic weight of the latter),[2] functions very much as recently defined by Simon Goldhill in his introduction to *Being Greek under Rome: Cultural Identity, the Second Sophistic, and the Development of Empire*. It is part of a "complex picture. . . . Affiliations to Greekness are seen—explored, contested, projected—. . . in a proclaimed communality of *paideia*, a shared system of reference and expectation [linking the elite of the empire]." In this context, what it meant to be Greek was "implicit in claims to tradition and the past; in the study of philosophy, rhetoric and medicine; the performance of ritual; in building projects; in sport and other entertainments." Most important, "Greek becomes a language of advancement and a key sign of the cultivated citizen. The Greek language transcends—and provokes debate about—ethnic origin in the determination of affiliation and status." Hence, Greekness as part of paideia was a crucial component of the "complex process of self-placement" in the society of the later Roman empire.[3] With that in mind, it is almost time to bring Julian and Gregory into dialogue.

However, before delving into a short summary of Julian's first proclamations as Augustus between 361 and 363, and Gregory's response in the years 362 and 363–64, I would like to step back for a moment to discuss the endlessly fascinating and always crucial topic that holds such a central place in the work of Elizabeth A. Clark, and which has profited so enormously from her analysis: historiography. More specifically, I will focus on the kind of historiographic persona scholarship has assigned to Julian and Gregory respectively as well as some of the underlying methodological assumptions that have led to the creation of these personae. Of course, the reasons for the historiographic assessments of our dramatis personae are complex and have a long intellectual history. Therefore, the following will only provide a brief overview.[4]

To begin with Julian, a short list of some significant recent titles is revealing: *Julian the Apostate, Julian and Hellenism, Julian's Gods: Religion and Philosophy in the Thought and Action of Julian the Apostate*.[5] "Apostate" or deserter is a polemical term, denoting a person who has abandoned his or her original religion—in Julian's case Christianity in favor of "paganism." Hence, by denoting him as such, Christianity sets the agenda from which Julian "deviates." However, almost all the works on Julian, including those that feature "Apostate" in the title, approach Julian from the opposite vantage point, that is, they focus, to a greater and lesser degree, on the viability of Hellenism and the "paganism" of which Julian is seen as the embodiment.[6] Hence, Julian figures prominently in works discussing pagan survival, Hellenism, or Hellenic religions in late antiquity in general. Yet, in this context Julian represents a historiographic paradox: though he epitomizes the paradigm of a pagan Neoplatonist, his paganism is frequently seen as "inauthentic" and "idiosyncratic," flawed by the emperor's Christian youth.[7]

The scholarly portraits of Julian and his reign comment implicitly or explicitly on the crucial pagan-Christian relationship, and here the underlying notion of the battle to death of "two religious systems" is hard to overcome, even in studies that privilege the concept of a slow and complex transformation.[8] Paganism and Christianity remain on either side of "the divide," whereby, historiographically speaking, paganism is all too frequently defined as the entire religious universe delineated by our late fourth- and early fifth-century Christian sources as being not Christian.[9]

In this context, late antique Hellenism occupies, at first glance, a middle ground.[10] On the one hand, it is something that Porphyry, Iamblichus, and certainly Julian considered a religion.[11] However, late antique Hellenism is also a "quality" shared by at least some Christians, since, to cite Isocrates, "the name Hellenes is given rather to those who share our *paideia* than to those who share a common blood."[12] Consequently, taking their cue from studies of "classic" Hellenism (i.e., the complex notion of a "period in a region," the Greek-speaking East after Alexander and prior to Roman dominance), many scholars have a very nuanced and comprehensive definition of late antique Hellenism, which incorporates notions of ethnicity and culture.[13] Thus, Glen Bowersock states in his fundamental work, *Hellenism in Late Antiquity*:

> I have tried to open up a new approach to Greek culture in the Christian empire, to determine why and how it survived as it did and why it was so regularly identified with paganism (despite the indignation of certain fathers of the Church). The study of late Hellenism reveals a pagan culture that is far from moribund. It is rather a living culture responding as sensitively to its Christian environment as Christianity itself responded to the pagan world in which it grew to maturity.[14]

This underscores my point. Most scholars consider paganism and Hellenism a priori as synonymous. Both are seen as essentially different from Christianity, which, as Robin Lane Fox claims, had "very distinctive roots."[15] This view does by no means negate the fact that Christianity and Hellenism share a tradition. However, the act of conversion to Christianity effectively marks the end of the effects of that tradition for historiographical purposes: since Hellenism remains in the final analysis synonymous with paganism, it is opposed to Christianity. Therefore, a postconversion influence not only of the "culture" but also of the belief systems associated with Hellenism on Christians need not be discussed—it falls under the rubric of Christianity.[16] Conversely, the impact of Christian beliefs on later "paganism" remains understudied—despite Glen Bowersock's observation (in the same work) that art historians such as Kurt Weitzmann have long since pointed to shared inheritances and mutual enrichment.[17] For example, while acknowledging that Julian was brought up as a Christian, no study on Julian cites any work by a Christian author (except the *Invectives*) which might have influenced Julian's Christianity, or, at the very least, attempts a discussion of the kind of Christianity prevalent in Asia Minor and Gaul during the later years of Constantius.[18]

After Constantine, the historiographical barriers harden. Even scholars who are fully conscious of the fact, so eloquently stated by Robert Markus, that "there just is not a different culture to distinguish Christians from their pagan peers, only their religion," shy away from positing even the potential for a mutual influence in matters of belief once this religious distinction has been made.[19]

What is the picture like once we shift the perspective? What role does Julian play for those who discuss Gregory of Nazianzus? Like his contemporary Julian, Gregory of Nazianzus, too, is a composite of several historiographic personalities. The most dominant persona, overshadowing all else, is that of Gregory the Christian. Within the circumference of that super-persona, one may discern several subpersonae, of which Gregory "the Theologian" and coarchitect of neo-Nicene orthodoxy, and Gregory as the abject ecclesiastical failure, are the most important ones in the present context.[20] As far as the persona "Gregory the Theologian" is concerned, the only Julian to make a cameo appearance in its construction is Julian the "Apostate" and imperial legislator. Julian and his reign are seen as an interlude of mercifully short duration, which briefly interrupted Gregory's seamless move toward his destiny as a theologian by forcing him to write two invectives against the (recently deceased) emperor.[21] No scholarly work on Gregory that I know of includes more than a cursory mentioning of Julian's philosophical writings, even though Frederick Norris, for example, in his excellent study of Gregory's theological orations states explicitly that "Nazianzen and Julian shared so many common features that their differences needed emphasis."[22] However, this statement addresses solely Julian and Gregory's mastery of rhetorical technique.[23] Shared *paideia*, here interpreted in its most restrictive sense, remains devoid of any content that could have influenced Gregory's religious thought.[24]

Again, these observations reflect underlying conceptualizations of the meaning of Hellenism in a fourth-century context, now seen, however, from the "Christian" perspective.[25] In that context, Gregory functions with regard to "Christian Hellenism" just as Julian does with regard to paganism. But whereas Julian measures the time remaining until the eventual death of paganism, Gregory is used to judge the degree to which Christianity did or rather ought to have remained "alien" from its surrounding Greek culture.[26]

Again like Julian, Gregory becomes an indicator of purity, this time of the "Christian message."[27] How the relationship of Gregory's message to "Christian Hellenism" is understood depends, in the majority of scholarly discussions, on the scholar's own judgment of what this relationship ought to have been—a subject that far exceeds the limits of the present essay.

At this point, the combination of Gregory's historiographic superpersona "Christian" with that of the "ecclesiastical failure" becomes relevant. Nearly the entire scholarly literature on Gregory, excluding the work of Neil McLynn but including, for example, John McGuckin's recent *Saint Gregory of Nazianzus: An Intellectual Biography*, has characterized Gregory, to quote Raymond van Dam, as "a man whom contemporaries and subsequent readers admired for the fluency of his theological treatises about the nature of the Trinity, . . . but who 'stuttered' as he remembered and recorded memories about himself."[28] The reconciliation of this duality—here the most fluently rhetorical theologian, there a man who stuttered when writing about himself and his choice of the philosophical life—poses, of course, a historiographic problem. The root of this problem lies in the very manner in which Gregory wrote his own life and one of the central themes of that work, namely, the continuing struggle between the *bios theoretikos* and the *bios praktikos*. In short, at stake for Gregory from his very first to his last writings was the nature of "true" philosophical life as the correct and appropriate mixture of retreat and involvement in the affairs of the community. Yet, in Gregory's case the exegesis of this classic Platonic and Aristotelian theme, for centuries a mandatory exercise for just about everyone belonging to the educated and therefore governing classes of the Greco-Roman world, has given rise to numerous discussions (more often than not thinly disguised attempts at psychology), because it has been read exclusively in "Christian" terms: as the struggle of a man burning with desire for ascetic retreat yet forced against his will into priestly office and the nasty world of church politics. Gregory's seeming preference for solitary asceticism is then interpreted, for example, as the result of a young man's resistance to his overbearing (formerly pagan) father and overidentification with his (always Christian) mother;[29] as the musings of a sensitive soul or a *romantique avant la lettre*; or as the shortcomings of a pusillanimous, indecisive man. All scholars agree, however, that Gregory's somewhat excessive desire for retreat rendered him problematic as a bishop, since he was so evidently incapable of holding an office and "sticking" with it.[30] Because Gregory is considered above all a Christian, his discussions of the philosophical life have been read and translated into "Christian" terms—as debating the monastic life exclusively. Therefore, and on that basis justifiably so, they have remained hermetically sealed off from other debates of the "true philosophical life" occurring at the same time among Gregory's non-Christian contemporaries. Foremost among those contemporaries was, of course, the emperor Julian, and with that it is finally time to return to the years between 361 and 364 and the dialogue between the two men.

In February 360 "barbarian" troops stationed in Paris acclaimed their commander, the Caesar Flavius Claudius Julianus, as Augustus. Constantius, the ruling emperor and Julian's uncle, was not pleased. In May 361 Constantius declared Julian a public enemy (*hostis publicus*), to which Julian responded with a publicity campaign to justify the impending civil war. He wrote several official letters to the citizens of Athens, Corinth, Sparta, Rome, and Constantinople, of which only the ones to the Athenians and to the Constantinopolitan senator-philosopher Themistius have been preserved.[31]

In his *Letter to the Athenians*, "so that it may become known to you and through you to the rest of the Greeks" (270b), Julian declared his uncle Constantius a criminal who had murdered most of his own and Julian's family in 337, and who had finished the job in 354 by eliminating his nephew and Julian's half-brother Gallus.[32] In the same letter Julian pointed out why he alone had been saved: "The Gods by means of philosophy" (272a) had spared his life, nurtured him throughout his youth, kept him "pure and untouched," and had granted him spectacular military victories in Gaul so that he would, as he elaborated shortly thereafter in his *Oration 7 Against the Cynic Heraclius*, restore the "ancestral temples, which . . . had been despised and stripped of the votive offerings."[33]

But the gods had done more. Zeus and Helios, in concert with Athena, had chosen Julian as their son, and had revealed his divine parentage while Julian had been captured in "a slumber of trance" (Or. 7.230b). When he had awoken from this slumber and fallen into despair in light of the sheer magnitude of his task, Hermes, the god of eloquence, had come to his rescue.

In short, Julian's letter to the (militarily insignificant) Athenians, written on the march toward Constantinople, was both autobiography and *apologetikos logos*, intended to demonstrate that he, the usurper, was in fact the legitimate ruler, whereas his uncle, the Augustus, was a criminal. Julian, though born to the same dynasty as Constantius and Constantine, was in effect a son of Helios, chosen by the gods to rectify the crimes of his earthly family through divinely inspired philosophy. Philosophy, not dynastic tradition, was the legitimization of his rule.

But what kind of philosophy did Julian have in mind? Lest there should be any doubt, Julian issued another letter on his way toward Constantinople, addressed to the philosopher Themistius. Themistius had been one of Julian's teachers, especially of Plato and Aristotle. Further, a few years previously, Constantius had made Themistius a member of the Constantinopolitan senate—a body now on Julian's mind.[34] Julian's letter responds to an earlier one (now lost) sent by the philosopher in his official capacity, in which Themistius had encouraged Julian to "shake off all thought of leisure and inactivity" and to rival Alexander or Marcus Aurelius, "men of old who [had been] at once philosophers and kings [*philosophountes homou kai basileuontes*]" (253b–54b).

Julian professed amazement at such a suggestion. It sounded to him as if Themistius, the specialist on Aristotle and no slouch on Plato, had misread the masters' teachings regarding the proper balance between the theoretical life of retreat and the political one of action (257d–59b). Indeed, by suggesting that he, Julian, prefer a life of action, Themistius had incorrectly equated Aristotle's "lawgivers and political philosophers" with emperors. In Julian's reading Aristotle had done no such thing, and he proceeds to distinguish clearly between those who were "leaders and champion of philosophers"— Julian's own goal—and "emperors" like Constantius (260d–62d).[35] Further, Julian was of the firm opinion that Socrates performed greater tasks than Alexander, because he had true opinions about the gods as a result of the philosophical life devoted to theory, and this is the life Julian wishes to champion (264c, 266a–b). Julian's true philosophical life was therefore the life of theory, and not the active philosophical life as advocated by the "political philosopher" Themistius—who had been sponsored by Constantius.

To summarize, by late 361 the contender Julian had declared publicly that he was the sole legitimate ruler because the gods had chosen him "by means of philosophy." These gods were Zeus and Helios, and the philosophy in question was, first, divinely inspired and, second, one that privileged theory and retreat over practice and involvement.

Constantius died on 3 November 361, while on his way to Constantinople to face his nephew. On his deathbed he declared Julian his legitimate heir.[36] Six weeks later, on 11 December 361, Julian entered Constantinople.[37] In January 362 he issued edicts that restituted all temples and their properties, and permitted all Christian clergy who had been exiled as a result of Constantius's various decisions to return to their country. At the same time, he sent letters inviting a variety of philosophers to court, from Cynics to strict Platonists, and including the Aristotelian Aetius and Basil of Caesarea, both

Christians.[38] In addition, he acquired a new chief court physician or *archi-atros*, a Cappadocian called Caesarius, who was none other than Gregory of Nazianzus's younger brother.[39]

During the early months of 362 the emperor, in public debates with many of the philosophers now at court, elaborated the themes just outlined further in three orations. Julian used one of these orations, the *Hymn to the Mother of the Gods*, which he wrote on the occasion of Cybele's festival in late March 362, to present his city and the *oikoumenê* with his thoughts on the nature of the gods.[40] According to Julian, his gods, Zeus/Helios, their mother, and her lover Attis-Logos (*Hymn* 179c) were truly universal. They—to condense his thought rather drastically—shared one divine essence, that is, they were one, though manifest in different *hypostaseis* (or persons). This one supreme, divine being, multiple yet one, was the "God of all," and its universality was proven—among other things—in the progression of the worship of the Mother of the Gods (whom he never calls Cybele) among the peoples. There-fore, Julian opens his *Hymn* with a discussion of the reasons why the Mother of the Gods "was . . . introduced in the beginning among us Romans" (159a).

In Julian's retelling of the familiar story of her triumphant arrival in Rome, the Great Mother Goddess is the paragon of his understanding of Greek *Romanitas*. Though originally from Phrygia, the Mother of the Gods had first been worshipped by the Greeks, "and not by any ordinary Greeks but by Athenians" upon the suggestion of Apollo through the oracle at Delphi. The very same god through the same oracle had then advised the transfer of the goddess's statue from Phrygia, specifically from Pergamon, to Rome, where her arrival had led to victory over Carthage and thus initiated Rome's glorious expansion (*Hymn* 159a–61b). The goddess, "who was that very Deo whom they worship, and Rhea and Demeter too" (159b), and her worship thus mirrored the progress of the Roman *oikoumenê*. Combining in her person the very essence of Phrygia, Pergamon, Athens, and Rome, the goddess embodied the correct mixing and merging of "us . . . and the Greeks, who are of the same parentage as we are," as Julian said shortly thereafter in his *Against the Galilaeans* (200a).[41] By celebrating her entry into Rome just after *his own* triumphant *adventus* into Constantinople, Julian thus made clear that *his* Constantinople was not Constantius's "new" Rome. It was the "ancient" Byzantium of Asia Minor, the land in which the goddess had originated and where she was now celebrating the universality of her "Greek *Romanitas*."[42]

Julian's other two orations delivered in the first months of his rule were prompted by debates with Cynic philosophers.[43] They focus once more on the crucial issue of the "true" philosophical life, as prescribed by the gods. According to Julian, philosophers were priests. Since true philosophy correctly practiced was the sole path toward the divine, the correct interpretation of the writings of divine men such as Plato, Aristotle, Diogenes, Porphyry, and Iamblichus was an act of piety vis-à-vis the gods, and a guarantee of the good order of society. Consequently, it was essential that those who practiced and taught philosophy undergo the proper training in "the art of arts and the science of sciences" (Or. 6.183a). According to Julian, leisure was the precondition enabling the philosopher to acquire a sound knowledge of the Greek language, rhetoric, and literary genres as the preparation for philosophical "know thyself," which in turn led to a merging with the divine to the most complete extent possible. Furthermore, such training was the best defense against those who perverted the philosophical life through populist actions of display, driven by vanity and greed: uneducated Cynics, and the "apotaktistai, a name applied to certain persons by the impious Galilaeans" (Or. 7.224b).[44]

Within weeks of this last statement, Julian issued an edict, followed by an imperial letter, in which he declared that philosophy and belief in "our" gods—that is, those of the Greeks and Romans—were one.[45] The only man who could teach the "right paideia" was the man who understood clearly that words and their content were likewise one.[46] Those who thought otherwise should "expound the Gospel of Matthew and Luke in the churches of the Galilaeans."

Among those now relegated to being a "Galilaean" was the brother of Julian's court physician Caesarius: Gregory, the young Cappadocian who had just announced his decision to lead the philosophical life. What was Gregory's reaction? We will, of course, never know what exactly Gregory said on that Easter celebration in 362. But we possess the published version of his oration, which he circulated late in 362 or early in 363. In the current numbering of his orations this is the second, though the majority of manuscript collections numbers it as the first, usually under the heading "apology for his flight to Pontus and on the priesthood."[47] Indeed, as mentioned above, Gregory delivered the oration on the occasion of his ordination as priest at the hands of the bishop, his father. He had also spent the first three months of 362 at the estate of his friend Basil in Pontus, ostensibly upon learning of his father's wish to ordain him.

However, as Gregory says in his opening paragraphs, this retreat or flight had not been caused by idleness or lack of education (apaideutos kai asynetos [Or. 2.3]). Rather (and here he evokes more or less the same passages from

Plato's *Laws* and Aristotle's *Politics* that Julian had used to refute Themistius),[48] Gregory had gone to Pontus because he was all too aware that the requirements for good governance were so stringent that anyone of sound mind and good character had to be highly reluctant to accept such a daunting responsibility. Therefore, when suddenly faced with the prospect of having to accept such a responsibility, namely, the public office of priesthood, Gregory had been instantly gripped by "an overwhelming desire for the beauty of tranquility and retreat" (*eros tou kalou tes hesychias kai tes anachoreseos*) (*Or.* 2.5–6).

However, irrespective of the intensity of his desires (he continues), he was back, ready to take action and assume office. Gregory's reasons for so doing were twofold. First, a "war" had broken out against "the sublime and divine word" about which "the entire world in our days philosophizes" (*tou theiou kai hypselou, kai hon pantes philosophousin*) (*Or.* 2.35). The *oikoumenê* was in deep crisis, caused by none other than the "ferocious beast" Julian (*Or.* 2.87). Therefore, good leadership was now essential. The quintessential precondition for such leadership—and this was Gregory's second point—was the philosophical life. Only philosophers could be priests, because no one should "be placed at the command of people in order to legislate" who had not been thoroughly prepared through the philosophical life (*Or.* 2.53–56, 69–70). Leisure and retreat were essential for such preparation. Only retreat—like Gregory's months spent in Pontus—permitted the philosopher, as priest, to acquire the sound basis in Greek language, rhetoric, and philosophy that was indispensable to understanding Scripture. Only those who had thus been thoroughly trained were capable of understanding God's words, and therefore only they, as philosophers and priests, were capable of leading the community toward the divine (*Or.* 2.48–76).

Gregory, in short, demanded a philosophical life of action, especially since in the current situation of crisis it was "urgently necessary to preserve God as one and to profess three *hypostaseis* [persons], each with its own characteristics" (*Or.* 2.39). In sharp contrast to Julian, who had just advocated the more Platonic interpretation of the philosophical life privileging theory over active involvement, Gregory did the opposite, much like Themistius, who had come into prominence under Constantius as a political philosopher. And Gregory proceeded accordingly: he accepted public office as a priest, persuaded his friend Basil of Caesarea to do the same, and both embarked upon a writing campaign which incorporated Scripture into Greek learning to the most comprehensive degree possible, with fundamental consequences for Byzantine thought.

Gregory's forceful call for the philosophy of action, the inaugural oration I have just summarized, is the very same text that has given rise to the dominant historiographical persona of Gregory as the sensitive soul, passionately devoted to the solitary ascetic life, unwilling and ultimately incapable of holding office. As discussed above, this interpretation has maintained such a tenacious hold only because it is the only plausible one as long as Gregory remains hermetically sealed within his Christian bubble. My reinterpretation of Gregory is the direct result of the suspension of the categories "pagan" and "Christian." It reveals Gregory as an active participant in the contemporary debates of the true philosophical life, and reveals him as someone who is almost the exact opposite of his historiographic persona. Only the context of Julian's postulation that the (neo) Platonic philosophical life of theory was the sole path toward the universal God illuminates Gregory's countercall for a philosophical life of active involvement, a life, not accidentally, much like that advocated by Constantius's political philosopher Themistius.

Gregory felt called to action to defend his universal God, who had inspired philosophy, "the art of arts and science of sciences" (Or. 2.15). Therefore, Gregory's philosophical life as outlined in his inaugural oration was the true one. Given Julian's proclamations at the time, it is no wonder that Gregory's decision to announce his choice of the philosophical life of action was difficult to make and came as a surprise to some. This is especially understandable, considering that he circulated his announcement after Julian had issued an imperial proclamation declaring that those who did not believe in the gods of the Greeks (and Romans) could not teach philosophy since they were Galilaeans.

A few months later, in three books written in the winter of 362–63, Julian made it clear that those who believed that the Galilaean Jesus was a god rather than a human being were deserters, "apostates," from "us . . . and the Greeks, who are of the same parentage as we are" (pros Hellenas, tous hêmeterous syggeneis) (C. Gal. 235b, 200a).[49] It was a serious accusation. Not only had they deserted "the common master of all things" for the much more limited God of the Jews, but they had abandoned even that limited deity for, at best, "the tutelary divinity of a very small realm," and at worst, a mere corpse (C. Gal. 148a). In abandoning the universal God, such persons had willfully abandoned the essence of Greekness within Rome. Though they had once been Greek, they were now no longer so: they were Galilaeans. Those were among the emperor's last words. In May of that same year he found his death on the battlefields of Persia.

Gregory responded immediately. Upon receiving the news of the emperor's death—at least that is the *mise en scène*—he wrote an invective in three parts: *Against Julian* (Or. 4 and 5), which he circulated probably in early 364.[50] Following the rules of the genre, Gregory used Julian as the negative foil to highlight four principal points: first, "all peoples [*panta ta ethnê*], men of all origin and ages, indeed, all powers of the universe," rejoice, because Julian's death proves unequivocally that the God of the Christians is the truly universal one (Or. 4.1). Secondly, Constantius had been the ideal ruler and Julian the tyrant (Or. 4.3). Thirdly—and this is the bulk of the invective—Gregory's philosophy is the true one. Christian philosophy is the "science of sciences" because its practitioners, such as Gregory, understand the language of the divine correctly. They have correctly interpreted the teachings of Plato and Aristotle, in particular the latter's theory of language—in sharp contrast to Julian.[51] Therefore, fourthly, those who follow the Christian philosophy practice the most sublime form of Greekness. Simply put, Gregory sets out to disprove Julian's claim that word and content are always one, in this case, that "Greekness" always denotes belief in Greek and Roman gods.

Gregory begins his argument by challenging Julian's mistaken notion that "to use Greek words [*hellena logon*] is a matter of belief, and not simply of language [*tês glossês*]" (Or. 4.5). In fact, Gregory enters into a full-scale discussion of the relationship between content and word, arguing that a word need not have a permanent semantic field or be inextricably linked to a precise "historical" reference point, that "religion" is not a defining characteristic of culture—by resorting, of course, to the classic argument that "Greekness" and hence Greek learning are itself the product of "non-Greek" influences.[52] Indeed, not even the Greek language belongs to the Greeks, assuming that Julian was capable of deciding which Greek he denied the Christians: low, middle, or Atticizing (Or. 4.105):

> For how are we to take this "Greekness"—with that word, how should it be called, and how should it be understood? Let me show you—you, who clings to homonyms—the power of a name. . . . Do you want Greekness to mean a religion, or, and the evidence seems to point that way, a people—those who first discovered the power of dialectic? . . . If you do not claim [Greekness] to be a religion, but a language which belongs only to you, and which you deny us like a heritage to which we have no claim, then I do not know what you want to argue, nor, how you can then attribute this language to the gods. Because the fact that the same people use the Greek language, who also profess Greek reli-

gion, does not mean that the words belong therefore to the religion, and that we are then naturally excluded from using them. This is not a logical conclusion, and does not agree with your own teachers of [Aristotelian] logic [*technologoi*]. If two terms address the same thing that does not make the two identical. (*Or.* 4.103–5)

Julian had forced the issue: the correct nature of Greekness within Rome. Who could claim to be truly universal, who represented the correct mixture of Greek learning and Roman universalism? Julian and the philosophical life he represented, or the philosophy of Constantius, who had abandoned the "old" gods for the sake of the new Christian one? For Julian, the answer was clear: Constantius had been wrong. No one who followed the god of the Galilaeans could lay claim to the universalism of Greece and Rome as represented in its divinely inspired philosophy.

For Gregory the answer was equally clear. Whoever equated Greekness and Greek learning—that is, philosophy—exclusively with belief in the Greek gods denied the universality of Greekness, itself the perfect mixture of the best of all the peoples within the Roman *oikoumenê*.[53] Obviously, Julian's misunderstanding of Greek learning as made evident in his faulty application of Aristotelian dialectic to the word "Greek" revealed a profound misunderstanding of philosophy, and hence of the true nature of the God who had inspired it: the Christian God, one yet manifest in three hypostaseis. In short, for Gregory, Greekness and Greek learning, once properly guided toward the correct divinity, were integral to being Christian, and the demonstration of that fact became his lifelong pursuit.

Themistius, in his panegyric to Julian's successor Jovian delivered in Ancyra on 1 January 364, put it slightly differently. As he pointed out, "[T]he Creator of the universe takes pleasure in diversity. He wishes the Syrians to organise their affairs in one way, and the Greeks in another, the Egyptians in another" (*Or.* 5.70a).[54] Christians, for him, were Syrians, by tradition participants in the universal "Greekness" of the Roman *oikoumenê* and hence almost, but not quite, Greek.

Suspending the categories "pagan" and "Christian" and permitting Julian and Gregory to enter into dialogue has not produced any earth-shattering revelations. Gregory was still Christian and Julian pagan. However, it has brought a number of issues into much sharper relief. First and foremost, during the middle of the fourth century, before Constantinople was the undisputed capital, and Theodosius's lengthy reign had not yet stabilized the realm, the meaning of Christianity was hotly debated. The debate, in which both Julian and Gregory participated, was carried out employing terminology that had a long tradition and a crucial place in the politics of the ancient world. Accordingly, neither Julian nor Gregory was an idiosyncratic oddity, but rather central in these debates. Further, as far as Gregory is concerned, the man who has emerged as a result of being placed into his wider context is, I think, a much more plausible candidate for the enormous influence he was to exert as the Theologian and active political philosopher, who became a model for Justinian as much as for Gregory the Great. And, as his "marriage of Hellenism and Christianity" attests, Greekness or Hellenism was not, at least then, the same as paganism. Indeed, Hellenism only could have become a synonym for paganism because Gregory made Greekness essential to Christianity. Or, in Constantine Cavafy's words, "that we've broken their statues, / that we've driven them out of their temples, / doesn't mean that all the gods are dead."[55]

Notes

An earlier version of this essay was given in the Department of Classics and the Center for Hellenic Studies at Princeton University. I would like to thank the members of both, especially Alexander Nehamas and Christian Wildberg, for their many stimulating suggestions. Most of all, however, I would like to thank the editors for permitting me to express my great affection, admiration, and appreciation of Liz Clark in this manner. Unless otherwise noted, the English translations in the following are my own.

1. Cameron, "Empress and the Poet," 239.
2. See, e.g., Saïd, ed. [Hellenismos].
3. Goldhill, ed., Being Greek under Rome, 13–14. The subject of Greekness, i.e., of ethnicity and identity, in particular as expressed in the so-called Second Sophistic, has received a great deal of renewed attention recently, not least as a result of postcolonial studies. For the ancient world see, e.g., Swain, Hellenism and Empire; Malkin, ed., Ancient Perceptions; Hall, Ethnic Identity; Richter, "Plutarch on Isis and Osiris"; Elm, "Isis' Loss"; Woolf, "Becoming Roman, Staying Greek"; Francis, Subversive Virtue; and Hahn, Der Philosoph und die Gesellschaft. For theoretical works, see, e.g., Ashcroft, Griffiths, and Tiffin, eds., Empire Writes Back; Breckenridge, Pollock, and Bhabha, eds., "Cosmopolitanism"; Bhabha, "Of Mimicry and Man."
4. For Julian especially, see also Braun and Richer, eds., L'empereur Julien, vol. 1.
5. Bowersock, Julian the Apostate; Browning, Emperor Julian; Klein, ed., Julian Apostata. For a bibliographical overview prior to 1977, see ibid., 509–617; Athanassiadi, Julian and Hellenism; Smith, Julian's Gods.
6. Much scholarly argument centers on the degree to which Julian's attempts to stem the tide of advancing Christianity were tragic or misguided. Bowersock,

Julian the Apostate, following Gibbon, sees Julian as misguided, whereas Browning, *Emperor Julian*, 219–35, following Bidez, *La vie de l'empereur Julien*, xii, sees him rather as a "tragic figure, a man of infinite promise, cut off before his time."

7. Julian's relationship to Hellenism is the second emphasis of the secondary literature, as exemplified by Bouffartigue, *L'empereur Julien*; Smith, *Julian's Gods*; and Athanassiadi, *Julian and Hellenism*. A third area of scholarly interest encompasses aspects of Julian's governance of the empire. In addition to Browning, *Emperor Julian*, see, e.g., Ensslin, "Kaiser Julians Gesetzgebungswerk"; Pack, *Städte und Steuern*.

8. The citations are from works that occupy diametrically opposed points on the historiographic pagan vs. Christian scale. See MacMullen's *Christianity and Paganism in the Fourth to Eighth Centuries*, 19, a work seething with anger at the destructive force of the impudently advancing Christianity; and Cameron's *Christianity and the Rhetoric of Empire*, 121–29, 220–29, which is scrupulously conscious of the methodological perils of precisely this "divide." The same binary focus prevails in other historiographic traditions, such as the French and German distinction between *antiquité/Antike* and *christianisme/Christentum*, for example, when discussing the "keineswegs unproblematische Synthese zwischen diesen beiden geistigen Mächten," Speyer, *Frühes Christentum im antiken Strahlungsfeld*, 1. Works emphasizing the lengthy process of a slow transformation include Fox's *Pagans and Christians*, 7, 11; and, of course, Brown's studies, e.g., *Making of Late Antiquity*.

9. See Markus's eloquent discussion, *End of Ancient Christianity*, 28–29, and in particular his introduction: "Talk about 'pagan survival' is the obverse of an uncritical use of the notion of 'Christianisation': pagan survivals are seen simply as what resists the efforts of the Christian clergy to abolish, transform or control" (9). Examples of other recent voices critical of such convenient assumptions are Frankfurter, *Religion in Roman Egypt*, 33–36; and Athanassiadi and Frede, eds., *Pagan Monotheism in Late Antiquity*, esp. the introduction (1–20).

10. As Gruen notes, " 'Late antique Hellenism' is *a priori* a different phenomenon from the much studied 'classical' Hellenism, which denotes, historiographically, a period and a region as well as a culture" (*Hellenistic World* 1:1–5); and see esp. 250–355 for ambivalent receptions of "Hellenism." For recent assessments of the field of "classical" Hellenism, see Cartledge, Garnsey, and Gruen, eds., *Hellenistic Constructs*, especially Cartledge's introduction (1–19); Funck, ed., *Hellenismus*. Studies of Hellenism in late antiquity are far less numerous.

11. Smith, "Iamblichus' Views"; Athanassiadi, *Julian and Hellenism*, 4–8.

12. Isocrates, *Panegyricus*, 50. Fowden, *Empire to Commonwealth*, 8–9, 58–59; Suzanne Saïd, "The Discourse of Identity in Greek Rhetoric from Isocrates to Aristides," in Malkin, ed., *Ancient Perceptions*, 275–99.

13. Cartledge, introduction to *Hellenistic Constructs*, 1–19; von Staden, "Affinities and Elisions"; Clover and Humphreys, eds., *Tradition and Innovation*, 7–10: "under Constantinople's aegis, imperial Hellenism, decidedly Greek in form and outlook, replaced the old Greco-Roman culture as the dominant way of life in the Roman Empire" (10).

14. Bowersock, *Hellenism in Late Antiquity*, xi, xii, 1–13. Bowersock's discussion of the

usage of *Hellenikos* (9–12) is crucial, but I disagree with his historical "order." W. Koch, "Comment l'empereur Julien tâche," *Revue belge de philosophie et d'histoire* 7 (1928): 539.

15. Fox, *Pagans and Christians*, 7.

16. Trombley, *Hellenic Religion and Christianization*, avoids the issue by adopting a minimalist view, i.e., he concentrates on "religious behavior," not "beliefs," predominantly of "the ordinary folk" (introduction and passim). See also Markus, *End of Ancient Christianity*, 10–13.

17. Bowersock, *Hellenism in Late Antiquity*, 64.

18. Bowersock, ibid., 6, summarizes thus: "only Julian seriously conceived of paganism in opposition to Christianity. And the reason for this is obvious, although it is rarely stated: Julian was raised as a Christian. He turned to paganism with the zeal of a convert, and his view of paganism was conditioned by his Christian upbringing" (see also 15–24). Bouffartigue, *L'empereur Julien*, and Smith, *Julian's Gods*, 183–218, briefly assess the direct Christian literary influences on Julian's oeuvre, restricted however to the *Contra Galilaeos*. Sources for a direct influence are not overabundant. However, Eusebius of Nicomedia, later bishop of Constantinople, is not unknown; and Julian's request for the library of George of Cappadocia after his murder as bishop of Alexandria in 361 is a second point of departure. See Julian, *Ep.* (= Epistula) 23 (Bidez 107), 38 (Bidez 106). Julian's complete extant works have most recently been edited by Bidez and Cumont, *Imp. Caesaris Flavii Clavdii Ivliani epistvlae.* In the following I will be referring, unless otherwise noted, to the English translation with Greek text of Julian's orations (hereafter *Or.*), selected fragments, and selected letters (hereafter *Ep.*) by Wright, *Works of the Emperor Julian*; the letters are in vol. 3. References to the letters in the following will be to the numbers in Wright, with the Bidez numbers in parentheses to facilitate cross-reference to the complete corpus in that edition. No modern author on Julian cites other works written by the same Christian authors who wrote invectives against the emperor, especially Gregory of Nazianzus, Ephrem of Nisibis, John Chrysostom, and Cyril of Alexandria. While the neglect of such admittedly peripheral figures is excusable when dealing with an emperor, these observations are nonetheless indicative. Still fundamental for Julian's adaptation of Christian structures is Koch, "Comment l'empereur Julien tâcha." Unfortunately, Andreotti's excellent "L'opera legislativa ed amministrativa," has not found sufficient echo.

19. Markus, *End of Ancient Christianity*, 12. He then distinguishes "sacred" from "secular" within a "culture," rather than distinguishing "religion" from "culture" (13).

20. See Susanna Elm, "The Diagnostic Gaze: Gregory of Nazianzus' Theory of Orthodox Priesthood in his Oration 6 'De pace' and 2 'Apologia de Fuga sua,' " in Elm, Rebillard, and Romano, eds., *Orthodoxie, christianisme, histoire*, 83–100; and Elm, "Programmatic Life."

21. Bernardi, *Grégoire de Nazianze*. Bernardi, *La Prédication des pères cappadociens*, 94 and 254, omits *Or.* 4 and 5 *Against Julian* entirely from his discussion of Gregory's orations as irrelevant to his subject, a Christian preacher. The tone of these invectives, to some ears unsuitable for a "Christian Theologian," is excused by

(a) self-defense against the nastiness of Julian's anti-Christian actions (which, after all, even the pagan Ammianus criticized); and (b) Gregory's excitable temperament.

22. Norris, *Faith Gives Fullness*, 5; and Kertsch, *Die Bildersprache*.

23. Kennedy, *Greek Rhetoric*, 141–49; Ruether, *Gregory of Nazianzus*; Masson-Vincourt, *Les allusions à la mythologie*; Pyykkö, *Die griechischen Mythen*; Trisoglio, "Uso ed effetti" and "Figurae, sententiae e ornatus." Trisoglio emphasizes the contextual qualities of Gregory's use of classic figures, whereas Masson-Vincourt and Pyykkö judge these to be mere rhetorical exempla-collections.

24. Cameron, *Christianity and the Rhetoric of Empire*, 1–14; Kertsch, "Eine Libanius-Reminiszens"; Demoen, "Attitude towards Greek Poetry," 238.

25. For a discussion of some of the historiographic parameters shaping the notion of Christian Hellenism, especially in a second-century context, as well as the impact of these notions on the historiography of the office of the bishop, see Elm, "Historiographic Identities," 225–57. For an excellent summary, see Lyman's discussion in *Christology and Cosmology*, 10–36, with bibliography.

26. Young, *Biblical Exegesis*; Garrison, *Graeco-Roman Context*. Very constructive is Cook's "Protreptic Power."

27. For the degree to which such notions of "purity" reflect ancient sources, both non-Christian and Christian, see Swain, *Hellenism and Empire*, 17–42.

28. See McLynn, "Self-Made Holy Man"; McLynn, "Voice of Conscience"; McGuckin, *Saint Gregory of Nazianzus*; and van Dam, "Self-representation," 140.

29. McGuckin, *Saint Gregory*, 1–34 and passim.

30. Rousseau, *Basil of Caesarea*, 86–87; for bibliographic details, see Elm, "Programmatic Life."

31. Julian, *Epistula ad senatum populumque Atheniorum* (hereafter *Ep. ad Ath.*) 282b–d; *Epistula ad Themistium philosophum* (hereafter *Ep. ad Them.*). As mentioned above, references to Julian's works are to the Loeb translation by Wright. However, since Wright uses a Greek text edited by F. C. Hertlein (Leipzig, 1875–76) for Julian's orations, of which the *Ep. ad Ath.* and the *Ep. ad Them.* form a part, the numerical citations, following convention, are to the pagination of the Greek text, e.g., 282b–d. In the following, wherever there is close textual analysis, these numerical citations will be included in the body of my text. For discussions of the circumstances of Julian's letters to the cities and to Themistius in contemporary authors, see Libanius, *Orationes* 12.58–61 and 18.90–102, English translation with Greek text by Norman, *Libanius*, here vol. 1; numbers refer to the Greek paragraphs. Ammianus Marcellinus, *Res Gestae* 20.4.1–3, English translation with Latin text by Rolfe; numbers refer to the Latin books and paragraphs. Zosimus, *Historia Nova* 13.10.11–16, ed. with French translation by Paschoud, *Zosime*; numbers refer to the Greek books and paragraphs. Drinkwater, " 'Pagan Underground,' " esp. 370–83; Matthews, *Roman Empire of Ammianus*, 93–103; Wiemer, *Libanios und Julian*, 28–32; and Lieu, ed., *Emperor Julian*, xii–xiv. On these letter exchanges as well as Julian's speedy advance, see now Ando, *Imperial Ideology*, 196–200.

32. See Julian, *Ep.* 8c (Bidez 26) to Maximus, written in November 361 from Naissus,

according to which his entire army was now sacrificing to the gods. For the date of the *Letter to the Athenians*, see Zosimus, *Historia Nova* 3.10.3 (Sirmium); Ammianus Marcellinus, *Res Gestae* 21.12.22; 22.2.1; 21.12.23–25; Libanius, *Or.* 12.64 and 14.29; Matthews, *Roman Empire of Ammianus*, 105–6; Szidat, "Zur Ankunft Julians"; Bowersock, *Julian the Apostate*, 60.

33. As Julian elaborated a few months later in his *Or.* 7 to the Cynic Heraclius (228c–30d).

34. The dating of the letter is controversial. Bradbury, "Date of Julian's *Letter to Themistius*," argued for a date prior to 360; Vanderspoel, *Themistius*, 117–19, for publication in 360; whereas Smith, *Julian's Gods*, 27; Bouffartigue, *L'empereur Julien*, 198, esp. n. 283; and Prato and Fornaro, eds., *Giuliano imperatore*, viii–ix; all following Dagron, "L'émpire romain d'orient," 220, propose late 361, a dating I am following as well. In general, see Criscuolo, "Sull'epistola di Giuliano imperatore"; and Brauch, "Themistius and the Emperor Julian."

35. Julian quotes Plato's *Laws* 709b and 713–714 nearly verbatim; also *Theaetetus* 153; Aristotle, *Politics* 3.15. 1286 and 3.16.1287a nearly verbatim, and 7.3.1325b.

36. Julian, *Ep. ad Ath.* 269d, 281b; *Ep.* 9 (Bidez 28); Ammianus Marcellinus, *Res Gestae* 20.8.18–9.1, 21.7–15.2, 22.2.1. See Socrates, *Historia ecclesiastica* 11.2–3, ed. Hansen; Philostorgius, *Historia ecclesiastica* 6.5, ed. Bidez and Winkelmann; in both cases numbers refer to the Greek books and paragraphs. Also see Bowersock, *Julian the Apostate*, 18, 58–65; Matthews, *Roman Empire of Ammianus*, 104–10; Smith, *Julian's Gods*, 4; Athanassiadi, *Julian and Hellenism*, 82–86.

37. Ammianus Marcellinus, *Res Gestae* 20.8.18–9.1, 21.7–15.2, 22.2.1. Seeck, *Regesten*, 208–9; Matthews, *Roman Empire of Ammianus*, 92–105; Barnes, *Ammianus Marcellinus and the Representation of Historical Reality*, 143–62.

38. Julian, *Ep.* 26 and 15 (Bidez 46 and 32) and *Ep.* 43, 44 (Bidez 34 and 35); Eunapius, *Vitae sophistarum*, English translation with Greek text by Wright; numbers refer to Greek pagination. Schlange-Schöningen, *Kaisertum und Bildungswesen*, 77–80.

39. Gregory of Nazianzus, *Or.* 7.10–11 and *Ep.* 7, in *Grégoire de Nazianze: Discours 6–12*, ed. with French translation by Calvet-Sébasti; Gallay, ed., *Gregor von Nazianz: Briefe*.

40. The hymn to Cybele was written overnight. Libanius, *Or.* 18.157; 17.16–17; Fontaine, *Giuliano Imperatore*, xlv–l, 43–44; Smith, *Julian's Gods*, 8, 49–50; Bouffartigue, *L'empereur Julien*, 308–9, 359–79.

41. Julian, *Contra Galilaeos*, hereafter cited parenthetically by Greek pagination and abbreviated as *C. Gal.*

42. This aspect, i.e., Julian's *Romanitas* and Hellenism respectively, has of course caused many scholarly debates. But as mentioned above, they tend to occur within a "Julianic" sphere, i.e., referring back to "pagan" arguments regarding Hellenism rather then seeking to contextualize his remarks vis-à-vis his own contemporaries, with some exceptions. Bouffartigue, *L'empereur Julien*, 658–65, 669–73; Smith, *Julian's Gods*, 163–78; Athanassiadi, *Julian and Hellenism*, 141–43. See also Jean-Pierre Weiss, "Julien, Rome et les Romains," in Braun and Richer, eds., *L'empereur Julien*, 125–40, esp. 129–30.

43. Julian, *Or.* 6 and 7. Chronologically, *Or.* 7 precedes *Or.* 5, which is followed by *Or.*

6 (in Wright's numbering). Billerbeck, "Ideal Cynic from Epictetus to Julian"; Bouffartigue, *L'empereur Julien*, 308–9, 359–79; Bouffartigue, "Le cynisme."

44. Julian uses largely stock themes regarding the false philosophers. Goulet–Cazé, "Le cynisme à l'époque impériale"; Bouffartigue, *L'empereur Julien*, 120–36; Smith, *Julian's Gods*, 55–79.

45. The law is preserved in the *Codex Theodosianus* 13.3.5, ed. Mommsen with Meyer and Krueger; and Julian's *Ep.* 36 (Bidez 61). The edict reached Spoletium on August 29 (Ammianus Marcellinus, *Res Gestae* 22.10.7; Libanius, *Or.* 18.157–60). Both edict and letter have received a great deal of scholarly attention: Banchich, "Julian's School Laws"; Bouffartigue, *L'empereur Julien*, 600–603; Klein, "Julians Rhetoren–und Unterrichtsgesetzt"; Pack, *Städte und Steuern*, 261–300, with bibliography; Smith, *Julian's Gods*, 18–19 and 199.

46. Accordingly, professors (*magistros studiorum doctoresque*) had to have their moral standing certified by their peers (*curialium . . . optimorum . . . consensu*) and by the emperor himself (*ad me tractandum referetur*).

47. Bernardi, ed., *Grégoire de Nazianze: Discours 1–3*, 14–17, 24–28, 30, dates to late 362 against Mossay's dating to 364 or later, in "La date de l'Oratio II." I argue for 362 or early 363. For the manuscript tradition see Bernardi's introduction.

48. E.g., Plato, *Laws* 12.942c; *Phaedo* 80a; Aristotle, *Politics* 1.5.4–6, 4.1319b.

49. See Libanius, *Or.* 18.178, for the date, winter 362–63. See also Julian, *Ep.* 38 and 23 (Bidez 106 and 107).

50. Bernardi, ed., *Grégoire de Nazianze: Discours 4–5*; for dating, see ibid., 20–36; Kurmann, *Gregor von Nazianz*, 6–12. Jovian, a Christian officer with ties to Constantius, took Julian's place, though not for long. He died by accident on 17 February 364, in Dardastana, on the border between Bithynia and Galatia, on his way back to Constantinople. Ammianus Marcellinus, *Res Gestae* 24–25; Libanius, *Or.* 18.260; Zosimus, *Historia Nova* 3.30–36; Barnes, *Ammianus Marcellinus*, 162–65, with bibliography; Matthews, *Roman Empire of Ammianus*, 130–90; Smith, *Julian's Gods*, 8–9.

51. Julian is consistently defined as uneducated and untrained: Kurmann, *Gregor von Nazianz*, 16–26.

52. Gregory of Nazianzus, *Or.* 4.96–109; Libanius, *Or.* 18.157.

53. For the second-century context of such debates, see above.

54. Themistius, *Or.* 5.70a, in *Themistii Orationes*, ed. Schenkel, Downey, and Norman. The English translation of *Or.* 5 is by Heather and Moncur, *Politics, Philosophy, and Empire*. The numbering refers to the Greek pagination.

55. C. P. Cavafy, "Ionic," in *Collected Poems*, ed. G. Savidis, trans. E. Keeley and P. Sherrard (Princeton: Princeton University Press, 1975), 62–63.

✣   Knowing Theodoret:

Text and Self

PHILIP ROUSSEAU

As this volume suggests generally, a key problem in late ancient studies in recent years, especially for historians, has been the problem of access. As we examine the evidence remaining to us, are we truly getting in touch, so to speak, with the peoples of a remote past? Or are we condemned, rather, to be mere aesthetes, judging in the terms of our own times the structure, the beauty, the dramatic force of what lies to hand? The problem attaches in a precise way to written, and especially literary, sources; but perhaps the whole world must be viewed as a text, of which we are but readers and writers. I like to think of a text as a field of play, in which a writer declaims, while a reader explores. The question is, of course, whether a writer genuinely reveals anything, and whether a reader can discover what it is.

Let me take as an example the Letters of Theodoret, the fifth-century bishop of Cyrrhus in Syria. Theodoret wrote several substantial works, in a variety of styles; but one might imagine that a collection of letters—in his case a surprisingly large collection—would reveal something more intimate about their writer, and do so more immediately. The first question, therefore, is whether we as historians can engage with a bishop so long dead, engage with both his reflections and his actions. A second question is whether his letters tell us anything directly, either about his consciousness of himself or about his understanding of communication with others. Historians of late antiquity are divided on the issue of what consciousness of self could have meant at that time. So, our two questions cry out for precision and theoretical justification. What can we mean by saying that we "know" Theodoret? Can we discover what such knowledge (that is, knowledge of other persons) meant to Theodoret himself? Can we take his Letters as expressions of a "self" and as a field of play within which a writer and his readers genuinely met (and might still meet)? Seen in those terms, the writing and reading of letters become virtual exercises in epistemology.

I am tempted at this point to plunge straight into the material, prior to making tentative and consequent suggestions about the general issues I have just described. However, in the matter of "textuality" there are philosophical positions that contemporary historians cannot ignore, and in relation to which they must make their position clear.[1] Among the most famous is Jacques Derrida's famous judgment (delivered in 1967), "Il n'y a pas de hors-texte."[2] The phrase is often taken to mean, "There is nothing outside of the text."[3] However, both the word order and the hyphen are crucial: the phrase is better rendered (albeit in clumsier English), "There is no 'outside of text.'" Derrida meant (among other things) that one could not escape being a reader: the whole world is always experienced *as text*.[4] Reading does not lead one to *something else* ("autre chose")—something "outside of text [*hors texte*] . . . outside of language [*hors de la langue*] . . . outside of writing in general [*hors de l'écriture en général*]." There is no scope for a transcendent state, in which a reader can observe from above, as it were, a process whereby meaning is imparted to a separately observable reality. However, the limit applied there is a limit to what one can *say* rather than to what *is*. Working at the world text of experience, a reader still experiences that world as a whole; is not limited to the decipherment of scattered fragments fluttering in what is otherwise a great and unreadable void. Derrida did not mean that one would have no interest—that is, no *right* to an interest—in the world that the text disclosed.[5] It was simply that, for readers, there is only "l'écriture," the writing. Purportedly "real" events and persons have been affected in the telling—in Derrida's words, "se sont toujours déjà dérobés": they are always hidden, or distorted, or even whisked away. Consequently, "what opens up meaning and language is this writing [*cette écriture*], as if the natural presence [*la présence naturelle*] has disappeared."

There is profit in arming ourselves with that familiar and well-aged prolegomenon before we seize upon anything so apparently intimate and allusive as a letter. Derrida's analysis also provides clues to the philosophical traditions within which he worked—his focus on Rousseau, a misleadingly autobiographical "self"; on written accounts, in which Rousseau and others are "dérobés"; on the immediacy of the reading experience; on the meaning that could (or could not) be attached to a "présence naturelle" that had now "disappeared"; on the avoidance of the transcendental; and finally on a system of signs, the assigning of meaning, echoing Ferdinand de Saussure and the structuralist view of language that, earlier in the twentieth century, he had set in train. For Derrida, as for his philosophical predecessors, the immediate problem was how to conceive and describe the distance between, say, oneself and a writer such as Rousseau. Reading could seem as immediate an experience as meeting someone in the street. To read a text was to be immersed in circumstance. But to express to oneself what such a reading might mean—not least, what meaning it might impart *about* another person—was made difficult by the fact that the person had "slipped away." And one could not transcend, in privileged isolation, the differences between engagement and understanding. So, persons, texts, readings, experience, transcendence, and the controlling force of language all lie within Derrida's one paragraph.[6]

After that modicum of philosophy (some of which I shall recall), let me tackle Theodoret's prose. The prose needs first to be given its context. We are accustomed—and it is a justified habit—to think of the Christian empire as a "rhetorical" society, with a system of education geared to the production of orators expert in political ideology, forensic strategy, and homilies both public and private. I might have concentrated, therefore, on word usage; on what, in the case of letters, could be taken as the vocabulary and grammar of the inner life. However, if politics, law, and homiletic exegesis were already formal exercises, was a letter any less an artifice? Are we entitled to segregate letters from other literary genres? Can they provide us, for example, with "the texture of individual lives," as opposed to "conventions of stylised elevation"?[7] Theodoret was aware of the specificity of the epistolary genre. It had its proper measure: "I have written these things," he admitted apologetically in one instance, "as is proper to the measure of a letter."[8] To Ibas of Edessa, he acknowledged that a letter should not turn into an exhortation, a *parainesis*. Yet letters were appropriately designed, he thought, to display a writer's *gnômê*, his attitude or frame of mind.[9] The question for us is whether "display" can be taken to imply any "revelation," any openness of meaning in the sense allowed by Derrida.

I shall have more to say shortly about the distance effected by artifice. We can adopt, however, another approach to the issues. Christianity had developed an articulate culture of its own, a rhetoric proper to itself; but Theodoret, like most Christian thinkers, believed that there were truths *beyond* words, constituting a mystic and inexpressible treasury of *noêmata*, of things thought about in a richer sense.[10] The Arian controversy of the fourth century (especially in its later phases, dominated by the arguments of Eunomius) had done much to reinforce that belief; for the orthodox wished to retain access, to "know" in some meaningful way, a God who was nevertheless utterly transcendent, and Arian diminution of God the Son appeared to jeopardize such access. Theodoret clearly supposed that the treasury of *noêmata* was "real." He would never have imagined that it was the mind that created a meaningful cosmos. The function of the mind was to read and interpret the signs of God's presence and action within that cosmos. However, that was far from being naive realism. It still allowed for epistemological difficulties, for the possibility of accurate or inaccurate interpretation. It meant, therefore, identifying the criteria by which one's interpretation could be justified. So, here we have a man who distinguished on his own terms between the sayable and the unsayable and between meaning and sign. He felt that his words could induce in his hearers or readers recognition of what those words could not, on the other hand, directly or fully describe.[11] And nature gave grace to the words with which one attempted to describe it, even though it did not need to speak in its own defense.[12] To make such points was to take a stand against any suggestion that words could constitute reality.

Many of Theodoret's categories of interpretation turn out, therefore, to be quite modern in their tone. His "outward-looking" epistemology needs to be kept in mind when we examine his declared ability or inability to speak about the inner world. First, he remained aware of what was not or could not be communicated in a person's response to experience. He referred, for example, to a sense of being "filled to the brim with fear" when he witnessed others being punished.[13] Being "filled to the brim" points to a subjective component of experience; a component so unmediated, if not predominantly physical, that it could not be spoken of fully, but only by approximation. He described in the same letter how, when he remembered what orthodox exiles from Vandal and Arian Africa had suffered, he was afraid that he might suffer similarly—conjuring a series of inner events that ran alongside experience.[14]

None of that means, however, that Theodoret dealt in dichotomies. There was no obvious frontier between self and world. In the first place, the person undergoing all those experiences formed a unit. It is remarkable to what extent Theodoret avoided easy divisions between "body," "soul," and "mind." What many since Gibbon have found wearisome in Trinitarian and Christological controversy had at least the advantage of inducing care at the level of psychology and anthropology. The Christian combatants in those debates were not using traditional terminology (whether Platonist or Aristotelian) to clarify a biblically based belief but were using the belief to give new clarity to the terminology.[15] The way in which Theodoret understood and explained the Incarnation often allows us to glimpse how he mapped the inner dimension of human experience. He rejected, for example, Apollinarius's distinction between *psyché* and *nous* (roughly, soul and mind)—the notion that the divine Son had taken upon himself only a human mind. The apostles had taught, rather, that Christ assumed "with [human] flesh [*meta sarkos*]"—and here the conjunction of concepts was crucial—"a soul at once rational and knowing" (*psychên logikên te kai noeran*). The taking of the soul came first, with the taking of the body.[16] So, the determination not to "divide" Christ, as contemporary theological disputants would have put it, demanded a more integrated view of *any* human being. Beneath the theology of the Incarnation lay truths about all humanity. As Scripture put it (in Gen. 2:7), "Man became a single living soul."[17] The soul lay at the heart or root of the human person, and rational thought was a quality inherent in that soul.[18] Combining those two sets of observations—about the partially inexpressible levels of subjective experience and the singleness of being constituted by body and soul, reason and understanding—we see hints of a theme that will become increasingly important. An unbroken pathway lay between the self and the other, along which the human person might venture as it wished, adopting at one moment reticence, at another candor.

Theodoret lived, therefore, in a world of words, but in a world that words were unable to encompass entirely. He lived in a world of shared discourse, but in a world where much could not be shared, or at least where sharing was subject to choice. He had a clear sense, for example, that he gained from the act of writing a psychological benefit quite separable from the pleasure or difficulty of presenting thoughts for others to read.[19] Most striking here is the *combination* of engagement and disengagement. A letter contributed to that ambivalence in its special way. There could be much "going on" in a writer's circumstance that a letter need not—at times could not—make clear. Yet Theodoret felt able, even obliged, to mention precisely those "private" reflections. I put "private" in quotation marks, because we are dealing with proximity or distance along a single axis rather than with marked divisions between the physical and the mental, the tangible and the imagined. A sophist, for example, habitually found himself, according to Theodoret, in two situations: in company or at his desk. Theodoret's terminology, however, shows how complicated the distinction might be. While the sophist might "hold forth" among his colleagues (*dialegomenos*), he also "spoke" in his writings (*phthengomenos*).[20] A Christian bishop might play the sophist in a comparable way. Theodoret described how he opposed calumny (against himself) in two spheres: one the houses of friends, the other the churches in which he preached. In his case the settings were both oral but still distinct in their degree of intimacy.[21] There was always a potential overlap between word and letter and a varying degree of proximity to other persons. Let me provide a particularly rich example. According to the report of a certain Eusebius, a priest named John had praised Theodoret. Theodoret, therefore, wrote to John—that is, responded to Eusebius's oral account. John, he declared, would now have to write a reply to what Theodoret had written. That ironic triangle obviously mattered to Theodoret, since he described it at length: "You yourself started with words, I with writing; and I changed [êmeipsamên] the words by writing. It remains for you [to change] the *writing* by writing."[22] The use here of the verb *ameibô* suggests not only an "exchange" (of letters) but also a "changing," from one mode of address to another, so that words became writings.

It was still possible to hide within the coils of language. Much Christian criticism of contemporary pagan culture hinged on precisely that imputation of "unreality." I mentioned above Theodoret's reaction to the sufferings of the orthodox in Vandal Africa. On another occasion, he recommended to the generosity of his acquaintances a refugee, Celestiacus, who had been cast adrift from that province. Only the "tragic tongue" could do justice, he wrote, to the man's misfortune. His former wealth, now lost, had taken on the guise of "myth," a tale stripped naked of all tangible reality, a *diêgma tôn pragmatôn gegymnomenôn*.[23] But social engagement, the reception of Celestiacus into the homes of Theodoret's friends, the "pragmatic" cancellation of his fabled misfortune, was precisely the antidote to literary escapism. It was in social interaction and sympathy, in discourse with others, therefore, that language would function to best effect; and it was in discourse with others that the written word could display its richest complexity. "Through what we write," Theodoret observed to an imperial official, "we neighbors call out to one another [prosphthengometha], signaling [sêmainontes] the gladness of heart that Easter gives rise to."[24] As with the sophist above, we have writing joined with the oral force of "calling out," the word *sêmainontes* standing as a marker on the pathway of exchange and transformation that lay between the inner quality of "gladness" and the outer "calling" of the voice, both of which writing had captured.

Theodoret rarely had recourse to the conceit, typical of his time, that one could see one's correspondents in their letters. One of the exceptions shows how, when coming close to such usage, he reached beyond convention. He assured Uranius of Emesa that letters could bring two people together. The union depended, however, on a preexisting harmony, a *diathesis*.[25] Such was the traditional understanding of friendship. A relationship that was *purely* epistolary was bound to be imperfect. Social groundwork had to be completed beforehand. In the case of Uranius, however, Theodoret was able to suggest that things would have been no different between them if they had met and spoken together.[26] Words, logoi, are allowed to hover here in the imagination (since they are not spoken or heard), while diathesis is made explicitly present in the written letter. Now, the exchange between Theodoret and Uranius was played out in the context of a misunderstanding. Theodoret had taken amiss what Uranius (on an earlier occasion) had appeared to recommend—namely, that Theodoret maintain a careful silence (in the face of his critics). The letter following in the series shows that Uranius had gone on to explain himself more agreeably. Theodoret now felt able to say, with subtlety as well as grace, that his misunderstanding of the original letter—his failure, as he put it, to "grasp the letter's mind"—had now prompted Uranius to make explicit the brotherly affection that he had at heart.[27] The locking together of many concepts here—writing (grammata), word (logos), disposition (diathesis) and mind (nous)—suggests a complex set of relations between what could be read and heard and what could only be hinted at.

I have tried so far to make three sets of points. First, there were difficulties: letters, apparently intimate, were in the public arena, governed by impersonal conventions; and there was much in any case that could not be written or said—about the world in general as well as particularly about the self as subject. Second, however, those difficulties did not arise because of some separation between world and self: one moved smoothly from disengagement to engagement; and, although they appeared to face a hurdle of their own, a distance apparently absent in speech, letters highlighted in a special way the mechanics of communication. Third, therefore, we observe a comparable absence of disjunction between letters and speech—comparable, I mean, to the continuity between world and self: they were interwoven one with the other, each playing the other's role in the enterprise of social engagement, and thus they made "public" in equal measure the partly inexpressible components of subjective experience.

Two concepts seem to introduce us more closely to that subjective arena: "conscience" (syneidos) and "mask" prosôpeion). However, both syneidos and prosôpeion were "public" in their implications, as well as subjective in character. Conscientiousness was played out on the public stage. Syneidos, therefore, referred to action—especially moral action—as well as to knowledge. That was why Theodoret could insist that conscience needed cultural support. Anyone who stole offerings made to God, for example, would need no accusers. Their own consciences would prove a lasting embarrassment; they would be "compelled by conscience" (hypo tou syneidotos).[28] Similarly, human nature had reason as its greatest ornament, which made possible an unmediated grasp of duty—*Autê kath' heautên to deon heuriskei*. Yet both the natural endowment and the inherent capacity for self-criticism had to be boosted by *paideia*.[29] It was thanks to his paideia, for example, that Pericles (in contrast to the "naturally virtuous" Themistocles) both "knew" what was demanded and could "explain" it to his audience.[30] Indeed, more than explanation is implied: Theodoret's use of the verb *hermêneuô* adds a note of interpretation, even of translation. Pericles was able to transform the known—that is, what was known to himself—into the intelligible, for the sake of his hearers.[31] Here was another species of "change" and "exchange," bringing a hidden insight into the political forum.[32]

One can detect, therefore, ambiguity in the term *syneidos*. Theodoret's conscience was not entirely hidden. However, the presence of self to self was involved. Writing to the *patricius* Nomos, Theodoret indulged in self-deprecation. He had written letters but Nomos had remained silent. At first, piqued, he had decided to be silent in return, but then he turned to the exercise of self-knowledge (*hemauton te gnônai*), in order to see what fault of his own might have caused the breakdown in communication.[33] What stirred him to write after all was his sense of being guiltless, the fruit of that self-knowledge.[34] It was possible, he admitted, to be at fault in spite of oneself; but he was willing to trust his conscience, or rather the "witness" of his conscience (*hê tou syneidotos martyria*: a gloss that will prove important).[35] What exactly was he talking about? He used the same vocabulary of "trust" in a closely associated letter.[36] There, however, he expanded the framework by bringing in the "witness" of God.[37] His turn inward, therefore, was more than a mental rumination: it was, rather, a dialogue with God, who could "see" him actually thinking.[38] That awareness of God's presence seems to have been essential to the awareness of self. Inner experience and outward action were linked with the judgment of God, and, as a result, belief in God became a way of defining the "reality" of what was hidden in the life of mortals.

Theodoret made the matter particularly clear in a letter to Domnus of Antioch, written early in what was for him a troubled year, 448. He described the two choices open, as he saw it, to himself and his supporters. Either one could rebel against God and violate one's conscience or one could fall subject to the unjust accusations of one's fellow men.[39] Such had been the choice facing Susanna, ensnared by the lascivious elders. Where Theodoret wrote about the first choice—rebellion and violation—he seems to have made them almost one and the same act. To deny the convictions of one's conscience was to attack God himself. That elision is confirmed in the way he wrote about Susanna: "She chose to be trapped in the snares of a false accusation rather than hold in contempt the just judge."[40] So, the judgment of God and the judgment one brought to bear upon oneself were virtually indistinguishable. However, the choices themselves—to submit to slander or to despise God—*were* distinguishable. Keeping faith with God was an inner commitment, while slander was a visible consequence; but one did have to choose. One could not adopt both options, as if they operated at two levels; one could not maintain an honest stance in the face of God and at the same time escape the condemnation of the unjust. Contrived deceit, therefore, was inevitably yoked with inner guilt. We have here another declaration that the inner and the outer life were not amenable to rigid distinction. As a moral being, one stood or fell within a single set of circumstances, subject to a single criterion and a single judgment.

All that helps us to identify Theodoret's central preoccupation. He left room for the inexplicit. The continuous axis between self and world still made some "places" along that axis less accessible than others to the observation of one's peers. For example, one could hide the truth—the truth about what one really believed—in the "storehouse" of one's soul.[41] It was also possible to keep hidden those faults that one did not consider the proper concern of ecclesiastical accusers. Theodoret knew of such faults in himself, but saw no need to make them an issue in public controversy.[42]

So much for what might be unspoken. Yet Theodoret was not intent on mapping out an essentially inaccessible realm of selfhood. He was making an ethical judgment, not articulating a principle of epistemology or an account of how the self was constructed. The story of Susanna made it clear that choice was what mattered, and the submission of choice to judgment. Not all human beings endured successfully the suffering imposed upon them by nature. Success depended on choice, on a willingness to endure.[43] So, possessing one nature, human beings adopted a variety of avocations and pursued a variety of moral goals.[44] That was why Christ—and again the theology of the Incarnation comes to our rescue—could be at once human in nature and yet sinless. His sinlessness was a matter of choice, otherwise he would not have been fully human.[45]

For that reason, action was, for Theodoret, the most obvious symptom and declaration of a conscientious decision.[46] He believed that there would be no inquiry, at the final judgment, into what he called "performance in a range of styles" (*schêmatôn hypokrisis*) (which I take to be a theatrical allusion), but rather into the genuineness of what one had actually *done*.[47] I mentioned previously the significance of legal vocabulary, such as that of "witness," and the extent to which awareness of God as a scrutinizer of thought was essential to a development of conscious selfhood. Allusion to the final judgment, therefore, widens our inquiry. Jill Harries warns us against basing too much on literary references to late Roman judges: "The various representations of this both feared and indispensable figure in Roman society are therefore often more relevant to the creator of texts and the cultural perceptions of late antiquity than to the actual functioning both of *iudices* themselves and, more broadly, of the judicial system of the time."[48] She also asserts, however, that the obviously good and the obviously bad were not the problem. *Iudices* were chiefly concerned with *ambiguitas*, which made them more like God than one might have expected. Resolving *ambiguitas*, for God as much as for a human judge, was a matter of assessing intention. The truth about what anyone had actually *done* was not, therefore, handed to one on a plate. Indeed, seeing only the things done was, for ordinary mortals, precisely the problem. God saw the intention (*skopos*) and judged with reference to intentions rather than to deeds.[49] He would disclose on the last day the man who had made "the better choice."[50]

There may have remained, therefore, a species of "gap" between decision and action, so that Theodoret could place over against visible performance a range of "hidden" processes. Yet his understanding of *syneidos* implied that attempt and success were two qualities of a single human act. His use of the term *prosôpeion*, "mask," formed, together with the image of the judge, a powerful framing technique within his correspondence.[51] Theatrical associations (combined with problematic implications about appearance and reality) have already been suggested by the phrase "performance in a range of styles." After discussing God's focus on intention, Theodoret turned, as if with a natural logic, to Paul's declared aim in 1 Corinthians (9:22) to be "all things to all men." The apostle, he insisted, had not made himself thereby a deceiver. The varied manner in which he presented himself was a variation of address only, adapted to aid each party. Theodoret's phrasing is careful and revealing: "he used the masks [in the plural] of an actor." That acting (here *hypokrisis*) could be superficial—that is, a matter of surface alone—did not make it "hypocritical" as we might understand the word. Paul's intentions were not the issue. Rather, he was pragmatic, offering practical help; and to that end his role playing was pedagogic, an instrument of instruction.[52]

Just as we habitually think of late Roman society as a society built upon "rhetoric," so also we think of it as deeply theatrical—indeed, the two qualities were connected. Of the *rhêtôr* Athanasios, Theodoret wrote, "His speech gives grace to his tongue, his behavior to his speech."[53] A *rhêtôr* was both a professor and a practitioner of rhetoric; and he was judged by how well he spoke his lines and went about his "business" (to use the jargon of the theater). But the apparent distinctions had to be handled with subtlety. An *archôn*, for example, exercising public authority in a community, would properly (and skillfully) induce fear in those beneath him. That was the role assigned to him. But beneath that appropriate "mask" of power, the "real" *archôn* might be entirely meek. There was gentleness inherent in the *archôn* himself, whereas his mask represented only the abstraction "governance," *archê*.[54] Even a monk—meek, one would hope—must learn to maintain an authoritative presence, since too much self-effacement might undermine the force of his address.[55] However, that interplay between the hidden and the revealed was not allowed to harden into divorce. Theodoret laid upon public actors a moral task, which demanded consistency. Governance, for example, had to reflect personal principle. Writing to another *archôn*, Theodoret insisted that the exercise of authority resided in more than style. Power had to be just, and suited to the needs of the governed.[56]

Theodoret was himself a dramatic self-presenter, at least in his letters, and immensely repetitive: certain phrases occur again and again in letters written during his period of greatest trial, in the late 440s. Although the repetition may be more obvious to us than it was to his scattered correspondents, it hints at calculation. We are invited to picture a man who adhered consistently to the teaching of the apostles, who would happily embrace silence, who carried a heavy burden of sin; a man condemned in his absence (which recalls our legal allusions) and robbed of an opportunity to face his accusers, contrary to law both human and divine.[57] Thus, one assumes, Theodoret thought of himself.

Those points bring us to the threshold of my final observations; but what has been the outcome of our analysis of *syneidos* and *prosôpeion*? I have already discussed the "public" and yet inhibited character of both the written and the spoken word and the absence of a clear separation between disengagement and engagement. The nature of both the written and the spoken word might have seemed at first to make such a separation inevitable; but what they had in common did more to achieve firmer connections and, for all the exigencies of circumstance and convention, one could overcome the distance between self and world. I spoke, therefore, of "an unbroken pathway," "a single axis," along which one lived out one's selfhood. The singleness of the human person as both thinker and agent guaranteed that continuity. Theodoret's handling of *syneidos* and *prosôpeion* confirms and expands those contentions. *Syneidos* was a species of action and therefore another example of how one might transform subjective experience into visible achievement. The transformation depended in part, however, on a keen sense of inner presence, which included the presence of God as a judge of one's intentions. Choice was the most characteristic symptom of selfhood. As for *prosôpeion*, the ideal was to achieve another form of transformation, so that one's visible role genuinely reflected one's intimate character.

The most important element in that summary is the ability to create a harmony between self and circumstance; a harmony effected and preserved by the singleness of the human person. I want to suggest now how social and exposed the process proved to be. Theodoret can seem to have hinted at dichotomy, at a lack of harmony. His phraseology in one notable instance is characteristically difficult to translate: "words often provide a living picture of the characteristics of souls and reveal their unseen forms."[58] Let us note at once that we are talking here about the effect and content of words, about what words *do* ("provide a living picture" and "reveal"). Now, the two terms—"characteristics" and "forms"—are in the plural, which means that they cannot refer to a single distinguishing quality or essence (such as "soul," for example, might stand for). Those "characteristics" (or "marks") and "forms" (or "shapes") are something *other* than the person whom the word "soul" would encompass. However, the phrase "their unseen forms" is immediately paradoxical, because "form" (*eidos*) would normally suggest a *visible* form. Finally, the word *zôgraphousi* (translated above as "provide a living picture") means literally "they draw [or paint] from life," which suggests that words can refer to the characteristics and forms of the soul, as if to models; which implies in turn that the speaker—we are talking about words, about socially audible words—occupies the *same setting* as the characteristics and forms that he or she describes. On all three scores, any simple dichotomy has been dissolved.[59]

On the subject of harmony between self and circumstance, Theodoret's letter to Marcellus, the superior of a monastery in Constantinople (the home of the so-called *Akoimêtoi*, "the ever watching ones") invites another range of reflections. Those who fabricated lies against him, he wrote, were talking in a sense to themselves, short-circuiting genuine communication: "they blather on [*lalousin*] about their own ideas, and do not speak [*legousin*] as we do."[60] There were literary precedents for distinguishing between the "blather" implied by the verb *lalein* and the measured address implied by the verb *legein*. I detect also a reminiscence of John 8:44 (where the same form of words is used): "You are sprung from your father the devil and you want to do what your father desires. He has been the death of humankind since the beginning and he does not take his stand upon truth: there is no truth in him. When he blurts out falsehood, it is his own language he is speaking, for he is a liar and the father of lies." What is the alternative force of Theodoret's phrase "they do not speak as we do"? What does it mean to say, as the passage states literally, "they are not speaking our things"? What are "our things"?[61] Theodoret may have meant simply "our party" or those whom he considered orthodox; but his recollection of John may also have been operating still. If so, he was laying claim to truth (as opposed to lies) in the way that Jesus did: "I, however, speak [legô] the truth," legô being contrasted with the devil's lalei. One may conclude that the difference between truth and falsehood, in Theodoret's eyes, was laid bare by a difference in the ways they were expressed. There was no question of "hypocrisy," of a dichotomy between heart and tongue, since telling the truth and telling a lie were both telling, a way of speaking. A letter to the monks of Constantinople adds to the force of the argument. Lies were another example of the short circuit. They were stale and predictable—"Those who arm their tongues against our God and Savior achieve nothing new or remarkable"—whereas truth could carry one onto new ground. And the effect of falsehood's sterility was insidious, precisely because it was not always immediately obvious: "Offering their services to the well-disposed, they pierce them with their lies."[62]

The portrayal of "characteristics," therefore, and the expression of false-hood and truth, show that we are dealing with a predominantly social experience, a setting within which things were seen and words were heard. The self was embodied and moved among other bodies.[63] It acted deliberately (from its own point of view) and intelligibly (from the point of view of others) within a community. A mutual relationship, a synapheia, between tongue and ear and between speech and hearing provided a model also for the harmony between Theodoret and his correspondents. (One may recall the presuppositions at work between Theodoret and Uranius of Emesa.) There was a close link between conversation and social unity; a link—again, a synapheia—that overcame the disjointed physics, the actio in distans, of speaking and hearing—where "the tongue projects the words and the ear receives them."[64]

Striking, finally, is the specificity given to such a model of social experience by the activities and perceptions of a Christian bishop. Theodoret observed that for him to maintain silence could arouse suspicion—that is, a suspicion of what others could see—and rightly, since silence could disguise heterodoxy. He, however, had spoken out in church before great numbers of people, and they would be able to bear witness to his purity of doctrine.[65] The assertion is by no means as simple as it may seem. How could even great numbers of people be certain that heterodoxy was not lodged invisibly even within one who spoke out in an apparently orthodox manner? The only quality distinguishing the second situation (Theodoret's own), apart from the great numbers "bearing witness," seems to have been the fact that he was "preaching in church."[66] Certainty as to what was "going on in someone's head" could not depend, therefore, on arguments for a reliable correspondence between what one could and could not see. The crucial distinction was between speech and silence. *Once one opened one's mouth* (for it was silence that aroused suspicion), the manner of one's address would attest to the acceptability of one's teaching and make it unnecessary to "wonder what he is really thinking." And it seems to have been precisely the *setting* that generated confidence in the authenticity of the declared sentiments.[67] In another letter written at the same time, Theodoret made much of the fact that his "witnesses" had been brought together by his catechesis, by his having baptized them, by his preaching to them in church. Their identity as witnesses was forged within a liturgical setting.[68] And they were fully active—were in some ways the chief agents—in the dialogue between themselves and the preacher: "they listened attentively [*epaïontes*] to the arguments put forward in churches."[69] Actually, the verb *epaïô* moves through a range of meanings, beginning with attentive listening but moving toward deep understanding. One can detect in its use here a steadily rising pitch of response: as Theodoret spoke in church, his hearers, exercising their liturgical identity, gave full substance to what he said.

What can we deduce from these reflections? What, in particular, can we carry away as partial answers to our original questions—about Theodoret's own understanding of subjectivity and discourse and about the availability of Theodoret himself in the texts that we read in our own day? Let me briefly list the reflections again: the public conventionality of word and script; the inadequacies of language; one's associated inability to express oneself fully; the avoidance, however, of a "hidden" self; the singleness of the human person and the unbroken axis of engagement; the positive ambiguities of *syneidos* and *prosôpeion* and the associated importance of morality and judgment; and finally the dependence of the self on a social arena.

Now, I do not wish to suggest that Theodoret was a phenomenologist *manqué*, the Heidegger of his time. He does display, however, epistemological sophistication. In particular, he seems to have overcome the debilitating barriers between self and world. He was no Cartesian, and his most striking assertions may be those concerning the singleness of the self. Given a common prejudice against the psychology of that age, it is refreshing to find someone who refused to be hidden away inside his body. Theodoret's body was the place where he engaged with others, where he made himself clear. I suspect that the theology of the Incarnation, which absorbed so much of his attention, was in that regard a stimulus and model. So, there was an unembarrassed immediacy about his relationship with the world; an immediacy that was never naïve but fully conscious of the difficulties and moral challenges involved. I would emphasize again the degree to which a moral concern at once defined and released Theodoret's inner being and gave it the independent dignity of a soul subject to judgment.

He also had interesting things to say about the relation between speech and writing, which makes him seem equally "modern" in his interests and solutions. As a letter writer, he was preoccupied with the communicative capacity of texts. We are just as much the recipients of those letters as were his contemporaries. He would never have envisaged that his writings might fall into the hands of people like ourselves, and we read them in a context radically different from his, which controls our reading in important ways.[70] Nevertheless, the *content* of each letter endures through time. Given what we may now say about Theodoret's commitment to immediacy and a shared social context, and given his sense that the written word spoke with the voice of the writer, I believe that in his correspondence he is not entirely hidden— *dérobé*, as Derrida put it—and that we can find in that correspondence (again, to quote Derrida) something of a *présence naturelle.*

Postscript

The *Letters* fall into three groups. First, there is the large body of material originally edited by Jacques Sirmond and published in 1642, which is more or less what we have in Migne, *Patrologia Graeca* (hereafter PG) 83, though numbered differently by Azéma (in vols. 2 and 3 of his *Théodoret de Cyr, Correspondance*). Second, there is Ioannes Sakkelion's edition of a unique Patmos manuscript, published in 1885 (reproduced in Azéma's volume 1). Third, there are letters drawn from conciliar collections (reproduced in Azéma's volume 4), of which four are in Migne, *Patrologia Graeca* (150, 151, 169, and 171). The conciliar material dates to the years 431–35. Four of the letters (the four in Migne) survive in Greek, of which two are in the Collectio Atheniensis (169 and 171) and one in the Collectio Vaticana (150). The other thirty-two survive only in Latin, in the Collectio Casinensis. Some of those were contained in the earlier Collectio Turonensis, which was formed before 553; the rest were translated in a Synodicon by the Roman deacon Rusticus (nephew of Pope Vigilius), drawing on material he found in the monastery of the *Akoimêtoi* in Constantinople. Those last are to some extent tendentious: Rusticus himself was intent upon exposing what he regarded as the injustice of Theodoret's condemnation in the "Three Chapters" controversy; but the letters he reproduced from the monastic library had originally formed part of a collection drawn up to exonerate Nestorius, by his friend the *comes* Irenaeus. Azéma provides all the details and I have adopted his numbering. (One must not confuse *ep.* IV, from the Sakellion series, with *ep.* IV, 1, 2, 3, and so on, from the conciliar series). I have not considered the Latin material in this paper—not because it is unimportant, since it contains rich theological material, but because one is able to place much less weight on a Latin term for which one has no immediate Greek equivalent (even though a guess might often be justified).

Notes

1. Professor Clark has been a salutary skeptic and guide in such matters, and I gladly acknowledge both her warnings and her encouragement. See most obviously her *Reading Renunciation*, together with my review in *Journal of Ecclesiastical History*.
2. Italicized in the original. For quotations here and immediately below, see Derrida, *De la grammatologie*, 227–28.
3. So the standard English translation by Spivak, *Of Grammatology*, 158—although Spivak is careful to add in brackets, "there is no outside-text."
4. I say "the whole world," because Derrida wanted the insight to apply to *any* system of what he called "signs."
5. "And that is not because we have no immediate interest in the life of Jean-Jacques or in the existence of Maman or of Thérèse *as such*, nor because we have access to their so-called 'real' life only in the text." He was discussing *Émile* and the *Confessions*.
6. For clarity on the traditions involved, see Gutting, *French Philosophy*; Bell, *Problem of Difference*; and Strozier, *Foucault, Subjectivity and Identity*.
7. A question posed by Stephen Halliwell, "Traditional Greek Conceptions of Character," in Pelling, ed., *Characterization and Individuality*, 57. For caution about "the way in which 'character' . . . is embedded in the form and structure of the literary work as a whole," see Christopher Gill in the same collection, "The Character-Personality Distinction," 8–9. Simon Goldhill makes a similar point in his contribution to the volume: "If the figures of drama cannot be separated—as bounded individuals—from the (figural) language of the narrative, neither can they be separated from the literary tradition in which they also inevitably play a

part," "Character and Action, Representation and Reading: Greek Tragedy and Its Critics," 108.

8. Theodoret of Cyrrhus, *epistula* (*ep.*) 65. Unwillingness to exceed that measure was almost a topos among late Roman letter-writers. For the text, see *Théodoret de Cyr, Correspondance*, ed. Azéma (in four volumes), 2: 146.17. In my references to the *Letters*, I have indicated the place of the relevant phrase in the Greek text. For further details about the structure and numbering of the collection, see "Postscript," the final section of my essay,

9. Ep. 133, ed. 3: 126.8–12. (Letters with Arabic numbers from Azéma, vols. 2 and 3, are those reproduced in Migne, although numbered differently.) Note the use of the word *poiôn* here, suggesting that a text is an act.

10. Ep. XII, ed. 1: 84.20–85.2. (Letters with Roman numbers from Azéma, vol. 1, are from Sakkelion's Patmos MS: see "Postscript.")

11. Ep. XXX, ed. 1: 96.21–23.

12. Ep. 22, ed. 2: 78.8–11.

13. *Anapimplasthai deous*, *ep.* 52, ed. 2: 128.9–10.

14. Ibid., ed. 2: 128.16–18. Putting matters the other way about, he stated, in a festal letter of the late 440s, that he wanted now to forget what he had learned (to his own cost) "from experience," *ep.* 54, ed. 2: 132.9.

15. See Rist, "Platonic Soul."

16. Ep. 104, ed. 3: 28.7–8. See also, for example, *ep.* 145, ed. 3: 164.10–11; *ep.* IV, 4, ed. 4: 104.1–2. (Letters numbered in this last form—Roman numeral, Arabic numeral—from Azéma, vol. 4, are from the "conciliar" collection: see "Postscript.")

17. Ep. 146, ed. 3: 182.10–11.

18. See Ware, "Soul in Greek Christianity," 54–56.

19. "Writing is, for me, a medicine that sets my soul in motion [*pharmakon psychagôgias*]," *ep.* 58, ed. 2: 134.21–136.1—an old Platonic notion and two-edged into the bargain. Compare *ep.* 144, ed. 3: 158.28–160.2.

20. Ep. XXXI, ed. 1: 97.7–9. Writing and rhetoric were mutual reinforcements against injustice: *ep.* 10, ed. 2: 36.18–21.

21. Ep. 146, ed. 3: 174.18–19. Compare *ep.* 90. ed. 2: 238.19–23.

22. Ep. 62, ed. 2: 142.14–16.

23. Ep. 33, ed. 2: 94. 6, 12–13.

24. Ep. 72, ed. 2: 158.8–10.

25. Ep. 122, ed. 3: 84.24–25.

26. Ep. 122, ed. 3: 84.25–86. 1.

27. Ep. 123, ed. 3: 88.16–19. Compare *ep.* 131, ed. 3: 112.8–9.

28. Ep. IX, ed. 1: 82.3–5.

29. Ep. XIX, ed. 1: 90.18–19. *Paideia* is hard to translate briefly: it refers to the instruction of the young in the values and practices of their culture. Compare *ep.* 20, ed. 2: 66.23–24.

30. Ep. 73, ed. 2: 158.19–21. In respect of Themistocles' "natural virtue" (*physikên . . . aretên*) (ibid., 16–17), we have to acknowledge that no tradition was entirely consistent in such matters: "The term *phusis* . . . is often used to present a person's character as a matter of that which is most intrinsic and integral to him;

where appropriate, the superiority of the natural over the acquired is an additional implication. Yet this poses a paradox, for character is also commonly conceived, as the etymology of *êthos* suggests, in terms of dispositions induced by habit, practice, and training." Halliwell, "Greek Conceptions of Character," 46–47.

31. God was in a comparable position—in one respect wise, in another good. As wise, he "knew," like Pericles, what was appropriate; as good (that being, therefore, his "active" quality), he made appropriate action possible for human beings, *ep.* 18, ed. 2: 66.12–13.

32. Theodoret almost suggested in one letter (*ep.* 51, ed. 2: 126.17–19) that talking about virtue was at least as good as possessing it—a telling comment on his *Historia religiosa*, in which putting virtue into words is itself conceived of as an act of virtue. See Krueger, "Hagiography as an Ascetic Practice."

33. *Ep.* 96, ed. 3: 10.2–6.

34. For a more formal description of an "examination of conscience," see *ep.* 135, ed. 3: 130.9–10. Had he maintained his orthodoxy? Had he been generous to those in need?

35. *Ep.* 96, ed. 3: 10.7–8,14–15.

36. *Ep.* 99, ed. 3: 16.14.

37. Ibid., ed. 3: 16.14–15.

38. Compare *ep.* 104, ed. 3: 24.15–16.

39. *Ep.* 110, ed. 3: 38.15–17.

40. Ibid., ed. 3: 38.13–15.

41. *Ep.* 136, ed. 3: 134.4–5.

42. *Ep.* 138, ed. 3: 140.11–12.

43. *Ep.* 65, ed. 2: 144.25–146.1.

44. *Ep.* 145, ed. 3: 162.4–5.

45. *Ep.* 113, ed. 3: 60.1.

46. "The mutually explanatory correspondence between character and action . . . acquires a distinctive Greek complexion through association with an ethical outlook which locates the finest human excellences in overt, publicly recognizable activities," and "[t]he psychological workings of the mind are rarely conceived in the Greek tradition as an enclosed world of their own (though they may sometimes *conceal* or dissemble their contents), but rather as the source and springs of ethically significant action." Halliwell, "Greek Conceptions of Character," 52, 58–59.

47. *Ep.* 141, ed. 3: 152.13–14.

48. Harries, "Constructing the Judge," 215–16.

49. *Ep.* 3, ed. 2: 22.21–24.2. See *ep.* IV, 3a, dating back to 431, ed. 4: 82.27–29. Later in *ep.* 3, Theodoret distinguished between deeds and inclinations (*enthumêmata*), which are more evocative of emotion or impulse. Compare *ep.* 146, ed. 3: 176.3–4.

50. *Ep.* 3, ed. 2: 28.27–30.2.

51. For a discussion of Mauss on the transition "from *persona* as mask to *persona* as a juridical notion," see Momigliano, "Marcel Mauss and the Quest," 83.

52. *Ep.* 3, ed. 2: 24.5–9.

53. Ep. 19, ed. 2: 66.17–18.

54. Ep. XXXVI, ed. 1: 101.7–9.

55. Ep. XLIII, ed. 1: 107.2–5.

56. Ep. XXXVII, ed. 1: 101.21–22. For a comparable relationship between visible power and inherent wisdom, again echoing the harmonized skills of a Pericles, see *ep.* XLVI, ed. 1: 111.15–17.

57. See, e.g., *ep.* 88 to the *patricius* Tauros, ed. 2: 236.4–5. Ep. 113 to Leo of Rome and *ep.* 119 to the *patricius* Anatolios make at length his general point about not being heard publicly. See also *epp.* 138, 139 (to Anatolios again). On the factors that induced him to eschew silence and speak out, *ep.* 134 is particularly explicit.

58. I have kept for the moment to a fairly literal translation: *ep.* 50, ed. 2: 126.5–6.

59. Another example of a shared setting: Theodoret assured the *patricius* Anatolios that he carried the "memory" (*mnêmê*) of Anatolios perpetually "in both his thoughts and his words," suggesting that "memory" could straddle any divide between the two: *ep.* 119, ed. 3: 80.23–24.

60. Ep. 143, ed. 3: 158.6–7.

61. Azéma renders the phrase into French thus: "ne parlent pas notre langage à nous," ed. 3: 159.

62. Ep. 146, ed. 3: 172.21–23. See another splendid image in the same letter, ed. 3: 174.15–16.

63. Phenomenology was wedded to that notion of a shared physical environment. Merleau-Ponty was more explicit than his predecessors and helped Foucault to recognize, at least at first, the dichotomies that phenomenology was trying to overcome. See Gutting, *French Philosophy*, 195, 273.

64. Ep. 75, ed. 2: 162.6–8.

65. Ep. 90, ed. 2: 238.19–23. Compare *ep.* 146, ed. 3: 176.6–13, with its added emphasis that he had both preached and written, ed. 3: 176.13–16.

66. As the passages cited in the previous note suggest, weight of numbers affected texts as well as words. If there was doubt whether Theodoret had written what he truly thought, his other writings would be sufficient to prove it (they would, as he put it again, "bear witness"), *ep.* 83, ed. 2: 218.12–13. One was entitled to suggest, in other words, that texts *by sheer volume* acquired a cumulative effect.

67. Thus speaker and audience in Theodoret's situation could be compared with those in other settings—for example, a sophist and his pupils: the sophist was recommended by his pupils' eloquence, *ep.* XXXVII, ed. 1: 95.3. Compare *ep.* XXXV.

68. A comparable progression is depicted in Theodoret's *Cure for Hellenic Maladies*, 1.109. For a full picture of his achieving such effects, see *ep.* 146, ed. 3: 178.11–15. Similarly, at an earlier date and on another bishop's patch, *ep.* IV, 3a, ed. 4: 84.45–53 and 88.83–85. In the latter case, Theodoret was fully aware of his effect on the people, which led, indeed, to a riot.

69. Ep. 94, ed. 2: 246.17–18.

70. I want to make clear my subscription to remoteness and *étrangeté*. I do not share Momigliano's belief that "our style of describing persons derives from the classical tradition of biography and accepts its basic presuppositions about the need of

evidence and about the techniques of transition from external signs to internal qualities," "Marcel Mauss and the Quest," 89. For greater caution, see Christopher Gill, "The Character-Personality Distinction," and Simon Goldhill, "Character and Action," although Stephen Halliwell, "Greek Conceptions of Character," will risk talking about "fundamental factors in human experience": all in Pelling, ed., *Characterization and Individuality*, 6, 35, 100–101. Several of the contributors to that collection have published more recent works that develop their line of thought—for example, Pelling, *Literary Texts*; Gill, *Personality*; and Halliwell, *Aesthetics of Mimesis*.

✝   Damasus and the Invention
      of Early Christian Rome

DENNIS E. TROUT

In 1864 Giovanni Battista de Rossi (1822–94) dedicated the first volume of *La Roma sotterranea cristiana* to Rome's "second Damasus," the Risorgimento pope, Pius IX (1846–78).[1] The comparison is still striking. The new Christian archaeology, then so furiously revealing subterranean shrines and ancient tombs originally discovered or lavishly embellished by the "first" Damasus (366–84), owed as much in practical terms to Pius's patronage as to de Rossi's tireless excavations. Twelve years before, in January 1852, Pius had approved the Commissione di Archeologia Sacra, whose mandate included "the systematic and scientific exploration" of the Roman catacombs. Two years after that, on 11 May, he joined de Rossi (as he would elsewhere on other occasions) to view San Callisto's papal crypt, where a month earlier de Rossi had recovered the precious fragments of two large marble tablets elegantly inscribed with Damasus's name and verses.[2] But most significant, perhaps, Pius had urged de Rossi to produce the magisterial study that quickly replaced Antonio Bosio's *Roma sotterranea*, published in 1632.[3] With some justice, then, this pope, so opportunistic and energetic in changing times, assumed the role that in de Rossi's eyes the fourth-century bishop had played in the Roman underground's first age of discovery.[4]

But Damasus's name was no less magical for de Rossi's disciples, who inherited his hunt for "i monumenti più famosi dell'età eroica del cristianesimo," for the pursuit, they could imagine, had truly begun in the days of Damasus.[5] Orazio Marucchi's (1852–1931) handbook of Christian archaeology not only proclaimed Damasus the premier "poète des martyrs" but also pronounced him "nearly" the first Christian archaeologist.[6] Sévère Charrier, in turn, openly applauded Damasus's entanglement of research and mission. Charrier's "premier archéologue chrétien" may have recovered and adorned the tombs of the saints to honor these "héros de la foi" and preserve their endangered history, but he also enlisted their help in the still pressing struggle against the forces of heresy, schism, and paganism.[7] Even so, Charrier supposed, Damasus's most enduring legacy was to be found in the guidance and instruction that his elegantly inscribed *elogia*, ringing the city, had offered to so many generations of pilgrims to Roma *sotterranea cristiana*.[8]

And, indeed, Damasus's elogia did educate several centuries of late antique and early medieval visitors to Rome's vast network of suburban catacombs. By the mid-fifth century, when the heyday of expansion and new burial was over, these subterranean galleries had become a meandering history exhibit. Thereafter late antique and medieval *itineraria* and *syllogae* attest not only to the continuing allure of these halls of fame but also to the resonant vitality of Damasus's ubiquitous monumental texts.[9] Nevertheless, these days it is Damasus the impresario of the saints, not the historical archaeologist, who grips our imagination. There is no longer an unobstructed approach to Rome of the martyrs through catacomb *cubicula* refurbished and decorated by a fourth-century bishop whose energetic articulation of the cult of Peter and Paul was an unabashed assertion of Roman primacy, or whose hagiographic poetry constructed models of episcopal leadership and church unity deemed apposite for a Christian flock rent by schism and discord.[10] Moreover, scholars who acknowledge the general will of commemoration to erase as well as preserve portions of the past, or who recognize the complex polysemy of late antique Rome's Christian cityscape, are not likely to collude unwittingly with a polemically adroit churchman's recovery and revival of Rome's early Christian story, especially one operating in an age of acute identity crisis.[11] And yet, Damasus's archaeology draws us in.

Excavating Identity

Past and present (as well as visions of the future) collided abruptly in mid-fourth-century Rome. The collision was the collateral damage of a Constantinian miracle that in a few short years thrust Christianity from persecuted to favored status. And though repercussions would long reverberate, the immediately post-Constantinian decades were summoned to respond first. Eventually, of course, Rome would become comfortable as Roma *christiana*. Across the fifth century, Roman time would take on the rhythms of Christian time, the festivals of the saints and high holy days gradually replacing public games and rites keyed to the cults of the old gods and deified emperors.[12] The Roman cityscape, though more slowly, would come to reflect fully the priorities of Christian building programs and liturgical needs:

the church of Santi Cosmas and Damian would finally be set adjacent to the Roman Forum in the late 520s, and in 609 Boniface IV would reassign Hadrian's Pantheon to Santa Maria ad Martyres, the first papal rededication of a major temple.[13] Long before then, however, Christian impresarios of the Roman heritage had blazed trails back though the great divide that Constantine had thrown across Roman "history," for fourth-century Romans truly first confronted, publicly and en masse, the problem of being both Roman and Christian, which meant, for them, somehow renegotiating a civic identity that, for a millennium, had given no time or place to Christian cult or history.

The hagiographic elogia that Damasus installed in Rome's suburban martyrial shrines preserve the first steps of a resolution that would, in the event, prove flexible as well as durable. If it was not the sole purpose of Damasus's elogia to (re)write history in the service of contemporary identity, for his pontificate was troubled by various challenges that threatened to unseat him till the very end,[14] it was surely the effect of this poetry to offer Rome's Christians (and christianizing Romans) an alternate vision of the past. At a moment when the future was nearly as uncertain as real knowledge of the (actual) past, when the mass migration of the Roman aristocracy to the new religion of the emperors (excepting Julian) was only about to begin,[15] and when Christian literature was still, in the eyes of most Roman nobles, an oxymoron, Damasus's poetic vision of early Christian Rome—echoing Vergil, fashioning virtuous heroes, and promoting new celestial guardians— would operate as the base camp for exploring new modes of Roman self-understanding. Excavations of this sort might indeed be capable of reshaping civic identity and public memory.[16]

Such archaeology had been successfully practiced at Rome long before Damasus took to the catacombs. For nearly a millennium, Romans had been rediscovering themselves in a past of their own making. Rome was already well established as a city "endlessly rewritten," and Roman collective memory, embodied in public monuments as well as traditions and historical reflection, had long been evolving in tandem with the "ethical and political dispositions" of each age.[17] But no other period of Roman history, before the fourth century, had so generously displayed itself excavating and restaging its "past" as did Augustan Rome, which, perched between republic and empire, straddling oligarchy and autocracy, faced its own brand of identity crisis.[18]

Home to a *princeps* adept at the "invention of tradition" and well supplied with writers sensitive to the "acceleration of history," Augustan Rome harbors valuable lessons.[19] Herein, famously, Vergil mused upon the central dilemmas of his time by imagining the bronze-age history that had summoned them into being. Meanwhile, Livy suggested that the legends of early Rome, as he recast them, could rejuvenate a Roman nobility hamstrung by three generations of civil war, amending the delinquency of the day and abetting the formulation of a civic ideology that could accommodate the dispositions of his recognizably new era.[20] Like the literature of the age, so too the more democratic media of sculpture and architecture. Thus the Ara Pacis Augustae, commissioned by the Senate and dedicated in 9 B.C.E., expressed a city's hopes for peace and plenitude by juxtaposing images of Aeneas, Mars, and Romulus with a processional frieze of contemporary Romans that included Aeneas's reigning descendant and the city's newest founder, Augustus.[21]

Indeed, just as images in later Rome's martyrial shrines would telescope past and present in order to imply historical continuity, the monuments of the Augustan city repeatedly looked back to venerable landmarks.[22] The mausoleum of Augustus, for example, was a bridge, built up through four decades, over which selectively recast elements of the republican heritage were carried forward into the autocratic present: When construction of the mausoleum began in 28 B.C.E., Octavian (not yet Augustus) was a recent triumvir and still a military dynast, and the hulking tumulus recalled the funerary monuments of Hellenistic monarchs. When he died more than forty years later, however, the nostalgically revisionist *Res Gestae*, inscribed before his tomb, transformed Augustus's mausoleum into a monument to the city's long-lived princeps, the first citizen of the restored republic.[23] Yet by 14 C.E., when Augustus finally abandoned earth for the heavens, an even more elegant example of historical reenactment had already been papering over the fissures of historical discontinuity for more than a decade. In the prominently sited Forum of Augustus, a host of legendary founders and heroes, Aeneas and Romulus (again) among them, rubbed shoulders with such more recent men of war and politics as Sulla and Caesar.[24] This parade of venerable figures, summed up in the statues and archaizing elogia that lined the Forum's flanking porticoes, might recall the remarkable achievements of the Roman people and suggest, in unison if not harmony with Livy, the continued relevance of ancient exemplars, but it also culminated in an image of Augustus, stationed as *pater patriae* and (most likely) *triumphator* in a *quadriga* in the Forum's piazza.[25] This "pepped up" Roman history,[26] proceeding from Aeneas and backlit by the glow from multiple images of the divine Julian ancestors, Venus and Mars, like Vergil's subterranean parade of great Romans, led naturally to the arrangements of the new era.

Some three and a half centuries later, Damasus began to excavate another past, one that might make sense for (and of) his Roman present. Recovered, decorated, and inscribed with res gestae, the tombs of the martyrs and confessors would eventually anchor an updated foundational myth and provide the landmarks for a redrawn sacred cityscape. Peter, Paul, and Lawrence would be the fathers of a Christian patria becoming coterminous with Roman society itself. They would assume the city's celestial guardianship, replacing such former heavenly transplants as Romulus-Quirinus, the Dioscuri, and the deified emperors.

Although this urban transformation, demonstrable in time, is more elusive in origin, Damasus's elogia reveal the mechanisms of appropriation and subversion that underwrote it from the outset.[27] It was not (and never could be) a matter of the simple rejection of all that the old past had to offer christianizing Romans; Damasus's invention of early Christian Rome around the tombs of the saints relied as heavily upon remembering as forgetting. Roman heritage, expressed in the phrases and verses of revered poets and in the venerable lexicon of elite commemoration, was at once claimed, manipulated, and transposed in order to make real Romans of the new patres patriae. Consequently Damasus's elogia are not only the literary forerunners of Prudentius's classicism but also the moral foundations of the supreme self-confidence with which the latter poet's Lawrence would demand the retro-conversion of even Iulus, Romulus, and Numa.[28]

To such ends Damasus ransacked the classical poets to create verses that might be aesthetically acceptable and conceptually challenging to Rome's christianizing elite, surrounding the martyrs with allusions to Vergil.[29] The dictates of metrical convenience surely encouraged sampling Vergil's hexameters, but Damasus's art also advanced a subtler agenda. The echoes of earlier poets in Damasus's elogium for Stephen and Tarsicius, for example, subvert as they recall the original context.[30] When Damasus celebrated Stephen for carrying off "the trophy from the enemy" (ex hoste tropaeum), he shifted a snippet of Vergilian praise (Georgics 3.32) from Octavian to the protomartyr. Similarly, Damasus's description of a persecuting Roman mob as "mad dogs" (canibus rabidis) redeployed words Virgil had used to characterize the hounds of Iulus, driven to madness by the Fury Allecto (Aeneid 7.493–94). But line 7 of this poem, "when a raving mad gang was pressing [Tarsicius] to reveal [the sacramenta] to the uninitiated" (cum male sana manus premeret vulgare profanis), was constructed out of an especially striking conflation of Virgil and Ovid. "Male sana" was Vergil's reproach of Dido (Aeneid 4.8), while in the second book of the Ars Amatoria Ovid had asked, "Who would dare to reveal the rites of Ceres to the uninitiated?" (*quis Cereris ritus ausit vulgare profanis?*). Thus Damasus sketched the specter of the deranged Dido, who had tried to derail an earlier tale of Roman destiny, behind the enraged anti-Christian mob and trumped the mysteries of Eleusis with the *sacramenta Christi*.[31]

In this elogium, as in others, Damasus offered educated readers verses worthy of the reflection that was the necessary first stage of a salvage archaeology intended to summon the shades of highly revered (pagan) poets while simultaneously interrogating their assumptions about sacrilege and sanctity, triumph and defeat.[32] The strategy had, in a sense, already been employed by Juvencus as later it would inspire Prudentius and Paulinus of Nola.[33] But here, at a crucial juncture in Rome's history, the public verses of the city's socially prominent bishop first demonstrated how Christian poets and their readers might keep their Vergil and their Ovid while continuing to polish and display their own literary sensibilities in acceptable fashion. Literary love and theft made possible both the embrace and disavowal of cultural performances that were potentially dangerous because too closely identified with the "other."[34] By a parallel kind of thinking, Prudentius would later advocate revering pagan cult statues as works of art.[35]

In a similar manner, Damasus manipulated language that had long been at home in the arena of aristocratic self-definition. When necessary, he first naturalized the early church's heroes: with their Roman martyrdoms the Carthaginian Saturninus and the Greek Hermes earned a Roman *patria*; though sent by the East, Peter and Paul became Rome's special citizens (*suos cives*).[36] More crucially Damasus's martyrs reveal themselves as exemplars of deeply embedded notions of manly excellence traceable from the epitaphs of the republican-age tomb of the Scipios, through the elogia of the Forum of Augustus, to the eulogistic epigrams composed by Damasus's contemporary, the pagan senator Avianius Symmachus.[37] In the catacombs of Domitilla, the soldier-martyrs Nereus and Achilles toss aside their shields and weapons and rejoice to carry the "triumphs of Christ" (*Christi portare triumfos*) (*Epig. Dam.* 8). In the catacombs of Praetextatus, the deacons Felicissimus and Agapitus, comrades of the unconquered cross (*hi crucis invictae comites*), stick by their *dux*, the bishop Sixtus, and win the "triumphs of Christ" (*Christi meruere triumphos*) (*Epig. Dam.* 25). Along the Via Salaria Nova, Felix and Philippus, martyrs equal in *virtus*, win the "coronas of Christ," recalling military laurels as well as athletic honors (*Epig. Dam.* 39). In San Callisto's papal crypt, the martyred *comites* of Sixtus, like Stephen before them, carry off trophies from the enemy, *ex hoste tropaea* again, while the same tomb's "pious" throng includes nobles (*proceres*), young and old alike, who display the venerable qualities of *pudor* and *castitas* (Epig. Dam. 16). Elsewhere, Crisantius and Daria commute *damna* into *honor* and *decus* (Epig. Dam. 45). Yet, surpassing the merely secular *fama* usually allowed to republican heroes, the true rewards awaiting Damasus's martyrs are the *praemia vitae*, a celestial afterlife more reminiscent of the apotheosis reserved for good emperors (Epig. Dam. 17).

One effect of this strategy of commemoration is the sublimation, if not erasure, of real differences. Historical outsiders, Greeks and criminals (at best) as the Romans once saw them, are recast as Damasus's elogia dress a peripheral early Christian subculture in the normative language of classical poetry and elite approbation. Simultaneously a once marginal historical narrative, for Roma christiana was an unlikely survivor from a Flavian or Antonine perspective, is brought closer to center stage, where for many it now belonged, amid the new arrangements of the post-Constantinian world. Thus Damasus's suburban *martyria*, refurbished and adorned, painted and inscribed, now challenged the version of civic identity still proclaimed by the statues and elogia of the city's *fora*. But they also took aim at the loftier reaches of old Rome's self-understanding.

In a cult area of the Basilica Apostolorum (San Sebastiano) on the Appian Way, Damasus installed a seven-verse cenotaph in honor of Peter and Paul, the city's premier immigrant saints.[38] Their missionary itinerary—beginning in the East ("Oriens"), leading through Rome, and concluding in the starry heavens—is pressed into the poem's three central lines (3–5), at whose structural and ideological center stand the martyrdoms that launched Peter and Paul heavenward (*per astra*). This "travelogue" is framed by four lines, two (1–2) that verify the saints' former "residence" at the very spot being memorialized (an emphatic *hic*); and two (6–7) that authorize, over Damasus's signature, not only Rome's adoption of Peter and Paul as "her own citizens" but also the city's right to address them as her "new stars."

The challenge issued by this elogium is not aimed at the legendary mortal agents of Roman destiny but rather at those whose merits, like Peter and Paul's, won them victory over death and the responsibilities of astral guardianship. That might suggest Augustus and other deified emperors who took up starry afterlives, but a more likely target of this elogium's counterclaim is an earlier pair of apotheosized eastern heroes, Castor and Pollux.[39] The legends and cult of the Dioscuri were ancient at Rome, but these heavenly twins, who entered Roman history at the early fifth-century battle of Lake Regillus and were honored with one of the earliest monumental temples of the Roman Forum, still had a vital purchase on the fourth-century city.[40] Carved in high relief and star-crowned, they greeted all who walked the busy Via Lata through Diocletian's Arcus Novus;[41] on coins of Maxentius they had stood, stars on their caps, shielding the wolf-suckling Romulus and Remus; as disembodied stars they hovered above the same scene on coins of Constantine and his sons;[42] their *dies natalis* (8 April) was recorded in the calendar of 354 and celebrated with circus races;[43] and in 359, in the midst of a food shortage, Rome's urban prefect performed a (successful) sacrifice at their temple in Ostia.[44] Peter and Paul, likewise arrivals from the East, were now imagined (and perhaps represented) as similarly ensconced in the "realms of ether," where they could be called upon as the city's "new stars."[45] As the apotheosized agents of Christ, they were at least positioned to drive the Dioscuri from the field.[46]

These observations about fourth-century Rome's revised sense of history, with new (but not unfamiliar) heroes and guardians, are not meant to imply that there is no "actual" history of pre-Constantinian Roman Christianity. In fact, that history may be better known now than it was to most fifth- and sixth-century Romans. The point, rather, is that this fourth-century archaeology of Rome of the martyrs, whose best-known impresario is Damasus, offered contemporaries a vision of their past that was both palatable and worthy of the new age. Enshrined and monumentalized, this "history" made available to the growing body of Romano-Christians a well-heeled "myth of origins," crucial to the construction of a viable civic identity. And as it happened, just as Charrier noted nearly a century ago, because Damasus's elogia possessed the durability and commanded the reach of monuments, they would shape public memory for centuries to come.

National Cemeteries and Public Memory

Henri Lefebvre has suggested, and Roman imperial funerary monuments seem to confirm, that the impulse to civic "self-presentation and self-representation" readily lodges in sites where death can be both "represented and rejected."[47] For this reason, perhaps, the tombs of deified emperors encouraged proclamations about history and identity. The mausoleum of Divus Augustus was topped by his colossal image but also housed his mortal remains in a circular burial chamber. Once prefaced by the *Res Gestae*, the mausoleum retrospectively justified the life and career of the princeps, while initiating a series of imperial funerary monuments that similarly "told Romans how their city should now be seen."[48]

A century after Augustus's death, a golden urn containing Trajan's ashes was placed in the base of the extraordinary column he had constructed, within the *pomerium*, at the northwestern end of his forum.[49] The column's sculpted frieze, unwinding in 23 whorls, with 2,639 figures (including 59 Trajans), had for several years already been announcing the Dacian res gestae of this *optimus* princeps while also testifying anew to the religious piety and military capacity of the Roman people.[50] With its reception of Trajan's ashes, however, the column also began to proclaim yet another hero-emperor's apotheosis.[51] But while Divus Traianus, perched atop his tomb (like Augustus atop his), was "reaching for the sky,"[52] pulling Rome with him, his urn, apparently highlighted by a window in the monument's base, attested to death's reality and the city's continuing claims. A generation later, Antoninus Pius and his wife, Faustina, mounted on the back of a winged male figure, even more emphatically soared heavenward from the base of their funerary column (a cenotaph).[53] Nevertheless, like Augustus and Trajan, these *divi* were not to escape the responsibilities attached to the grant of apotheosis. They remained firmly tethered to the sightlines of both a personified Campus Martius, where the ceremonies of cremation and consecration took place,[54] and a helmeted Roma, her arm resting lightly upon a shield embossed with a wolf-suckling Romulus and Remus, her feet nestled in a heap of arms and armor. Monuments like these graphically linked heaven and earth and thus interwove history and destiny. Before them imperial Romans might well remind themselves who they were and sense how their city should be seen.

The same bivalency of presence and absence that charges imperial funerary monuments also gave distinct meaning and handbook authority to late antique Rome's catacomb shrines. The martyrs, as bodies, bone, and ash, may have been fully present at their graves, but they had also been swept heavenward, where their unfettered souls enjoyed the rewards of virtue in the starry palace of heaven. Damasus's elogia insist on this polarity with a sense of urgency that underscores the paradoxical force of their claims. The saints were simultaneously here and there, intimately available (rather unlike the divi) yet powerfully remote. Seven lines of an elogium for the saints of San Callisto's papal crypt begin with *hic*: "Here collected lies a heaped up throng of saints. . . . Here the comrades of Sixtus. . . . Here young men and boys."[55] On the Via Labicana "this tomb" (*hic tumulus*) holds the limbs of Gorgonius, as Maurus's grave on the Via Salaria Nova (*hic tumulus* again) sheltered his *pia membra* (*Epig. Dam.* 32.1, 44.1). Even notable events might hallow ground. "Here [*hic*] once dwelt," began Damasus's elogium of Peter and Paul; while

Sixtus II, his elogium declared, was "in this very spot [hic positus], sitting down," at the exact moment of his martyrdom.[56]

Yet, the Christ-given "rewards of (eternal) life" had to override the gravity of the tomb; bodies might be earthbound but souls shot upward.[57] The *animae* of San Callisto's *turba piorum* thus lived on in the "palace of heaven."[58] So, too, Felicissimus and Agapitus, similarly snatched up.[59] As the victorious Peter and Paul had followed Christ per astra, the martyr Tiburtius claimed heaven's heights in Christ's company.[60] Damasus's monuments, that is, were no less determined than imperial mausolea to crystallize history and identity in the very same tension between death acknowledged and death rejected that holds in balance the tomb of the apotheosized hero.[61] No matter that the triumphs here commemorated were those of alternative heroes. Soon enough these forms of expression would leak from the tombs of the martyrs to the epitaphs of contemporary Christians who were prepared to relate their own merits and to imagine their own astral immortality.[62]

That the shrines of the martyrs, hemmed in by countless other ancient and more recent graves, were so well poised to charge life and history with new meaning may, however, have more to do with the catacombs' resemblance to national cemeteries than to any parallels between the *martyria* themselves and the grand and isolated tombs of the Roman emperors. Certain private tombs (where the ghosts live on)—Scipio Africanus's at Liternun, Robert Johnson's in the Mississippi Delta, Elvis Presley's at Graceland—do become sites of pilgrimage where potentially dynamic cross-generational connections of social identity are forged or reinforced.[63] But monuments looming over hillsides carpeted with the graves of "hero-martyrs," like memorials set upon ennobled battlefields, may tap a deeper, if more diffuse, vein of the collective consciousness.[64] And met in the solemn stillness of ground hallowed by self-sacrifice, well-chosen words, like the morally charged exegesis of civic space, will have an uncanny ability to bind (at least for the moment) personal identity to "national memory."[65]

At classical Athens, it was the custom for a leading citizen to deliver a *logos epitaphios* in the *kerameikos* over the remains of those who died in the service of the city-state.[66] Each such speech, exemplified now by the oration of Thucydides' Pericles, was "a lesson in patriotism."[67] And although such orations endlessly restaged the city's political myths, constantly reverting to well-worn images of Marathon and promoting idiosyncratic visions of Athenian democracy, the history they taught was thereby no less "true for the Athenians."[68] More than two millennia later, at the dedication of the Gettysburg battlefield cemetery, Abraham Lincoln redefined America at a moment of seemingly irremediable identity crisis by reimagining his country's story. Sidestepping the Constitution and rooting the sacrificial carnage of Gettysburg in a principle of human "equality" expressed in the Declaration of Independence, Lincoln's *logos epitaphios* not only refigured the issues behind the American Civil War but also "remade" America.[69] That the revisionism of Lincoln's "American scripture" was a "swindle," and "one of the most daring acts of open-air sleight-of-hand ever witnessed by the unsuspecting" matters little, for its "truths," inscribed widely across the land, still help Americans define themselves.[70]

In fourth-century Rome, the catacombs became the Christian city's national cemeteries. In this "imagineered protogeography" history would be pulled forward and reflection turned back; here, while the future became "a thing of the past," the past was also restaged to keep pace with the present.[71] If Damasus's elogia must surely have provoked charges of foul play in some quarters, as permanent features of the catacombs' sacred topography they too eventually became "true for Romans."[72] Read, reinscribed, and copied for generations, elaborated as *acta* and *passiones*, they ever announced the inherited obligations that are the load-bearing elements of civic identity.[73] When so much else falls into silence, monuments remain. Two decades after Damasus's death, as Prudentius explored the Roman catacombs, he encountered innumerable mute or reticent graves. It was, he told Valerian of Calagurris, the responsibility of the more forthcoming tombs of the saints to speak on their behalf (*Peristephanon* 11.7–23). Damasus's elogia had become a fundamental link between the Christian city and its heroic age.

The First Christian Archaeologist

In one sense, then, de Rossi's disciples were right. Damasus did stand in the vanguard of an archaeological enterprise that would be long engaged in recovering the history of early Christian Rome. But like Livy and Augustus before him, Damasus was also a present-minded agent of the Roman past, re-presenting (if not discovering) new stars, revamping the cityscape both to bring it into line with the times and to make its (newer) past more accessible.[74] Early in the fourth century, entering the dark and terrifying catacombs to visit the tombs of the martyrs and apostles had been like going "down living to hell."[75] By century's end, however, Prudentius had to jostle the crowds to get a look at the subterranean shrine of Hippolytus on the Via Tiburtina. The catacombs' corridors had become a chiaroscuro of dark splashed by pools of sunlight, while the saints' *aediculae* glittered with polished marble and precious metals (*Peristephanon* 11.155–68). Damasus had been busy. Most of the major catacomb complexes show signs of his intervention. New stairways, retrofit light wells, expanded galleries, and enlarged cubicula reveal his handiwork in the catacombs of San Callisto, Domitilla, Generosa, *ad duas lauros*, and elsewhere around the city.[76] And it was in these refurbished cubicula and underground basilicas that Damasus installed the inscribed tablets of marble that proclaimed the martyrs' merits and rewards.

This Rome of the martyrs first excavated in earnest by Damasus would be further revealed and elaborated in the decades ahead, though not necessarily in a well-coordinated manner. While Damasus's elogium installed at Lawrence's Via Tiburtina tomb, for example, had offered little more than a shop of horrors—scourging, mangling, flames, tortures, and chains—Prudentius soon fleshed out the tale with dialogue and action and staged a more ambitious assault on public memory. His Lawrence, slowly roasting to death, delivered the lengthy speech on the providential nature of pre-Christian Roman history that included his summons to Iulus, Romulus, and Numa to join the faithful. With similar optimism the *Peristephanon*'s contemporary Rome is a virtually uncontested *urbs Romula christiana* where the Quirites pour out their tears and count their blessings over the "bones" of the martyrs (2.310, 2.532–36, 2.561–65).

Yet, at the other end of late antiquity, the vision of Prudentius's written Rome was, in fact, essentially realized and the aims of Damasus's archaeology seemingly met. During the years when Gregory the Great (590–604) was assuring an overly acquisitive eastern empress that the saints still displayed their dreadful power at their tombs, a certain John was apparently in Rome operating as an agent of the Lombard queen, Theodelinda.[77] His assignment was to collect oil from the lamps burning in the Roman martyria and transport this precious cargo to the Lombard court at Monza.[78] For Theodelinda, and the empress Constantina, the essence of the city, and the sources of its image and identity, now lay outside its walls. Rome of the martyrs, the Roma sotterranea first opened to the public in the fourth century, was the Rome that now commanded nearly undivided attention.

Notes

1. Rossi, *La Roma sotterranea cristiana*, frontispiece: "Pio IX Pont. Max. alteri Damaso . . . auctor d. d." Elements of this essay have been presented at Brown University, Pennsylvania State University, Duke University, The Catholic University of America, and Iowa State University. Thanks to Joe Pucci, Paul Harvey Jr.,

Elizabeth Clark, Philip Rousseau, and David Hunter for invitations; to the anonymous reader who helped me trim my sails; and to the following for pointing directions: Pietri, "Concordia apostolorum"; and J. Fontaine, "Damase poète théodosien: l'imaginaire poétique des *Epigrammata*," in *Saecularia Damasiana*, 113–45. The present essay was completed while enjoying the benefits of a National Endowment for the Humanities Fellowship.

2. Ferrua, *Epigrammata Damasiana*, nos. 16 and 17 (hereafter *Epig. Dam.*). Ferrua's edition remains standard, though a new one is under way.

3. See Giuliani, ed., *Giovanni Battista de Rossi*, with 62–65 on Pius. Background at Frend, *Archaeology of Early Christianity*, 76–81, 160–64; L. Rutgers, *Subterranean Rome*, 9–41.

4. Kelly, *Oxford Dictionary of Popes*, 309–11; and see de Rossi, *Roma sotterranea*, 212–13.

5. Ibid., 213.

6. Marucchi, *Éléments d'archéologie chrétienne*, 1:227: "On pourrait presque l'appeler le premier archéologue chrétien."

7. Charrier, "Le premier archéologue chrétien."

8. Ibid., 572: "Ces épitaphs sacrées devaient guider et instruire les pèlerins."

9. On such syllogae, see Ferrua, *Epig. Dam.* 13–17. For the Roman *itineraria*, see *Itineraria et Alia Geographica*; and Valentini and Zucchetti, *Codice topografico*, vol. 2. For the distribution of the elogia, see Guyon, "Damase et l'illustration des martyrs," fig. 1.

10. Pietri, "Concordia apostolorum," 309: "L'intérêt de Damase pour les martyrs n'était pas seulement celui d'une pieuse archéologie." Cf. Pietri, *Roma Christiana*, 1590–96; and the well-illustrated Donati, ed., *Pietro e Paolo*. Février, "Un plaidoyer pour Damase."

11. E.g., Hedrick, *History and Silence*. Curran, *Pagan City and Christian Capital*, with Damasus at 142–55.

12. Salzman, *On Roman Time*; Salzman, "Christianization of Sacred Time and Sacred Space," in Harris, ed., *Transformations of Urbs Roma*, 123–34.

13. See Salzman's overview, "Christianization of Sacred Time"; on Cosmas and Damian, see Krautheimer, *Corpus Basilicarum*, 1.3:137–43; S. Episcopo, "Ss. Cosmas et Damianus, basilica," in Steinby, *Lexicon Topographicum*, 1:324–25; and on the Pantheon, F. Tommasi, "S. Maria ad Martyres," ibid., 3:218.

14. For an overview with a Roman slant, see C. Pietri, "Damase, Évêque de Rome," in *Saecularia Damasiana*, 31–58. Ammianus Marcellinus, *Rerum gestarum libri* 27.3.12–13, records the bloody beginning, but Damasus's ecclesiastical opponents long denounced him. Cf. *Collectio Avellana* 1.2 and 1.9–10 and 4 (*praefatio*) with "ambitione corruptus" and "quem in tantum matronae diligebant, ut matronarum auriscalpius diceretur." The praefatio (or *quae gesta sunt inter Liberium et Felicem*) introduced the *Libellus precum* addressed to Valentinian, Theodosius, and Arcadius in 384 by the Luciferians Marcellinus and Faustus. The Altar of Victory affair escalated in the last months of Damasus's episcopate. See Symmachus, *relatio* 3, in *Q. Aurelii Symmachi quae supersunt*, 280–83, with Damasus's role at Ambrose, *Epistula* 10.72.10, in *Epistulae et acta* (= Migne, *Patrologia Latina* [hereafter PL] 16, *Epistula* 17.10).

15. For review of the question see Hedrick, *History and Silence*, 54–56; with quantitative support and recognition of "significant advances" beginning in the pontificate of Damasus at Salzman, *Making of a Christian Aristocracy*, 73–80. See also Sághy, "Patrons and Priests."

16. See working definitions in Peterson, *Lincoln in American Memory*, 35; and Filene, *Romancing the Folk*, 5–8, emphasizing a public remembrance of the past "less concerned with establishing its truth than with appropriating it for the present" and the recursive processes that revisit and reevaluate the past "in the light of the present." See also Lowenthal, "Fabricating Heritage." My reading on the debate over the concept's validity includes Halbwachs, *On Collective Memory*; Nora, "Between Memory and History"; Knapp, "Collective Memory"; and Gedi and Elam, "Collective Memory."

17. Edwards, *Writing Rome*, xi; Knapp, "Collective Memory," 123.

18. Augustan writers dominate Edwards's *Writing Rome*, but see also Zanker, *The Power of Images*; Raaflaub and Toher, eds., *Between Republic and Empire*; Galinsky, *Augustan Culture*; and Habinek and Schiesaro, eds., *Roman Cultural Revolution*.

19. Begin, still, with Hobsbawm and Ranger, eds., *Invention of Tradition*. Augustus's recreation of the *Fratres Arvales* is a case in point, but Augustan revivalism generally appears as "a process of formalization and ritualization, characterized by reference to the past, if only by imposing repetition" (4). Nora's metaphor, "Between Memory and History," 7, describes the "rapid slippage of the present into a historical past that is gone for good." Nora's essay is richly suggestive, although his modern *lieux de mémoire* are shrinking preserves while the fourth-century *memoriae* of the saints are colonizing outposts.

20. Livy, *Ab urbe condita, praefatio*, 6–10. On "identity" as a prominent Livian theme see, e.g., Miles, *Livy*; Jaeger, *Livy's Written Rome*; Fox, *Roman Historical Myths*; and Chaplin, *Livy's Exemplary History*.

21. Richardson, *New Topographical Dictionary*, 287–89; Kleiner, *Roman Sculpture*, 90–99; Galinsky, *Augustan Culture*, 141–55; M. Torelli, "Pax Augusta, Ara," in Steinby, *Lexicon Topographicum*, 4:70–74.

22. E.g., the sixth-century "portrait" of Turtura in the catacombs of Commodilla in which the deceased joins the martyrs Felix and Adauctus beside Mary and the Christ child: Deckers, Mietke, and Weiland, *Die Katacombe "Commodilla,"* 1:61–65.

23. Initiation dated to 28 B.C.E. by Suetonius, *Divus Augustus* 100.4. Richardson, *Topographical Dictionary*, 247–49; Zanker, *Power of Images*, 72–77; von Hesberg and Panciera, *Das Mausoleum des Augustus*; Magness, "The Mausolea"; with Davies, *Death and the Emperor*, 49–67 on the mausoleum's "multivalency." On this aspect of the *Res Gestae*, see Suetonius, *Divus Augustus* 101; and J. Elsner, "Inventing Imperium: Texts and the Propaganda of Monuments in Augustan Rome," in Elsner, ed., *Art and Text*, 32–53.

24. Zanker, *Forum Augustum*; Richardson, *Topographical Dictionary*, 160–62; and V. Kockel, "Forum Augustum," in Steinby, *Lexicon Topographicum*, 2:289–95; with Zanker, *Power of Images*, esp. 193–215; and Kleiner, *Roman Sculpture*, 99–102.

25. On the forum's exemplary status, see Suetonius, *Divus Augustus* 31.5; T. J. Luce, "Livy, Augustus, and the Forum Augustum," in Raaflaub and Toher, *Between Repub-*

lic and Empire, 123–38. For the elogia, see Degrassi, Inscriptiones Italiae 13.3. On Augustus's image, see Zanker, Forum Augustum, 12. Note Res Gestae Divi Augusti 35, where recall of the quadriga and the title, pater patriae, culminates that document.

26. Stephen Kinzer, "George Washington: Mr. Excitement? Mount Vernon, Alarmed by Fading Knowledge, Seeks to Pep Up His Image," New York Times (29 July 2002): B1: "Their goal is to reposition the father of the country for a new era."

27. The pre-Damasan stages of such shifts in consciousness are now barely visible as, for example, are the earlier "lives" of many of the martyrs commemorated by Damasus.

28. Prudentius, Peristephanon (hereafter Perist.) 2.443–44, in Prudentius, Carmina: "fiat fidelis Romulus, / et ipse iam credat Numa"; 2.455–56: "agnoscat ut verum Deum / errans Iuli caecitas." Not purely metaphorical.

29. See Ferrua's individual commentaries in Epig. Dam.

30. Epig. Dam. 15; also Inscriptiones Christianae Urbis Romae (hereafter ICUR) 4.11078; preserved only in transcription.

31. Premeret vulgare, however, is de Rossi's emendation of the manuscript's prericret pulgare. All translations are my own unless otherwise noted.

32. Pleasure may be another matter. Modern readers have often been unsympathetic, e.g., Ferrua, Epig. Dam., 12, but Jerome thought Damasus "elegans in versibus componendis" (De viris illustribus 103). See positive assessments at Fontaine, Naissance de la poésie, 111–25; and Fontaine, "Damase poète théodosien."

33. See Juvencus, Evangeliorum libri quattuor.

34. Cf. Lott, Love and Theft.

35. Prudentius, Contra Symmachum 1.502–5, in Prudentius, Carmina.

36. Epig. Dam. 46.4–5: "sanguine [Saturninus] mutavit patriam nomenque genusque / Romanum civem sanctorum fecit origo." Epig. Dam. 48.1–2: "te [Hermetem] Graecia misit; / sanguine mutasti patriam." Epig. Dam. 20.6–7 (Peter and Paul): "Roma suos potius meruit defendere cives. / Haec Damasus vestras referat, nova sidera, laudes." Cf. Pietri, "Concordia apostolorum," 297–98. Late antique Rome may have been a city of immigrants; see N. Purcell, "The Populace of Rome in Late Antiquity," in Harris, ed., Transformations of Urbs Roma, 137–44.

37. On Damasus's "baptism" of the genre of the elogium, see Fontaine, "Damase poète théodosien," 143; Trout, "Verse Epitaph(s)," 168–70.

38. Epig. Dam. 20; also E. Diehl, ed., Inscriptiones Latinae Christianae Veteres 951; and ICUR 5.13273; preserved only in transcriptions: "Hic habitasse prius sanctos cognoscere debes / nomina quisque Petri pariter Paulique requiris. / (3) Discipulos Oriens misit, quod sponte fatemur; / sanguinis ob meritum Christumque per astra secuti / aetherios petiere sinus regnaque piorum. / (6) Roma suos potius meruit defendere cives. / Haec Damasus vestras referat, nova sidera, laudes."

39. Kraus, "Dioskuren,"in Reallexikon für Antike und Christentum (1957): 3:1135; Pietri, "Concordia Apostolorum," 314–17.

40. Livy, Ab urbe condita 2.20.12, 2.42.5; Dionysius of Halicarnassus, Roman Antiquities 6.13; Richardson, Topographical Dictionary, 74–75; I. Nielsen, "Castor, Aedes, Templum," in Steinby, ed., Lexicon Topographicum 1:242–45. The Dioscuri were also venerated early at the Forum's Lacus Iuturnae; see Nash, Pictorial Dictionary,

2:11–12; Geppert, *Castor und Pollux*, 134–37. The dictator A. Postumius, who "aed[em Castoris . . .] ex s[poliis hostium vovit]" was honored with an elogium in the Forum Augustum (Degrassi, ed., *Inscriptiones Italiae* 13.3.10).

41. Nash, "Arcus Novus," in Nash, *Pictorial Dictionary*, 1:120–25; Kleiner, *Roman Sculpture*, 409–13; Geppert, *Castor und Pollux*, 180 (R 15) and 120–21, on the "pilos und/oder stern" iconography.

42. Robertson, *Roman Imperial Coins*, 5:112 (Maxentius), 5:278–80 (Constantine; an Urbs Roma series). For the contorniate medallions, see Alföldi and Alföldi, *Die Kontorniat-Medaillons*, 2:126 (Nr. 45).

43. Degrassi, *Inscriptiones Italiae* 13.2, p. 245: "N(atalis) Castor(is) et Pollu(ci)s, C(ircenses), m(issus) XXIIII." Cf. Salzman, *On Roman Time*, 118–31, 156.

44. Ammianus, *Rerum gestarum libri* 19.10.4.

45. See, e.g., the fourth-century gold-glass token depicting Agnes flanked by two stars (Elsner, *Imperial Rome*, illus. 159); cf. Donati, *Pietro e Paolo*, no. 91, and the epiphany scene of Santa Maria Maggiore.

46. They did not go quietly. Prudentius's assault on Roman religion's great deception (*Contra Symmachum* 1.164–244 with 1.227–28, in *Carmina*) denounced them as the bastard sons of a fallen woman ("Gemini quoque fratres / corrupta de matre nothi"), but in the late fifth century Gelasius was still complaining at *Adversus Andromachum contra lupercalia* 18. See *Collectio Avellana*, 459; Gelasius, *Lettre*, 177: "Castores vestri certe, a quorum cultu desistere noluistis." Shortly the martyr twins Cosmas and Damian joined the fray (Kraus, "Dioskuren," 1135–36).

47. Lefebvre, *Production of Space*, 34–35.

48. For the quote see Elsner, "Inventing Imperium," 40. Further insights at Beard and Henderson, "The Emperor's New Body."

49. Lancaster, "Building Trajan's Column"; Jones, *Principles of Roman Architecture*, 161–75. In the fourth century the oddity still provoked comment, e.g., Eutropius, *Breviarium*, 8.5: "Inter divos relatus est solusque omnium intra Urbem sepultus est."

50. The column was dedicated in 113 C.E.; Trajan died in Cilicia in the late summer of 117. For review of questions regarding the column's funerary status, see Davies, *Death and the Emperor*, 30–34. On the column's frieze as res gestae, see V. Huet, "Stories One Might Tell: Reading Trajan's Column and the Tiberius Cup," in Elsner, *Art and Text*, 9–31. Religious piety is evident in the column's scenes of ritual and sacrifice.

51. On the association of *intra pomerium* burial with hero cult, see Davies, *Death and the Emperor*, 32.

52. Modifying Beard and Henderson, *Classical Art*, 181.

53. Their ashes were in Hadrian's mausoleum: *Corpus Inscriptionum Latinarum*, 6:986; also Dessau, *Inscriptiones Latinae Selectae*, 346; *Scriptores Historiae Augustae*, *Marcus* 7.10; Davies, *Death and the Emperor*, 40–43. Titus had already appeared in the vault of his arch ascending by eagle.

54. Richardson, "Ustrinum Domus Augustae," and "Diva Faustina Maior, Ara," in *Topographical Dictionary*, 404, 149. V. Jolivet, "Ustrinum Augusti," in Steinby, ed., *Lexicon Topographicum*, 5:97.

55. *Epig. Dam.* 16: "Hic congesta iacet quaeris si turba piorum. . . . Hic comites Xysti. . . . Hic iuvenes puerique."

56. *Epig. Dam.* 20.1: "Hic habitasse prius"; *Epig. Dam.* 17: "hic positus . . . sedentem."

57. *Epig. Dam.* 17.8–9 (Sixtus II): "Ostendit Christus, reddit qui praemia vitae, / pastoris meritum."

58. *Epig. Dam.* 16.2–3: "corpora sanctorum retinent veneranda sepulcra / sublimes animas rapuit sibi regia caeli."

59. *Epig. Dam.* 25.1–2: "Aspice, et hic tumulus retinet caelestia membra / sanctorum subito rapuit quos regia caeli."

60. *Epig. Dam.* 31.3: "aetheris alta petit Christo comitante beatus."

61. We know less about how pictorial representation reinforced this theme. Hippolytus's shrine included a painting depicting his burial; see Prudentius, *Peristephanon* 11.145–52. The early sixth-century mosaic from the apse of Santi Cosmas e Damian shows Peter and Paul introducing the two martyrs to Christ, who points to a phoenix and star, a corollary to the apotheosis scene of Antoninus and Faustina that merits further consideration. Krautheimer, *Corpus Basilicarum Christianarum Romae*, 1.3:137–43.

62. More in Trout, "Verse Epitaph(s)." Pope Felix built Cosmas and Damian "ut aetheria vivat in arce poli."

63. Livy, *Ab urbe condita* 38.56.1–4, and Seneca, *Epistulae* 86, both visitors. Provocative insights at Jaeger, *Livy's Written Rome*, 164–72; and Henderson, *Morals and Villas*. Notably the confusion over Scipio's burial place, as over Johnson's (e.g., Wyman, *Blues Odyssey*, 217), yielded multiple funerary sites.

64. E. Everett refers to "hero-martyrs" in his Gettysburg address (19 Nov. 1863) when describing the Athenian dead buried at Marathon and the Union dead of Gettysburg; Everett, *Orations and Speeches*, 4:623. Alcock, *Archaeologies*, 74–81.

65. Jaeger, *Livy's Written Rome*, 14.

66. Camp, *Archaeology of Athens*, 163–64, 261–64.

67. Loraux, *Invention of Athens*, 20.

68. Loraux, *Invention of Athens*, 132–71, at 171, emphasis in original.

69. Wills, *Lincoln at Gettysburg*.

70. Ibid., 38, noting contemporary grumbling. See most recently commemorations of the first anniversary of 11 September 2001. See Ignatieff in "What We Think of America," for whom "the power of American scripture [citing the Gettysburg Address] lies in this constant process of democratic reinvention" (49). On the dissemination of the Gettysburg address through inscription, classroom memorization, performance, and recasting, see Bullard, *Lincoln in Marble and Bronze*, too early to include the text's third inscription in the Gettysburg cemetery alone (on the Kentucky Monument of 1975); Bradon, *Building the Myth*; and Schwartz, *Abraham Lincoln*, 133, 241.

71. The quotations are from, respectively, Soja, "Los Angeles," 427, on Disneyland; and Bob Dylan, "Bye and Bye," *Love and Theft* (CD, Sony Music, 2001), on the burdens of the past from a writer deeply invested in the American imaginary. See further Marcus, *Invisible Republic*, Filene, *Romancing the Folk*, 204–32; and Dale, "Stolen Property," whose medieval Venetians "periodically reinvented the mem-

ory" of Mark's Venetian advent in accord with the evolution of their civic institutions (220).

72. Witness the pagan Praetextatus's sarcasm on another issue: Jerome, *Contra Joannem Hierosolymitanum ad Pammachium* 8 (PL 23:377C).

73. Several Damasan texts damaged during the sieges of the earlier sixth century were repaired or recarved by his episcopal successors; e.g., Vigilius's efforts (537–55) at *Epig. Dam.* 18.2 and 41. On the elogia as the seedbeds of *acta* and *passiones*, see *Epig. Dam.* 37; with Prudentius, *Peristephanon* 14; and *Bibliotheca Hagiographica Latina*, s.v. "Agnes."

74. Favro, *Urban Image of Augustan Rome*; and on Damasus's intramural building, see Curran, *Pagan City and Christian Capital*, 142–46.

75. Jerome's memory in action at *Commentarii in Ezechielem*, 12.40.5–13 (CCSL 75:556–57), with citation of Ps. 54:16: "descendant ad infernum viventes."

76. See the catalogue by Barbini in Pergola, *Le catacombe romane;* and the articles by A. Nestori, U. M. Fasola, P. Pergola, J. Guyon, and L. Reekmans in *Saecularia Damasiana*.

77. See Gregory the Great, *Registrum epistularum* 4.30 (CCSL 140:248–50): Constantina had requested "caput eiusdem sancti Pauli aut aliud quid de corpore ipsius" (248.5); she was offered *brandea* instead.

78. CCSL 175:284–95, with a reading to be tested elsewhere.

Adkin, Neil. "Ambrose and Jerome: The Opening Shot." *Mnemosyne* 46 (1993): 364–76.

——. "Jerome on Ambrose: The Preface to the Translation of Origen's Homilies on Luke." *Revue Bénédictine* 107 (1997): 5–14.

Aesop. *Aesopi Fabulae* 2.347–48. Edited by Aemilius Chambry. 2 vols. Paris: Belles Lettres, 1925–26.

Agapitos, P. "Teachers, Pupils and Imperial Power in Eleventh-Century Byzantium." In *Pedagogy and Power: Rhetorics of Classical Learning*, edited by Y. Lee Too and N. Livingstone, 170–91. Cambridge: Cambridge University Press, 1998.

Alcock, S. *Archaeologies of the Greek Past: Landscapes, Monuments, and Memories.* Cambridge: Cambridge University Press, 2002.

Aldama, José A. de. "La condenación de Joviniano en el sínodo de Roma." *Ephemerides Mariologicae* 13 (1963): 107–19.

Alexakis, A. *Codes Parisinus Graecus 1115 and Its Archetype.* Washington, D.C.: Dumbarton Oaks, 1996.

Alexander, P. "Religious Persecution and Resistance in the Byzantine Empire of the Eighth and Ninth Centuries: Methods and Justifications." *Speculum* 52 (1977): 238–64.

Alföldi, A., and E. Alföldi. *Die Kontorniat-Medaillons.* 2 vols. Berlin: de Gruyter, 1976–90.

Alon, Gedalyahu. "Rabban Joḥanan B. Zakkai's Removal to Jabneh." In *Jews, Judaism and the Classical World: Studies in Jewish History in the Times of the Second Temple and Talmud*, translated by Israel Abrahams, 269–313. Jerusalem: Magnes Press, 1977.

Amar, Joseph P. *The Syriac "Vita" Tradition of Ephrem the Syrian.* Ann Arbor: University Microfilms, 1988.

Ambrose. *Epistulae et acta.* Edited by O. Faller. 4 vols. Corpus Scriptorum Ecclesiasticorum Latinorum 82. Vienna: Hoelder-Pinchler-Tempsky, 1968–96.

——. *De virginibus.* In *Sant'Ambrogio, Opere morali II/I: Verginità e vedovanza*, edited by Franco Gori. 2 vols. Rome: Città Nuova Editrice, 1989.

Ammianus Marcellinus. *Ammianus Marcellinus: The Later Roman Empire* (A.D. 354–378). Translated by Walter Hamilton. London: Penguin, 1986.

——. *Rerum gestarum libri*. Edited by C. U. Clark. 2 vols. Berlin; Weidmann, 1910–15.

——. *Res Gestae*. Edited and translated by John C. Rolfe. 3 vols. Loeb Classical Library. Cambridge: Harvard University Press, 1969.

Ando, C. *Imperial Ideology and Provincial Loyalty in the Later Roman Empire*. Berkeley and Los Angeles: University of California Press, 2000.

Andreotti, Roberto. "L'opera legislativa ed amministrativa dell'imperatore Giuliano." *Nuova Rivista Storica* 14 (1930): 236–73.

Angold, Michael. *Church and Society in Byzantium under the Comneni, 1081–1261.* Cambridge: Cambridge University Press, 1995.

Anson, John. "The Female Transvestite in Early Monasticism: The Origin and Development of a Motif." *Viator* 5 (1974): 1–32.

Apophthegmata patrum. In *Patrologiae cursus completus: Patrologia Graeca*, edited by J.-P. Migne, 65:71–440.

——. *Les apophthegmes des pères: Collection systématique, chapitres I–IX.* Edited by Jean-Claude Guy. Sources chrétiennes 387. Paris: Éditions du Cerf, 1993.

——. "Histoire des solitaires égyptiens (MS Coislin 126, fol. 158f)." Edited by François Nau. *Revue d'orient chrétien* 13 (1908): 47–57, 266–83; 14 (1909): 357–79; 17 (1912): 204–11, 295–301; 18 (1913): 137–46.

——. *Sentences des pères du désert: Nouveau recueil*. Translated by Lucien Regnault. Sablé-sur-Sarthe: Abbaye de Solesmes, 1970.

——. *Les sentences des pères du désert: Série des anonymes*. Translated by Lucien Regnault. Sablé-sur-Sarthe: Abbaye de Solesmes, 1985.

Apuleius. *Florida*. Edited by P. Vallette. Paris: Les Belles Lettres, 1924.

Apuleius. *Metamorphoses*. 2 vols. Edited by J. A. Hanson. Loeb Classical Library. Cambridge: Harvard University Press, 1989.

——. *Metamorphoses*. Translated by E. J. Kenney. London: Penguin, 1998.

Arnold, Matthew. *Culture and Anarchy*. Edited with introduction by J. Dover Wilson. Cambridge: Cambridge University Press, 1932.

Artemidorus. *Oneirocritica*. Translated by Robert J. White as *The Interpretation of Dreams*. Park Ridge: Noyes Press, 1975.

Ashcroft, Bill, Gareth Griffiths, and Helen Tiffin, eds. *The Empire Writes Back: Theory and Practice in Post-Colonial Literatures*. 2nd ed. London: Routledge, 2002.

Athanasius of Alexandria. *Athanase d'Alexandrie: Vie d'Antoine*. Edited and translated by G. J. M. Bartelink. Sources chrétiennes 400. Paris: Éditions du Cerf, 1994.

——. "Athanasiana Syriaca I: 'Un *Logos peri parthenias* attribué à Saint Athanase d'Alexandrie.'" Edited and translated by J. Lebon. *Le Muséon* 40 (1927).

——. "Athanasiana Syriaca II: Une lettre attribuée à Saint Athanase d'Alexandrie." Edited and translated by J. Lebon. *Le Muséon* 41 (1928): 169–216.

——. *Athanasius: The Life of Antony and the Letter to Marcellinus*. Translated by Robert C. Gregg. Classics of Western Spirituality. New York: Paulist Press, 1980.

——. *The Canons of Athanasius, Patriarch of Alexandria, ca. 293–373.* Edited and translated by William Riedel and Walter E. Crum. Texts and Translation Society 9. London: William and Norgate, 1904; reprint, Amsterdam: Philo Press, 1973.

Badger, Carlton Mills, Jr. "The New Man Created in God: Christology, Congregation and Asceticism in Athanasius of Alexandria." Ph.D. diss., Duke University, 1990.

Baker, Cynthia M. *Rebuilding the House of Israel: Architectures of Gender in Jewish Antiquity.* Stanford, Calif.: Stanford University Press, 2002.

Baker, Steve. *Picturing the Beast: Animals, Identity and Representation.* Manchester: Manchester University Press, 1993.

Banchich, Thomas M. "Julian's School Laws: *Cod. Theod.* 13.3.5 and *Ep.* 42." *The Ancient World* 24 (1993): 5–14.

Bardy, Gustave. "Athanase." In *Dictionnaire de spiritualité ascétique et mystique, doctrine et histoire,* 1.2.1047–52. Paris: G. Beauchesne et ses fils, 1935.

——, ed. *Les trophées de Damas: controverse judéo-chrétienne du VIIe siècle.* Patrologia Orientalis 15. Paris: Firmin-Didot, 1927.

Barnes, Timothy D. *Ammianus Marcellinus and the Representation of Historical Reality.* Ithaca, N.Y.: Cornell University Press, 1998.

——. "Christians and the Theater." In *Roman Theater and Society,* edited by William J. Slater, 174–80. Ann Arbor: University of Michigan Press, 1996.

Barrell, John. *The Dark Side of Landscape: The Rural Poor in English Painting, 1730–1840.* Cambridge: Cambridge University Press, 1980.

Barton, Carlin. "Savage Miracles: The Redemption of Lost Honor in Roman Society and the Sacrament of the Gladiator and the Martyr." *Representations* 45 (1994): 41–71.

——. *The Sorrows of the Ancient Romans: The Gladiator and the Monster.* Princeton: Princeton University Press, 1993.

Basil of Caesarea. *Lettres.* Edited and translated by Yves Courtonne. 3 vols. Paris: Belles Lettres, 1957–66.

Batiffol, Pierre. "Le *peri parthenias* du pseudo-Athanase." *Römische Quartalschrift* 7 (1893): 275–76.

——. "Recension." *Revue biblique* 3 (1906): 295–99.

Bauer, J. B. "Novellistisches bei Hieronymus Vita Pauli 3." *Wiener Studien* 74 (1961): 130–37.

Beard, M., and J. Henderson. *Classical Art from Greece to Rome.* Oxford: Oxford University Press, 2001.

——. "The Emperor's New Body: Ascension from Rome." In *Parchments of Gender: Deciphering the Bodies of Antiquity,* edited by M. Wyke, 191–219. Oxford: Oxford University Press, 1998.

Bell, Catherine. *Ritual Theory, Ritual Practice.* New York: Oxford University Press, 1992.

Bell, H. Idris. *Jews and Christians in Egypt: The Jewish Troubles in Alexandria and the Athanasian Controversy.* Reprint. Westport, Conn.: Greenwood Press, 1972.

Bell, Jeffrey A. *The Problem of Difference: Phenomenology and Poststructuralism.* Toronto and Buffalo: University of Toronto Press, 1998.

Berger, John. "Why Look at Animals?" In *About Looking.* London: Writers and Readers Publishing Cooperative, 1980.

Bermingham, Ann. *Landscape and Ideology: The English Rustic Tradition, 1740–1860.* Berkeley and Los Angeles: University of California Press, 1986.

——. *La Prédication des pères cappadociens: Le prédicateur et son auditoire.* Paris: Presses Universitaires de France, 1968.

Bhabha, Homi. "Of Mimicry and Man: The Ambivalence of Colonial Discourse." In *Tensions of Empire: Colonial Cultures in a Bourgeois World*, edited by Frederick Cooper and Ann Laura Stoler, 152–60. Berkeley and Los Angeles: University of California Press, 1997.

Bidez, Joseph. *La vie de l'empereur Julien.* Paris: Belles Lettres, 1930.

Billerbeck, Margarete. "The Ideal Cynic from Epictetus to Julian." In *The Cynics: The Cynic Movement in Antiquity and Its Legacy*, edited by R. Bracht Branham and Marie-Odile Goulet-Cazé, 216–20. Berkeley and Los Angeles: University of California Press, 1996.

Bloch, Marc. *The Historian's Craft: Reflections on the Nature and Uses of History and the Techniques and Methods of Those Who Write It.* New York: Vintage Books, 1953.

Boccaccini, Gabriele. *Beyond the Essene Hypothesis: The Parting of the Ways between Qumran and Enochic Judaism.* Grand Rapids, Mich.: W. B. Eerdmans, 1998.

Bonnell, Victoria E., and Lynn Hunt, eds. *Beyond the Cultural Turn: New Directions in the Study of Society and Culture.* Berkeley and Los Angeles: University of California Press, 1999.

Bouffartigue, Jean. "Le cynisme dans le cursus philosophique au VIe siècle: Le témoignage de l'empereur Julien." In *Le cynisme*, edited by Marie-Odile Goulet-Cazé, 339–58. Paris: Presses Universitaires de France, 1993.

——. *L'empereur Julien et la culture de son temps.* Paris: Études Augustiniennes, 1992.

Bourdieu, Pierre. *Distinction: A Social Critique of the Judgement of Taste.* Translated by Richard Nice. Cambridge: Harvard University Press, 1984.

——. *The Logic of Practice.* Translated by Richard Nice. Stanford: Stanford University Press, 1990.

Bowersock, Glen. *Hellenism in Late Antiquity.* Cambridge: Cambridge University Press, 1990.

——. *Julian the Apostate.* London: Duckworth, 1978.

Boyarin, Daniel. *Carnal Israel: Reading Sex in Talmudic Culture.* The New Historicism: Studies in Cultural Poetics 25. Berkeley and Los Angeles: University of California Press, 1993.

——. "The Diadoche of the Rabbis: Judah the Patriarch at Yavneh." In *Jewish Culture and Society under the Christian Roman Empire*, edited by Richard Kalmin and Seth Schwartz, 285–318. Louvain: Peeters, 2003.

——. "Justin Martyr Invents Judaism." *Church History* 70 (2001): 427–61.

——. "On the Status of the Tannaitic Midrashim." *Journal of the American Oriental Society* 113 (1993): 455–65.

Bradbury, Scott. "The Date of Julian's *Letter to Themistius.*" *Greek, Roman, and Byzantine Studies* 28 (1987): 235–51.

Bradon, W. *Building the Myth: Selected Speeches Memorializing Abraham Lincoln.* Urbana: University of Illinois Press, 1990.

Braidotti, Rosi. *Nomadic Subjects: Embodiment and Sexual Difference in Contemporary Feminist Theory.* New York: Columbia University Press, 1994.

———. *S. Athanase: Lettres festales et pastorales en copte*. Edited and translated by L.-Th. Lefort. Corpus Scriptorum Christianorum Orientalium 150–51. Louvain: L. Durbecq, 1955.

———. *St. Athanasius: The Life of Saint Antony*. Translated by Robert T. Meyer. Ancient Christian Writers 10. New York: Newman Press, 1950.

Athanassiadi, Polymnia, and Michael Frede, eds. *Pagan Monotheism in Late Antiquity*. Oxford: Clarendon Press, 1999.

Athanassiadi, Polymnia. *Julian and Hellenism*. Oxford: Oxford University Press, 1981. Reprinted as *Julian: An Intellectual Biography*. London: Routledge, 1992.

Aubineau, Michel. *Grégoire de Nysse: Traité de la virginité*. Sources chrétiennes 119. Paris: Éditions du Cerf, 1966.

———. "Les écrits de saint Athanase sur la virginité." *Revue d'Ascétique et de Mystique* 31 (1955): 140–73.

Auerbach, Erich. *Mimesis: The Representation of Reality in Western Literature*. Translated by Willard R. Trask. Princeton: Princeton University Press, 1953.

———. *Scenes from the Drama of European Literature*. New York: Meridian, 1959.

Augustine. *De civitate Dei*. In *Sancti Aurelii Augustini episcopi de civitate Dei*, edited by B. Dombart and A. Kalb. Stuttgart: B. G. Teubner, 1981.

———. *Confessiones*. Edited by M. Skutella et al. Stuttgart: B. G. Teubner, 1981.

———. *Confessions*. Edited by James J. O'Donnell. 3 vols. Oxford: Clarendon Press, 1992.

———. *Confessions*. Translated by Maria Boulding. Hyde Park, N.Y.: New City Press, 1997.

———. *De doctrina Christiana*. Edited and translated by R. P. H. Green. Oxford: Clarendon Press, 1995.

———. *De fide et symbolo, De fide et operibus . . .* Edited by J. Zycha. Corpus Scriptorum Ecclesiasticorum Latinorum 41. Vienna: Tempsky, 1900.

———. *De genesi ad litteram*. Edited by J. Zycha. Vienna: Tempsky, 1894.

———. *Epistulae*. Edited by A. Goldbacher. Corpus Scriptorum Ecclesiasticorum Latinorum 34, 44, 57, 58. Vienna: Tempsky, 1895–1923.

———. *Oeuvres de Saint Augustin: Lettres 1-29*. Edited by Johannes Divjak. Bibliothèque Augustinienne 46B. Paris: Études Augustiniennes, 1987.

———. *Retractationes*. Edited by A. Mutzenbecher. Corpus Christianorum, series latina 37. Turnhout, Belgium: Brepols, 1984.

———. *Sancti Aurelii Augustini episcopi de civitate Dei libri XXII*. 5th ed. 2 vols. Edited by B. Dombart and A. Kalb. Stuttgart: B. G. Teubner, 1981.

———. *Saint Augustine: Letters*. Vols. 1–5, translated by Wilfrid Parsons (Fathers of the Church 12, 18, 20, 22, and 32). Vol. 6, translated by Robert Eno (Fathers of the Church 81). Washington: Catholic University of America, 1964–89.

———. *S. Aureli Augustini Hipponensis Episcopi Epistulae*. Edited by A. Goldbacher. Corpus Scriptorum Ecclesiasticorum Latinorum 34, 44, 57, and 58. Vienna: Tempsky, 1895–98.

———. *The Works of Saint Augustine: A Translation for the Twenty-first Century*. Vol. 2.1, *Letters 1–99*. Edited by John Rotelle. Translated by Roland J. Teske. Hyde Park, N.Y.: New City Press, 2001.

Brakke, David. *Athanasius and the Politics of Asceticism.* Oxford Early Christian Studies. Oxford: Clarendon Press, 1995.

——. "The Authenticity of the Ascetic Athanasiana." *Orientalia* 63 (1994): 17–56.

——. "The Early Church in North America: Late Antiquity, Theory, and the History of Christianity." *Church History* 71 (2002): 473–41.

——. "The Problematization of Nocturnal Emissions in Early Christian Syria, Egypt, and Gaul." *Journal of Early Christian Studies* 3 (1995): 419–60.

Brandes, Wolfram. "Orthodoxy and Heresy in the Seventh Century: Prosopographical Observations on Monotheism." In *Fifty Years of Prosopography: Rome, Byzantium, and Beyond,* edited by Averil Cameron, 105–20. Oxford: Oxford University Press for the British Academy, 2003.

Brauch, T. "Themistius and the Emperor Julian." *Byzantion* 63 (1993): 79–115.

Braun, René, and Jean Richer, eds. *L'Empereur Julien.* Vol. 1, *De l'histoire à la légende (331–1715).* Paris: Belles Lettres, 1978.

Breckenridge, Carol A., Sheldon Pollock, and Homi K. Bhabha, eds. *Cosmopolitanism.* Special issue of *Public Culture* 12.3 (2001).

Brock, Sebastian P. *Bride of Light: Hymns on Mary from the Syriac Churches.* Kottayam, Kerala: St. Ephrem Ecumenical Research Institute, 1994.

——. "Dramatic Dialogue Poems." In *IV Symposium Syriacum,* edited by H. J. W. Drijvers, R. Lavenant, C. Molenberg, and G. J. Reinink, 135–47. Orientalia Christiana Analecta 229. Rome: Pontificum Institutum Studiorum Orientalium, 1987.

——. *The Luminous Eye: The Spiritual World Vision of Saint Ephrem the Syrian.* Kalamazoo: Cistercian Publications, 1992.

——. "Mary and the Eucharist: An Oriental Perspective." *Sobornost* 1 (1979): 50–59.

——. "Mary in Syriac Tradition." In *Mary's Place in Christian Dialogue,* edited by A. Stacpoole, 182–91. Slough: St. Paul Publications, 1982.

——. "Syriac Dispute Poems: the Various Types." In *Dispute Poems and Dialogues in the Ancient and Mediaeval Near East: Forms and Types of Literary Debates in Semitic and Related Literature,* edited by G. J. Reinink and H. L. J. Vanstiphout, 109–20. Orientalia Lovaniensia Analecta 42. Leuven: Peeters, 1991.

Brock, Sebastian, and Susan Ashbrook Harvey. *Holy Women of the Syrian Orient.* Berkeley and Los Angeles: University of California Press, 1987.

Brown, Peter. *Augustine: A Biography.* Berkeley and Los Angeles: University of California Press, 1967.

——. *The Body and Society: Men, Women, and Sexual Renunciation in Early Christianity.* Lectures on the History of Religions 13. New York: Columbia University Press, 1988.

——. "Images as a Substitute for Writing." In *East and West: Modes of Communication (The Transformation of the Roman World 5),* edited by Evangelos Chrysos and Ian Wood, 15–34. Leiden: Brill, 1999.

——. *The Making of Late Antiquity.* Cambridge: Harvard University Press, 1978.

——. "The Notion of Virginity in the Early Church." In *Christian Spirituality: Origins to the 12th Century*, edited by Bernard McGinn and John Meyendorff, 427–43. New York: Crossroad, 1985.

——. "The Rise and Function of the Holy Man in Late Antiquity." *Journal of Roman Studies* 61 (1971): 80–101.

——. "The Rise and Function of the Holy Man in Late Antiquity, 1971–1997." *Journal of Early Christian Studies* 6 (1998): 353–76.

——. *The World of Late Antiquity, AD 150–750*. London: Thames and Hudson, 1971.

Browning, Robert. *The Emperor Julian*. London: Weidenfeld and Nicolson, 1975.

——. "Enlightenment and Repression in Byzantium in the Eleventh and Twelfth Centuries." *Past and Present* 69 (1975): 3–23.

Brubaker, Leslie, ed. *Byzantium in the Ninth Century: Dead or Alive?* Aldershot: Ashgate, 1998.

Buell, Denise Kimber. *Making Christians: Clement of Alexandria and the Rhetoric of Legitimacy*. Princeton: Princeton University Press, 1999.

Bullard, F. *Lincoln in Marble and Bronze*. New Brunswick, N.J.: Rutgers University Press, 1952.

Buonaiuti, Ernesto. "Evagrio Pontico e il De Virginitate pseudo-Atanasiano." In *Saggi sul cristianesimo primitivo*, 242–54. Castello: Il Solco, 1923.

Burch, H. Vacher. "An Early Witness to Christian Monachism." *American Journal of Theology* 10 (1906): 738–43.

Burns, J. Patout. "On Rebaptism: Social Organization in the Third Century Church." *Journal of Early Christian Studies* 1 (1993): 367–403.

Burrus, Virginia. *Begotton, Not Made: Conceiving Manhood in Late Antiquity*. Stanford: Stanford University Press, 2000.

——. "Is Macrina a Woman? Gregory of Nyssa's Dialogue on the Soul and the Resurrection." In *The Blackwell Companion to Postmodern Theology*, edited by Graham Ward, 249–64. Oxford: Blackwell, 2001.

——. *The Making of a Heretic: Gender, Authority, and the Priscillianist Controversy*. The Transformation of the Classical Heritage 24. Berkeley and Los Angeles: University of California Press, 1995.

——. *The Sex Lives of Saints: An Erotics of Ancient Hagiography*. Philadelphia: University of Pennsylvania Press, 2004.

Burrus, Virginia, and Catherine Keller. "Confessing Monica." In *Feminist Interpretations of Augustine*, edited by Judith Chelius Stark. University Park: Pennsylvania State University Press, forthcoming.

Burton-Christie, Douglas. *The Word in the Desert: Scripture and the Quest for Holiness in Early Christian Monasticism*. Oxford: Oxford University Press, 1993.

Butler, Judith P. *Antigone's Claim*. New York: Columbia University Press, 2000.

——. *Bodies That Matter: On the Discursive Limits of "Sex."* New York: Routledge, 1993.

——. *Gender Trouble: Feminism and the Subversion of Identity*. New York: Routledge, 1990.

Cadell, H., and R. Rémondon. "Sens et emplois de *to oros* dans les documents papyrologiques." *Revue des études greques* 80 (1967): 343–49.

Caltabiano, Matilde. *Litterarum Lumen: Ambienti culturali e libri tra il IV e il V secolo.* Rome: Institutum Patristicum Augustinianum, 1996.

Camelot, P. Thomas. "Les traités 'de virginitate' au IVe siècle." In *Mystique et continence: Travaux scientifiques du VIIe Congrès international d'Avon*, 273–292. Études Carmélitaines 13. Bruges: Desclée de Brouwer, 1952.

Cameron, Alan. "The Empress and the Poet: Paganism and Politics at the Court of Theodosius III." In *Later Greek Literature*, edited by John J. Winkler and Gordon Williams, 217–89. Cambridge: Cambridge University Press, 1982.

Cameron, Averil. "Apologetics in the Roman Empire—A Genre of Intolerance?" In *"Humana sapit": Études d'antiquité tardive offertes à Lellia Cracco Ruggini*, edited by Jean-Michel Carrié and Rita Lizzi Testa, 219–27. Bibliothèque de l'Antiquité Tardive 3. Turnhout: Brepols, 2002.

———. "Blaming the Jews: The Seventh-Century Invasions of Palestine in Context." *Travaux et Mémoires* 14 (2002): 57–78.

———. *Christianity and the Rhetoric of Empire: The Development of Christian Discourse.* Berkeley and Los Angeles: University of California Press, 1991.

———. "Disputations, Polemical Literature, and the Formation of Opinion." In *Dispute Poems and Dialogues in the Ancient and Mediaeval Near East*, edited by G. J. Reinink and H. L. J. Vanstiphout, 91–108. Orientalia Lovaniensia Analecta 42. Leuven: Peeters, 1991.

———. "Jews and Heretics—A Category Error?" In *The Ways That Never Parted*, edited by Annette Yoshiko Reed and Adam Becker. Texts and Studies in Ancient Judaism. Tübingen: Mohr Siebeck, 2003.

———. *The Mediterranean World in Late Antiquity* AD *395–600*. London and New York: Routledge, 1993.

———. "On Defining the Holy Man." In *The Cult of Saints in Late Antiquity and the Middle Ages: Essays on the Contribution of Peter Brown*, edited by James Howard-Johnston and Paul Antony Hayward, 27–43. Oxford: Oxford University Press, 1999.

———. "On Naming: The Trouble with Heresy." Paper presented at the 13th International Conference on Patristic Studies, Oxford, August 1999.

———. "Texts as Weapons: Polemic in the Byzantine Dark Ages." In *Literacy and Power in the Ancient World*, edited by Alan K. Bowman and Greg Woolf, 198–215. Cambridge: Cambridge University Press, 1994.

Cameron, Averil, and Peter Garnsey, eds. *Cambridge Ancient History.* Vol. 13, *The Late Empire*, A.D. *337–425*. Cambridge: Cambridge University Press, 1998.

Cameron, Averil, and Amelie Kuhrt, eds. *Images of Women in Antiquity.* London: Croom Helm, 1983.

Camp, J. *The Archaeology of Athens.* New Haven: Yale University Press, 2001.

Caner, Daniel. *Wandering, Begging Monks: Spiritual Authority and the Promotion of Monasticism in Late Antiquity.* The Transformation of the Classical Heritage 33. Berkeley and Los Angeles: University of California Press, 2002.

Canivet, P. *Histoire d'une entreprise apologétique au Ve siècle.* Paris: Bloud and Gay, 1957.

Caplan, Jane, ed. *Written on the Body: The Tattoo in European and American History*. Princeton: Princeton University Press, 2000.

Cartledge, Paul, Peter Garnsey, and Erich Gruen, eds. *Hellenistic Constructs: Essays on Culture, History, and Historiography*. Berkeley and Los Angeles: University of California Press, 1997.

Cassian, John. *Johannis Cassiani Opera: Conlationes XXIIII*. Edited by Michael Petschenig. Corpus Scriptorum Ecclesiasticorum Latinorum 13. Vienna, 1886.

———. *John Cassian: The Conferences*. Translated by Boniface Ramsey. New York: Newman Press, 1997.

———. *John Cassian: The Institutes*. Translated by Boniface Ramsey. New York: Newman Press, 2000.

Castelli, Elizabeth. " 'I Will Make Mary Male': Pieties of the Body and Gender Transformation of Christian Women in Late Antiquity." In *Bodyguards: The Cultural Politics of Gender Ambiguity*, edited by Julia Epstein and Kristina Straub, 29–49. New York: Routledge, 1991.

———, ed., with Rosamond C. Rodman. *Women, Gender, Religion: A Reader*. New York: Palgrave, 2001.

Cavafy, C. P. "Ionic." In *Collected Poems*, edited by G. Savidis, translated by E. Keeley and P. Sherrard, 62–63. Princeton: Princeton University Press, 1975.

Cavallera, Ferdinand. *Saint Athanase. La pensée chrétienne*. Paris: Librairie Bloud, 1908.

———. *Saint Jérôme: Sa vie et son oeuvre*. Louvain: Bureaux, 1922.

Chaney, David. *The Cultural Turn: Scene-Setting Essays on Contemporary Cultural History*. London and New York: Routledge, 1994.

Chaplin, J. *Livy's Exemplary History*. Oxford: Oxford University Press, 2000.

Charlesworth, J. H. *The Old Testament Pseudepigrapha*. New York: Doubleday, 1985.

Charrier, S. "Le premier archéologue chrétien: Saint Damase." *Revue Augustinienne* 8 (1906): 569–78.

Chrysos, E. *He ekklesiastike politike tou Ioustinianou*. Thessaloniki: Patriarchikon Hidryma Paterikon Meleton, 1969.

———. "Konzilsakten und Konzilsprotokolle vom 4. bis 7. Jahrhundert." *Annuarium Historiae Conciliorum* 15 (1983): 30–40.

Clark, Elizabeth A. *Ascetic Piety and Women's Faith: Essays on Late Ancient Christianity*. Lewiston and Queenston: Edwin Mellen, 1986.

———. *Clement's Use of Aristotle: The Aristotelian Contribution to Clement of Alexandria's Refutation of Gnosticism*. New York: Edwin Mellen, 1977.

———. "Foucault, The Fathers, and Sex." *Journal of the American Academy of Religion* 56 (1988): 619–41.

———. "Holy Women, Holy Words: Early Christian Women, Social History, and the 'Linguistic Turn.' " *Journal of Early Christian Studies* 6 (1998): 413–30.

———. "Ideology, History, and the Construction of 'Woman' in Late Antique Christianity." *Journal of Early Christian Studies* 2 (1994): 155–84.

———. *Jerome, Chrysostom, and Friends: Essays and Translations*. New York: Edwin Mellen, 1979.

——. "The Lady Vanishes: Dilemmas of a Feminist Historian after the 'Linguistic Turn.'" *Church History* 67 (1998): 1–31.

——. *The Life of Melania the Younger: Introduction, Translation, Commentary.* New York: Edwin Mellen, 1984.

——. *The Origenist Controversy: The Cultural Construction of an Early Christian Debate.* Princeton: Princeton University Press, 1992.

——. *Reading Renunciation: Asceticism and Scripture in Early Christianity.* Princeton: Princeton University Press, 1999.

——. "Rewriting Early Christian History: Augustine's Representation of Monica." In *Portraits of Spiritual Authority: Religious Power in Early Christianity, Byzantium and the Christian Orient,* edited by Jan Willem Drijvers and John W. Watt, 3–23. Leiden: Brill, 1999.

——. "Rewriting Early Christian History." In *Theology and the New Histories,* edited by Gary Macy, 89–111. College Theology Society Annual Volume 44 (1998). Maryknoll, N.Y.: Orbis, 1999.

——. "Theory and Practice in Late Ancient Asceticism." *Journal of Feminist Studies in Religion* 5, no. 2 (fall 1989): 25–46.

——. "Women, Gender, and the Study of Christian History." *Church History* 70 (2001): 395–426.

——. "Women in the Early Christian World: New Directions in Scholarship." Paper delivered at the University of St. Thomas (Minn.), April 20, 1999.

Clark, Elizabeth A., and Everett Ferguson. "Editors' Note." *Journal of Early Christian Studies* 1 (1993): v–vi.

Clark, Gillian. "The Fathers and the Animals: The Rule of Reason?" In *Animals on the Agenda: Questions about Animals for Theology and Ethics,* ed. Andrew Linzey and Dorothy Yamamoto, 67–79. Chicago: University of Illinois Press, 1998.

Clement of Alexandria. *Stromata.* In *Clément d'Alexandrie: Les Stromates,* edited by Claude Mondésert. Sources chrétiennes 38. Paris: Editions du Cerf, 1954.

Cloke, Gillian. *"This Female Man of God": Women and Spiritual Power in the Patristic Age, 350–450.* London: Routledge, 1995.

Clover, Frank M., and R. Stephen Humphreys, eds. *Tradition and Innovation in Late Antiquity.* Madison: University of Wisconsin Press, 1989.

Collectio Avellana. Edited by O. Guenther. Corpus Scriptorum Ecclesiasticorum Latinorum 35. Vienna: F. Tempsky, 1895.

Constas, Nicholas. "Weaving the Body of God: Proclus of Constantinople, the Theotokos, and the Loom of the Flesh." *Journal of Early Christian Studies* 3 (1995): 169–94.

Conybeare, Catherine. *Paulinus Noster: Self and Symbols in the Letters of Paulinus of Nola.* Oxford: Oxford University Press, 2000.

Cook, John G. "The Protreptic Power of Early Christian Language: From John to Augustine." *Vigiliae Christianae* 48 (1994): 105–34.

Coon, Lynda L. *Sacred Fictions: Holy Women and Hagiography in Late Antiquity.* Philadelphia: University of Pennsylvania Press, 1997.

Cooper, Kate. *The Virgin and the Bride: Idealized Womanhood in Late Antiquity.* Cambridge: Harvard University Press, 1996.

Copeland, Rita. *Pedagogy, Intellectuals, and Dissent in the Later Middle Ages: Lollardy and Ideas of Learning.* Cambridge: Cambridge University Press, 2001.

Corbier, Mireille. "The Ambiguous Status of Meat in Ancient Rome." *Food and Foodways* 3 (1989).

Corrigan, K. *Visual Polemics in the Ninth-Century Byzantine Psalters.* Cambridge: Cambridge University Press, 1992.

Courcelle, Pierre. "La correspondance avec Paulin de Nole et la genèse des 'Confessions.' " In *Les Confessions de saint Augustin dans la tradition littéraire*, 559–607. Paris: Études Augustiniennes, 1963.

Cox, Patricia. *Biography in Late Antiquity: A Quest for the Holy Man.* The Transformation of the Classical Heritage 5. Berkeley and Los Angeles: University of California Press, 1983.

Criscuolo, Ugo. "Sull'epistola di Giuliano imperatore al filosofo Temistio." *Koinonia* 7 (1983): 89–111.

Cummings, Charles. "In Praise of the Desert: A Letter to Hilary of Lérins, Bishop, by Eucher of Lyons." *Cistercian Studies* 11 (1976): 60–72.

Curran, J. *Pagan City and Christian Capital: Rome in the Fourth Century.* Oxford: Oxford University Press, 2000.

Cyril of Jerusalem. *S. Cyril of Jerusalem; S. Gregory Nazianzen.* Translated by Charles Gordon Browne and James Edward Swallow. Select Library of the Nicene and Post-Nicene Fathers of the Christian Church, 2nd ser., vol. 7. 1893. Reprint, Grand Rapids, Mich.: Eerdmans, 1978.

Cyril of Scythopolis. *Vita sancti Sabae; Vita sancti Theodosi; Vita sancti Euthymii.* In *Kyrillos von Skythopolis, Texte und Untersuchungen zur Geschichte der altchristlichen Literatur*, edited by E. Schwartz. Leipzig: Hinrichs, 1939. Translated by R. M. Price in *Lives of the Monks of Palestine.* Cistercian Studies 114. Kalamazoo: Cistercian Publications, 1991.

Dagron, Gilbert. *Emperor and Priest: The Imperial Office in Byzantium.* Translated by Jean Birrell. Cambridge: Cambridge University Press, 2003.

———. "Judaïser." *Travaux et Mémoires* 11 (1991): 359–80.

———. "L'empire romain d'orient au IVe siècle et les traditions politiques de l'Hellénisme: Le témoniage de Thémistios." *Travaux et mémoires* 3 (1968): 1–242.

———. "Les moines et la ville: Le monachisme à Constantinople jusqu'au concile de Chalcédoine (451)." *Travaux et mémoires* 4 (1970): 250–52.

Dale, T. "Stolen Property: St Mark's First Venetian Tomb and the Politics of Communal Memory." In *Memory and the Medieval Tomb*, edited by E. del Almo and C. Pendergast, 205–25. Aldershot, England: Ashgate, 2000.

Davies, P. *Death and the Emperor: Roman Imperial Funerary Monuments from Augustus to Marcus Aurelius.* Cambridge: Cambridge University Press, 2000.

Davies, William David. *The Setting of the Sermon on the Mount.* Cambridge: Cambridge University Press, 1976.

Davis, Stephen J. "Crossed Texts, Crossed Sex: Intertextuality and Gender in Early Christian Legends of Holy Women Disguised as Men." *Journal of Early Christian Studies* 10 (2002): 1–36.

Dawson, John David. *Christian Figural Reading and the Fashioning of Identity.* Berkeley and Los Angeles: University of California Press, 2002.

DeBruyne, D. "Les anciennes collections et la chronologie des lettres de saint Augustin." *Revue Bénédictine* 43 (1931): 83–85.

Deckers, J. G., G. Mietke, and A. Weiland. *Die Katacombe "Commodilla": Repertorium der Malereien.* 3 vols. Vatican City: Pontificio Istituto di Archeologia Cristiana, 1994.

Degrassi, A. *Inscriptiones Italiae.* 13 vols. Rome: Libreria dello stato, 1931–63.

Delmaire, Roland. "Contributions des nouvelles lettres de saint Augustin à la prosopographie du Bas-Empire romain." In Claude Lepelley, *Les lettres de saint Augustin decouvertes par Johannes Divjak: Communications présentées au colloque des 20 et 21 septembre 1982.* Paris: Études Augustiniennes, 1983.

Demoen, Kristoffel. "The Attitude towards Greek Poetry in the Verse of Gregory of Nazianzus." In *Early Christian Poetry,* edited by Jan den Boeft and Anton Hilhorst, 235–52. Leiden: Brill, 1993.

Derrida, Jacques. *De la grammatologie.* Paris: Minuit, 1967.

———. *Of Grammatology.* Translated by Gayatri Chakravorty Spivak. Baltimore: Johns Hopkins University Press, 1976.

Dessau, H. *Inscriptiones Latinae Selectae.* 3 vols. in 5. 1892. Reprint, Zurich: Weidmann, 1997.

Donati, A., ed. *Pietro e Paolo: La storia, il culto, la memoria nei primi secoli.* Milan: Electa, 2000.

Douglas, Mary, and David Hull, eds. *How Classification Works: Nelson Goodman among the Social Sciences.* Edinburgh: Edinburgh University Press, 1992.

Douglas, Mary. *How Institutions Think.* London: Routledge and Kegan Paul, 1987.

Draguet, René. "L'inauthenticité du proemium de l'histoire lausiaque." *Muséon* 59 (1946): 529–34

———. "Un nouveau témoin du texte G de l'histoire lausiaque (Ms. Athènes 281)." *Analecta Bollandiana* 67 (1949): 300–308.

Drijvers, H. J. W. "The 19th Ode of Solomon." *Journal of Theological Studies* 31 (1980): 337–55.

Drinkwater, J. F. "The 'Pagan Underground,' Constantius II's 'Secret Service,' and the Survival, and the Usurpation of Julian the Apostate." In *Studies in Latin Literature and Roman History III,* edited by Carl Deroux, 348–87. Brussels: Latomus Revue d'Études Latines, 1983.

Dubrov, Gregory W. "A Dialogue with Death: Ritual Lament and the *threnos theotokou* of Romanos Melodos." *Greek, Roman, and Byzantine Studies* 35 (1994): 385–405.

Dummer, J. "Ein naturwissenschaftliches Handbuch als Quelle für Epiphanius von Constantia." *Klio* 55 (1973): 289–99.

Duval, Yves-Marie. *L'affaire Jovinien: D'une crise de la société romaine à une crise de la pensée chrétienne à la fin du IVe et au début du Ve siècle.* Rome: Institutum Patristicum Augustinianum, 2003.

Edwards, C. *Writing Rome: Textual Approaches to the City.* Cambridge: Cambridge University Press, 1996.

Elm, Susanna. "Historiographic Identities: Gregory of Nazianzus and Julian, the

Emperor." *Journal of Ancient Christianity | Zeitschrift für Antikes Christentum* 7 (2003): 249–66.

———. "Introduction." *Journal of Early Christian Studies* 6 (1998): 343–51.

———. "Isis' Loss: Gender, Dependence, and Ethnicity in Synesius' *De Providentia* or Egyptian Tale." *Journal of Ancient Christianity* 1 (1997): 96–115.

———. " 'Pierced by Bronze Needles': Anti-Montanist Charges of Ritual Stigmatization in Their Fourth-Century Context." *Journal of Early Christian Studies* 4 (1996): 409–39.

———. "The Polemical Use of Genealogies: Jerome's Classification of Pelagius and Evagrius Ponticus." *Studia Patristica* 33 (1997): 311–18.

———. "A Programmatic Life: Gregory of Nazianzus' Orations 42 and 43 and the Constantinopolitan Elites." *Arethusa* 33 (2000): 411–27.

———. " 'Sklave Gottes': Stigmata, Bishöfe und anti-häretische Propaganda im vierten Jahrhundert." *Historische Anthropologie: Kultur/Gesellshaft/Alltag* 8 (1999): 345–63.

———. *"Virgins of God": The Making of Asceticism in Late Antiquity.* Oxford Classical Monographs. Oxford: Clarendon Press, 1994.

Elm, Susanna, Éric Rebillard, and Antonella Romano, eds. *Orthodoxie, christianisme, histoire | Orthodoxy, Christianity, History.* Rome: École Française de Rome, 2000.

Elsner, J., ed. *Art and Text in Roman Culture.* Cambridge: Cambridge University Press, 1996.

———. *Imperial Rome and Christian Triumph.* Oxford: Oxford University Press, 1998.

Ensslin, Werner. "Kaiser Julians Gesetzgebungswerk und die Reichsverwaltung." *Klio* 18 (1922): 104–99.

Ephrem Syrus. *Ephrem the Syrian, Hymns.* Translated by Kathleen McVey. Mahweh, N.J.: Paulist Press, 1989.

———. *Des heiligen Ephraem des Syrers Hymnen de Nativitate (Epiphania).* Edited by Edmund Beck. Corpus Scriptorum Christianorum Orientalium 186–87 and Scriptores Syri 82–83. Louvain: Secrétariat du CorpusSCO, 1959.

———. *St. Ephrem the Syrian, Hymns on Paradise.* Translated by Sebastian P. Brock. Crestwood, N.Y.: St. Vladimir's Seminary Press, 1990.

Epiphanius. *Panarion.* Edited by K. Holl. In *Ancoratus und Panarion.* Griechische Christliche Schriftsteller. 3 vols. Leipzig: J. C. Hinrichs, 1915–33. Rev. ed., edited by J. Dummer, Berlin: Akademie Verlag, 1980, 1985.

———. *Panarion.* Translated by F. Williams. 2 vols. Leiden: Brill, 1987.

———. *The Panarion of St. Epiphanius, Bishop of Salamis.* Partial translation by P. Amidon. New York: Oxford University Press, 1990.

Eucherius of Lyon. *Sancti Eucherii Lugdunensis Epistula de laude heremi.* Edited by Karl Wotke. Corpus Scriptorum Ecclesiasticorum Latinorum 31. Prague, 1894.

———. *Eucherii De laude eremi.* Edited by Salvator Pricoco. Catania: Centro di Studi Sull'Antico Cristianesimo, 1965.

Eunapius. *Vitae sophistarum.* Edited and translated by Wilber Cave Wright. Loeb Classical Library. Reprint, Cambridge: Harvard University Press, 1989.

Evagrius of Pontus. *The Greek Ascetic Corpus.* Translated by Robert E. Sinkewicz. Oxford Early Christian Studies. Oxford: Oxford University Press, 2003.

——. *Kephalaia Gnostica*. In *Les six centuries des "Kephalaia Gnostica" d'Évagre le Pontique*, edited by Antoine Guillaumont. Paris: Firmin-Didot, 1958.

——. *Praktikos*. In *Évagre le Pontique: Traité pratique, ou, Le moine*, edited by Antoine and Claire Guillaumont. Sources chrétiennes 171. Paris: Éditions du Cerf, 1971.

——. *Sententiae ad virginem*. In *Nonnenspiegel und Mönchsspiegel des Euagrios Pontikos*, edited by Hugo Gressmann. Leipzig: J. C. Hinrichs, 1913.

——. *Skemmata*. Translated by William Harmless, S.J., and Raymond R. Fitzgerald, S.J., in "The Sapphire Light of the Mind: The *Skemmata* of Evagrius Ponticus," *Theological Studies* 62 (2001): 498–529.

Everett, Edward. *Orations and Speeches on Various Occasions*. 4 vols. Boston: Little, Brown, 1892.

Favro, D. *The Urban Image of Augustan Rome*. Cambridge: Cambridge University Press, 1996.

Ferrua, A. *Epigrammata Damasiana*. Vatican City: Pontificio Istituto di Archeologia Cristiana, 1942.

Festugière, André-Jean. See *Historia monachorum in Aegypto*.

Février, P.-A. "Un plaidoyer pour Damase: Les inscriptions des nécropoles romaines." In *Institutions, société et vie politique dans l'empire romain au IVe siècle ap. J.-C.*, edited by M. Christol et al., 497–506. Rome: École française de Rome, 1992.

Filene, B. *Romancing the Folk: Public Memory and American Roots Music*. Chapel Hill: University of North Carolina Press, 2000.

Fiorenza, Elisabeth Schüssler. *Bread Not Stone: The Challenge of Feminist Biblical Interpretation*. Boston: Beacon, 1984.

——. *In Memory of Her: A Feminist Theological Reconstruction of Christian Origins*. New York: Crossroads, 1983.

Fitzgerald, Allan D., ed. *Augustine through the Ages: An Encyclopedia*. Grand Rapids, Mich., and Cambridge, England: Eerdmans, 1999.

Flemming, Rebecca. "*Quae Corpore Quaestum Facit*: The Sexual Economy of Female Prostitution in the Roman Empire." *Journal of Roman Studies* 89 (1999): 39–50.

Fontaine, Jacques. *Giuliano Imperatore: Alla madre degli dei e altri discorsi*. Edited by Carlo Prato. Translated by Arnaldo Marcone. Milan: Fondazione Lorenzo Valla, 1987.

——. *Naissance de la poésie dans l'occident chrétien*. Paris: Études Augustiniennes, 1981.

Ford, J. Massynbaerde. "Bookshelf on Prostitution." *Biblical Theology Bulletin* 23 (1993): 128–34.

Foucault, Michel. *The Use of Pleasure*. Vol. 2 of *The History of Sexuality*. New York: Random House, 1986.

——. "What Is an Author?" In *Language, Counter-Memory, Practice: Selected Essays and Interviews*, edited by Donald F. Bouchard, 124–27. Ithaca: Cornell University Press, 1977.

Fowden, Garth. *Empire to Commonwealth: Consequences of Monotheism in Late Antiquity*. Princeton: Princeton University Press, 1993.

Fox, M. *Roman Historical Myths: The Regal Period in Augustan Literature*. Oxford: Oxford University Press, 1996.

Fox, Robin Lane. *Pagans and Christians.* London: Harmondsworth, 1986.

Francis, James. *Subversive Virtue: Asceticism and Authority in the Second-Century Pagan World.* University Park: University of Pennsylvania Press, 1999.

Frank, Georgia. "Macrina's Scar: Homeric Allusion and Heroic Identity in Gregory of Nyssa's *Life of Macrina.*" *Journal of Early Christian Studies* 8 (2000): 511–30.

——. *The Memory of the Eyes: Pilgrims to Living Saints in Christian Late Antiquity.* The Transformation of the Classical Heritage 30. Berkeley and Los Angeles: University of California Press, 2000.

Frank, K. Suso. "Antonius Aegyptius Monachus." In *Augustinus-Lexikon,* edited by Cornelius Mayer, 1:382–83. Basel: Schwabe, 1986–94.

Frankenburg, W. *Euagrios Ponticus.* Berlin: Weidmann, 1912.

Frankfurter, David. *Religion in Roman Egypt.* Princeton: Princeton University Press, 1998.

Fredriksen, Paula. "Paul and Augustine: Conversion Narratives, Orthodox Traditions, and the Retrospective Self." *Journal of Theological Studies* n.s. 37 (1986): 3–34.

Frend, W. H. C. *The Archaeology of Early Christianity: A History.* Minneapolis: Fortress Press, 1996.

Funck, Bernd, ed. *Hellenismus.* Tübingen: J. C. B. Mohr, 1996.

Gafni, Isaiah M. *Land, Center and Diaspora Jewish Constructs in Late Antiquity.* Journal for the Study of the Pseudepigrapha, Supplement series. Sheffield: Sheffield Academic Press, 1997.

Gager, John G. *Kingdom and Community: The Social World of Early Christianity.* Englewood Cliffs: Prentice Hall, 1975.

Galen. *De alimentorum facultatibus.* In *Claudii Galeni Opera Omnia,* edited by C. G. Kühn, vol. 6. Hildesheim: G. Olms, 1965.

——. *Quod animi.* In *Claudii Galeni Opera Omnia,* edited by C. G. Kühn. Hildesheim: G. Olms, 1965.

Galinsky, K. *Augustan Culture.* Princeton: Princeton University Press, 1996.

Gallagher, Catherine, and Stephen Greenblatt. *Practicing New Historicism.* Chicago: University of Chicago Press, 2000.

Gambero, Luigi. *Mary and the Fathers of the Church: The Blessed Virgin Mary in Patristic Thought.* Translated by Thomas Buffer. San Francisco: Ignatius Press, 1999.

Garber, Marjorie. *Vested Interests: Cross-Dressing and Cultural Anxiety.* New York: HarperCollins, 1992.

Garrison, Ramon. *The Graeco-Roman Context of Early Christian Literature.* Sheffield: Sheffield Academic Press, 1997.

Garsoian, N. G. "Byzantine Heresy: A Reinterpretation." *Dumbarton Oaks Papers* 25 (1971): 87–113.

——. *The Paulician Heresy.* The Hague: Mouton, 1967.

Gedi, N., and Y. Elam. "Collective Memory—What Is It?" *History and Memory* 8 (1996): 30–50.

Gelasius. *Lettre contre les Lupercales et dix-huit messes du sacramentaire leonine.* Edited and translated by G. Pomarès. Sources chrétiennes 65. Paris Éditions du Cerf, 1959.

Geppert, S. *Castor und Pollux: Untersuchung zu den Darstellungen der Dioskuren in der römischen Kaiserzeit.* Münster: Lit, 1996.

Giannarelli, Elena. "La biografia femminile: Temi e problemi." In *La donna nel pensiero cristiano antico,* edited by Umberto Mattioli, 223–45. Genoa: Marietti, 1992.

——. "Women and Miracles in Christian Biography (ivth–vth Centuries)." *Studia Patristica* 25 (1993): 376–80.

——. "Women and Satan in Christian Biography and Monastic Literature (ivth–vth centuries)." *Studia Patristica* 30 (1997): 196–201.

Gill, Christopher. *Personality in Greek Epic, Tragedy, and Philosophy: The Self in Dialogue.* Oxford and New York: Clarendon Press, 1995.

Giuliani, Raffaella, ed. *Giovanni Battista de Rossi e le catacombe romane: Mostra fotografica e documentaria in occasione del 1 centenario della morte di Giovanni Battista de Rossi (1894–1994).* Vatican City: Pontificia Commissione di Archeologia Sacra, 1994.

Gleason, Maud W. *Making Men: Sophists and Self-Representation in Ancient Rome.* Princeton: Princeton University Press, 1994.

——. "Visiting and News: Gossip and Reputation-Management in the Desert." *Journal of Early Christian Studies* 6 (1998): 501–21.

Goehring, James, ed. *Ascetics, Society, and the Desert: Studies in Early Egyptian Monasticism.* Studies in Antiquity and Christianity. Harrisburg, Pa.: Trinity Press International, 1999.

——. "The Encroaching Desert: Literary Production and Ascetic Space in Early Christian Egypt." *Journal of Early Christian Studies* 1 (1993): 281–96. Reprinted in Goehring, ed., *Ascetics, Society, and the Desert,* 73–88.

——. "Melitian Monastic Organization: A Challenge to Pachomian Originality." *Studia Patristica* 25 (1993): 388–95. Reprinted in Goehring, ed., *Ascetics, Society, and the Desert,* 187–95.

——. "Monastic Diversity and Ideological Boundaries in Fourth-Century Christian Egypt." *Journal of Early Christian Studies* 5 (1997): 61–84. Reprinted in Goehring, ed., *Ascetics, Society, and the Desert,* 196–218.

——. "Withdrawing to the Desert: Pachomius and the Development of Village Monasticism in Upper Egypt." *Harvard Theological Review* 89 (1966): 267–85. Reprinted in *Ascetics, Society, and the Desert,* 89–109.

Goldenberg, Robert. "Is 'the Talmud' a Document?" In *The Synoptic Problem in Rabbinic Literature,* edited by Shaye J. D. Cohen. Brown Judaic Studies. Providence: Brown Judaic Studies, 2000.

Goldhill, Simon, ed. *Being Greek under Rome: Cultural Identity, the Second Sophistic, and the Development of Empire.* Cambridge: Cambridge University Press, 2001.

——. *Foucault's Virginity: Ancient Erotic Fiction and the History of Sexuality.* Cambridge: Cambridge University Press, 1995.

Goodblatt, David. "The Beruriah Traditions." *Journal of Jewish Studies* 26 (1975): 68–86.

——. "From History to Story to History: The Rimmon Valley Seven." In *The Talmud Yerushalmi and Graeco-Roman Culture,* edited by Peter Schäfer, 1:173–99. Texte und Studien Zum Antiken Judentum 71. Tübingen: Mohr Siebeck, 1998.

Goodman, Nelson. *Ways of Worldmaking*. Indianapolis: Hackett, 1978.

Goody, Jack. *Cooking, Cuisine and Class: A Study in Comparative Sociology*. Cambridge: Cambridge University Press, 1982.

Gouillard, J. "L'hérésie dans l'empire byzantine des origines au xiie siècle." *Travaux et Mémoires* 1 (1965): 299–324.

——. "Le procès officiel de Jean l'Italien, les Actes et leurs sous-entendus." *Travaux et Mémoires* 9 (1985): 133–73.

——, ed. "Le Synodikon d'orthodoxie." *Travaux et mémoires* 2 (1967): 1–313.

Goulet–Cazé, Marie-Odile. "Le cynisme à l'époque impériale." In *Aufstieg und Niedergang der römischen Welt* II. 36. 4, edited by Walter Haase and Hildegard Temporini, 2720–2833. Berlin: de Grüyter, 1990.

Graham, William A. *Beyond the Written Word: Oral Aspects of Scripture in the History of Religion*. Cambridge: Cambridge University Press, 1987.

Grant, Robert M. *Early Christians and Animals*. London: Routledge, 1999.

Green, William Scott. "What's in a Name? the Problematic of Rabbinic Biography." In *Approaches to Ancient Judaism: Theory and Practice*, edited by William Scott Green, 1.77–96. Missoula, Mont.: Scholars Press, 1978.

Gregg, Robert C., and Dennis E. Groh. *Early Arianism: A View of Salvation*. Philadelphia: Fortress Press, 1981.

Gregory of Nazianzus. *Grégoire de Nazianze: Discours 1–3*. Edited by Jean Bernardi. Sources chrétiennes 247. Paris: Éditions du Cerf, 1978.

——. *Grégoire de Nazianze: Discours 4–5 contre Julien; Introduction, texte critique, et notes*. Edited by Jean Bernardi. Sources chrétiennes 309. Paris: Éditions du Cerf, 1983.

——. *Grégoire de Nazianze: Discours 6–12*. Edited and translated by Marie-Ange Calvet-Sébasti. Sources chrétiennes 405. Paris: Éditions du Cerf, 1995.

——. *Lettres [par] Saint Grégoire de Nazianze*. Edited and translated by Paul Gallay. 2 vols. Paris: Belles Lettres, 1964–67. German edition: *Gregor von Nazianz: Briefe*, edited by Paul Gallay. Griechische christliche Schriftsteller der ersten Jahrhunderte. Berlin: Akademie-Verlag, 1969.

——. *S. Cyril of Jerusalem; S. Gregory Nazianzen*. Translated by Charles Gordon Browne and James Edward Swallow. Select Library of the Nicene and Post-Nicene Fathers of the Christian Church, 2nd ser., vol. 7. 1893. Reprint, Grand Rapids, Mich.: Eerdmans, 1978.

Gregory of Nyssa. *Ascetical Works*. Translated by Virginia Woods Callahan. Washington, D.C.: Catholic University of America Press, 1967.

——. *Grégoire de Nysse: Vie de Sainte Macrine*. Translated by Pierre Maraval. Paris: Éditions du Cerf, 1971.

Gribomont, Jean. "Eustathe de Sébaste." *Dictionnaire de spiritualité* 4 (1961): 1708–12.

——. "Eustathe de Sébaste." *Dictionnaire d'histoire et de géographie ecclésiastiques* 16 (1967): 26–33.

——. "Le monachisme au IVe s. en Asie Mineure: De Gangres au Messalianisme." *Studia Patristica* 2 (1957): 400–15.

Grodzynski, D. "Tortures mortelles et categories sociales: Les *summa supplicia* dans le droit romain aux IIIe et IVe siècles." In *Du châtiment dans la cité:supplices corporels et peine du mort dans la monde antique*, 361–403. Collection de l'École Française de Rome 79. Rome: École Française de Rome, 1984.

Grubbs, Judith Evans. " 'Pagan' and 'Christian' Marriage: The State of the Question." *Journal of Early Christian Studies* 2 (1994): 361–412.

Gruen, Erich. *The Hellenistic World and the Coming of Rome.* 2 vols. Berkeley and Los Angeles: University of California Press, 1984.

Gsell, S. *Inscriptions latines de l'Algérie.* Vol. 1. Paris, 1922; reprint, Rome: "L'Erma" di Bretschneider, 1965.

Gustafson, Mark. "*Inscripta in Fronte*: Penal Tattooing in Late Antiquity." *Classical Antiquity* 16 (1997): 79–105.

Gutting, Gary. *French Philosophy in the Twentieth Century.* Cambridge and New York: Cambridge University Press, 2001.

Guy, Jean-Claude. See *Apophthegmata patrum.*

Guyon, J. "Damase et l'illustration des martyrs: Les accents de la dévotion et l'enjue d'une pastorale." In *Martyrium in Multidisciplinary Perspective: Memorial Louis Reekmans*, edited by M. Lamberigts and P. Van Deun, 157–78. Leuven: Leuven University Press, 1995.

Habinek, T., and A. Schiesaro, eds. *The Roman Cultural Revolution.* Cambridge: Cambridge University Press, 1997.

Hadot, Pierre. *Marius Victorinus: Recherches sur sa vie et ses oeuvres.* Paris: Études Augustiniennes, 1971.

Hagendahl, Harald. *Augustine and the Latin Classics.* 2 vols. Göteborg: Acta Universitatis Gothoburgensis, 1967.

Hägg, Tomas, and Philip Rousseau, eds. *Greek Biography and Panegyric in Late Antiquity.* The Transformation of the Classical Heritage 31. Berkeley and Los Angeles: University of California Press, 2000.

Hahn, Johannes. *Der Philosoph und die Gesellschaft: Selbstverständnis, öffentliches Auftreten und populäre Erwartungen in der hohen Kaiserzeit.* Stuttgart: Steiner, 1989.

Hajjar, J. *Le synode permanente (synodos endemousa) dans l'église byzantine des origines au Xie siècle.* Orientalia Christiana Analecta 164. Rome: Pontifical Institute, 1962.

Halbwachs, M. *On Collective Memory.* Edited and translated by L. Coser. Chicago: University of Chicago Press, 1992.

Hall, Jonathan. *Ethnic Identity in Greek Antiquity.* Cambridge: Cambridge University Press, 1997.

Haller, Wilhelm. *Iovinianus: Die Fragmente seiner Schriften, die Quellen zu seiner Geschichte, sein Leben und seine Lehre.* Leipzig, 1897.

Halliwell, Stephen. *The Aesthetics of Mimesis: Ancient Texts and Modern Problems.* Princeton: Princeton University Press, 2002.

Hamel, Gildas. *Poverty and Charity in Roman Palestine, First Three Centuries C.E.* Berkeley: University of California Press, 1990.

Hamilton, Janet, and Bernard Hamilton. *Christian Dualist Heresies in the Byzantine World, c. 650–c. 1405.* Manchester: Manchester University Press, 1998.

Harmless, William, S.J. *Desert Christians: An Introduction to Early Monastic Literature.* New York: Oxford University Press, 2004.

Harpham, Geoffrey Galt. *The Ascetic Imperative in Culture and Criticism*. Chicago: University of Chicago Press, 1987.

——. *On the Grotesque: Strategies of Contradiction in Art and Literature*. Princeton: Princeton University Press, 1982.

Harries, Jill. "Constructing the Judge: Judicial Accountability and the Culture of Criticism." In *Constructing Identities In Late Antiquity*, edited by Richard Miles, 214–33. London and New York: Routledge, 1999.

Harris, W. V., ed. *The Transformations of Urbs Roma in Late Antiquity*. Journal of Roman Archaeology, Supp. Ser. 33, 1999.

Harrison, S. J. *Apuleius: A Latin Sophist*. Oxford: Oxford University Press, 2000.

Hartog, François. *The Mirror of Herodotus: The Representation of the Other in the Writings of History*. Translated by Janet Lloyd. Berkeley and Los Angeles: University of California Press, 1988.

Harvey, Paul B. Jr. "Mary the Egyptian: Sources and Purpose and New Notes." Unpublished manuscript.

Harvey, Susan Ashbrook. "Feminine Imagery for the Divine: The Holy Spirit, the Odes of Solomon, and Early Syriac Tradition." *St. Vladimir's Theological Quarterly* 37 (1993): 111–39.

——. "Sacred Bonding: Mothers and Daughters in Early Syriac Hagiography." *Journal of Early Christian Studies* 4 (1996): 27–56.

——. "Spoken Words, Voiced Silence: Biblical Women in Syriac Tradition." *Journal of Early Christian Studies* 9 (2001): 105–31.

——. "Women in Early Byzantine Hagiography: Reversing the Story." In *That Gentle Strength: Historical Perspectives on Women in Christianity*, edited by Lynda L. Coon, Katherine J. Haldane, and Elisabeth W. Sommer, 36–59. Charlottesville: University Press of Virginia, 1990.

——. "Women's Service in Ancient Syriac Christianity." *Kanon* 16 (2000): 226–41.

Hasan-Rokem, Galit. *The Web of Life—Folklore in Rabbinic Literature: The Palestinian Aggadic Midrash Eikha Rabba*. Translated by Batya Stein. Contraversions: Jews and Other Differences. Stanford: Stanford University Press, 2000.

Heather, Peter, and David Moncur. *Politics, Philosophy, and Empire in the Fourth Century: Selected Orations of Themistius*. Liverpool: Liverpool University Press, 2001.

Hedrick, C. *History and Silence: Purge and Rehabilitation of Memory in Late Antiquity*. Austin: University of Texas Press, 2000.

Helm, Rudolf. "Hieronymus' Zusätze in Eusebius' Chronik und ihr Wert für die Literaturgeschichte." *Philologus* Supplementband 21 (1929).

Henderson, J. *Morals and Villas in Seneca's Letters: Places to Dwell*. Cambridge: Cambridge University Press, 2004.

Henry, Nathalie. "The Song of Songs and the Liturgy of the *Velatio* in the Fourth Century: From Literary Metaphor to Liturgical Reality." In *Continuity and Change in Christian Worship: Papers Read at the 1997 Summer Meeting and the 1998 Winter Meeting of the Ecclesiastical History Society*, edited by R. N. Swanson, 18–28. Woodbridge, England: Boydell, 1999.

Herodas. *Mimes*. In *Theophrastus, "Characters"; Herodas, "Mimes"; Cercidas and the Cho-*

Iiambic Poets, edited and translated by Ian C. Cunningham, A. D. Knox, and Jeffrey Rusten. 2nd ed. Loeb Classical Library. Cambridge: Harvard University Press, 1993.

Hill, Robert C. "St. John Chrysostom's Homilies on Hannah." St. Vladimir's Theological Quarterly 45 (2001): 319–38.

Hillerbrand, Hans. "Introduction." Present Trends in the Study of Christian History. Special issue Church History 71.3 (2002): 471–72.

Historia monachorum in Aegypto. Edited by André-Jean Festugière. Subsidia Hagiographica 53. Brussels: Société des Bollandistes, 1971.

———. The Lives of the Desert Fathers. Translated by Norman Russell. Kalamazoo: Cistercian Publications, 1980.

Hobsbawm, E., and T. Ranger, eds. The Invention of Tradition. Cambridge: Cambridge University Press, 1983.

Hopkins, Keith. "Novel Evidence for Roman Slavery." Past and Present 138 (1993): 3–27.

Huber-Rebenich, Gerlinde. "Hagiographic Fiction as Entertainment." In Latin Fiction: The Latin Novel in Context, edited by Heinz Hofmann, 187–212. London: Routledge, 1999.

Hunt, Lynn, ed. The New Cultural History. Berkeley and Los Angeles: University of California Press, 1989.

Hunter, David G. "Clerical Celibacy and the Veiling of Virgins: New Boundaries in Late Ancient Christianity." In The Limits of Ancient Christianity: Essays on Late Antique Thought and Culture in Honor of R. A. Markus, edited by William E. Klingshirn and Mark Vessey, 139–52. Ann Arbor: University of Michigan Press, 1999.

———. "Helvidius, Jovinian, and the Virginity of Mary in Late Fourth-Century Rome." Journal of Early Christian Studies 1 (1993): 47–71.

———. "Resistance to the Virginal Ideal in Late-Fourth-Century Rome: The Case of Jovinian." Theological Studies 48 (1987): 45–64.

———. "The Virgin, the Bride, and the Church: Reading Psalm 45 in Ambrose, Jerome, and Augustine." Church History 69 (2000): 281–303.

Husmann, Heinrich. "Syrian Church Music." In New Grove Dictionary of Music and Musicians, edited by Stanley Sadie, 18:472–81. Washington: Groves Dictionaries of Music, 1980.

Ignatieff, M. "What We Think of America." Granta 77 (2002): 47–50.

Inglebert, Hervé. "L'histoire des hérésies chez les hérésiologues." In L'historiographie de l'Église des premiers siècles, edited by B. Pouderon and Y.-M. Duval, 105–25. Théologie historique 114. Paris: Beauchesne, 2001.

———. Les Romains chrétiens face à l'histoire de Rome: Histoire, christianisme et romanités en Occident dans l'antiquité tardive (IIIe-Ve siècles). Paris: Études Augustiniennes, 1996.

Inscriptiones Christianae Urbis Romae septimo saeculo antiquiores. New series. Edited by A. Silvagni et al. 10 vols. Vatican City: Pontificio Istituto di Archeologia Cristiana, 1922–92.

Inscriptiones Latinae Christianae Veteres. Vols. 1–3, edited by E. Diehl. Berlin: Weidmann, 1925–31; rev. ed., 1961. Vol. 4, Supplementum, edited by J. Moreau and H. I. Marrou. Berlin: Weidmann, 1967.

Isocrates. *Panegyricus* 50. In Isocrates, *Operae*, edited by Friedrich Blass. 2 vols. Leipzig, 1889–98.

Itineraria et Alia Geographica. Corpus Christianorum, series latina 175. Turnhout, Belgium: Brepols, 1965.

Jacob of Serug. "A Metrical Homily on Holy Mar Ephrem by Mar Jacob of Serug." Edited and translated by Joseph P. Amar. *Patrologia Orientalis* 47 (1995): 5–76.

———. *Jacob of Serug on the Mother of God*. Translated by Mary Hansbury. Crestwood, N.Y.: St. Vladimir's Seminary Press, 1998.

———. *Jacob of Serugh: Select Festal Homilies*. Translated by Thomas Kollamparampil. Rome: Centre for Indian and Inter-religious Studies, 1997.

———. *S. Martyrii, qui et Sahdona, quae supersunt omnia*. Edited by Paul Bedjan. Paris and Leipzig: Otto Harrassowitz, 1902.

Jaeger, M. *Livy's Written Rome*. Ann Arbor: University of Michigan Press, 1997.

Jeanjean, Benoît. *Saint Jérôme et l'hérésie*. Paris: Études Augustiniennes, 1999.

Jerome. *Chronicon*. Edited by R. Helm. Die griechischen christlichen Schriftsteller der ersten drei Jahrhunderte 33. Berlin: Akademie-Verlag, 1957.

———. *De viris illustribus*. Edited by E. C. Richardson. *Texte und Untersuchungen zur Geschichte der altchristlichen Literatur* 14:1. Leipzig: J. C. Hinrichs, 1896.

———. *Epistulae*. In *Eusebius Hieronymi Epistulae*, edited by Isidorus Hilberg. Vindobonae: Verlag der Österreichischen Akademie der Wissenschaften, 1996.

John Moschos. *Pratum Spirituale* (PG 87.iii). Translated by John Wortley as *The Spiritual Meadow of John Moschos*. Cistercian Studies 139. Kalamazoo: Cistercian Publications, 1992.

John of Damascus. *Jean Damascène: Écrits sur l'Islam*. Edited by Raymond Le Coz. Sources chrétiennes 383. Paris: Éditions du Cerf, 1992.

Jones, A. H. M., J. R. Martindale, and J. Morris. *The Prosopography of the Later Roman Empire*. Cambridge: Cambridge University Press, 1971.

Jones, M. W. *Principles of Roman Architecture*. New Haven: Yale University Press, 2000.

Julian. *Contra Galilaeos*. Edited by Emanuela Massaracchia. Rome: Edizioni dell'Ateneo, 1990.

———. *Giuliano imperatore: Epistola a Temistio*. Edited by Carlo Prato and A. Fornaro. Lecce: Milella, 1984.

———. *Imp. Caesaris Flavii Clavdii Ivliani epistvlae, leges, poemata, fragmenta varia*. Edited by Joseph Bidez and Franz Cumont. Paris: Belles Lettres, 1922.

———. *The Works of the Emperor Julian*. 3 vols. Loeb Classical Library. Translated by Wilmer Cave Wright. Cambridge: Harvard University Press, 1962–69.

Juvencus. *Evangeliorum libri quattuor*. Edited by I. Huemer. Corpus Scriptorum Ecclesiasticorum Latinorum 24. Vienna: F. Tempsky, 1891.

Kalmin, Richard. *Sages, Stories, Authors, and Editors in Rabbinic Babylonia*. Brown Judaica Studies 300. Atlanta: Scholars Press, 1994.

Karras, Ruth Mazo. "Holy Harlots: Prostitute Saints in Medieval Legend." *Journal of the History of Sexuality* 1 (1990): 3–32.

Kelly, J. N. D. *Jerome: His Life, Writings, and Controversies*. New York: Harper and Row, 1975.

———. *The Oxford Dictionary of Popes*. Oxford: Oxford University Press, 1986.

Kennedy, George A. *Greek Rhetoric under Christian Emperors*. Princeton: Princeton University Press, 1983.

Kertsch, Manfred. *Die Bildersprache bei Gregor von Nazianz: Ein Beitrag zur spätantiken Rhetorik und Populärphilosophie*. Graz: Institut für ökumenische Theologie, 1978.

———. "Eine Libanius-Reminiszens bei Gegror von Nazianz, Or. 4, 99?" *Vigiliae Christianae* 46 (1992): 80–82.

Keufler, Mathew. *The Manly Eunuch: Masculinity, Gender Ambiguity, and Christian Ideology in Late Antiquity*. Chicago: University of Chicago Press, 2001.

Kinzer, Stephen. "George Washington: Mr. Excitement? Mount Vernon, Alarmed by Fading Knowledge, Seeks to Pep Up His Image." *New York Times*, 29 July 2002, B1.

Klein, Richard, ed. *Julian Apostata*. Darmstadt: Wissenschaftliche Buchgesellschaft, 1978.

———. "Julians Rhetoren–und Unterrichtsgesetzt." *Römische Quartalschrift* 76 (1981): 73–94.

Kleiner, D. *Roman Sculpture*. New Haven: Yale University Press, 1992.

Klutz, Todd E. "The Rhetoric of Science in *The Rise of Christianity*: A Response to Rodney Stark's Sociological Account of Christianization." *Journal of Early Christian Studies* 6 (1998): 162–84.

Knapp, S. "Collective Memory and the Actual Past." *Representations* 26 (1989): 123–49.

Knauer, G. N. *Psalmenzitate in Augustins Konfessionen*. Göttingen: Vandenhoek and Ruprecht, 1955.

Koch, W. "Comment l'empereur Julien tâcha de fonder une église païenne." *Revue belge de philosophie et d'histoire* 6 (1927): 123–46; 7 (1928): 49–82, 511–50; 1363–85.

Kolbaba, T. *The Byzantine Lists: Errors of the Latins*. Urbana: University of Illinois Press, 2000.

Kondoleon, Christine. *Antioch: The Lost Ancient City*. Princeton: Princeton University Press, 2000.

Kraemer, Ross S. *Maenads, Martyrs, Matrons, Monastics: A Sourcebook on Women's Religions in the Greco-Roman World*. Philadelphia: Fortress, 1988.

Kramer, Bärbel, and John C. Shelton. *Das Archiv des Nepheros und verwandte Texte*. Mainz: Philipp von Zabern, 1987.

Kraus, W. "Dioskuren." In *Reallexikon für Antike und Christentum*, 3:1135. Stuttgart: A. Hiersemann, 1957.

Krautheimer, R. *Corpus Basilicarum Christianarum Romae*. 5 vols. Vatican City: Pontificio Istituto di Archeologia Cristiana, 1937–77.

Krawiec, Rebecca. *Shenoute and the Women of the White Monastery: Egyptian Monasticism in Late Antiquity*. New York: Oxford University Press, 2002.

Krueger, Derek. "Hagiography as an Ascetic Practice in the Early Christian East." *Journal of Religion* 75 (1999): 216–32.

———. "Writing and the Liturgy of Memory in Gregory of Nyssa's *Life of Macrina*." *Journal of Early Christian Studies* 8 (2000): 483–510.

Kurmann, Alois. *Gregor von Nazianz: Oratio 4 gegen Julian; ein Kommentar.* Basel: F. Reinhardt, 1988.

LaCapra, Dominick. *History and Reading: Tocqueville, Foucault, French Studies.* Toronto and Buffalo: University of Toronto Press, 2000.

Lake, Kirsopp, and Robert P. Casey. "The Text of the *De Virginitate* of Athanasius." *Harvard Theological Review* 19 (1926): 173–90.

Lancaster, L. "Building Trajan's Column." *American Journal of Archaeology* 103 (1999): 419–39.

Lardinois, André, and Laura McClure, eds. *Making Silence Speak: Women's Voices in Greek Literature and Society.* Princeton: Princeton University Press, 2001.

Lebon, J. "Pour une édition critique des oeuvres de Saint Athanase." *Revue d'histoire ecclésiastique* 21 (1925).

Le Boulluec, Alain. *La notion d'hérésie dans la littérature grecque IIe–IIIe siècles.* 2 vols. Paris: Études Augustiniennes, 1985.

Le Goff, Jacques, ed. *Hérésies et sociétés dans l'Europe préindustrielle, 11e–18e siècles.* Colloque du Royaumont 27–30 May 1962. Paris: Mouton, 1968.

Le Coz, R. *Jean Damascène: Écrits sur l'Islam.* Sources chrétiennes 383. Paris: Éditions du Cerf, 1992.

Ledit, Joseph. *Marie dans la liturgie de byzance.* Théologique historique 39. Paris: Éditions Beauchesne, 1976.

Lefebvre, H. *The Production of Space.* Translated by D. Nicholson-Smith. Oxford: Blackwell, 1991.

Lefort, L.–Th. "Athanase, Ambroise, et Chenoute 'Sur la virginité.'" *Le Muséon* 48 (1935): 55–75.

Lemerle, P. "L'histoire des Pauliciens d'Asie Mineure d'après les sources grecques." *Travaux et Mémoires* 5 (1973): 1–144.

Lepelley, Claude. *Les cités de l'Afrique romaine au Bas-Empire.* 2 vols. Paris: Études Augustiniennes, 1979–81.

Levi, Doro. *Antioch Mosaic Pavements.* Rome: L'Erma di Bretschneider, 1971.

Lévi-Strauss, Claude. *The Savage Mind.* London: Weidenfeld and Nicolson, 1966.

Leyerle, Blake. "John Chrysostom on the Gaze." *Journal of Early Christian Studies* 1 (1993): 159–74.

——. "Monastic Formation and Christian Practice: Food in the Desert." In *Educating People of Faith: Exploring the History of Jewish and Christian Communities,* edited by John Van Engen, 85–112. Grand Rapids: Eerdmans Press, 2004.

——. *Theatrical Shows and Ascetic Lives: John Chrysostom's Attack on Spiritual Marriage.* Berkeley: University of California Press, 2001.

Libanius. *Epistulae.* In *Opera,* edited by Richardus Foerster. Hildesheim: Georg Olms, 1963.

——. *Libanius: Selected Works.* 3 vols. Edited by A. F. Norman. Loeb Classical Library. Cambridge: Harvard University Press, 1969.

Liebeschuetz, J. H. W. G. *Antioch: City and Imperial Administration in the Later Roman Empire.* Oxford: Clarendon Press, 1972.

Lieu, S. N. C. *Manichaeism in Mesopotamia and the Roman East.* Leiden: Brill, 1994.

——. *Manichaeism in the Later Roman Empire and Medieval China*. Rev. ed. Tübingen: J. C. B. Mohr, 1992.

Lieu, Samuel N. C., ed. *The Emperor Julian: Panegyric and Polemic; Claudius Mamertinus, John Chrysostom, Ephrem the Syrian*. Liverpool: Liverpool University Press, 1989.

Life of Onnophrius. In *Coptic Martyrdoms, etc., in the Dialect of Upper Egypt*, edited by E. A. Wallis Budge. London: British Museum, 1914; reprint, New York: AMS Press, 1977.

——. In *Histories of the Monks of Upper Egypt and the Life of Onnophrius*, translated by Tim Vivian, 145–66. Kalamazoo: Cistercian Publications, 1993.

——. In *The Life of the Jura Fathers*, translated by Tim Vivian. Kalamazoo: Cistercian Publications, 1999.

——. In *Vie des pères du Jura*, edited and translated by François Martine. Sources chrétiennes 142. Paris: Éditions du Cerf, 1968.

Lim, Richard. "Christian Triumph and Controversy." In *Late Antiquity: A Guide to the Postclassical World*, edited by G. W. Bowersock, Peter Brown, and Oleg Grabar, 196–218. Cambridge: Harvard University Press, 1999.

——. *Public Disputation, Power, and Social Order in Late Antiquity*. The Transformation of the Classical Heritage 23. Berkeley and Los Angeles: University of California Press, 1995.

Limberis, Vasiliki. *Divine Heiress: The Virgin Mary and the Creation of Christian Constantinople*. New York: Routledge, 1994.

Livy. *Ab urbe condita*. Vol. 1, books 1–5. Edited by R. M. Ogilvie. Oxford: Oxford University Press, 1974.

Loos, M. *Dualist Heresy in the Middle Ages*. Prague: Akademia, 1974.

Loraux, N. *The Invention of Athens: The Funeral Oration in the Classical City*. Translated by A. Sheridan. Cambridge: Harvard University Press, 1986.

Lott, E. *Love and Theft: Blackface Minstrelsy and the American Working Class*. New York: Oxford University Press, 1993.

Louth, Andrew. *St. John Damascene: Tradition and Originality in Byzantine Theology*. Oxford: Oxford University Press, 2002.

——. *The Wilderness of God*. Nashville: Abingdon Press, 1997.

Lowenthal, D. "Fabricating Heritage." *History and Memory* 10 (1998): 5–24.

Ludwig, C. "Paulicians and Ninth-Century Byzantine Thought." In *Byzantium in the Ninth Century: Dead or Alive?* edited by Leslie Brubaker, 23–35. Aldershot: Ashgate, 1998.

Lyman, J. Rebecca. *Christology and Cosmology: Models of Divine Activity in Origen, Eusebius, and Athanasius*. Oxford: Clarendon Press, 1993.

——. "Historical Methodologies and Ancient Theological Conflicts." In *The Papers of Henry Luce III Fellows in Theology*, edited by Matthew Zyniewicz, 3:75–96. Atlanta: Scholars Press, 1999.

——. "Origen as Ascetic Theologian: Orthodoxy and Heresy in the Fourth-Century Church." In *Origeniana Septima: Origenes in den Auseinandersetzungen des 4. Jahrhunderts*, edited by W. B. Bienert and U. Kühneweg, 187–94. Leuven: Peeters, 1999.

——. "The Making of a Heretic: The Life of Origen in Epiphanius, *Panarion* 64." *Studia Patristica* 31 (1997): 445–51.

———. "A Topography of Heresy: Mapping the Rhetorical Creation of Arianism." In *Arianism after Arius: Essays on the Development of the Fourth-Century Trinitarian Conflicts*, edited by Michel R. Barnes and Daniel H. Williams, 45–62. Edinburgh: T. and T. Clark, 1993.

Macherey, Pierre. *A Theory of Literary Production*. Translated by Geoffrey Wall. London: Routledge and Kegan Paul, 1978.

MacKendrick, Karmen. *Word Made Skin: Figuring Language at the Surface of Flesh*. Bronx, N.Y.: Fordham University Press, 2004.

MacMullen, Ramsay. *Christianity and Paganism in the Fourth to Eighth Centuries*. New Haven: Yale University Press, 1997.

———. "Some Pictures in Ammianus Marcellinus." *Art Bulletin* 46 (1964): 435–55.

Magness, J. "The Mausolea of Augustus, Alexander, and Herod the Great." In *Hesed Ve-Emet: Studies in Honor of Ernest S. Frerichs*, edited by J. Magness and S. Gitin, 313–27. Atlanta: Scholars Press, 1998.

Maier, Harry O. "Purity and Danger in Polycarp's Epistle to the Philippians: The Sin of Valens in Social Perspective." *Journal of Early Christian Studies* 1 (1993): 229–47.

———. *The Social Setting of the Ministry as Reflected in the Writings of Hermas, Clement and Ignatius*. Waterloo, Canada: Wilfrid Laurier University Press, 1991.

Malina, Bruce J. *The New Testament World: Insights from Cultural Anthropology*. Atlanta: John Knox, 1981.

Malkin, Irad, ed. *Ancient Perceptions of Greek Ethnicity*. Cambridge: Harvard University Press, 2001.

Mandouze, André, and Anne-Marie La Bonnardière. *Prosopographie chrétienne du Bas-Empire*. Vol. 1, *Prosopographie de l'Afrique chrétienne (303–533)*. Paris: CNRS, 1982.

Marcus, G. *Invisible Republic: Bob Dylan's Basement Tapes*. New York: Henry Holt, 1997.

"The Markings of Heresy: Body, Text, and Community in Late Ancient Christianity." Special issue. *Journal of Early Christian Studies* 4 (1996): 403–513.

Markus, Robert A. *The End of Ancient Christianity*. Cambridge: Cambridge University Press, 1990.

———. "Evolving Disciplinary Contexts for the Study of Augustine, 1950–2000: Some Personal Reflections." *Augustinian Studies* 32 (2001): 189–200.

———. *Signs and Wonders: World and Text in Ancient Christianity*. Liverpool: Liverpool University Press, 1996.

Marrou, Henri-Irénée. *A History of Education in Antiquity*. Translated by G. Lamb. London: Sheed and Ward, 1956.

———. "La vie intellectuelle au forum de Trajan et au forum d'Auguste." *Mélanges de l'École Française de Rome* 49 (1932): 93–110.

———. *Mousikos aner: Étude sur les scènes de la vie intellectuelle figurant sur les monuments funéraires romains*. Grenoble: Didier and Richard, 1938; reissued with postface, Rome: "L'Erma" di Bretschneider, 1964.

Martin, Dale B. "Contradictions of Masculinity: Ascetic Inseminators and Menstruating Men in Greco-Roman Culture." In *Generation and Degeneration: Literature and Tropes of Reproduction*, edited by Valeria Finucci and Kevin Brownlee, 81–108. Durham: Duke University Press, 2001.

——. "Social Scientific Criticism." In *To Each Its Own Meaning: An Introduction to Biblical Criticisms and Their Applications*, edited by Steven L. McKenzie and Stephen R. Haynes, 125–41. Rev. and expanded, Louisville: Westminster John Knox Press, 1999.

——. *Slavery as Salvation: The Metaphor of Slavery in Pauline Christianity*. New Haven: Yale University Press, 1990.

Martin, René. "Apulée, Virgile, Augustin: Réflexions nouvelles sur la structure des *Confessions*." *Revue des Études Latines* 68 (1990): 136–50.

Martyn, James Louis. *History and Theology in the Fourth Gospel*. Nashville: Abingdon, 1979.

Marucchi, H. *Éléments d'archéologie chrétienne*. 2nd ed. 3 vols. Paris: Desclée, Lefebvre, 1905.

Masson-Vincourt, M.-P. *Les allusions à la mythologie et à la religion païenne dans les ouevres de Grégoire de Nazianze*. Lille: Librairie de l'Université, 1973.

Matthews, John. "Peter Valvomeres, Re-arrested." In *Homo Viator: Classical Essays for John Bramble*, edited by Michael Whitby et al., 277–84. Bristol: Bristol Classical Press / Oak Park, Ill.: Bolchazy-Carducci, 1987.

——. *The Roman Empire of Ammianus*. London: Duckworth, 1989.

Mauser, Ulrich. *Christ in the Wilderness*. Naperville, Ill.: Alec R. Allerson, 1963.

McClure, J. M. "Handbooks against Heresy in the West, from the Late Fourth to the Sixth Century." *Journal of Theological Studies* n.s. 30 (1979): 186–97.

McClure, Laura R. *Spoken Like a Woman: Speech and Gender in Athenian Drama*. Princeton: Princeton University Press, 1999.

McGuckin, John. *Saint Gregory of Nazianzus: An Intellectual Biography*. Crestwood, N.Y.: St. Vladimir's Press, 2001.

McLeod, Frederick G., ed. and trans. *Narsai's Metrical Homilies on the Nativity, Epiphany, Passion, Resurrection and Ascension*. Patrologia Orientalis 40. Turnhout, Belgium: Brepols, 1979.

——. "A Self-Made Holy Man: The Case of Gregory of Nazianzen." *Journal of Early Christian Studies* 6 (1998): 463–83.

McLynn, Neil B. "Augustine's Roman Empire." *Augustinian Studies* 30 (1999): 29–44.

——. "Seeing and Believing: Aspects of Conversion from Antoninus Pius to Louis the Pious." In *Conversion in Late Antiquity and the Middle Ages: Seeing and Believing*, edited by Kenneth Mills and Anthony Grafton, 224–70. Rochester, N.Y.: University of Rochester Press, 2003.

——. "The Voice of Conscience: Gregory Nazianzen in Retirement." In *Vescovi e pastori in epoca Teodosiana*, [no editor], 2:299–308. Rome: Institutum Augustinianum, 1997.

Meeks, Wayne A. *The First Urban Christians: The Social World of the Apostle Paul*. New Haven: Yale University Press, 1983.

——. "The Irony of Grace." In *Shaping a Theological Mind: Theological Context and Methodology*, edited by Darren C. Marks, 45–57. Aldershot: Ashgate, 2002.

——. "The Man from Heaven in Johannine Sectarianism." *Journal of Biblical Literature* 91 (1972): 44–72.

Merlo, G. G., ed. *Eretici e eresia medievali nella storiografia contemporanea*. Atti del XXXII

Convegno di Studi sulle reforme e i movimenti religiosi in Italia, Bollettino delle Società di Studi Valdensi 174. Torre Pellici: n.p., 1994.

Migne, J.-P., ed. *Patrologiae cursus completus: Patrologia Graeca.* 161 vols. in 166. Paris, 1857–1866.

——. *Patrologiae cursus completus: Patrologia Latina.* 221 vols. in 222. Paris, 1844–1865.

Miles, G. *Livy: Reconstructing Early Rome.* Ithaca, N.Y.: Cornell University Press, 1995.

Miles, Margaret R. *Desire and Delight: A New Reading of Augustine's Confessions.* New York: Crossroad, 1992.

Miller, Patricia Cox. "The Blazing Body: Ascetic Desire in Jerome's Letter to Eustochium." *Journal of Early Christian Studies* 1 (1993): 21–45.

——. "Desert Asceticism and 'The Body from Nowhere.'" *Journal of Early Christian Studies* 2 (1994): 137–53.

——. *Dreams in Late Antiquity: Studies in the Imagination of a Culture.* Princeton: Princeton University Press, 1994.

——. "Jerome's Centaur: A Hyper-Icon of the Desert." *Journal of Early Christian Studies* 4 (1996): 209–33. Reprinted in Miller, *The Poetry of Thought in Late Antiquity.*

——. *The Poetry of Thought in Late Antiquity: Essays in Imagination and Religion,* 75–99. Aldershot: Ashgate, 2001.

Mimouni, Simon Claude. *Dormition et Assomption de Marie: Histoire des traditions anciennes.* Théologiques historiques 98. Paris: Beauchesne, 1995.

Mitchell, W. J. T. *Landscape and Power.* Chicago: University of Chicago Press, 1994.

——, ed. *On Narrative.* Chicago: University of Chicago Press, 1981.

Momigliano, Arnaldo. "Marcel Mauss and the Quest for the Person in Greek Biography and Autobiography." In *The Category of the Person: Anthropology, Philosophy, History,* edited by Michael Carrithers, Steven Collins, and Steven Lukes, 83–92. Cambridge and New York: Cambridge University Press, 1985.

——. *On Pagans, Jews, and Christians.* Middletown, Conn.: Wesleyan University Press, 1987.

Mommsen, Theodor, ed., with Paul M. Meyer and Paul Krueger. *Codex Theodosianus.* 2 vols. in 3. Berlin: Weidmann, 1905; reprint, 1962.

Monceaux, P. "Saint Augustin et saint Antoine: Contribution à l'histoire du monachisme." In *Miscellanea Agostiniana,* 2:61–89. 2 vols. Rome: Tipografia Poliglotta Vaticana, 1931.

Mondzain-Baudinet, M.-J. *Nicephore: Discours contre les iconoclastes.* Paris: Klincksieck, 1989.

Moore, Stephen D., and Susan Lochrie Graham. "The Quest of the New Historicist Jesus." *Biblical Interpretation* 5 (1997): 437–63.

Moore, R. I. *The Formation of a Persecuting Society: Power and Deviance in Western Europe, 950–1250.* Oxford: Oxford University Press, 1987.

Moschos, John. *The Spiritual Meadow.* Translated by John Wortley. Cistercian Studies Series 139. Kalamazoo, Mich.: Cistercian Publications, 1992.

Mossay, Justin. "La date de l'*Oratio* II de Grégoire de Nazianze et celle de son ordination." *Le Muséon* 77 (1964): 175–86.

Motyer, Stephen. *Your Father the Devil?: A New Approach to John and "the Jews."* Paternoster Biblical and Theological Studies. Carlisle, England: Paternoster Press, 1997.

Mullett, Margaret. "The 'Other' in Byzantium." In *Strangers to Themselves: The Byzantine Outsider*, edited by Dion C. Smythe, 1–22. Aldershot: Ashgate, 2000.

Munitiz, Joseph A. "Synoptic Greek Accounts of the Seventh Council." *Revue des études byzantines* 32 (1974): 147–86.

Murray, Robert. "Mary, the Second Eve in the Early Syriac Fathers." *Eastern Churches Review* 3 (1971): 372–84.

——. *Symbols of Church and Kingdom: A Study in Early Syriac Tradition.* Cambridge: Cambridge University Press, 1975.

Nagel, Peter. "Action-Parables in Earliest Monasticism: An Examination of the *Apophthegmata Patrum*." *Hallel* 5 (1977–78): 251–61.

Nash, E. *Pictorial Dictionary of Ancient Rome.* 2 vols. London: A. Zwemmer, 1962.

Nau, François. See *Apophthegmata patrum.*

Nautin, Pierre. "Études de chronologie hiéronymienne (393–397) (suite et fin)." *Revue des études augustiniennes* 20 (1974): 251–84.

Neusner, Jacob. *The Canonical History of Ideas: The Place of the So-Called Tannaite Midrashim.* University of Southern Florida Studies in the History of Judaism. Atlanta: Scholars Press, 1990.

——. *The Documentary Foundation of Rabbinic Culture: Mopping Up after Debates with Gerald L. Bruns, S. J. D. Cohen, Arnold Maria Goldberg, Susan Handelman, Christine Hayes, James Kugel, Peter Schaefer, Eliezer Segal, E. P. Sanders, and Lawrence H. Schiffman.* Atlanta: Scholars Press, 1995.

——. "The Formation of Rabbinic Judaism: Yavneh (Jamnia) from A.D. 70 to 100." In *Aufstieg und Niedergang der Römischen Welt: Principat: Religion (Judentum: Pälastinisches Judentum [Forts.])*, edited by Wolfgang Haase, 3–42. Berlin: de Gruyter, 1979.

——. "Judaism after the Destruction of the Temple: An Overview." In *Formative Judaism: Religious, Historical, and Literary Studies, Third Series; Torah, Pharisees, and Rabbis*, 83–98. Chico, Calif.: Scholars Press, 1983.

——. *Reading and Believing: Ancient Judaism and Contemporary Gullibility.* Atlanta: Scholars Press, 1986.

Nissen, Theodor. "Unbekannte Erzählungen aus dem *Pratum Spirituale*." *Byzantinische Zeitschrift* 38 (1938): 358–59.

Nora, P. "Between Memory and History: Les Lieux de Mémoire." *Representations* 26 (1989): 7–25.

Norris, Frederick W. *Faith Gives Fullness to Reasoning: The Five Theological Orations of Gregory of Nazianzus.* Leiden: Brill, 1991.

O'Daly, Gerard. *Augustine's "City of God."* Oxford: Clarendon Press, 1999.

O'Donnell, James J. "Augustine's Classical Readings." *Recherches Augustiniennes* 15 (1980): 144–75.

——. "The Authority of Augustine." *Augustinian Studies* 22 (1991): 7–35.

Oberhelman, S. M. "Jerome's Earliest Attack on Ambrose: *On Ephesians*, Prologue (ML 26: 469D–70A)." *Transactions of the American Philological Association* 121 (1991): 377–401.

Obolensky, D. *The Bogomils*. Cambridge: Cambridge University Press, 1948.

Oldfather, W., et al. *Studies in the Text Tradition of St. Jerome's Vitae Patrum*. Urbana: University of Illinois Press, 1943.

Pachomian Koinonia: The Lives, Rules, and Other Writings of Pachomius and His Disciples. Translated by Armand Veilleux. 3 vols. Vol. 1, *The Life of Saint Pachomius and His Disciples*. Vol. 2, *Pachomian Chronicles and Rules*. Cistercian Studies Series 45–46. Kalamazoo: Cistercian Publications, 1980–81.

Pack, Edgar. *Städte und Steuern in der Politik Julians: Untersuchungen zu den Quellen eines Kaiserbildes*. Brussels: Éditions Latomus, 1986.

Packer, James E. *The Forum of Trajan in Rome: A Study of the Monuments*. 2 vols. Berkeley and Los Angeles: University of California Press, 1997.

Palladius of Helenopolis. *Historia lausiaca*. English translation, *The Lausiac History of Palladius*. Edited by Edward Cuthbert Butler. 1898; reprint, Hildesheim: Georg Olms, 1967.

——. *Palladius: The Lausiac History*. Translated by Robert T. Meyer. New York: Newman Press, 1964.

Patlagean, Evelyne. "Aveux et désaveux d'hérétiques à Byzance (xie–xiie siècle)." In *L'Aveu: Antiquité et Moyen Âge*, 243–60. Collection de l'École Française de Rome 88. Rome: École Française de Rome, 1986.

——. "L'histoire de la femme déguisée en moine et l'évolution de la sainteté féminine à Byzance." In Evelyne Patlagean, *Structure sociale, famille, chrétienté à Byzance*, 597–623. London: Variorum, 1981.

Patrich, Joseph. *Sabas, Leader of Palestinian Monasticism: A Comparative Study in Eastern Monasticism, Fourth to Seventh Centuries*. Washington: Dumbarton Oaks, 1995.

Patterson, Annabel. *Fables of Power: Aesopian Writing and Political History*. Durham: Duke University Press, 1991.

Paulinus. *Epistulae*. Edited by G. Hartel. Corpus Scriptorum Ecclesiasticorum Latinorum 29. Vienna: Tempsky, 1894.

Pelling, Christopher, ed. *Characterization and Individuality in Greek Literature*. Oxford: Clarendon Press; New York: Oxford University Press, 1990.

——. *Literary Texts and the Greek Historian*. London and New York: Routledge, 2000.

Pergola, P. *Le catacombe romane: Storia e topografia*. Rome: Carocci, 1997.

Perkins, Judith. *The Suffering Self: Pain and Narrative Representation in the Early Christian Era*. London: Routledge, 1995.

Peskowitz, Miriam. *Spinning Fantasies: Rabbis, Gender, and History*. Contraversions. Berkeley and Los Angeles: University of California Press, 1997.

Peterson, M. *Lincoln in American Memory*. New York: Oxford University Press, 1994.

Petitmengin, Pierre, et al. *Pélagie la pénitente, metamorphoses d'une légende*. Vol. 1, *Les textes et leur histoire*. Paris: Études Augustiniennes, 1984.

Petronius. *Satyricon*. Translated by E. H. Warmington, W. H. D. Rouse, and Michael Heseltime. Loeb Classical Library. Cambridge: Harvard University Press, 1988.

Philostorgius. *Historia ecclesiastica*. Edited by Joseph Bidez and Friedrich Winkelmann. Griechische christliche Schriftsteller der ersten Jahrhunderte. Berlin: Akademie-Verlag, 1972.

Piccirillo, Michele. *Chiese e Mosaici di Madaba*. Jerusalem: Franciscan Printing Press, 1989.

Piccirillo, Michele, and Eugene Alliata. *Mount Nebo: New Archaeological Excavations 1967–1997*. Jerusalem: Studium Biblicum Franciscanum, 1998.

Pietri, C. "Concordia apostolorum et renovatio urbis (Culte des martyrs et propagande pontificale)." *Mélanges de l'École Française de Rome, Antiquité* 73 (1961): 275–322. Reprinted in C. Pietri, *Christiana respublica*, 2:1085–1133. 3 vols. Rome: École Française de Rome, 1997.

——. *Roma Christiana: Recherches sur l'Eglise de Rome, son organisation, sa politique, son idéologie de Miltiade à Sixte III (311–440)*. Rome: École Française de Rome, 1976.

Pinches, Charles, and Jay B. McDaniel. *Good News for Animals?: Christian Approaches to Animal Well-Being*. New York: Orbis, 1993.

Pollmann, Karla. *Doctrina christiana: Untersuchungen zu den Anfängen der christlichen Hermeneutik unter besonderer Berücksichtigung von Augustinus, De doctrina christiana*. Freiburg, Switzerland: Universitätsverlag, 1996.

——. "Zwei Konzepte von Fiktionalität in der Philosophie des Hellenismus und in der Spätantike." In *Zur Rezeption der hellenistischen Philosophie in der Spätantike*, edited by Therese Fuhrer and Michael Erler, 261–78. Stuttgart: Franz Steiner, 1999.

Pomper, Philip, Brian Fay, and Richard T. Vann, eds. *History and Theory: Contemporary Readings*. Malden, Mass.: Blackwell, 1998.

Possidius. *Vita Augustini*. Edited by A. A. R. Bastiaensen. In *Vita dei Santi*, edited by Christine Mohrman, vol. 2. Milan: Fondazione Lorenzo Valla, 1974.

Pourkier, A. *L'Hérésiologie chez Epiphane de Salamine*. Paris: Beauchesne, 1992.

Power, Kim. *Veiled Desire: Augustine on Women*. New York: Continuum, 1996.

Prudentius. *Carmina*. Edited by M. Cunningham. Turnhout, Belgium: Brepols, 1966.

Pseudo-Athanasius. *De virginitate*. In *Logos sôtêrias pros tên parthenon (De virginitate): Eine echte Schrift des Athanasius*, edited by Eduard F. von der Goltz. Texte und Untersuchungen 29, 2a. Leipzig: J. C. Hinrichs, 1905.

——. *Discours de salut à une vierge*. Translated by Chanoine J. Bouvet. Spiritualité orientale 9. Begrolles-en-Mauge: Abbaye Notre Dame de Bellefontaine, 1972.

——. "Pseudo-Athanasius: Discourse on Salvation to a Virgin." Translated by Teresa M. Shaw. In *Religions of Late Antiquity in Practice*, edited by Richard Valantasis, 82–99. Princeton: Princeton University Press, 2000.

——. *Pseudo-Athanasius on Virginity*. Edited and translated by David Brakke. Corpus Scriptorum Christianorum Orientalium 592–93 (Scriptores Syri, 232–33). Louvain: Peeters, 2002.

——. *Vita et gesta Sanctae beataeque magistrae Syncleticae*. In J.-P. Migne, *Patrologiae cursus completus: Patrologia Graeca*, vol. 28.

Puech, Aimé. *Histoire de la littérature grecque chrétienne*. Paris: Belles Lettres, 1930.

Pyykkö, V. *Die griechischen Mythen bei den grossen Kappadokiern und bei Johannes Chrysostomus*. Turku, Finland: University of Turku Press, 1991.

Raaflaub, K., and M. Toher, eds. *Between Republic and Empire: Interpretations of Augustus and His Principate*. Berkeley and Los Angeles: University of California Press, 1990.

Raes, Alphonse. "Aux origines de la fête de l'Assomption en Orient." *Orientalia Christiana Periodica* 12 (1946): 262–74.

Rapp, Claudia. "Story-Telling as Spiritual Communication in Early Greek Hagiography: The Use of Diegesis." *Journal of Early Christian Studies* 6 (1998): 431–48.

Rebenich, Stefan. "Asceticism, Orthodoxy and Patronage: Jerome in Constantinople." *Studia Patristica* 33 (1997): 358–77.

Regnault, Lucien. See *Apophthegmata patrum*.

Reinink, G. J. and H. L. J. Vanstiphout, eds. *Dispute Poems and Dialogues in the Ancient and Mediaeval Near East: Forms and Types of Literary Debates in Semitic and Related Literature*. Orientalia Lovaniensia Analecta 42. Leuven: Peeters, 1991.

Richardson, L. *A New Topographical Dictionary of Ancient Rome*. Baltimore: Johns Hopkins University Press, 1992.

Richter, Daniel S. "Plutarch on Isis and Osiris: Text, Culture, and Cultural Appropriation." *Transactions of the American Philological Association* 131 (2001): 191–216.

Riggi, C. *Epifanio contro Mani*. Rome: Pontificium Institutum Altioris Latinitatis, 1967.

Rist, J. M. "Platonic Soul, Aristotelian Form, Christian Person." In *Self, Soul, and Body in Religious Experience*, edited by A. I. Baumgarten, J. Assmann, and G. G. Stroumsa, 347–62. Leiden and Boston: Brill, 1998.

Robertson, A. S. *Roman Imperial Coins in the Hunter Coin Cabinet, University of Glasgow*. 5 vols. Oxford: Oxford University Press, 1962–82.

Roldanus, Johannes. *Le Christ et l'homme dans la théologie d'Athanase d'Alexandrie*. Leiden: E. J. Brill, 1968.

Romm, James S. *The Edges of the Earth in Ancient Thought*. Princeton: Princeton University Press, 1992.

Rossi, Giovanni Battista de. *La Roma sotterranea cristiana*. Rome: Cromo-litografia Pontificia, 1864.

Rousseau, Philip. *Ascetics, Authority, and the Church in the Age of Jerome and Cassian*. Oxford: Oxford University Press, 1978.

——. *Basil of Caesarea*. The Transformation of the Classical Heritage 20. Berkeley and Los Angeles: University of California Press, 1994.

——. Review of Elizabeth A. Clark, *Reading Renunciation: Asceticism and Scripture in Early Christianity* (Princeton: Princeton University Press, 1999). *Journal of Ecclesiastical History* 52 (2001): 342–44.

Rousselle, Aline. *Porneia: On Desire and the Body in Antiquity*. Translated by Felicia Pheasant. Oxford: Basil Blackwell, 1988.

Rubenson, Samuel. *The Letters of St. Antony: Monasticism and the Making of a Saint*. Studies in Antiquity and Christianity. Minneapolis: Fortress Press, 1995.

Ruether, Rosemary R. *Gregory of Nazianzus: Rhetor and Philosopher*. Oxford: Oxford University Press, 1969.

Rufus of Ephesus. *Oeuvres de Rufus d'Ephèse*. Edited by C. Dremberg and C. E. Ruelle. Paris, 1897. Reprint, Amsterdam: Adolf M. Kakkert, 1963.

Russell, Norman, trans. *The Lives of the Desert Fathers*. Kalamazoo: Cistercian Publications, 1980.

Rutgers, Leonard. *Subterranean Rome*. Leuven: Peeters, 2000.

Saecularia Damasiana: Atti del convegno internazionale per il XVI centenario della morte di Papa Damaso I. [No editor] Vatican City: Pontificio Istituto di Archeologia Cristiana, 1986.

Sághy, M. "Patrons and Priests: The Roman Senatorial Aristocracy and the Church A.D. 355–384." Ph.D. diss., Princeton University, 1998.

Saïd, Suzanne, ed. [Hellenismos]: *Quelques jalons pour une histoire de l'identité grecque*. Leiden: Brill, 1991.

Saller, Sylvester J., and Bellarmino Bagatti. *On Roman Time: The Codex Calendar of 354 and the Rhythms of Urban Life in Late Antiquity*. Berkeley and Los Angeles: University of California Press, 1990.

———. *The Town of Nebo and Other Ancient Christian Monuments in Transjordan*. Jerusalem: Franciscan Press, 1949.

Salzman, Michele Renee. *The Making of a Christian Aristocracy: Social and Religious Change in the Western Roman Empire*. Cambridge: Harvard University Press, 2002.

———. *On Roman Time: The Codex Calendar of 354 and the Rhythms of Urban Life in Late Antiquity*. The Transformation of the Classical Heritage 17. Berkeley: University of California Press, 1990.

Sanders, Jack T. *Schismatics, Sectarians, Dissidents, Deviants: The First One Hundred Years of Jewish-Christian Relations*. London: SCM Press, 1993.

Sargent, Anne Marie. "The Penitent Prostitute: The Tradition and Evolution of the Life of St. Mary the Egyptian." Ph.D. diss., University of Michigan, 1977.

Sauneron, S., and J. Jacquet. *Les Ermitages chrétiens du désert d'Esna*. Vol. 1, *Archéologie et inscriptions*. Cairo: Institut Français d'Archéologie Orientale du Caire, 1972.

Saussure, Ferdinand de. *Course in General Linguistics*. Rev. ed. Charles Bally et al. Translated by Wade Baskin. London: Fontana, 1974.

Schlange-Schöningen, Heinrich. *Kaisertum und Bildungswesen im spätantiken Konstantinopel*. Stuttgart: Steiner, 1995.

Schneemelcher, Wilhelm, ed. *New Testament Apocrypha*. Rev. ed. Translated by R. M. Wilson. Louisville, Ky.: Westminster John Knox Press, 1991.

Scholes, Robert, and Robert Kellogg. *The Nature of Narrative*. New York: Oxford University Press, 1966.

Schwartz, B. *Abraham Lincoln and the Forge of National Memory*. Chicago: University of Chicago Press, 2000.

Schwartz, Seth. *Imperialism and Jewish Society from 200 B.C.E. to 640 C.E.* Princeton: Princeton University Press, 2001.

Scriptor(es) Historiae Augustae (Firmus 1.2). Edited by D. Magie. 3 vols. Loeb Classical Library. Cambridge: Harvard University Press, 1921–32.

Segal, Alan F. *Two Powers in Heaven: Early Rabbinic Reports about Christianity and Gnosticism*. Studies in Judaism in Late Antiquity. Leiden: E. J. Brill, 1977.

Séminaire d'histoire des textes de l'École normale supérieure. *Pélagie la Pénitente: Métamorphoses d'une légende*. Vol. 1, *Les textes et leur histoire*. Paris: Études Augustiniennes, 1981.

Severus of Antioch. "Les Homiliae cathedrales de Sévère d'Antioche: Hom. 118." Edited and translated by Maurice Brière. In *Patrologia Orientalis* 26:357–74. Paris: Firmin-Didot, 1948.

Shaw, Brent. "African Christianity: Disputes, Definitions and 'Donatists.'" In *Orthodoxy and Heresy in Religious Movements: Discipline and Dissent*, edited by M. R. Greenshields and T. A. Robinson, 5–34. Lewiston, N.Y.: Edwin Mellen, 1992.

Shaw, Teresa M. "*Askêsis* and the Appearance of Holiness." *Journal of Early Christian Studies* 6 (1998): 485–99.

———. *The Burden of the Flesh: Fasting and Sexuality in Early Christianity*. Minneapolis: Fortress Press, 1998.

———. "The Virgin Charioteer and the Bride of Christ: Gender and the Passions in Late Ancient Ethics and Early Christian Writings on Virginity." In *The Feminist Companion to the Early Church*, edited by Amy-Jill Levine. Sheffield: Sheffield Academic Press, forthcoming.

Shoemaker, Stephen J. "Rethinking the 'Gnostic Mary': Mary of Nazareth and Mary of Magdala in Early Christian Tradition." *Journal of Early Christian Studies* 9 (2001): 555–95.

Shumate, Nancy. *Crisis and Conversion in Apuleius' "Metamorphoses."* Ann Arbor: University of Michigan Press, 1996.

Sillet, Helen. "Culture of Controversy: The Christological Disputes of the Early Fifth Century." Ph.D. diss., University of California at Berkeley, 1999.

Simpson, Jane. "Women and Asceticism in the Fourth Century: A Question of Interpretation." *Journal of Religious History* 15.1 (June 1988): 38–60.

Smid, H. R. *Protevangelium Jacobi, A Commentary*. Translated by G. E. Van Baaren-Pape. Assen: Van Gorcum, 1965.

Smith, A. "Iamblichus' Views on the Relationship of Philosophy to Religion in *De Mysteriis*." In *The Divine Iamblichus: Philosopher and Man of Gods*, edited by Henry J. Blumenthal and E. G. Clark, 74–86. London: Bristol Classical Press, 1993.

Smith, Mark. *Culture: Reinventing the Social Sciences*. Buckingham: Open University Press, 2000.

Smith, Rowland. *Julian's Gods: Religion and Philosophy in the Thought and Action of Julian the Apostate*. London: Routledge, 1995.

Smith, Warren S. "Apuleius and Luke: Prologue and Epilogue in Conversions Contexts." In *A Companion to the Prologue of Apuleius' "Metamorphoses,"* edited by Ahuvia Kahane and Andrew Laird, 88–99. Oxford: Oxford University Press, 2001.

Smythe, Dion. "Alexios I and the Heretics." In *Alexios I Komnenos* Vol. 1, *Papers*, edited by M. Mullett and D. Smythe, 232–59. Belfast: Belfast Byzantine Texts and Translations, 1996.

———. "Outsiders by *Taxis*: Perceptions of Non-conformity in Eleventh and Twelfth-Century Literature." In *Conformity and Non-conformity in Byzantium*, edited by L. Garland, 229–49. Amsterdam: Hakkert, 1997.

Socrates. *Historia ecclesiastica*. Edited by Günther Christian Hansen. Griechische christliche Schriftsteller der ersten Jahrhunderte. Neue Folge 1. Berlin: Akademie-Verlag, 1995.

Soja, Edward. "Los Angeles, 1965–1992: From Crisis-Generated Restructuring to

Restructuring-Generated Crisis." In *The City: Los Angeles and Urban Theory at the End of the Twentieth Century*, edited by A. Scott and E. Soja, 426–62. Berkeley and Los Angeles: University of California Press, 1996.

Speck, P. *Ich bin's nicht: Kaiser Konstantin ist es gewesen; die Legenden vom Einfluss des Teufels, des Juden und des Moslem auf den Ikonoklasmus*. Bonn: Habelt, 1990.

Speyer, Wolfgang. *Frühes Christentum im antiken Strahlungsfeld*. Tübingen: J. C. B. Mohr, 1989.

Steinby, E. *Lexicon Topographicum Urbis Romae*. 5 vols. Rome: Quasar, 1993–99.

Stemberger, Günter. *Jews and Christians in the Holy Land: Palestine in the Fourth Century*. Edinburgh: T. and T. Clark, 1999.

Stewart, Columba. "Imageless Prayer and the Theological Vision of Evagrius Ponticus." *Journal of Early Christian Studies* 9 (2001): 173–204.

———. *Working the Earth of the Heart: The Messalian Controversy in History, Texts and Language to A.D. 431*. Oxford: Clarendon Press, 1991.

———. *The World of the Desert Fathers*. Kalamazoo, Mich.: Cistercian Publications, 1986.

Stock, Brian. *After Augustine: The Meditative Reader and the Text*. Philadelphia: University of Pennsylvania Press, 2001.

———. *Augustine the Reader: Meditation, Self-Knowledge, and the Ethics of Interpretation*. Cambridge: Harvard University Press, 1996.

Stoyanov, Y. *The Hidden Tradition in Europe: The Secret History of Medieval Christian Heresy*. London: Arkana, 1994. Rev. as *The Other God: Dualist Religions from Antiquity to the Cathar Heresy*. New Haven: Yale University Press, 2000.

Stroumsa, G. G. "Aspects de la polémique antimanichéenne dans l'antiquité tardive et dans l'Islam primitif." In *Savoir et Salut*, edited by G. G. Stroumsa, 355–77. Paris: Éditions du Cerf, 1992.

———. *Barbarian Philosophy: The Religious Revolution of Early Christianity*. Tübingen: Mohr Siebeck, 1999.

Stroumsa, G. G., and O. Limor, eds. *Contra Iudaeos: Ancient and Medieval Polemics between Christians and Jews*. Tübingen: J. C. B. Mohr, 1996.

Strozier, Robert M. *Foucault, Subjectivity and Identity: Historical Constructions of Subject and Self*. Detroit: Wayne State University Press, 2002.

Swain, Simon. *Hellenism and Empire: Language, Classicism, and Power in the Greek World, A.D. 50–250*. Oxford: Clarendon Press, 1996.

Symmachus. *Epistulae*. Edited by J. P. Callu. Paris: Belles Lettres, 1972.

———. *Q. Aurelii Symmachi que supersunt*. Edited by O. Seeck. Monumenta Germaniae Historica, Auctores Antiquissimi 6. Berlin: Weidmann, 1883.

Szidat, Joachim. "Zur Ankunft Julians in Sirmium 361 n. Chr. auf seinem Zug gegen Constantius II." *Historia* 24 (1975): 375–78.

Tanner, Kathryn. *Theories of Culture: A New Agenda for Theology*. Minneapolis: Fortress, 1997.

Taylor, Mark C. *Hiding*. Chicago: University of Chicago Press, 1997.

Theissen, Gerd. *The Social Setting of Pauline Christianity*. Philadelphia: Fortress, 1982.

———. *Sociology of Early Palestinian Christianity*. Philadelphia: Fortress, 1978.

Themistius. *Themistii Orationes*. Edited by H. Schenkel, G. Downey, and A. F. Norman. 3 vols. Leipzig: Teubner, 1965–74.

Theodoret of Cyrrhus. *Curatio*. Edited by P. Canivet. Sources chrétiennes 52. Paris: Éditions du Cerf, 1958.

——. *Eranistes*. Edited by G. Ettlinger. Oxford: Clarendon Press, 1975.

——. *Théodoret de Cyr, Correspondance*. Edited by Yvan Azéma. 4 vols. Sources chrétiennes 40, 98, 111, 429. Paris: Éditions du Cerf, 1955, 1964, 1965, 1998.

Theognostos. *Theognosti Thesaurus*. Corpus Christianorum, series graeca 5. Turnhout, Belgium: Brepols / Leuven: University Press, 1979.

Theophanes Confessor. *Chronographia*. Edited by Carl de Boor. 2 vols. Hildesheim: G. Olms, 1963–65; reprint of 1883 edition.

Tompkins, Ian. "The Relations between Theodoret of Cyrrhus and His City and Its Territory, with Particular Reference to the Letters and *Historia Religiosa*." D.Phil. diss., University of Oxford, 1993.

Torp, H. "Les murs d'enceinte des monastères coptes primitifs." *Mélanges d'archéologie et d'histoire* 76 (1964): 173–200.

Toynbee, J. M. C. *Animals in Roman Life and Art*. Baltimore: Johns Hopkins University Press, 1973.

Trisoglio, Franco. "Figurae, sententiae e ornatus nei discorsi di Gregorio di Nazianzo." *Orpheus* 34 (1987): 71–86.

——. "Uso ed effetti delle figurae elocutionis nei discorsi di Gregorio di Nazianzo." *Orpheus* 33 (1986): 254–71.

Trombley, Frank. *Hellenic Religion and Christianization*. 2 vols. Leiden: Brill, 1995.

Trout, Dennis. *Paulinus of Nola: Life, Letters, and Poems*. The Transformation of the Classical Heritage 27. Berkeley and Los Angeles: University of California, 1999.

——. "Re-Textualizing Lucretia: Cultural Subversion in the *City of God*." *Journal of Early Christian Studies* 2 (1994): 53–70.

——. "The Verse Epitaph(s) of Petronius Probus: Competitive Commemoration in Late-Fourth-Century Rome." *New England Classical Journal* 28 (2001): 157–76.

Urbainczyk, Theresa. *Theodoret of Cyrrhus: The Bishop and the Holy Man*. Ann Arbor: University of Michigan Press, 2002.

Valantasis, Richard. "Constructions of Power in Asceticism." *Journal of the American Academy of Religion* 63 (1995): 775–821.

——. "Is the Gospel of Thomas Ascetical? Revisiting an Old Problem with a New Theory." *Journal of Early Christian Studies* 7 (1999): 55–81.

Valentini, R., and G. Zucchetti. *Codice topografico della città di Roma*. 4 vols. Rome: Tipografia del Senato, 1940–53.

Vallée, G. *A Study in Anti-Gnostic Polemics: Irenaeus, Hippolytus, and Epiphanius*. Studies in Judaism and Christianity 1. Waterloo, Canada: Wilfrid Laurier University Press, 1981.

Valli, Francesco. *Gioviniano: Esame delle fonti e dei frammenti*. Urbino: Università di Urbino, 1953.

Van Dam, Raymond. "Self-Representation in the Will of Gregory of Nazianzus." *Journal of Theological Studies* 46 (1995): 118–48.

Van Esbroeck, Michel. *Aux origines de la Dormition de la Vierge: Études historique sur les traditions orientales.* Brookfield, Vt., and Aldershot: Variorium, 1995.

——. "La date et l'auteur du *De Sectis* attribué à Léonce de Byzance." In *After Chalcedon: Studies in Theology and Church History Offered to Professor Albert Van Roey for His Seventieth Birthday,* edited by C. Laga, J. A. Munitiz, and L. van Rompay, 415–24. Leuven: Peeters, 1985.

Vann, Richard T. "Turning Linguistic: History and Theory and *History and Theory,* 1960–1975." In *A New Philosophy of History,* edited by Frank Ankersmit and Hans Kellner, 40–69. Chicago: University of Chicago Press, 1995.

Vessey, Mark. "Conference and Confession: Literary Pragmatics in Augustine's 'Apologia contra Hieronymum.' " *Journal of Early Christian Studies* 1 (1993): 175–213.

——. "The Forging of Orthodoxy in Latin Christian Literature." *Journal of Early Christian Studies* 4 (1996): 495–513.

——. "Jerome's Origen: The Making of a Christian Literary Persona." *Studia Patristica* 28 (1993): 135–45.

——. "Reading like Angels: Derrida and Augustine on the Book." In *Augustine and Postmodernism: Confession and Circumfession,* edited by John D. Caputo and Michael J. Scanlon. Bloomington: Indiana University Press, forthcoming.

Vivian, Tim, et al., trans. *The Life of the Jura Fathers.* Kalamazoo, Mich.: Cistercian Publications, 1999.

Von Hesberg, H., and S. Panciera. *Das Mausoleum des Augustus: Der Bau und seine Inschriften.* Munich: Bayerischen Akademie der Wissenschaften, 1994.

Von Staden, Heinrich. "Affinities and Elisions: Helen and Hellenocentrism." *Isis* 83 (1992): 578–95.

Vööbus, Arthur, ed. and trans. *The Canons Ascribed to Maruta of Maipherqat and Related Sources.* Corpus Scriptorum Christianorum Orientalium 349–40 and Scriptores Syri 191–92. Leuven: Peeters, 1982.

——. *Syriac and Arabic Documents Regarding Legislation Relative to Syrian Asceticism.* Stockholm: Estonian Theological Society in Exile, 1960.

Walsh, P. G. "The Rights and Wrongs of Curiosity (Plutarch to Augustine)." *Greece and Rome* 35 (1988): 73–85.

Walter, C. "Heretics in Byzantine Art." *Eastern Churches Review* 3 (1970): 40–49.

——. *L'iconographie des conciles dans l'art byzantin.* Archives de l'orient chrétien 13. Paris: Institut Français d'Etudes Byzantines, 1970.

Ward, Benedicta, trans. *Harlots of the Desert.* Kalamazoo, Mich.: Cistercian Publications, 1987.

——. *The Sayings of the Desert Fathers: The Alphabetical Collection.* Rev. ed. Kalamazoo, Mich.: Cistercian Publications, 1984.

——. *The Wisdom of the Desert Fathers.* New ed. Oxford: SLG, 1986.

Ware, Kallistos. "The Soul in Greek Christianity." In *From Soul to Self,* edited by M. James C. Crabbe, 49–69. London and New York: Routledge, 1999.

Weingarten, Susan. "Jerome and the *Golden Ass.*" *Studia Patristica* 33 (1997): 383–89.

Weitzmann, Kurt. *Late Antique and Early Christian Book Illumination.* New York: George Braziller, 1977.

White, Carolinne. *Christian Friendship in the Fourth Century.* Cambridge: Cambridge University Press, 1992.

White, Hayden. *Figural Realism: Studies in the Mimesis Effect.* Baltimore: Johns Hopkins University Press, 1999.

——. "The Value of Narrativity in the Representation of Reality." In *On Narrative,* edited by W. J. T. Mitchell, 1–24. Chicago: University of Chicago Press, 1981.

White, Robert J. *The Interpretation of Dreams.* Park Ridge: Noyes Press, 1975.

Whitmarsh, Tim. *Greek Literature and the Roman Empire: The Politics of Imitation.* Oxford: Oxford University Press, 2001.

Wiemer, Hans-Ulrich. *Libanios und Julian.* Munich: Beck, 1995.

Wiesen, David. *St. Jerome as a Satirist.* Ithaca: Cornell University Press, 1964.

Wilken, Robert. " 'In novissimus diebus': Biblical Promises, Jewish Hopes, and Early Christian Exegesis." *Journal of Early Christian Studies* 1 (1993): 1–19.

Wilkins, John, David Harvey, and Mike Dobson, eds. *Food in Antiquity.* Exeter: University of Exeter Press, 1995.

Williams, Michael. *Rethinking Gnosticism: An Argument for Dismantling a Dubious Category.* Princeton: Princeton University Press, 1996.

Williams, Raymond. *Keywords: A Vocabulary of Culture and Society.* Rev. ed. London: Fontana, 1983.

Wills, Garry. *Lincoln at Gettysburg: The Words That Remade America.* New York: Simon and Schuster, 1992.

Wimbush, Vincent L., ed. *Ascetic Behavior in Greco-Roman Antiquity: A Sourcebook.* Minneapolis: Fortress Press, 1990.

Wimbush, Vincent L., and Richard Valantasis, eds. *Asceticism.* New York: Oxford University Press, 1995.

Winkler, John J. *Auctor and Actor: A Narratological Reading of Apuleius's "The Golden Ass."* Berkeley and Los Angeles: University of California Press, 1985.

Winlock, H. E., and W. E. Crum, *The Monastery of Epiphanius at Thebes.* Vol. 1, *The Archeological Material.* New York: Metropolitan Museum of Art, 1926; reprint, Arno Press, 1973.

Wittgenstein, Ludwig. *Philosophical Investigations.* Translated by G. E. M. Anscombe. 2d ed. Reprint, Cambridge, Mass.: Blackwell, 1997.

Woolf, Gregg. "Becoming Roman, Staying Greek: Culture, Identity, and the Civilizing Process in the Roman East." *Proceedings of the Cambridge Philological Society* 40 (1994): 116–43.

——. Review of Averil Cameron, *Christianity and the Rhetoric of Empire: The Formation of Christian Discourse* (Berkeley and Los Angeles: University of California Press, 1991). *Journal of Roman Studies* 83 (1993): 257–58.

Wyman, B. *Blues Odyssey.* London: DK Publishers, 2001.

Young, Frances M. *Biblical Exegesis and the Formation of Christian Culture.* New York: Cambridge University Press, 1997.

——. "Did Epiphanius Know What He Meant by 'Heresy'?" *Studia Patristica* 17.1 (1982): 199–205.

——. *From Nicaea to Chalcedon.* London: SCM Press, 1983.

Young, Steven. "Being a Man: The Pursuit of Manliness in *The Shepherd of Hermas*."
  Journal of Early Christian Studies 2 (1994): 237–55.
Zafiropoulos, Christos A. *Ethics in Aesop's Fables: The Augustana Collection*. Leiden: Brill,
  2001.
Zanker, P. *Forum Augustum: Das Bildprogramm*. Tübingen: E. Wasmuth, 1968.
——. *The Power of Images in the Age of Augustus*. Translated by A. Shapiro. Ann Arbor:
  University of Michigan Press, 1990.
Zosimus. *Zosime: Nouvelle Histoire*. Edited and translated by François Paschoud. 3
  vols. in 5. Paris: Belles Lettres, 1971–89.
Zucchetti, Fausta. "Il sinodo di Gangra e uno scritto pseudo-Atanasiano." *Ricerche
  Religiose* 1 (1925): 548–51.

✢ CONTRIBUTORS

DANIEL BOYARIN is Taubman Professor of Talmudic Culture in the Department of Near Eastern Studies and Rhetoric at the University of California, Berkeley.

DAVID BRAKKE is a professor of religious studies and professor of history at Indiana University.

VIRGINIA BURRUS is a professor of early church history at the Theological School and Caspersen School of Graduate Studies, Drew University.

AVERIL CAMERON is the professor of late antique and Byzantine history at the University of Oxford, and Warden of Keble College.

SUSANNA ELM is a professor of history at the University of California, Berkeley.

JAMES E. GOEHRING is a professor of religion at the University of Mary Washington, Fredericksburg, Virginia.

SUSAN ASHBROOK HARVEY is a professor of religious studies at Brown University.

DAVID G. HUNTER is a professor of religious studies and Monsignor James A. Supple Professor of Catholic Studies at Iowa State University.

BLAKE LEYERLE is an associate professor of theology and associate professor of classics at the University of Notre Dame, Notre Dame, Indiana.

DALE B. MARTIN is a professor and chair of the Department of Religious Studies at Yale University.

PATRICIA COX MILLER is W. Earl Ledden Professor of Religion at Syracuse University.

PHILIP ROUSSEAU is Andrew W. Mellon Professor of Early Christian Studies at the Catholic University of America, Washington.

TERESA M. SHAW is vice provost and an associate professor of religion at Claremont Graduate University.

MAUREEN A. TILLEY is an associate professor of religious studies at the University of Dayton, Ohio.

DENNIS E. TROUT is an associate professor of classics at the University of Missouri, Columbia.

MARK VESSEY is an associate professor of English and Canada Research Chair in Literature / Christianity and Culture at the University of British Columbia.

Elm, Susanna, 4, 105, 228
Elsner, J., 305
Erasmus, Desiderius, 216
Everett, E., 314 n.64

Ferguson, Everett, 9–10
Filene, B., 311 n.16
Finley, Moses, 2
Foucault, Michel, 8, 9, 12, 171 n.88, 296 n.63
Fox, Robert Lane, 261
Frank, George, 104
Fredriksen, Paula, 256 n.54

Gager, John, 4
Gallagher, Catherine, 91
Garber, Marjorie, 33–34
Geertz, Clifford, 5, 10
Gill, Christopher, 293 n.7
Goehring, James E., 11, 228–229, 230, 236 n.61
Goldenberg, Robert, 190 n.26
Goldhill, Simon, 259–260, 293 n.7
Goltz, Eduard von der, 216, 224–227, 232 n.19, 235 n.50
Goodblatt, David, 190 n.29
Goulliard, Jean, 195, 209 n.48
Grant, Robert, 19 n.6, 169 n.73
Greenblatt, Stephen, 91
Gregg, Robert C., 141
Groh, Dennis E., 141
Grubbs, Judith Evans, 11
Gruen, Erich, 273 n.10
Gustafson, Mark, 105, 115 n.16, 115 n.17, 115 n.19

Hägg, Thomas, 87
Hall, Jonathan, 180–181, 183–184, 187–188
Halliwell, Stephen, 293 n.7, 294 n.30, 295 n.46, 297 n.70
Harpham, Geoffrey Galt, 92, 94, 95, 96, 97, 99 n.14, 101 n.54
Harries, Jill, 287

Harvey, Susan Ashbrook, 11, 92, 93, 100 n.39
Henry, Nathalie, 126
Herrin, Judith, 92
Hillerbrand, Hans, 19 n.11,
Humphreys, R. Stephen, 273 n.13

Jones, A. H. M., 2
Jones, C. P., 106

Karras, Ruth Mazo, 97
Kelly, J. N. D., 121
Kolbaba, T., 212 n.88
Kondoleon, Christine, 152
Krawiec, Rebecca, 39 n.41
Kristeva, Julia, 12
Krueger, Derek, 109–110

LaCapra, Dominick, 184, 191 n.35
Le Boulluec, Alain, 213, 229
Lefebvre, Henri, 305
Levi, Doro, 157
Lieu, S. N. C., 211 n.73
Lim, Richard, 203, 211 n.73
Lincoln, Abraham, 307–308
Lyman, J. Rebecca, 218

MacKendrick, Karmen, 110
MacMullen, Ramsay, 2, 273 n.8
Maier, Harry O., 10,
Malina, Bruce, 4
Markus, Robert A., 3, 262, 273 n.9, 274 n.19
Marucchi, Orazio, 298
Masson-Vincourt, M.-P., 275 n.23
McGuckin, John, 263
McLynn, Neil, 263
Meeks, Wayne, 4
Merleau-Ponty, Maurice, 296 n.63
Miles, Margaret, 59
Miller, Patricia Cox, 12, 28, 111, 165 n.22
Mitchell, W. J. T., 136–137, 146
Momigliano, Arnaldo, 115 n.21, 296 n.70
Munitiz, Joseph A., 209 n.48

Neusner, Jacob, 176, 178, 181, 182, 190 n.29
Nora, P., 311 n.19
Norris, Frederick, 262

O'Donnell, James J., 237, 255 n.40

Patterson, Annabel, 156
Pietri, C., 310 n.10
Pollmann, Karla, 255 n.33
Pourkier, Aline, 198
Puech, Aimé, 220
Pyykkö, V., 275 n.23

Rossi, Giovanni Battista de, 298
Rostovtzeff, M. I., 2
Rousseau, Jean-Jacques, 279–280
Rousseau, Philip, 87
Rousselle, Aline, 92
Ruether, Rosemary Radford, 164 n.5

Schüssler Fiorenza, Elizabeth, 11
Schwartz, Seth, 178
Segal, Alan, 182
Shaw, Brent, 201
Shaw, Teresa, 92, 93, 153, 170 n.78
Smith, Mark, 6
Smith, Rowland, 274 n.18
Soja, Edward, 308
Speck, P., 210 n.55

Speyer, Wolfgang, 273 n.8
Spivak, Gayatri, 293 n.3
Stock, Brian, 237, 256 n.44

Tanner, Kathryn, 7, 16, 17, 190 n.26
Taylor, Mark, 111
Tester, Keith, 150
Theissen, Gerd, 4
Tompkins, Ian, 200
Toynbee, J. M. C., 151
Trisoglio, Franco, 275 n.23
Trombley, Frank, 274 n.16
Trout, Dennis, 10

Valantasis, Richard, 14–15, 28
Vallée, G. A., 198
Vessey, Mark, 128

Walter, C., 210 n.53
Ward, Benedicta, 90
White, Hayden, 179–180, 185
Wilken, Robert, 10
Williams, Raymond, 6
Wimbush, Vincent, 13, 14
Winkler, John J., 251, 256 n.50, 256 n.53
Woolf, Gregg, 194

Young, Frances, 197–198
Young, Steve, 12

Canons Ascribed to Maruta, 86 n.40
Canons of the Quinisext Council, 197
Cassian, John, 27
Clement of Alexandria, 209 n.37
  Stromateis, 132 n.3
Codex Theodosianus, 133 n.21
Collectio Avellana, 310 n.14
Cyril of Scythopolis
  Vita sancti Sabae, 154, 162
  Vita sancti Theodosii, 154

Damasus
  Epigrammata, 298–309
Didache, 224

Epiphanius of Salamis, 195
  Ancoratus, 198
  Ethiopian Collection, 156
  Panarion, 193, 197–199
Ephrem Syrus, 63
  Hymns on the Nativity, 64–72, 81–
    82
Eucherius of Lyon
  De laude heremi, 145–146
Eusebius
  Chronicle, 242, 244
Euthymius Zigabenus, 195
Eutropius
  Breviarium, 313 n.49
Evagrius Ponticus
  Antirrheticus, 33
  Kephalaia Gnostica, 35
  Sententiae ad virginem, 35, 224, 229,
    231 n.10
  Skemmata, 34

Galen
  De alimentorum facultatibus, 155
Germanus of Constantinople
  De haeresibus et synodis, 200, 201
Gerontius
  Life of Melania the Younger, 98 n.7
Gregory of Nazianzus, 258–272
  Concerning Himself, 98 n.7

Epistulae, 144, 266
Orationes, 266, 267–269, 270
Gregory of Nyssa
  Vita Macrinae, 98 n.7, 103–104, 108–
    113
Gregory the Great
  Registrum epistularum, 309

Herodas
  Mimes, 106–107, 109
Herodotus, 176
Hesiod, 158
Hippolytus
  Syntagma, 197
Historia monachorum in Aegypto, 33, 36–
    37, 153, 224–225, 228
Homer
  Odyssey, 104, 144
Horace
  Epodes, 158

Irenaeus
  Adversus Haereseis, 197
Isocrates
  Panegyricus, 261

Jacob of Serug
  Homilies, 63, 77–81, 82, 83 n.5
Jerome
  Adversus Jovinianum, 125, 127, 130–
    131, 133 n.18
  Apologia contra Rufinum, 132 n.10
  Chronicon, 241–247, 250, 252
  Commentarii in Ezechielem, 308
  Contra Helvidium, 128
  Contra Joannem Hierololymitanum ad
    Pammachium, 315 n.72
  De viris illustribus, 128–129, 239, 312
    n.32
  Epistulae, 43, 45, 62 n.30, 120, 121,
    128, 129–130, 131, 133 n.19, 133
    n.25, 156, 244, 255 n.31
  Praef. in omelias super Lucam evange-
    listam, 129

De virginitate (*Discourse on Salvation*),
214–230
Vita Syncleticae, 224, 231 n.10, 236
n.54

Rabbula Canons, 83 n.5
Rufinus
Apologia contra Hieronymum, 134 n.42,
n.43

Seneca
Epistulae, 314 n.63
Siricius, Bishop of Rome
Epistolae, 119–123, 134 n.33
Socrates
Historia ecclesiastica, 276 n.36
Soghyatha, 63, 73–77, 82
Sophronius
Synodical Letter, 200
Suetonius
Divus Augustus, 311 n.23, n.25
De viris illustribus, 242
Symmachus
Epistulae, 253 n.10, 310 n.14
Synodikon of Orthodoxy, 194, 196, 205

Talmud, 190 n.26, 191 n.29
Babylonian, 180, 191 n.29
Palestinian, 180
Tatian, 209 n.37
Themistius, 265
Orationes, 271
Theodoret of Cyrrhus, 200, 278–293
Compendium of Heretical Fables, 193,
199, 200
Epistulae, 200, 278–293
Remedy for Pagan Maladies, 193, 296
n.68
Theognostos
Treasury, 210 n.55
Timothy of Constantinople, 193, 197
Tosefta, 180
Trophies of Damascus, 204

Varro, 247–248, 250
Vergil, 300–303
Aeneid, 245, 302
Eclogues, 158
Georgics, 302

Zosimus
Historia Nova, 275 n.31, 277 n.50

SCRIPTURES
Genesis
2:7, 282
Leviticus
19:28, 107
1 Samuel
2:1–10, 67
Psalms, 239
138 (139), 253 n.6
Proverbs
12:25, 34
Song of Songs
1:5–6, 94
4:12, 95, 126
Isaiah
11:7, 159
Daniel
1:3–16, 221
Matthew
1:1–16, 84 n.20
2, 74
10:26, 30, 99 n.24
21:1–9, 95
Luke, 79
1, 73
1:43, 67
1:46–55, 67, 84 n.20
7:37–38, 94
14:26, 137–138
24:22–25, 30
John
4:7–39, 289–290

Library of Congress Cataloging-in-Publication Data

The cultural turn in late ancient studies : gender,

asceticism, and historiography / Dale B. Martin and

Patricia Cox Miller, editors.

p. cm.

Includes bibliographical references and index.

ISBN 0-8223-3411-9 (cloth : alk. paper)

ISBN 0-8223-3422-4 (pbk. : alk. paper)

1. Church history—Primitive and early church, ca. 30–600.

2. Christianity—Influence. 3. Civilization, Western.

4. Gender. 5. Asceticism. 6. Historiography. I. Martin, Dale

B., 1954– II. Miller, Patricia Cox, 1947–

BR162.3.C85   2005

270.2—dc22   2004019863